D1564819

In Babel's Shadow

In Babel's Shadow

Language, Philology, and the Nation in Nineteenth-Century Germany

TUSKA BENES

WAYNE STATE UNIVERSITY PRESS
DETROIT

KRITIK

German Literary Theory and Cultural Studies
Liliane Weissberg, Editor

A complete listing of the books in this series can be found online at wsupress.wayne.edu

© 2008 by Wayne State University Press,
Detroit, Michigan 48201. All rights are reserved.
No part of this book may be reproduced without formal permission.

12 11 10 09 08 5 4 3 2 1

Library of Congress Cataloging-in-Publication Data
Benes, Tuska, 1971–
In Babel's shadow : language, philology, and the nation in nineteenth-century Germany / Tuska Benes.
p. cm. — (Kritik : German literary theory and cultural studies)
Includes bibliographical references and index.
ISBN 978-0-8143-3304-4 (cloth : alk. paper)
1. German language—19th century. 2. German language—Philology.
3. Nationalism—Germany—History—19th century 4. Indo-European languages—History I. Title.
PF3085.B46 2008
409.43—dc22
2008025000

∞ The paper used in this publication meets the minimum requirements of the American National Standard for Information Sciences—Permanence of Paper for Printed Library Materials, ANSI Z39.48-1984.

To Jane and Peter

Contents

Illustrations

Acknowledgments

A NUMBER OF GRANTS sustained the research for this book, as well as the writing and revision of chapters. The German Academic Exchange Service (DAAD) funded my first years in Berlin with an annual grant and an extension from 1996 to 1998. A fellowship from the Studienstiftung des Abgeordnetenhauses von Berlin allowed me to join in 1999–2000 a comprehensive program supporting scholars from the former Allied countries of the Second World War. The following academic year the Stiftung Luftbrückendank, established to honor the American, British, and French pilots who lost their lives airlifting supplies to West Berlin, once again extended my stay. For these generous opportunities to work and reside in Germany during a period of considerable historical change I am most grateful. Two terms teaching with the Berlin Program of the University of Washington's Comparative History of Ideas Program (CHID) likewise helped inscribe Berlin's libraries and cityscapes more intimately on my memory. In the early years of graduate school I profited from a Foreign Language and Area Studies (FLAS) Fellowship, as well as from a Chester Fritz Grant for International Exchange given by the University of Washington.

Two postdoctoral fellowships allowed me to take leave of the dissertation on which this book is based and to create a substantially revised manuscript. A Mellon Postdoctoral Teaching Fellowship in the Humanities and Social Sciences from 2002 to 2004 gave me two wonderful years at the University of Pennsylvania. Participating in a European-American Young Scholars Summer Institute called the "Concept of Language in the Academic Disciplines," funded by the Andrew W. Mellon Foundation and Alexander von Humboldt-Stiftung, in 2003 and 2004 was equally a treat, first at the National Humanities Center in North Carolina and then with the Wissenschaftskolleg zu Berlin. The tireless energies of the interlibrary loan staff at the College of William and Mary have meant that finding an academic home and starting a family have been compatible with intellectual productivity.

My intellectual debts far outweigh the aforementioned. Suzanne L. Marchand and John E. Toews will most readily see their own reflections in the pages that follow. Inspiring intellects and gentle critics, both substantially shaped the questions and themes guiding this book. The following friends, colleagues, and mentors commented generously on the entirety or sections of the manuscript: Jonathan M. Hess, David L. Hoyt, Jennifer Jenkins, Sarah Leonard, Jennifer Milligan, Karen Oslund, Peter K. J. Park, Uta G. Poiger, Sara Pritchard, Sara Pugach, Jonathan Steinberg, Liliane Weissberg, and George S. Williamson. Their contributions are invaluable and very much appreciated. Talbot J. Taylor, John E. Joseph, and the other participants in the "Concept of Language in the Academic Discourses" summer programs decisively shaped my understanding of linguistics.

To my family I am the most obliged. Ali Bonyadlou unknowingly provided the first inspiration for this project, taught me German, made Berlin my home, and unflinchingly endured my years of itinerancy. Like any good critic, Parvaneh dismantled draft chapters, parading around the house with pens and fragments of paper. My parents, Jane Montague Benes and Peter Benes, provided their scholar-daughter with the discipline, the example, and the emotional and material support necessary to complete this project. To them this book is dedicated. I take full responsibility for its faults.

Introduction

In 1843 the young French theology student Ernest Renan (1823–92) found himself "strangely fascinated" by what he termed the "peculiar spirit of Germany": he had just begun reading works in German philology that "astonished" him. For two years the aspiring scholar of Hebrew devoured volumes dedicated to the critical, historical exegesis of biblical texts. This "initiation to German studies" was enthralling, but it placed Renan in a difficult position. Philology, he claimed, "ruin[ed] the edifice of absolute truth" that his Catholic superiors invested in scripture. The revealed word of God seemed incommensurate with a critical reading of the Bible.[1] This realization propelled the would-be priest into a deep spiritual crisis. On October 6, 1845, Renan refused the tonsure, left the confines of the Saint-Suplice seminary, and embarked on a secular career as a philologist. His later reflections on *The Future of Science* (1848) credited German philology with awakening the "spirit of modernity." "The founders of the modern spirit are philologists," Renan ventured. "The day philology perishes, criticism will perish with her; barbarism will be born again, and the credulous will be masters of the world."[2]

Uninitiated readers might assume the philologist "only works with words." "What could be more frivolous?" Renan declared.[3] "Many may be tempted to laugh" on seeing how seriously the philologist "explicates grammatical idiosyncrasies, gathers commentaries, and compares editions of ancient authors" known only for their "caprice and mediocrity."[4] Renan defended his German authors from "the terrible accusation of pedantry."[5] Philology, he insisted, was more than "simple erudite curiosity." It was "an exact science of the human spirit."[6] "The true philologist, Renan asserted, was "at once linguist, historian, archaeologist, artist, philosopher. . . . Philology is not an end in itself. Its value is as a necessary condition for the history of the human spirit."[7] Language study lay at the heart of humanistic inquiry for Renan; the history and forms of language had a significance beyond their mere utility in the interpretation of texts.

In the nineteenth century, the field of philology encompassed varied forms of biblical criticism, art history, archaeology, and literary, cultural, and historical analysis, as well as the formal study of ancient languages and grammar. These pursuits were united by a critical-historical reading of texts and by an assembly of technical methods forged by Italian humanists in the early modern period.[8] Knowledge of language, including grammar and etymology, was key to the philological enterprise, both as a requisite for textual criticism and as a study in its own right. Comparative and historical analysis of Semitic tongues, for example, fueled Renan's criticism of the Bible. In 1848 he advanced a controversial thesis regarding the origins of monotheism. The rigid structure of Hebrew roots had supposedly curtailed the mythological imagination of its early speakers, suggesting to Hebrews the existence of a one and only God. For Renan, as for many of his contemporaries, each national tongue provided insight into the cultural and intellectual proclivities of its speakers. The history of languages likewise revealed the origins and ethnic affiliations of their speakers, transporting scholars to the most distant moments of the past.

Renan's grand ambitions suggest why the field of philology captivated the nineteenth century. Lectures on the science of language attracted large popular audiences in cities such as London, and philology intrigued some of the period's brightest minds.[9] Renan's remarks likewise recall Germany's prominence in the field. "Almost all the material work in philology is sustained . . . by Germans," he noted in 1857. "The true excellence of Germany is in the interpretation of the past. . . . Philology . . . is her creation. . . . The service rendered by Germany is to have elevated an organized science to new heights . . . and to have given philosophical meaning to a pursuit once imagined as a simple exercise in curiosity."[10] If Renan's faith in the language sciences was inflated, his debt to German precedents was real. German-speaking Europe was arguably the center of philology in the nineteenth century;[11] from Johann Gottfried Herder (1744–1803) and Jacob Grimm (1785–1863) to Friedrich Nietzsche (1844–1900) and Ferdinand de Saussure (1857–1913), philologists trained at German universities were influential, internationally renowned scholars.

The particular field of comparative-historical philology is the center of gravity around which this study draws together related German scholarship on language. At midcentury comparative philology distinguished itself from culturally and historically based textual analysis as *Sprachwissenschaft* (the science of language) or *Linguistik* (linguistics), although scholars of language were closely affiliated with various national philologies, especially Indology, through the Weimar Republic.[12] Born of the Oriental Renaissance, comparative philology prided itself on the ability to order the world's diverse tongues and peoples in genealogical formations. Its notable achievements include the massive grammars and dictionaries, mind-boggling in their detail and scope, that still dot library shelves. (Not atypical is Franz Bopp's 550-page *Comparative Grammar of the Sanskrit, Zend, Greek, Latin, Lithuanian, Gothic, German, and Slavonic Languages,* published in six parts from 1833 to 1852.) Comparative philologists were masters of little-known and often scarcely documented languages. Their concern was the historical reconstruction of tongues and the search for a lost, primordial Indo-European *Ursprache.*[13] Far from obscure, such research carried cultural weight, with implications for theology, philosophy, the pursuit of prehistory, and notions of nationhood and ethnicity. Especially among students of Semitic tongues and New Testament Greek, comparative research on language and the historicization of once sacred idioms was never far removed from highly controversial forms of biblical criticism. As Maurice Olender has shown, comparative philology attended closely to questions of race and religious identity, seeking in the distant past alternative models of Christianity, while distinguishing the supposed contributions "Aryans" and "Semites" made to European culture.[14]

The emergence of comparative philology as a field coincided with the upsurge of nationalist sentiment that spread across German-speaking lands from Köngisberg to Konstanz following Napoleon's defeat of the Holy Roman Empire in 1806. For this reason, the passion with which philology was practiced in Germany, especially within the fields of Germanics and Oriental studies, has also often been tied to national concerns.[15] Language scholars inspired over a century of historicist forays into the *Ur*-forms of German national culture and set a tradition of defining the nation according to three competing points of presumed origin in India, the Nordic lands, and classical Greece. Problems of nationhood closely intersected with the religious concerns of comparative philologists. As George Williamson has argued, research into the German national past was always framed within a narrative that engaged traditional Protestant, Catholic, or Jewish self-understanding.[16]

In contrast to fields such as anthropology or psychology, the history of linguistics has received remarkably little attention outside disciplinary circles.[17] This is surprising given the undeniable impact language study has had on the modern period. Language scholars contributed to the rise of European nationalism and the emergence of nineteenth-century notions of race and ethnicity. Comparative philology intervened in debates over the interpretation of scripture; it also contributed to the formation of academic disciplines and to the methodologies of humanistic inquiry. These are the chosen contexts of reception for this study. The entwinement of language scholarship in discussions of nationhood, religion, and the production of knowledge and culture is not coincidental. A German tradition of reflecting on the autonomous powers of language or the way words actively mold the human experience attributed to language almost mystical powers of creation. Nineteenth-century philologists imagined national tongues shaping communities and cultural practices, as well as the thought patterns and identities of those who spoke them.

The first aim of this study is to consider why language became a powerful and enduring metaphor for the representation of national culture in Germany. Germany represents the quintessential case of language study contributing to the rise of modern nationalism.[18] From the Napoleonic invasions until the founding of the German Empire in 1871, German speakers often asserted the right to national self-definition on linguistic, not political or territorial, grounds.[19] When Ernst Moritz Arndt demanded in 1813, "Where is the German's fatherland?" his reply echoed those of other nationalists: "Wherever is heard the German tongue, And German hymns to God are sung!" University professors and academics were key public figures in the Restoration and *Vormärz*. And language was an important venue in which they defined

German nationhood.[20] As Benedict Anderson has noted, professional philologists were "incendiaries" in the nationalist movements of central Europe. Their grammars and dictionaries produced new awareness of the European vernaculars, enabling speakers and readers to assert the unique value of their language and nation.[21]

Languages have not always marked national boundaries, however. There were no uniform spoken national tongues before the onset of general primary education. Nonliterate vernaculars provided only a weak basis for communal identification, language falling often secondary to and in conflict with other criteria for distinguishing group membership. In the late eighteenth century a small cultural elite had to invent the idea of a standardized national tongue and popularize the right to national self-determination on linguistic grounds.[22] Actual linguists have reconstructed processes of language standardization that allowed local idioms to claim the status of national tongues.[23] Compilations by Andreas Gardt and Claus Ahlzweig document the emergence of a "mother-tongue ideology" or a national linguistic consciousness among German-speakers.[24] Similarly, Michael Townson has sketched the political functions of language in Germany as a symbol and instrument of national solidarity and a creator of political realities.[25] This study establishes the intellectual foundations for defining the German nation as a linguistic community.

The second goal of the study is to contextualize the importance of linguistics to modern cultural studies. Specifically, it puts into historical perspective what has become known as the "linguistic turn" in today's social sciences and humanities. This term usually refers to an early-twentieth-century rejection of traditional notions of language, in which words were a transparent medium for the expression of ideas and emotions or for the description of an external world. As Martin Jay has argued, this rejection coincided with a new appreciation of the epistemological significance of language. In interwar England, for example, Ludwig Wittgenstein began to regard language as a social practice, suggesting that the meaning of words was determined by use and performative function. French philosophers, by contrast, explored a supposed deeper level of structural regularities that constituted language as an unintended and arbitrary system of diacritical signs. Structuralists and poststructuralists, including Michel Foucault (1926–84), claimed language to be an autonomous system that both conditioned and enabled the assertion of human subjectivity.[26] These scholars rejected the idealist assumption that concepts and identities originated in the activity of a sovereign consciousness. Rather, after the "linguistic turn," subjects themselves appeared to be constituted by linguistic infrastructures not readily accessible to the mind. The ramifications of this were considerable, shaking the foundations of carefully laid systems in a manner that recalls Renan's disillusionment with theological orthodoxy.

The shape of the linguistic turn in Germany depended, as Jay suggests, on a Protestant tradition of biblical exegesis. In his view, German scholars were most concerned with hermeneutics, the interpreting, translating, and explaining of texts. Jay rightly notes the early modern roots of German hermeneutics and its close ties to the Reformation. Protestant exegetes assumed that divine revelation came through speech, and the sacramental character of speech continued to inform later hermeneutic theory. In the twentieth century, German critical theorists, for example, including Jürgen Habermas, practiced an antinomian hermeneutics of suspicion and demystification, hoping to unmask ideology in language.[27] Jay's focus on meaning and hermeneutics, however, overlooks the rich, nineteenth-century tradition of comparative philology and the historical study of *language itself* in Germany.[28] It is here that the roots can be found of the characteristically French, poststructuralist attempt to deconstruct subjectivity based on a view of autonomous language.

My contention is that the centrality of language to the contemporary human sciences dates to the late Enlightenment. Language began to assume what the East Prussian Pietist J. G. Hamann termed "genealogical priority" in all questions of the mind during the last decades of the eighteenth century. I argue that this transformation occurred in a two-part process. On the one hand, the theory of signs presented by the French philosophe Étienne Bonnot de Condillac in 1746 gradually historicized language as the subjective expression of particular human communities. This move disrupted the representational function of language by detaching words from their ultimate reference points in previously existing physical or metaphysical realities. Language ceased to mirror universal rational forms, appearing instead as a contingent product of its own internal principles or of a national spirit. On the other hand, the German theologians J. G. Hamann and J. G. Herder evoked language in an influential critique of Kantian metaphysics during the 1790s. Their efforts, especially as continued among the followers of Wilhelm von Humboldt, set a tradition of pitting language against the claims of rationalism and the transcendental subject. Friedrich Nietzsche and Ferdinand de Saussure should, for this reason, not be seen as the autochthonous founders of a radically postmodern movement. As this study indicates, their interventions followed and engaged a century of philological reflection on the constructive powers of language.

Why was language such a potent object of analysis for nineteenth-century German intellectuals? The institutional context of the university is one consideration. The humanist reforms of the fifteenth and sixteenth centuries made training in language a mainstay of the European universities and a sine qua non for the human sciences. Of the seven liberal arts, grammar, rhetoric, and dialectic are concerned with the structure and use of language. The humanist curriculum subjected students to extensive linguistic drilling, as well as to arduous training in grammar and formal rhetoric. The fluency thus gained in a foreign language and literature was thought to bestow the skills necessary to become a model member of the community. Eloquence bred civic virtue and moral individuals by recalling the example of classical antiquity. As Anthony Grafton and Lisa Jardine have shown, grammarians did far more than relay formal rules of grammar and syntax. They introduced students to foreign cultures and presented them with a classical ideal of aesthetic and moral development.[29]

By the late eighteenth century, philology had established itself as the flagship discipline that set the standards of professionalism and science (*Wissenschaft*) that defined the modern research university.[30] As the founding of the Friedrich Wilhelm University in Berlin in 1810 testifies, philological seminars were the first to embrace research as their calling. A training ground for university and gymnasium teachers, philology attracted students in numbers comparable to those in theology and law. Its chief representatives, including the classicists Christian Gottlob Heyne, Friedrich August Wolf, and August Boeckh, were harbingers of a tradition of historicist thought, textual interpretation, and hermeneutic theory that sustained the cultural sciences through the late nineteenth century.[31] Classical studies, in particular, offered the German bourgeoisie a choice venue for social self-definition, bestowing through education or *Bildung* the rights to state service and cultural leadership.

Within the European tradition language had also long been a medium for reflecting on questions of epistemology and theology. Since antiquity language had been evaluated for its effectiveness in disclosing truths of various kinds. Plato's *Cratylus,* for example, asserted that names were tools or instruments of instruction, regardless of whether they had a natural or conventional relationship to the objects they represented. This dialogue considered whether etymology could shed light on the correctness of ideas by tracing them back to a mythical name giver. According to the Hebrew Bible, a thorough understanding of language could further one's knowledge of the physical world; the names Adam gave to Eve and the animals in the Garden of Eden maintained an essential bond to the things they represented. The mystical tradition of the Kabala likewise invested metaphysical and magical significance in the structures of the Hebrew language, the letters of the alphabet both constituting and embodying a divine order.[32]

Language study could also prove destabilizing and provoke anxiety about the certainty of truths it purported to uphold. A perceived crisis of linguistic representation plagued the seventeenth-century heirs to the rhetorical culture of Renaissance humanism. As Quentin Skinner has argued, the art of persuasive speech and its ability to sway listeners threatened moral ambiguity; eloquence could transform the reality of vice into apparent virtue. For John Locke and John Wilkens, language was likewise fallible. But it was also the tool best equipped to ensure stable meanings and a reliable correspondence of facts and definitions.[33] Locke, for example, assumed that speakers developed ideas independently of language; but he feared the confusion that arose when an individual arbitrarily selected linguistic signs to stand for ideas in the mind.[34] Thomas Hobbes, for this reason, proposed that the fiat of the sovereign should regulate meanings and definitions.[35] This perspective on language corresponded with a concern for the viability of the new discursive communities that grew up around the European vernaculars. Individual languages were expected to facilitate the exchange of ideas among all who mastered the standardized forms of national tongues and partook in the institutions of print culture and the public sphere.

Seventeenth-century natural philosophers likewise searched for a universal system of representation, a mathematical language capable of depicting accurately the laws of a divinely authored universe. As Robert Markley has shown, the Christian tradition contrasted God's ineffable word with the fallen languages of humankind. War, religious sectarianism, and political instability exacerbated anxieties about conventional language on the eve of the scientific revolution; experimental philosophy also revealed a supposed rupture between theological absolutes and a corrupt material world. The universal language schemes of the 1640s to 1680s attempted to "reverse Babel" by removing representation from history. If the fall into national tongues had marked a descent into sin and political instability, restoring the transparency of an ideal language could repair the damage done by human presumption.[36]

Biblical criticism proved to be the most contentious application of philology in Europe from Renaissance times on. Analysis of rhetoric enabled Christian humanists, such as Desiderius Erasmus, to isolate universally valid theological teachings from culturally specific injunctions.[37] The historicization of sacred languages could also undermine orthodox readings of scripture. Sixteenth-century philologists interpreted the biblical text as a historical document and the product of specific cultural and social conditions. Old Testament exegetes tended to be professors of Hebrew or "Oriental" languages, such as Aramaic, Syriac, Arabic, or Ethiopian. In contrast to classicists, they did not adopt a formalist approach to language. Biblical scholars bound the meaning of words to cultural practice and regarded textual production as a social behavior. At first this transpired without secularizing scripture or questioning the mystical and miraculous.[38] But philology raised the problem of how God's word is transmitted to a fallen world. Was God's freedom of expression limited by the expressive possibilities of historical speakers in the first through third century?

By the end of the eighteenth century, philology had decisively weakened the bond between the Bible and theology. As Jonathan Sheehan has argued, Enlightenment philologists separated revelation or the word of God from the Old and New Testaments as texts. Historical criticism transformed the Bible into a local and temporal artifact, subject to degeneration and corruption, while God's word remained eternal. As this happened, the "Enlightenment Bible" assumed new meaning and authority as a cultural document.[39] By the nineteenth century the continued amalgamation of culture and religion placed theological debates within national frameworks. Christianity, for example, increasingly appeared as an expression of German culture, one that rejected its Jewish origins and repudiated contemporary Jews as culturally distinct.[40] Nineteenth-century philologists provided the material and tools necessary to unravel theological orthodoxies, entering heated debates on the relationship between theology and national heritage until the eve of World War I.

German philologists put particular emphasis on problems of origin and historical development when considering language. Their historicization of national tongues thus contributed to what John E. Toews terms the emergence of the historical principle as a dominant cultural form in the early nineteenth century.[41] Comparative philologists generally interpreted language as evidence of ethnic descent and wove myths of cultural origin around the perceived starting points of national tongues. The first moments in the emergence of a language or nation were considered to be formative; the organic unfolding of a first principle or underlying idea could explain subsequent historical development. This origin paradigm held sway over German linguistic thought through most of the nineteenth century. By contrast, French language scholars embraced a model of nationhood based on the idea of a discursive community, an open assembly of speakers united by shared patterns of communication and exchange. In revolutionary France, for example, knowledge of the mother tongue was thought necessary for citizens to participate in legal institutions, sustain a democratic government, and foster French literature and culture.[42]

In this respect, comparative philology epitomized the nineteenth-century German quest for origins. Language scholars worked feverishly to reconstruct the *Ursprache,* or the primordial linguistic forms from which the world's tongues supposedly evolved, especially within the Indo-European language family. Philologists ordered languages and ethnic groups based on the model of branching genealogy from a single point of origin.[43] "Family tree" figures were unusually prominent in German linguistics and the German social sciences generally. A stepped staircase or "scale of civilization," by contrast, in which successive forms progress through standardized evolutionary stages, dominated British social anthropology in the 1860s and 1870s.[44]

The concern for origins can partly be explained by the central role language played in German considerations of culture, community, and cognition. In the Judeo-Christian tradition, language is deeply embedded in the quintessential myth of origins, as well as in the most enduring account of the history of nations. In the beginning was the Word, according to the Gospel of John. The God of Genesis supposedly created earth and the heavens through a performative act of speech. Adam's first act in the Garden of Eden was to name the animals of creation and his female companion. The Pentateuch likewise defines the tribes that descended from Noah's three sons by tracing the genealogy of their national tongues.[45] German philologists, in this sense, worked in the shadow of Babel, searching for primordial tongues with a view to biblical accounts of their significance.

The importance comparative philology assigned to origins had two contradictory implications for German intellectual circles—one conservative, one critical. The discipline walked a fine line between two tendencies: affirming the exemplary aesthetic and moral value of past epochs, and conjuring powerful weapons of historical criticism. On the one hand, philology idealized distant moments in the past as models for German cultural rebirth. This sustained a quasi-religious longing for the salvation promised by providential history. A focus on formative foundations anchored what were often messianic narratives of fall and redemption.[46] The primeval past was likened to a Golden Age; the naïve innocence of youth enjoyed a moment of purity and respite before succumbing to an inevitable process of cultural degeneration. The prospect of return encouraged nationalists to model the imagined community on memories of archaic cultural essences. Origins could also provide a sense of epistemological security. *Ur*-forms offered a stabilizing locus of meaning and identity, an idealized moment of nostalgia that offset the otherwise unsettling effects of historical relativism.[47]

On the other hand, genealogy and the search for origins could disrupt established historical narratives and rob ethical claims of their universal validity. Renan's crisis of faith afflicted many who chose philology over theology in the nineteenth century. Comparative philology threatened to confront language scholars and other humanists with the implications of extreme historical and cultural relativism. Exposing the origins of metaphysical concepts, for example, could, as Friedrich Nietzsche argued, fatally unmask the contingent, nonbinding foundations of theology and ethics. German philology tended to affirm the notion that chance linguistic conventions shaped communities and their thought patterns independently of human desire or self-reflection. As such, a penchant for tracking origins and *Ur*-forms strengthened the power and perceived autonomy with which language molded the human experience. By contrast, examining distinct stages in the life of a language might have drawn attention to the synchronic dynamics of speech and communication and reinforced a discursive model of linguistic community. It might likewise have endowed individual speakers with greater authority to direct their use of language through conscious acts of communication and representation.

There was a tension in nineteenth-century German historicism, Toews has shown, between the perception that human identity was constituted by inherited patterns and an ethical ambition to forge new political and cultural communities in the present.[48] Linguists took various positions on whether speakers could consciously alter the autonomous inner laws regulating language change and on the degree to which external historical factors conditioned the evolution of language. Yet the prevalence of the origin paradigm tended to foreground the historically determined and ethnic nature of linguistic communities, while limiting the supposed ability of speaking subjects to express or even experience a sovereign consciousness outside of a national linguistic framework. This linguistic determinism transferred to historical tongues some of the autonomy and agency that other concepts of language reserved for human subjects. German comparativists conjured a vision in which national tongues could be independent, living beings endowed with their own internal principles of growth. The self-sufficient, inner laws governing the linguistic organism drew the act of representation away from the conscious intention of speakers. It also detached words from stable reference points in the external or metaphysical world. How the concept of linguistic agency that resulted from these transformations shaped ideas of nationhood and influenced the linguistic turn in twentieth-century continental philosophy is the subject of this study.

Language and National Genealogy

The story of Genesis opened the possibility of using language to trace national genealogies. Following the flood, the descendents of Noah's three sons, Shem, Ham, and Japheth, formed tribes speaking distinct tongues, and their division was often regarded as the first source of national and linguistic diversity. Long before the nineteenth century, German speakers defined their communities through language and history. During the Renaissance, for example, philologists applied their technical skills to craft fallacious myths of origin. The cities and states of fifteenth-century Europe felt the need for a primordial past that rivaled the ancient histories of Greece and Rome. Philologists thus forged "historical" texts that linked the biblical Middle East, Troy, and the peoples of northern Europe. One early-modern *Urgeschichte* curiously claimed that Friesland was founded by three Indian gentlemen, Friso, Saxo, and Bruno, who traveled west to study with Plato and fight for

Philip and Alexander of Macedon. Finally settling in Frisia, they drove away the aboriginal giants, all while speaking Sanskrit.[49]

Martin Luther's 1534 translation of the Bible helped standardize written High German and raised new expectations for the study of language in Germany. On the one hand, the philological act of translating scripture into the vernacular appeared to bring German readers closer to the divine truth of God's word. Luther's text extended to Protestants a more intimate relationship to God; it also suggested that the truest form of Christianity was a German cultural achievement.[50] Later generations likewise believed that translation could improve upon an original text by better explicating hidden or intended meanings. Thus, the early Romantics declared German speakers to have a proclivity for translation, being uniquely capable of interpreting and mediating the cultural patrimony of other nations. On the other hand, Luther's Bible gained symbolic weight as a foundational moment in the emergence of the German nation. Nineteenth-century scholars cited Luther as the bearer of a national language and literature. A masterpiece of philology supposedly created the language that united Germans; in Luther's tradition, German national culture was enriched and expanded through work on language.[51]

The experience of the Thirty Years War (1618–48) also attuned German intellectuals to the national cultural significance of language. Central Europe suffered devastation during this conflict, and the solidification of a German vernacular lagged behind other European idioms. Not surprisingly, baroque philologists, such as Justus Georg Schottelius (1612–76), equated the restoration of German culture, even German political authority, with establishing the mother tongue as a viable medium for literature and scholarship. As Markus Hundt has suggested, seventeenth-century language scholarship aimed to correct a perceived deficit in the development of German culture when compared to France, Italy, and Spain.[52] Schottelius's drama *FriedensSieg* (1642), for example, which was often performed after the Peace of Westphalia, bemoaned the intrusion of foreign words into the German language. Ancient German heroes returning to aid a seventeenth-century soldier found themselves unable to understand his corrupt idiom. For Schottelius, cultivating the German language was the only way to restore cultural and moral integrity to a war-torn land.[53]

Philologists and poets carried the German patriotic movement of the seventeenth century, especially in Protestant areas. The perceived instability of the German vernacular made for a situation in which speakers felt compelled to make claims about its heritage and significance. New societies, such as the Fruchtbringende Gesellschaft (1617), aimed to perfect the German language as a medium of artistic and literary expression. And asserting its practical, political, and poetic value over Latin required technical research. Lexicographers and grammarians, such as Christian Gueintz (1592–1650), consciously began constructing a standardized written tongue, contributing, as did Hieronymus Freyer (1675–1747) and Hans Jakob Christoph von Grimmelshausen (1625–76), to the development of New High German.[54] Schottelius himself published *Ausführliche Arbeit von der teutschen Haubt Sprache* (1663), as well as a grammar and commentaries on the supposedly depraved state of his mother tongue. These texts no longer treated German as the "maid of Latin," an aid for learning classical tongues, but insisted on its value for the nation. After Christian Thomasius defiantly announced his intention to hold lectures in German in Leipzig in 1687, this type of *Kulturpatriotismus* found a home in Germany's unusually high density of universities and attracted mobile members of the intellectual elite.[55]

Reference to the origins and great antiquity of the German language was in this period an important mechanism for legitimating its social and literary application. Schottelius countered the prevalent view that German was a relatively new language by tracing its genealogy to Babel. He proclaimed German to be the oldest *Ursprache* of the Celtic tongues, being at least three thousand years of age and of no relation to Greek or Latin.[56] According to Schottelius, German was a direct descendent of the Adamic language and as such had a divine character.[57] He stressed the affinities between German and Hebrew, then considered of closest relation to the divine language of revelation;[58] others, such as Leibniz, declared German itself most proximate to God's word.

Privileging German over the holy and classical languages had since the early modern period likewise been a means of undermining traditional forms of cultural authority. Philology could challenge, as well as stabilize, ruling elites. German humanists and church reformers turned the vernacular against the dictates of Rome. In the late eighteenth century, the emerging German middle class cultivated a standardized written idiom in literary and academic discourse as the basis for a new public sphere that challenged aristocratic and court culture. The numerous reading groups, patriotic societies, and literary journals that gave birth to modern civil society depended on written High German as a unifying bond.[59] Until the mid-nineteenth century, members of the *Bildungsbürgertum* (the educated middle class) in Germany relied on university training, rather than on economic or political achievement, for social recognition, so academic publications, scholarship, and literature were chief vehicles for class self-definition. Devotion to the vernacular enabled German intellectuals to define a public sphere of middle-class activity independent of the *Ständestaat* (corporative state) and to nurture a small but burgeoning national community. Benedict Anderson's notion that the emergence of print culture enabled disparate populations to imagine themselves as a community partaking in a collective fate holds true for German speakers, perhaps more so than for more homogeneous linguistic groups.

The political history of modern central Europe presented few alternatives to a linguistic conception of community. In contrast to states with a long tradition of central monarchy, the Holy Roman Empire of the German Nation lacked compelling institutions that might have united its many principalities and free cities; German speakers had no dominant urban center and few natural geographic boundaries. For most of the nineteenth century, Prince Klemens von Metternich's loose confederation of thirty-nine German states served only to buttress the political order of the old regime and silence nationalist or revolutionary forces. Until German unification in 1871, central Europe remained fragmented into tiny principalities that could not sustain a political vision of nationalism. Austria and Prussia, the two largest German territories and the most promising candidates for unification, were multiethnic states containing significant Polish-, French-, Danish-, and Czech-speaking minorities. Sizable German-speaking populations were also scattered across eastern Europe and Russia and could not readily be included in either a *groß-* or *kleindeutsch* political solution.

A particular concept of language emerged within this German context, one that favored the historically specific over the universal. At the most basic level, German comparativists held words and grammatical structures to be historical testaments to the communities that spoke them. The history of a language and its geographical expansion from a point of origin revealed the heritage of its speakers and their ethnic descent. Many philologists assumed that etymology could uncover how prehistoric peoples had lived, thought, and worshiped. Language scholars attributed peculiarities in a nation's religious practices or intellectual achievements to the thought patterns and worldviews produced by certain grammatical structures and vocabulary. The inner principle of growth attributed to each national tongue supposedly exerted a formative influence on its speakers, guiding their collective consciousness and communal life.

Another series of relationships drew together language, culture, and nationhood outside of Germany. Language scholars in France and Britain continued to embrace the tradition of general grammar well into the 1830s. According to this tradition, shared grammatical principles expressing universal laws of rationality lay hidden in the diversity of national tongues. Words spoke not to cultural particularities of their speakers, but to divinely inspired structures that permeated the mind and the empirical world. Scholars outside of Germany also retained greater concern for the contributions that individual speakers made to the evolution of national tongues. For Locke and others, language was an instrument of communication and sociability, one that bowed to the whims and intentions of its users. Imagining language as a system of signs set by consensus and convention tended to reinforce the agency and free will of speakers, and it drew attention to static language states rather than genealogical development.

German philologists made language study central to a historical definition of national culture and to an ethnographic project of establishing the genealogical relations among the world's peoples. In so doing, comparative philology built upon and altered the largely biblical and Christian terms by which cultural difference had previously been defined. New mechanisms for classifying languages and tracing their early histories raised the expectation of scientifically "correcting" the Pentateuch. German scholars reworked the tale of Babel into a historical explanation for the emergence of cultural diversity, applying secularized biblical narratives of cultural degeneration and salvation to a new history of nations.

This attempt to rewrite Babel produced three new national genealogies in German-speaking lands. Orientalists proposed that the first Germans hailed from a primordial homeland in India or central Asia. Scholars with theological concerns, often Catholics, generally favored this vision, wishing to uncover the origins of Christianity in a culture that predated Hebrew antiquity. Some Germanists suggested that modern German likely descended from Gothic speakers in the north. Their model of nationhood stood in opposition to the reactionary policies of local German princes and tended to advocate a Protestant, northern German solution to unification. Both views challenged the neohumanism of classicists who situated the cultural starting point of the German nation in ancient Greece.

The "tyranny of Greece over Germany" has been well documented in nineteenth-century German literature and aesthetic tastes, and at the start of the nineteenth century the Hellenic model of German nationhood commanded the greatest degree of cultural influence and credibility. The institutional strength of classical philology and the prominence of neohumanism in the schools upheld the supposedly universal aesthetic of classical antiquity as the preferred source for German self-styling.[60] Yet the humanist predilection for an idealized Greek aesthetic increasingly came under fire from Orientalists and Germanists who gave greater cultural authority to perceived lines of historical and ethnic descent.

Historians have often tied the German penchant for defining nationhood through language and descent to an expansionist and exclusionary vision of community. In this view, early nineteenth-century thinkers, such as J. G. Herder, provided fodder for a radical *völkisch* nationalism in the Wilhelmine period, with language serving as evidence of racial identity.[61] Others have claimed that the early conflation of language and race in German nationhood sustained a special path of development leading to the Third Reich. According to Leon Poliakov and George Mosse, the violent anti-Semitism of the Nazi period found its inspiration in the distinction language scholars drew between Semitic and Indo-European tongues.[62] While comparative philology was an important venue for the German invention of race, reducing the field to a precursor of National Socialism or, as Edward Said has implied, to the handmaiden of imperial expansion, ignores its complexities. As Thomas Trautmann has shown for British India, Aryan theory has had varying functions and cultural implications over time, including the marking of kinship between Britons and Indians. Europeans looked to an Aryan past to answer questions of religious, national, and political identity. These were specific to a nineteenth-century context, and religion was often a more pressing concern than race in the search for German origins.[63]

German statehood came from above in 1871 through blood, iron, and the *Realpolitik* of Prussian chancellor Otto von Bismarck (1815–98). Hardly inspired by the force of a common cultural patrimony, unification represented the triumph of new state structures, rather than the victory of popular, emancipatory nationalism.[64] Merely the largest of the German principalities, Prussia asserted its dominion over lesser states, adopting the rhetoric of nationalists who once sought liberal political reforms. Given the strength of other loyalties and identities, the Empire held limited appeal for the majority of its inhabitants.[65] And Bismarck largely rejected an ethnocultural definition for the *Kaiserreich,* initially protecting the status of linguistic minorities and resisting the type of eastward imperial expansion that his successors envisioned.

Nevertheless, the notion that Germany existed as a linguistic community or *Kulturnation* exercised a recurrent appeal, especially among a new brand of Wilhelmine nationalists. A far more popular conflation of language and race after 1890 justified the imperial and Pan-Germanic aspirations of powerful patriotic societies.[66] Their representatives heralded Fichte, Grimm, and other comparative philologists as evidence of a long-standing German tradition. Hellenic, Orientalist, and Germanic models of German nationhood likewise existed side by side through the mid-twentieth century. Historical novels, such as Gustav Freytag's *Die Ahnen,* and Richard Wagner's operas fixed in the popular imagination notions of German speakers' cultural origins that had been introduced over a century earlier.[67] Nineteenth-century philologists set the terms of a discourse whose relevance only increased as their exclusive control of it ceded to more dominant cultural figures within the newly established nation-state. Language did not create a German nation, but middle-class intellectuals did imagine the ideal forms it should take. The tale philologists told of a pure linguistic community that had primordial roots in Asia and the Germanic past influenced how political leaders, educators, artists, and authors defined the nation until the ultimate perversion of these ideas in the Aryan theory and Germanophilia of the Third Reich.

The Rise of Autonomous Language

If one tangent of this study leads toward Nazi Germany, the other resurfaces in postwar France. In 1966 the French philosopher Michel Foucault attributed pride of place to philology in his controversial history of the human sciences. While remaining on the "fringes of our historical awareness," he claimed in *The Order of Things: An Archaeology of the Human Sciences,* philology modified the modern manner of knowing "at the deepest level of its archaeological organization."[68] The work outlined the discursive formations that since the sixteenth century had guided the production of knowledge in the fields of labor, life, and language. According to Foucault, comparative philologists, such as Franz Bopp, Friedrich Schlegel, and Jacob Grimm, were major intellectual figures whose impact had yet to be recognized. Their historicization of language around the year 1800 destroyed, in his view, the illusion that words were transparent media of representation and communication.[69] Philology, in Foucault's interpretation, depicted national tongues as having an independent principle of inner development. And this life force actively shaped how speakers thought. Nineteenth-century observers wished speech to be their servant, he suggested, yet slowly realized that they expressed their ideas in words of which they were not the masters.[70] For Foucault, this foretold the "end of man." "Man is in the process of perishing," he concluded, "as the being of language continues to shine ever brighter upon our horizon."[71] The historically determined structures of language set the possibilities for the very articulation of human subjectivity.

Foucault's history served a philosophical agenda. A major figure in the "linguistic turn" of twentieth-century continental philosophy, Foucault presented in *The Order of Things* a genealogy of the concept of language underlying his own understanding of how discourse constitutes modern subjects. Comparative philology, he implied, decisively influenced the turn to language within modern thought. "It is clear that this 'return' of language is not a sudden interruption in our culture"; he asserted, "it is not the irruptive discovery of some long-buried evidence. . . . It is, in fact, the strict unfolding of Western culture in accordance with the necessity it imposed upon itself at the beginning of the nineteenth century."[72] Foucault lay claim to comparative philology as one of his own formative points of origin.

This study seeks to make more precise Foucault's claim that comparative philology developed the concept of language that sustained poststructuralist thought. It traces the rise of "autonomous" language from the late eighteenth century through Friedrich Nietzsche, one of the figures who most influenced Foucault. As Foucault suggests, comparative philologists began to imagine language as an independent force existing beyond the conscious control of speaking subjects. They depicted language as a system blindly obeying impersonal phonological rules at the expense of human values and experience.[73] This conception of language fueled an escalating crisis of subjectivity that culminated in Nietzsche's reducing the knowing subject to an illusion of grammar. In this way, linguistic analysis has rivaled psychology and historicism in its penchant for destabilizing the coherent, knowing subject supposedly exalted within the humanist tradition.[74] Twentieth-century observers questioned the ability of the subject to declare itself independent of the external conditions of its own possibility, whether those be linguistic, rooted in the body, or in historical and cultural contingencies.

Starting in the 1760s and 1770s, well before the turning point Foucault cited, two related theories of language gradually endowed words with the autonomous power to shape culture, community, and cognition. What Charles Taylor has termed an *expressive* theory of language came to replace a predominantly representative view of language. Words were thought to reveal more about the subjective character and spirit of their speakers than about the objects they represented.[75] The late-eighteenth century also witnessed the emergence of what Lia Formigari labels *constructivist* theories of language.[76] National tongues, in this view, cease to be passive instruments of thought, communication, and representation. Rather, they actively contribute to the way human subjects experience the world, engage in intersubjective relationships, and conceive of their own identities and cultural practices.

The autonomy that characterized language in both these conceptions derived from a profound shift in its presumed points of reference. The historicity of national tongues prevented both a natural and a purely conventional bond between a word and its referent. Words no longer marked stable structures that existed prior to the intervention of human observers or remained unchanged by their representation in language. An expressive theory of language assumed that national tongues referred to the subjective spirit of those who spoke them; an irreducible spiritual force motivated the act of linguistic signification. This endowed national languages with ethnological significance and elevated words themselves to sites of cultural memory. Conversely, constructivist theories held that language referenced nothing more than its own inner principles of organization and growth. Speakers were captive to the self-regulating systems of signification whose vast internal labyrinths determined what could be said, thought, and experienced at a given moment in time.

Linguistic historians have debated which figures and intellectual traditions are most responsible for historicizing language and thus binding it to questions of nationhood and cognition, and the battle lines fall in stubborn formations. A French camp led by Hans Aarsleff argues that the universalist tradition of general grammar, especially as influenced by Étienne de Condillac, coupled questions of language and the mind. In this view, both Wilhelm von Humboldt and Saussure expanded a late eighteenth-century concern for the role sign systems played in representation, reviving interest in how the mind distinguished linguistic elements to create meaning.[77] Germanists mustered by Konrad Koerner insist on the philosophical sensitivity of German language scholars. J. G. Herder and Humboldt translated their respect for cultural particularism into a theory of linguistic relativity and linguistic determinism. Considerations of Kant's transcendental philosophy, moreover, and the introduction of psychological principles to linguistics maintained a consistent German concern for the relationship between language and the mind.[78]

While acknowledging French precedents, this study highlights the German and especially the theological context to the rise of autonomous language. The French Enlightenment was a major source of German ideas about nationhood. German philologists, however, enhanced the expressive and constructivist functions of language as these were suggested by Condillac. Radical Pietists and liberal Protestants in Germany recalled the performative function language assumed in the Old Testament, endowing the "living word" with creative powers in a fallen world. God's word had brought into existence the earth and the firmament, according to Genesis. In the Gospel of John, the word of God acquired the life necessary to infuse a fallen world with divine truth. At the start of the nineteenth century, comparative philologists took the Promethean step of historicizing the world's tongues. Language ceased to be a gift of God. Yet in an ironic twist of fate, the creative powers of God's word survived to animate national tongues, while drawing the shadow of Babel over the autonomy of speaking subjects. The poststructuralist concern for language bears the mark of a distinctively religious paper trail; the modern critique of subjectivity echoes an earlier fall of man.

1

Words Alive!

Constructivist Theories of Language in Late-Enlightenment Prussia

In the winter of 1801–2, the Prussian nobleman Wilhelm von Humboldt (1767–1835) hastened to jot down some reflections on the Basque language. He had just returned to his Tegel estates after an expedition through the Spanish Pyrenees, and an ambitious intellectual project was brewing in his mind. The unpublished fragment evolved into a plan for transforming the study of language into "its own, systematically ordered subject, one distinct from all others." What a "rich, grand, and profitable" exercise it would be to compare "the diverse languages of ancient and present times." The young Humboldt elaborated his vision in the prophetic tones of a recent convert. Researchers would compile a "systematic encyclopedia" that arranged the world's tongues according to the degree of their linguistic affinity. This was hardly a novel proposal, as Humboldt himself recognized. Comparative philologists had taken steps in this direction, but he had a heightened sense of the historical and philosophical rewards such a project would reap. Humboldt held language to be "the imprint of a people's ideas" and their "collective spiritual energy." Documenting the historical relations among languages would therefore elucidate the "character" of the nations that spoke them, as well as their "past fate." It would also enable a "metaphysical analysis" of how the peculiarities of each national tongue stood in relation to the universal human capacity for thought.[1]

Reasoned reflection, Humboldt had long suspected, was not possible without language.[2] Philologists who charted the "landscape of all possible linguistic variety" could thus glean insight into the inner workings of the human mind.[3]

These words fell at the end of Humboldt's six year quest for an intellectual vocation. Recent stays among the German Romantics in Jena and the disciples of Étienne de Condillac in Paris had convinced him that "absolutely nothing is so important for a nation's culture as its language." While in Spain, the future Prussian statesman resolved to devote himself "more exclusively to the study of language" and to a "philosophically based comparison" of different national tongues.[4] Basque was an inspirational starting point because the language deviated so dramatically from its European neighbors. Humboldt hoped to discover whether the Iberian natives were indeed "a distinct tribe" and to "classify them correctly . . . in the genealogical table of all nations."[5] The topic departed markedly from previous forays into ancient Greece. As a student of the noted philologist Christian Gottlob Heyne, Humboldt had been trained in a canon of literary and aesthetic Hellenism. Now he insisted that the "raw and barbaric" languages many contemporaries dismissed as "wild" merited serious intellectual attention.[6] Within a year, he began perusing the grammars of Native American tongues that his brother, the biologist Alexander von Humboldt, had brought back to Europe. To these he later added Sanskrit, Hebrew, Farsi, Chinese, and the southeast Asian language Kawi.

Diplomatic responsibilities and service to the Prussian state prevented Wilhelm von Humboldt from devoting himself fully to philology. But his conception of the language sciences falls at an important juncture in the history of the discipline. Humboldt possessed the cultural foresight and political acumen necessary to launch comparative philology on its distinguished nineteenth-century career. This chapter reconstructs the intellectual pillars upon which comparative philology and philosophical reflection on language rested in nineteenth-century Germany. As Humboldt's remarks suggest, considerations of nationhood, cultural identity, epistemology, and language were closely related in the late eighteenth century. Exploring the epistemological concerns of the period is thus an important prerequisite for situating both the linguistic definition of German nationhood and the renewal of philosophical interest in language that occurred in Germany after 1850. The chapter distills a tradition of reflecting on the supposedly autonomous powers with which words and grammatical structures molded human subjects. Efforts to explain how historical tongues shaped nations and various forms of thought endowed language with a life and will of its own that gradually encroached on the perceived ability of speaking subjects to hold and express ideas independently of inherited linguistic frameworks.

The specter of autonomous language first arose in the French Enlightenment. An increasingly historical appreciation of the evolution of national tongues led late-Enlightenment observers to question the transparency with which language represented and communicated ideas. For this reason this chapter starts by sketching a gradual transformation in eighteenth-century conceptions of the epistemological significance attributed to language study. The creative powers of language acquired new depth and dimension, however, in the work of two East Prussian theologians: Johann Georg Hamann (1730–88) and his disciple Johann Gottfried Herder (1744–1803). Their Pietist Protestant background breathed life into a word that an earlier tradition still deemed a perfectible instrument of a person's rational control. It was in their hands that language evolved from being a pliable tool to an active and unwieldy subject in its own right. The "living word" embodied the creative power of an immanent God; it was also inspired by the collective souls of linguistic communities.

The late eighteenth-century German concern for the relationship between language and nationhood arose in the context of the political and religious debates surrounding Enlightenment absolutism and the Francophone culture of the Prussian court. Hamann and Herder turned against the universalist project of *Aufklärung* that Frederick the Great cultivated among rationalist elites interested in its utility at the level of the state. For Enlightenment scholars, the existence of uniform rational structures—outside of language—implied that a set of universal rules governed politics and the ideal state. The pair favored an alternative model of community that stressed the organic, historical growth of unique national communities founded upon the *Volksgeist,* as well as the formative power with which language imbued native speakers.

Hamann and Herder's insistence on the extent language molded the understanding brought them into conflict with the transcendental philosophy of Immanuel Kant (1724–1804) in the 1780s. This chapter also follows how the constructivist powers attributed to words evolved in response to German idealism. A late-Enlightenment attempt to factor language into Kant's theory of the mind introduced many of the philosophical concerns for language that have characterized the twentieth century.[7] Wilhelm von Humboldt was a key transitional figure whose posthumous legacy bridged these two periods. The constructivist aspects of his linguistic philosophy have their roots in the empirical tradition of French theorists, but also in the *Sprachkritik* that German scholars launched against Kant's metaphysical edifice.

Language and Cognition from Locke to Condillac

The novelty of late eighteenth-century associations of language and thought can best be appreciated with a brief retrospective. Only gradually did European thinkers come to regard language as a constructive force, even if it had factored prominently in earlier discussions of epistemology. The parameters for discussing the role of language in cognition during the Enlightenment were set by two theorists in the closing decades of the seventeenth century: the Englishman John Locke (1632–1704) and the German Gottfried Wilhelm Leibniz (1646–1716). Representatives of competing empiricist and rationalist traditions, both sought a basis for certainty in knowledge by perfecting the ability of words to convey ideas and facilitate thought. Locke's *Essay Concerning Human Understanding* (1689) introduced the notion that language could be a potentially transparent tool of communication and cognition, and the question of how to enhance knowledge by perfecting language resurfaced throughout the eighteenth century in the form of critical responses to this text. The ultimate goal of making language transparent to its representations, of rectifying its deficiencies and lifting the opaqueness with which it signified an external or subjective reality, remained at the core of language theory until the 1770s, although perceptions of the difficulties facing speakers in this matter led to a growing appreciation of the power words held over the human mind.

Unlike their eighteenth-century followers, neither Locke nor Leibniz viewed language as having a constitutive role in the acquisition of knowledge. For both, the ultimate possibility of words becoming effective vehicles of thought lay in the supposition that ideas existed prior to language and that the human mind, whether reacting to sense impressions or innate ideas, acquired knowledge on a prelinguistic level.[8] Thus, in Locke's view, "simple ideas of sensation," derived from the empirical world, and "simple ideas of reflection," based on the mind's processing of them, both existed first in prelinguistic form as a mental sign of a *thing*, and only at a second level of abstraction were they assigned words that became signs of the *ideas*.[9] For Leibniz, words likewise functioned merely as "slips or tokens," "markers" that "mirror[ed] the understanding."[10] He, however, sought a rational order, "something divine and eternal" in the multiplicity of national tongues and envisioned compiling a perfect artificial language that reduced reasoning to numerical calculation.[11]

Within this framework, Locke in particular emphasized the free will and agency of the speaker. For him language did not entail an abstract, external system or a preexisting set of rules that governed communication and might be thought of as evolving independently of human action. Rather, it consisted in the voluntary acts of individual speakers. Locke prioritized what Talbot Taylor terms the "semiotic agency" of the subject in the way he conceived the relationship between word and idea.[12] The speaker, Locke insisted, had the "inviolable liberty" to "make Words stand for what Ideas he pleases." This connection was not guided by an a priori correspondence between word and idea, but was something the individual forged. Specifically, Locke stipulated that the linguistic process of signification was arbitrary, voluntary, private, and individual. Neither language nor society could impose meaning on the free will of the speaker: "no one hath the Power to make others have the same Ideas in their Minds, that he has, when they use the same Words, that he does."[13] This situation was not entirely beneficial; it led to miscommunication and confusion. This was for Locke the main obstacle and source of error in the development of human understanding, and he suggested to later theorists that it would be possible to reason and use language more effectively if one inquired into the origins and evolution of signifying practices.

While there are indications that Leibniz at times questioned the arbitrary nature of the linguistic sign, the classical empirical tradition extending from John Locke is more directly responsible than the rationalists for assigning autonomous power to words.[14] The notions that linguistic signs had a constitutive role in the acquisition of knowledge and that historical fluctuations in the store of words available to the human mind affected the possibilities for cognition contributed in the eighteenth century to a new appreciation of the constructivist function of language. As an afterthought to his *Essay Concerning Human Understanding*, Locke proposed a "doctrine of signs" that evaluated "the signs the Mind makes use of . . . and the right ordering of them for its clearer Information."[15] His suggestion that signs played an inescapable role in cognition inspired later eighteenth-century theorists to make semiotics the foundation of epistemology.[16] In another widely read passage, Locke speculated that the complex vocabulary of any given national tongue developed as a metaphorical expansion from an original core of names for simple ideas of sensation. By implication, the growth of national vocabularies over time could be interpreted as an expansion in the store of ideas available to their respective cultural communities.[17]

Étienne de Condillac (1715–80) translated Locke's observations into a more rigorous analysis of how the historical growth of language influenced the progress of knowledge, as well as the formation of nations and their worldviews. The epistemological significance he and the French ideologues placed on the evolution of particular sign systems has led many to herald his work as the "source" of modern notions concerning the linguistic relativity of cognition, including claims that each national tongue generates its own worldview and accepted forms of knowledge.[18] Condillac's *Essay on the Origin of Human Understanding (1746*) did tie progress in knowledge to the historical development of language, thereby eliminating Locke's lingering rationalistic faith in humankind's a priori capacity for thought.[19] The linguistic sign, in his view, was not a supplementary instrument created to communicate thoughts that existed prior to language; rather, it had a constitutive role in cognition, "the use of signs" being "the principle which unfolds all our ideas."[20] Classical empiricism assigned an active role to language in the cognitive process and for this reason has rightly been considered one the forerunners in a constructivist theory of language.[21]

Specifically, Condillac's *Essay* sought to explain how individual national tongues evolved historically from what he considered to be an original language of gesture. Children abandoned on a desert island would have relied on nature, he believed, to draw from them the first cries and gestures. Physical responses to certain sensations, desires, and passions, and "accidental signs" that brought to mind objects based on contextual association, were both, according to Condillac, involuntary products of environmental stimuli and physiological determination. Only in a second stage of development did speakers themselves invent the type of linguistic sign that "insensibly enlarged and improved the operations of the mind."[22] "Institutional" or "artificial" signs evolved under the voluntary control of human beings and allowed them to engage in willful cognitive activity. For Condillac, all signs established connections between ideas. Yet humans only gained semiotic agency once the historical development of language made them "masters" of their own attention and enabled the mind to "dispose of itself, draw ideas which it owes only to itself." Without institutional signs the mind was "ruled by its environment," subject to the accidental and natural associations the material world established between ideas.[23]

Different patterns of signification produced for Condillac the linguistic diversity found across nations. While claiming that individual sign systems were "arbitrary," he also opened the possibility that languages developed their own "character." Specifically, Condillac wondered whether it was not "natural for each nation to combine its ideas according to its particular genius."[24] Discrepancies in the interests, needs, and circumstances of individual linguistic groups resulted in their processing sense impressions and associating ideas in a different manner. A preexisting feeling or sensibility characteristic of a community resulted in each national tongue developing its own unique "*génie de la langue*."[25] Condillac stressed that "each language expresses the character of the people who speak it"; the "genius of a language" reflected certain "passions" that a multitude could not conceal. National character was, however, not determined by language. It was a factor of two conditions: climate and government.[26] More pressing than the reciprocal relationship between language and nationhood was for Condillac whether linguistic peculiarities hindered or advanced progress in the arts and sciences.[27]

Condillac's notion that a group's language helped determine how its members think represents a reversal of the mentalist foundations of language proposed by Locke and Leibniz, in which linguistic expression is determined by an innate thought structure. Yet he stopped far short of assigning fully autonomous powers to language by maintaining the bonds between words and nature. In the *Essay,* arbitrariness appears to be the dominant feature of the institutional signs invented by man. But here, as in his later work, Condillac questioned the completely arbitrary nature of the linguistic sign, insisting that words were artificial but not lacking an intrinsic connection to their incorporeal ideas.[28] Like Locke, he maintained that "the most abstract terms" developed on the basis of natural analogical principles from "the first names that were given to sensible objects."[29] Metaphors provided the means of making the transition from primitive sounds to an expanding store of linguistic signs. Condillac, in other words, preserved a universal foundation for cognition in the physical nature of human sensation. The linguistic sign retained an intrinsic metaphorical meaning derived from the empirical world. And a language could become a perfect conduit for understanding if speakers took care to develop it analogically and without flaws from the original language of nature.[30] Words remained perfectible instruments in the hands of sovereign subjects until a more fully historicist theory of language made knowledge and sign systems relative to particular human communities.

J. D. Michaelis and the "Opinions of Peoples"

Condillac's understanding of language in relation to nationhood entered Germany under the auspices of the Francophone court of Frederick the Great. In 1746 the Prussian sovereign appointed Pierre-Louis Moreau de Maupertuis (1698–1759), one of Condillac's closest followers, president of the newly revitalized Academy of Sciences and Belles-Lettres. The reception of Maupertuis's and, by extension, Condillac's linguistic thought among many nascent German intellectuals was thus colored by its associations with absolute monarchy, Enlightenment rationalism, and French cultural hegemony. Adherents of the Enlightenment project, including the rationalist theologian Johann David Michaelis, welcomed both the cultural and political implications of Condillac's conception of language. His Pietist critics, J. G. Hamann and J. G. Herder, engaged fully with the questions raised by French linguistic thought, but their epistemological resistance to Condillac and Michaelis reveals a distinct agenda centered on the articulation of German difference and the advancement of an alternative notion of political community.

At stake was the question of how to reconcile Enlightenment faith in universal reason with the apparent diversity of national tongues. In the French tradition, sign systems were historically contingent and therefore arbitrary. Yet, by virtue of this very fact, the process of linguistic signification could be perfected. Individuals could amend specific instances of language use so that words corresponded more directly to preexisting rational structures. Hamann and Herder ascribed greater autonomy to national tongues, believing that speakers lacked a prelinguistic foundation for evaluating truth and accuracy. For them, the diversity of languages implied an extreme form of cultural relativism. Political institutions should be a natural outgrowth of a nation's inner spirit, just like its language, literature, laws, and mythology. In their view, the Prussian state slavishly followed the dictates of France, and absolutist rule threatened to eliminate uniquely German traditions.

Frederick the Great's vision of the enlightened state, as well as his disdain for German language and literature, shaped the Academy of Sciences that welcomed Maupertius. As his essay "On German Literature" (1780) suggests, the Prussian king feared his "native" tongue lacked the clarity, polish, purity, and taste necessary to be an effective vehicle of culture. Accordingly, he designed the academy to serve as "the official mouthpiece of French philosophy in Germany."[31] Its membership was predominantly foreign; publications and plenary sessions were held in French. Frederick, moreover, used the institution to assert his authority as an enlightened philosopher-king. The academy made manifest notions of the hierarchical relationships linking power, knowledge, and obligation that were typical of Prussian absolutism.[32] Maupertuis was a willing servant, styling himself as the enlightened despot of the academy and helping maintain the Enlightenment credentials of the king.[33]

Within this context, Maupertuis investigated how the diverse sign systems of national languages influenced the respective forms of peoples' thought. Like many in the eighteenth century, he was concerned with the relative cultural achievements of different human communities and suggested in his *Reflections on the Origin of Languages and the Signification of Words* (1748) that a comparison of the languages "to which each nation is accustomed" and their "fixing of signs. . . in this or that manner" might shed light on the way the "first human beings" developed their knowledge. His "Dissertation on the different means employed by men to express their ideas," read to the academy on May 13, 1756, urged German scholars to conduct empirical research on the epistemological nexus between national tongues and cognition.[34] At his behest one year later, the speculative-philological class of the academy hosted the first of its famous essay competitions on the topic "What is the reciprocal influence of the opinions of a people on the language and of language on opinions?"[35]

The academy competition dwelt primarily on the problem of how a comparison of national tongues could highlight defects that made language less effective as an instrument of cognition.[36] Participants were advised to consider based on examples how "the particular opinions held by the peoples" influenced the "many forms and bizarre expressions there are in languages." The successful response would also show how the preponderance of certain idioms and root words could be "sources of particular errors or the obstacles to the acceptance of particular truths." The goal of the essay was then to conclude generally how a "language in turn gives to the mind a more or less favorable inclination towards true ideas" so that "one could explore the most practicable means to remedy the short-comings of languages."[37] Reflection on language was to provide solutions to philosophical problems.[38] But the formulation of the question also suggests that the usefulness of particular sign systems could be evaluated against standards of truth that existed outside of language. Condillac himself expected the history of language to "uncover philosophical errors . . . at their causes" so that he might "prescribe a simple and easy procedure to attain certain knowledge" of the metaphysical world.[39]

The Göttingen theologian and Orientalist Johann David Michaelis (1717–91) submitted the winning essay. His *Dissertation on the Influence of Opinions on Language, and of Language on Opinions* (1759) explored what contributed to the relative "perfection, or imperfection of the languages of certain nations," situating their particular characteristics in relation to the "degrees of genius, understanding, and knowledge" that could be achieved by these peoples.[40] Michaelis took an anecdotal approach to the question, first citing cases where the influence of a people's opinions had impacted language. According to the biblical philologist, language had all the benefits and perils of a "democracy" where "use or custom is the supreme law." Nobody controlled the "immense heap of truths and errors of which the languages of the nations are the repositories," so the ideas of scholarly authorities often mixed with the knowledge of ordinary people.[41] This need not be disadvantageous. For example, the persistence of local names for plants among speakers of dialect could assist the learned botanist in his classifications. The remainder of the essay outlined those attributes that contributed to the relative "richness or poverty of a language." Michaelis showed how a "copiousness of terms and fecundity of etymologies and expressions" could further the advance of science by "preventing many errors and altercations about words."[42] Equivocation, on the other hand, spread the "kind of mist" that prevented a name from being "fully expressive of its object."[43]

The expectation of advancing knowledge by perfecting language suggests the extent that Michaelis believed words could be tools of an understanding that transcended nationality. The biblical philologist built his career interpreting the Old Testament as a historical product of the ancient nation of Israel. According to Jonathan Hess, he hoped to "de-Orientalize" contemporary Christianity by excerpting universally valid elements of the faith from what was otherwise a culturally specific product of the Hebrews.[44] The *Dissertation* is filled with examples of how the truths of divine revelation could be purged from the historical and social context in which scripture was written by identifying how nationally specific aspects of biblical languages might have altered the message of God.[45] Michaelis cautioned that some exegetes had perpetuated mistakes found in scripture because they falsely assumed that "the Hebrew people had never spoke a word but was inspired, or [that] the prophets writing in that language, had not been obliged to make use of popular expressions." His *Dissertation* suggested how the study of historical languages could rectify the literalness of such interpretations and remind readers just how alien the ancient world of the Hebrews had been.[46]

Michaelis likely suggested to Johann Gottfried Herder that languages were "an accumulation of the wisdom and genius of nations."[47] The *Fragments on Recent German Literature* (1767), in which Herder first explored the relationship between national languages and cognition, opened as a critique of Michaelis's assumption that reason was prior to and essentially independent of language. Earlier, the same assumption solicited disapproval from a fellow Orientalist, Johann Georg Hamann, who objected more generally to the understanding of language that the biblical philologist applied to the interpretation of scripture. Until this time, the goal of Enlightenment semiotics remained that of the doctrine of signs proposed by John Locke: to perfect language as a vehicle of communication and to reach an unequivocal understanding of words that might help foster the acquisition of knowledge. As will be seen, the new understanding of linguistic signification introduced by Hamann and Herder more thoroughly rooted words in the subjective consciousness of the historical subject and made human beings, not nature, the ultimate source of meaning and representation. Their notion that language was first and foremost the creative expression of a people's inner spirit brought an end to eighteenth-century attempts to reform language as a tool for enhancing and transmitting knowledge. Language study, as Hamann and Herder understood it, did not light the path to truth. Rather, it "carr[ied] a torch to the dark recesses of the human soul"[48] and illuminated the conditions under which the very standards for evaluating knowledge were constructed.

The "Living Word" of J. G. Hamann

The two theologians who came to stand as patrons of the German nationalist movement both rejected the Enlightenment project of Frederick the Great, as well as the related religious assumptions behind Michaelis's view of language. In the 1760s and 1770s, J. G. Hamann and J. G. Herder reconceived the relationship between individual languages, reason, and national culture based on the supposed role of "the word" in God's revelation to man. Responding to Michaelis's *Dissertation,* the pair declared nationality to be the result of linguistic diversity. They dismissed his instrumentalist view that language was a perfectible instrument under a person's rational control. Words, in their view, were not pliable tools, but active and autonomous subjects that helped forge culture and community. Hamann and Herder imagined national tongues to be living beings with their own laws of historical development. Languages embodied the creative power of God's word and supported more meaningful communities than those modeled on the Enlightened rational state. Reason, Hamann and Herder insisted, was the variable product of contingent linguistic structures, so too should be the political life of the nation.

Frederick the Great and his coterie of French philosophers were among the chief targets of Hamann's attack on the Berlin Enlightenment.[49] This animosity had both personal and intellectual roots. Hamann spent twenty years of his life employed as a clerk in the king's General Excise and Customs Administration, a government bureau adapted from French models. Charged with translating documents from French to German, he resented the foreign taxation practices as a constant reminder of German cultural subservience. In his polemic "To the Solomon of Prussia" (1772), Hamann demanded the king rid his realm of the foreigners who dominated the academy and recognize the genius of native sons. Like Solomon, Frederick was guilty of whoring after foreign gods, and Hamann urged him to break with his rationalistic favorites at the court.[50] For Hamann, an Enlightenment-rationalistic view of language corresponded with an overly abstract and disembodied notion of community.

Hamann's own theory of language emerged as fragments in reviews published in the *Crusades of a Philologist* (1761). Several of these reproached J. D. Michaelis with the passion of religious conviction. The animosity of the rhetoric likely stems from the differing responses each scholar had to the rationalist reforms of Enlightenment Prussia, as well as from the proximity of their intellectual projects as Orientalists and biblical exegetes. Both men had been born into Pietist strongholds and experienced a radical version of German Lutheranism that stressed the depth and sincerity of personal faith, inward reflection, and direct union with an immanent God. Michaelis had gained critical distance from the intellectual climate of his native Halle while abroad in England in 1741 and came to reject the notion that supernatural grace was working in human life. As professor for Oriental languages at the University of Göttingen, he favored a rationalist interpretation of scripture, denying the miraculous nature of Christian writings and the notion that the Holy Spirit guided exegesis of biblical texts.[51] Hebrew, Michaelis held, was a natural tongue that had to be read with the strict standards of philological criticism and interpreted based on its place within the larger Semitic language family. His rationalistic philosophy of language meshed well with the ambitious of the Francophile Berlin academy and its patron, Frederick the Great, but was a thorn in the side of their self-proclaimed enemy, the "Magus of the North."

Young Hamann's own attempts to find a niche in the Franco-Prussian cultural establishment had failed despite his early entrance into Königsberg's rising bourgeoisie. His father had been a surgeon-barber who had advanced in his career far enough to become the supervisor of a municipal bathhouse. Following a rather undistinguished tenure at the local university, Johann Georg had joined the household of rich Baltic merchants in Riga as the tutor to the ambitious Berens family. Hamann himself journeyed to London in 1758 to conduct secret negotiations on behalf of the family. But the departure from East Prussia resulted in his returning to his family's Pietist roots. For ten months Hamann reveled in raucous London living, an indulgence that propelled him into a prolonged spiritual crisis and depression. In debt and devastated to have discovered that his host had accepted money for illicit sexual favors, Hamann fled to a cheap boarding house to repent his sins. He found solace in reading the Bible from cover to cover. The transmitted word of God in scripture offered Hamann salvation and converted him to a mystical form of German Protestantism that profoundly shaped his appreciation of the power of language.

The particular object of dispute between Hamann and Michaelis

The portrait J. G. Hamann left to his parents upon leaving Königsberg to serve the family of Baroness von Budberg in 1752. The informal checkered scarf covered the hair loss he suffered following a childhood illness; in public settings Hamann preferred a wig. From Volkmar Hansen, ed. *Johann Georg Hamann, 1730–1788* (Düsseldorf: Goethe Museum, 2001). (Courtesy Goethe Museum Düsseldorf)

was the relationship of Old Testament Hebrew to Arabic and other "Oriental" tongues. Michaelis was the biblical philologist who had advanced the critical-historical interpretation of scripture by demonstrating how the study of Arabic, Aramaic, Chaldean, and Syriac could illuminate Hebrew texts. In 1761 he organized a scholarly expedition to the Arabian peninsula on behalf of the Danish crown, hoping to use contemporary ethnographic knowledge to illuminate the language and culture of an earlier period. In the *Aesthetica in Nuce* (1762), Hamann attacked Michaelis's plan to rob scripture of poetic mystery. Instead, a figurative crusade to the Levant designed to "resurrect the magic" of natural languages was in order. Mohammed may have been a "lying prophet" for Hamann, but knowledge of his words would help restore the mystical power of biblical texts.[52] Hamann himself studied Arabic, Hebrew, Chaldean, Aramaic, and dabbled in Armenian, Turkish, and Tibetan.[53] The early Romantics took from him the idea that "poetry [was] the mother tongue of the human race"[54] and that ancient eastern languages were the oldest and thus best expressed the literary and magical qualities of the divine.

The journal Hamann kept during his London conversion, later published as the *Diary of a Christian* (1758), offered an alternative account of God's presence in language. His view of scripture drew on the tradition of the Kabala and on arguments other Neo-Pietists launched against the rationalist theology of Christian Wolff (1679–1754). Specifically, Hamann adopted a type of "religious primitivism" in which the unspoiled relationship that people of early cultures had with nature was linguistic in character. Communion with a primordial language of nature offered uninhibited access to God.[55] "Every phenomenon of nature was a name," he explained, "the sign, the symbol, the promise of a fresh and secret and ineffable but all the more intimate chosen union, communication and communion of divine energies and ideas. All that man in the beginning heard, saw with his eyes, contemplated and touched with his hands, all this was a *living word* [*lebendiges Wort*]. For God was the Word."[56] For Hamann, the word of God had not been revealed in the abstract language of philosophers. Rather, God had been "the poet at the beginning of days."[57] Like the writers he inspired in the *Sturm-und-Drang* movement, Hamann insisted that inner experience, feeling, and freedom of expression were more important for apprehending the divine than reason.[58] In this he drew on the skepticism of David Hume, which held that the fallibility of the mind required faith to transcend criticism.[59] Hamann also resurrected traditional Lutheran themes regarding the authority of the Bible, the importance of a personal relationship to God, and the superrationality of faith. The creative power of the word had been the medium through which God had brought the world and all living creatures into existence; the same word, as revealed in the gospel, retained its generative force to redeem the spiritual life of man.[60]

For Hamann, all of history and creation thus presented itself in the secret language of the divine. The material world itself was a symbolic text that could be read as a poetic expression of God's grace. Hamann was an empiricist and a sensualist, assuming like Condillac that thought and reason emerged in the mind's response to external factors. But he insisted that sense impressions were always cloaked in aesthetic and poetic meaning. In this way, the natural languages of nations acquired elements of the same creative power through which God had brought the world into existence. Hamann also explained the presence of God's force in the historical tongues of specific human communities based on the traditional Lutheran doctrine of condescension and accommodation—the idea that the son had entered into the imperfect historical world of man to impart divine grace.[61] Language mediated between the divine and human for Hamann, bringing the powers of an immanent God into the mouths of historical subjects.

The creative power of God's word and the symbolic nature of historical experience framed how Hamann imagined the relationship between language, cognition, and human communities. On the one hand, he believed language existed as an object in time and space. The symbolic forms of language did not transcend their embodiment in the cultural life of particular human communities; rather, they were conditioned by the people who spoke them. As he wrote to his friend G. I. Lindner in 1759, this implied that "in the language of each *Volk* we find its very history."[62] On the other hand, historical tongues were inspired by God's creative power. Hamann believed that the divine elements of language were the source and possibility of all thought and action. Language was "the mother of reason and revelation, their alpha and omega."[63] As he wrote to Friedrich Jacobi: "without a word, no reason—no world."[64] Similarly, he depicted language as the "seducer of our understanding."[65] Thought had to be "impregnated" by the "seed of the divine Word" before taking form.[66]

The task of philosophy was not to measure the relative effectiveness with which language represented an empirical or metaphysical reality, but to acknowledge that the divinely inspired word of God was the creative source of all symbolic meaning. There was no prelinguistic form of knowledge, in Hamann's view, and thus no means for detecting error in language. A new language could not be invented to convey truth more exactly, because there were no independent rational structures that existed outside of words.

On these grounds, Hamann accused Michaelis of treating the influence language held over the opinions of a people superficially. His "Essay on an Academic Question" (1760) chided Michaelis for only showing anecdotally how deficits in language affected the possibility of reaching and communicating truth. His focus on error neglected to theorize how thought itself was substantially conditioned by language; Michaelis concentrated only on "the appearances" of this relationship. For Hamann there was a deeper connection between "our soul's faculty of perception and the body's ability to signify." A real treatment of the topic, its "main doctrine" would have been to investigate "the relationship of language" to "the means of communicating our thoughts and understanding the thoughts of others." It was not just a question of identifying the poverty or felicity with which a nation's forms allowed for the advance of knowledge. Words had a far more complex cognitive power that substantially determined thought.[67]

Significantly, Hamann's review of Michaelis proposed, as Herder would later, that language could be read as an artifact of the inner historical development of national peoples. In his view, words were the symbols in which the souls of human communities were expressed: "If . . . the soul is determined by the condition of the body; then the same may be applied to the body of an entire people [*Volk*]. The lineaments of their language will correspond with the tendencies in their way of thinking." According to Hamann, vernacular tongues documented the historical evolution of a people's inner spirit. When brought "in connection with time, place, and subject," different national languages could offer "a sea of observations" on "the history of particular peoples, societies, sects, and individuals."[68] Only through language could the nation, the deeper meaning of its poetry, and its public and institutional life be comprehended.

CHAPTER 1

Language and the *Volk:* J. G. Herder

Johann Gottfried Herder was a disciple and close friend of Hamann and shared his Pietist East Prussian upbringing. Their acquaintance dates to the English and Italian lessons Herder took from Hamann as a student at the University of Königsberg, and the pair remained in close contact until Hamann's death in 1788. Like his mentor, Herder harbored distaste for the rationalist court culture of Frederick the Great and opposed German subservience to French traditions. He likewise regarded as limited the abstract view that the state emanated from the power of a sovereign; he believed that a political community consisted of more than a central administrative body and its subjects. For Herder, language and a shared cultural legacy organically gave birth to a nation; its members were united from below by an elusive *Volksgeist.* An organic theory of language with roots in Pietist theology encouraged this brand of ethnocultural nationalism. The nation in Germany was first a religious concept before it was secularized by the generation of philologists who followed Herder.

Protestantism influenced Herder's reception of Enlightenment thought, as it did for Hamann. But he located God in the soul of national communities. God spoke not through the symbolic forms of language; rather, he made his presence felt in the human soul and encouraged people to create language from within. As will be seen, placing the act of linguistic signification in the soul of the *Volk* eliminated the effects of nature and divine revelation in cognition. The historical subject became the sole source of linguistic meaning as language lost its last claims to a stable, external foundation. Words no longer stood for ideas, rather they symbolized the mode or manner in which a national people gave meaning to objects. At the same time, language itself was transformed into a living organism whose inner principle of development was itself a force guiding the thought and spirit of a people.

Herder's first reflections on language likewise evolved as a criticism of Michaelis's academy essay. In the *Fragments on Recent German Literature* (1767–68), Herder argued that the "genius of language," a term adopted from Condillac, was also the "genius of a nation's literature." He lamented that no one had yet done for the German language what Michaelis had anecdotally done for others, to show the influence the mother tongue had on the opinions of its speakers. Herder confided that he intended to reflect on "a similar, but not the same problem" as the biblical philologist.[69] Language, he claimed, was "more than an instrument"; it was "at the same time the receptacle and content of literature." Earlier scholars had already recognized that language provided the "the form of the sciences . . . in which . . . thoughts are fashioned." Herder proclaimed that "it is much more than this"; language was the form "according to which" thoughts are formed. His goal in the *Fragments* was to characterize "the epochs . . . of our language" and to show how their historical progression had shaped four areas of German cultural life. This was the groundwork for identifying where the German language found itself in its own internal history and what type of literature it could support.[70] Three of language's cultural implications had been suspected by Michaelis: language influenced "abstract worldly wisdom, the literature of a people, and every single science." Herder had great expectations for what he considered to be "the best" insight language study provided: "knowledge of the soul." Semiotics, the study of words and signification, was, in his view, more than a tool in the service of philosophy, as it had been for Condillac and Michaelis. It aimed at "deciphering the human soul out of language."[71]

Herder's prize-winning treatise *On the Origin of Language* (1772) developed the anthropological implications of this perspective in greater detail. Inspired by a remark Michaelis made in his *Dissertation,* the Prussian Academy of Sciences had announced an essay contest in 1769 on the topic of whether man could have invented language when left to his own natural faculties. Shortly before, Maupertuis's own reflections on the origin of language had provoked Johann Peter Süßmilch to argue that the complexity and perfect ordering of language could only be explained as a direct gift of God, and the academy solicited refutations of this position.[72] Herder's response drew on an already established line of argumentation that the possession of reason and reflection, lacking in animals, provided the foundation of human language.[73] The essay topic presumed that contestants would deny the supernatural origins of language, but the opening sentence of Herder's response was still provocative: "while still an animal, man already has language."[74]

The novelty of his position derives from its rejection of Condillac's claim that nature had stimulated humanity's first words by provoking outcries of the emotions. Herder accused his predecessor of unjustly transforming animals into men when he described their gradual acquisition of institutional signs and the power to reflect. The uniqueness of humans lay for him in their being the "only creatures" endowed from the start with language and with the innate ability to reason at will. Language was "as essential to man as it is essential that he is man."[75] In Herder's view, it was a vicious circle of argumentation to claim that people could acquire words without already possessing reason or that they became reflective without the capacity for language. Condillac neglected to investigate the source of humans' representative consciousness: "words arose because words had arisen before they rose."[76]

Two decades earlier, in his *Discourse on the Origin of Inequality Among Men* (1753), Rousseau had pointed to the contradictions inherent in Condillac's argument. He was unable to resolve the question of what came first: language, society, or the capacity for reasoned thought.[77] Herder found his own way out of this dilemma by switching the focus of the origin of language debate from the problem of how nature could inspire abstract, verbal signs to an investigation of the human act of linguistic signification.[78] God had instilled the power to reflect in the human soul and thereby gave humanity the power and freedom to create language. Man, thus endowed, "learn[ed] to stand free, to find for himself a sphere of self-reflection, and seek his reflection in himself."[79] Key to understanding the origin of words was thus to delve into the representative consciousness of human beings themselves and uncover their "art of changing into sound what is not sound."[80] Here Herder relied on the soul's powers of perception and its capacity for reflection (*Besonnenheit*). Even as the senses were confronted with a "vast hovering dream of images," he argued, the reflective human mind could dwell on one perception at will and "select in it distinguishing marks [*Merkmale*]." This subjective act of perception generated the "sign through which the soul clearly remembered an idea."[81] As Herder explained in his famous example of the sheep ("the bleating-one"), man's reflective consciousness alone determined the name by which an object was to be known. Words stood in direct relation to the will of speakers and mirrored the inner force with which they imposed their subjective character on the world.

Hamann was distressed by his friend's decision to locate language in the soul of the *Volk*, criticizing Herder in several anonymous reviews and unpublished polemics. The mystic did not advocate a return to the rationalism of Süßmilch, for whom the divine origin of language was a rational truth, clear, distinct, and necessary, and not a leap of faith. But he feared Herder had wrongly asserted that human reflection had invented language in complete autonomy and in so doing denied the creative power of God. Herder himself insisted that the prospect that man invented language "reveal[ed] God in the light of a higher day: his work is a human soul which itself creates and continues to create its own language because it is his work, because it is a human soul."[82] An ordained Protestant minister at the court of Bückeburg and then Weimar, he expected to "implant in the hearts of men the word that can make souls holy."[83] Herder's theory of language showed God working within the human mind; as Arnd Bohm has suggested, he extended Adam's responsibility as a name-giver to mankind in general.[84] Significantly, Herder did not understand language as a mechanism of sociability;[85] the word emerged in an act of inwardness, of the soul expressing its essential human creativity.[86] Condillac's origin theory presumed a communicative event between two isolated children. For Herder, the "soul [of man] bleated in its interior as it were"; "the wild, lonely man in the forest would have had to have invented language for himself, even if he had never spoken."[87]

Herder's focus on the human act of linguistic signification had implications both for both ethnological study and for a new understanding of subjectivity. Language, on the one hand, was the privileged medium through which individuals and communities defined themselves. The mother tongue was inextricably linked to the "custom, character, and origin of the people" that spoke it.[88] On the other hand, as Charles Taylor has suggested, the possession of a representative consciousness implied that human activity could no longer be seen as the embodiment of an ideal external order or of a plan fixed independently of the subject, but only as the expression of a freely self-unfolding life force or soul. Herder assumed all living beings to be unified by an innate inner essence; their highest goal was attaining the full self-realization of this idea through history.[89]

Theories of language were critical to the historical consciousness that developed in the late eighteenth century, and it was language that offered Herder a model of organic growth and decay. In 1767 he proposed that each national tongue possessed "its own laws of change";[90] these revealed a language's "origin, history, and the true nature of its uniqueness."[91] Like other organic beings, languages traversed three developmental stages comparable to childhood, youth, and old age. These phases marked "the circular course of all things," and Herder suggested that language developed from "monosyllabic, rough, high tones," through a musical period of poetry and sensual imagery, to a masculine and grammatical age of philosophy and prose.[92] In his view, individuals and nations were also organisms with a higher purpose; their development was "genetic and organic" like that of language itself.[93]

The notion that language followed its own internal model of development implied that language itself could be an agent of historical transformation, an independent force that helped determine the character of a people, as well as how it exercised its powers of reason and reflection. Specifically, Herder imagined each national language (*Nationalsprache*) to be the "preserve" or "receptacle" for the "entire collection of a people's thoughts."[94] Through the centuries, each generation of speakers had borrowed and selected its defining ideas from the national treasure trove, altered them, and deposited new and refined traditions back into the mother tongue. The store of linguistic forms received by a community determined how its life force was expressed so that in language, not only was the "reason of a nation" but also "its character imprinted."[95] It was an illusion, Herder asserted, that man "had become all that he was by himself." The specific forms of a nation's linguistic expression were in the moment of their articulation always conditioned by a historical trajectory governed by the life force of language itself. Linguistic development took place within a historical community, and despite the subject's capacity for free self-expression, the articulation of the person's humanity was shaped by an extended "spiritual genesis formed by his education, parents, teachers, friends, . . . by his *Volk* and its fathers, ultimately by the entire chain of humanity."[96]

In subsequent works, Herder returned to the implications the organic growth of diverse languages had for the universality of reason and the formation of nationhood. National tongues marked for him "the beginning of reason and culture," and the historically contingent origins of their systems of signification undermined universalistic notions of truth. In his *Ideas on the Philosophy of the History of Mankind* (1785–87) Herder thus argued that no deeper metaphorical or essential relationship tied an object to the "arbitrary, completely immaterial sounds" with which it was represented in the soul. There was no "substantial connection between language and the thought" it designated.[97] This had the result that "the spirit of words and their art of abstraction is the most diverse among nations."[98] Linguistic diversity was also the basis on which Herder argued that "the landscape of nations has . . . endless gradations of color."[99] His belief in the pluralism and incommensurability of cultural values and societies rested in the differences separating national tongues. Language determined the character of a nation and was the organic force that guided its development from origins to old age. "He who was raised in a language," Herder wrote in 1795, "and learned to pour out his heart in her, express his soul in her, he belongs to the people [*Volk*] of this language . . . a nation is built and reared by means of language."[100]

This claim enabled philologists to place language studies at the core of research into the formation of culture and community. In the *Fragments,* Herder outlined an ambitious philological project on which nineteenth-century scholars with better understandings of grammar and etymology later embarked. He remarked on the difficult yet rewarding task of a "national philologist" who interpreted the history of words themselves for its greatest possible ramifications.[101] A true language scholar, Herder suggested, would be "a man of three heads" who combined philosophy, history, and philology. "Like a stranger," he would "wander through peoples and nations and learn foreign tongues and languages, so that he might speak intelligently about his own."[102] In the *Ideas,* Herder again raised the expectation that comparative philologists complete a massive ethnographic project of mapping human communities. Language was the "means to develop the humanity of our species." Therefore, "a comparison of different cultivated languages with the different revolutions of their peoples would reveal . . . a changing landscape of the manifold development of the human spirit."[103]

At the end of the eighteenth century, the philologists of the nation—most with classical training—still lacked the technical skills and linguistic materials necessary to complete what Herder envisioned as a "general physiognomy of nations based on their languages."[104] General theories on the origin of language were highly speculative in the absence of adequate data from actual languages, and despite the broad historical orientation of eighteenth-century linguistics, methods for establishing genealogical relations among languages were largely deficient. Most research concentrated on the historical connections between the vocabularies and grammatical structures of Latin and the Romance languages, but even here etymological evidence of lexical similarities was often obscured by a rigid classification of languages into syntactic types.[105] Eighteenth-century comparativists had compiled polyglot word lists, dictionaries, and texts, as well as linguistic atlases, but they were still in search of the missing link that Sanskrit or ancient Indic would provide between European and Asian languages. Comparative-historical philologists had the benefit of Sir William Jones when they took on Herder's project, but this was not before his philosophy of language came under attack from another man from Königsberg.

The Linguistic Turn in Transcendental Philosophy

The Copernican revolution that Immanuel Kant's transcendental philosophy unleashed on German thinkers at the end of the eighteenth century all but uncoupled language and thought as the relationship had emerged within the French empirical tradition. German idealists tended not to foreground the mediating function of language or to dwell on the significance of signs and grammatical structures in processes of representation. For an interesting moment at the turn of the century, however, Hamann, Herder, and a number of avowed Kantians tried to articulate how considerations of language meshed with transcendental philosophy. The linguistic critique of Kant produced among select German Romantics a conception of language in which the evolution of national tongues resembled the coming-into-being of an original idea or spirit in the historical world. This reinforced existing notions of language as a self-determining organic being, while challenging in some respects the very foundations of Kantian philosophy.

Most Kantians neglected to regard the cognitive process as a linguistic activity. The *Critique of Pure Reason* (1781) claimed to identify the a priori forms and categories that governed the human understanding. Kant hoped the work would help liberate reason from its dependence on sensual experience and thereby affirm the freedom and autonomy of the cognitive subject. Because he considered language to be an empirical condition of experience, it played little role in Kant's understanding of the a priori conditions that made knowledge possible and was never the subject of sustained discussion. Some of his followers assumed that the categories in which the phenomenal world was conceptualized could be found codified in any and all natural languages.[106] But twentieth-century critics have cited the omission of langauge as the chief weakness of transcendental philosophy. Kant neglected to address one of the main problems faced by Western thought since Plato and Aristotle. Moreover, any attempt to interpret the a priori categories of pure reason as the product of a specific historical tongue would have seriously compromised his claim to free knowledge from empirical conditioning.[107]

Hamann and Herder were the first to decry Kant's apparent silence on linguistic matters and, in so doing, forced the brief linguistic turn that transcendental philosophy took in the late eighteenth century. Four years younger than Kant, Hamann had known and lived within miles of the fellow Königsberg native for most of his life. The Berens family had unsuccessfully engaged Kant to reconvert Hamann to the cause of the *Aufklärung* in 1759; a series of philosophical confrontations between the two regarding the nature of human rationality followed. In 1781 Kant's publisher asked Hamann to review the *Critique of Pure Reason,* and he was the first to receive the galley sheets, turning to Herder for help in understanding the work. The result was a short essay titled the "Metacritique of the Purity of Reason" (1784), which took aim from a linguistic perspective at the transcendental foundations of Kant's philosophy. Until surreptitiously slipped to a publisher in 1799, the essay enjoyed an "underground existence," circulating to Friedrich Jacobi, Herder, and the third *Metakritiker,* Salomon Maimon.[108] "The major question still remains," Hamann insisted, "How is the capacity to think possible? No deduction is needed to prove the *genealogical priority of language* over the several holy functions of logical propositions and syllogisms."[109] He doubted that the categorical schemas underlying the analysis of experience were language independent. This prospect opened the possibility of rousing language in a radical critique of ontology and the coherence of the knowing subject.

The a priori categories that Kant claimed to constitute grounds for the possibility of experience were, according to Hamann, mere linguistic conventions. Foreshadowing Friedrich Nietzsche, Hamann suggested that Kant's metaphysical edifice was erected on nothing more than linguistic practice. "The entire capacity to think rests upon language," he insisted. In Hamann's view, language was "the first, last, and only organon and criterion of reason, which dismisses it with no . . . credit." Words were the ultimate pillars upon which transcendental categories could be built: "Sounds and letters" were, according to Hamann, "pure forms a priori . . . , they are the true 'aesthetic' elements of all human knowledge and reason."[110] He concluded that thinking was only the actualization of certain possibilities inherent in individual languages. Kant had falsely assumed that the categorical structures of experience were independent of historical existence and the latent possibilities present in concretely existing languages. In truth, the historical embodiment of national tongues set limits on what could be thought and experienced. Therefore, transcendental reason was no more than a construction based on the language in which it was articulated.[111]

Hamann's critique of transcendental philosophy highlighted one of the central problems that would preoccupy the first generation of post-Kantian thinkers. He blamed Kant's inability to address linguistic issues on an unnatural separation of the noumenal and phenomenal realms. Kant's distinction between understanding and sensibility, between a priori concepts and the forms of intuition, had artificially cut reason off from language.[112] "If sensibility and understanding as the two branches of human knowledge spring from one common root," Hamann questioned, "to what end such a violent, unauthorized and willful separation of that which nature has joined together! Will not both branches wither away and die through a dichotomy and division of their common root?"[113] Hamann suggested that language offered a unifying point of contact between the a priori concepts of the understanding and the intuitions of sensibility. In order to overcome Kant's dualism, Hamann suggested, philosophy must investigate the connection between thought and language. He was the first to identify the need to search for an inner unity between concepts and sense impressions. Subsequent idealists, including Friedrich Schleiermacher and G. W. F. Hegel, concurred with this analysis but substituted other mediating devices, such as religion and spirit, where Hamann relied on language.[114]

Herder's public break with his renowned former teacher was slower in coming. From 1762 to 1764 Herder had been Kant's most devoted and talented student. But Herder's friendship with Hamann slowly became the source of a growing tension between the pair, as did the critical reviews Kant published of the *Ideas*. In 1797 years of repressed animosity erupted in Herder, triggered by the impact Kant's philosophy was having on his theological students and by his own son's gravitating toward J. G. Fichte.[115] Herder showed open hostility toward Kant in his own *Metacritique of the Critique of Pure Reason* (1799). The book generated a commotion at the time, second only to the uproar caused by Fichte's being dismissed from the University of Jena on charges of atheism in the same year; it was widely read and debated among the early German Romantics.

Especially in the second section titled "Reason and Language," Herder argued that a critique of language, "the organon of our reason," was the only legitimate foundation for philosophy. He tried to shift the focus of Kant's project from defining reason in the realm of pure thought, which existed independently of linguistic expression, to the realm of language. Kant, in his view, had failed to show "how we arrive a priori at such concepts."[116] The only acceptable critique of cognition was for Herder "*Sprachkritik*"—a study of language that analyzed the conceptual resources available in natural tongues. "Metaphysics," he insisted, must "become a philosophy of human language. What an immense field! How much is there yet in it to observe, order, sow, and harvest! . . . it is the true critique of pure reason as well as of the imagination; it alone contains the criteria for the senses and for the understanding."[117] Like Hamann, Herder opposed developing distinct or specialized philosophical languages that claimed to rise above the language of experience. The grounds for the possibility of any philosophical discourse were already present in conventional language. Herder insisted more adamantly on the radically historical nature of language than either Hamann or Salomon Maimon. For him, the possibilities for cognition were historically and culturally relative to the evolution of natural languages through time.[118]

Early supporters of Kant found more affirming ways of integrating language into transcendental philosophy, arguing that he raised an intriguing set of new linguistic concerns. As Pietro Perconti has suggested, Kant stood on the threshold of a theory of language in that he reflected on the prelinguistic conditions that make linguistic meaning possible. To the extent that Kant contributed to a new theory of mental representation, he opened a space for his followers to discuss the formative role of symbolic systems in such tasks as recognizing objects and using empirical concepts.[119] Within the first post-Kantian generation there were a number of language theorists who deliberated on the role of words and grammatical structures within their mentor's theory of mental representation. Karl Leonard Reinhold (1758–1823), Georg Michael Roth (1769–1817), and August Ferdinand Bernhardi (1769–1820) interpreted language as the external presentation (*Darstellung*) of internal representations (*Vorstellungen*) by articulate sounds. In their view, language was an object of experience, but at the same time it was conditioned by the deep rules of the mind. They set out to discover the capacity of language to shape the mental faculty of representation and the connections it had to the a priori concepts of the understanding.[120]

Kant's best-known early interpreter, K. L. Reinhold, was one of the first to work out the linguistic implications of transcendental philosophy. In the *Critique of Judgment* Kant had suggested that perceptible symbols, such as language, were necessary to connect intuitions gained from sense impressions with the concepts of pure reason. Reinhold expanded this observation into his *Search for a New Theory of the Human Representational Faculty* (1789), a text that considered the role of verbal language in the rules for generating mental representations. In his view, the productive imagination had the capacity to create schemata, symbolic forms that bridged understanding and sensibility in knowledge of the natural world. Several years later, Roth adapted the seventeenth- and eighteenth-century tradition of universal grammar to analyze what such schemes might entail in linguistic terms. Port-Royal grammarians had supposed that all languages had the same essential structure derived from the universal forms of reason. In his *Antihermes or Philosophical Investigations into the Pure Concept of Human Language and General Linguistic Theory* (1795) Roth theorized the possibility of creating a *pure* universal grammar, one derived not from natural tongues but from a Kantian interpretation of human representational faculty.[121]

Johann Gottlieb Fichte (1762–1814), Kant's self-appointed spokesperson among the Jena Romantics, articulated the concept of language that became most characteristic of idealists, one derived from his readings of transcendental philosophy. Fichte had succeeded Reinhold at the local university in 1794 and credited his predecessor with suggesting to him that the Kantian dualism between the theoretical and practical realms could be overcome with a "first principle" that would systematize all philosophy.[122] Fichte's essay "Concerning the Faculty of Speech and the Origin of Language" (1795) derived language from people's inherent capacity to be rational. As Lia Formigari has argued, the piece marks an interesting moment of continuity between the naturalist linguistic theory of the French Enlightenment and nineteenth-century German idealism.[123] Like his empiricist predecessors, Fichte described the historical transformation of an original language

(*Ursprache*) from gestures and natural signs into arbitrary signs and complex forms of grammar and syntax, only he argued that all hypotheses regarding the origin of language had to be based on an ideal principle if they were to be considered valid. "One cannot rely," he explained "on the arbitrary suggestion of special circumstances under which a language *might* perhaps have arisen. . . . One cannot content himself with showing that and how a language *could* have been invented; rather, one must deduce the necessity of this invention from the nature of human reason: One must show that and how language *must* have been invented."[124] Fichte transformed the natural history of language into what he called "an *a priori* history of language" that traced the unfolding of the "idea of language" as such. The nature of the original language must be deduced from "a principle that itself lies in the nature of man"—humanity's rational capacity for speech.[125] The majority of Fichte's own essay was dedicated to explaining how the *Ursprache* as idea evolved into historical human speech and assumed grammatical form.

Idealist scholars among the German Romantics tended to regard language as a timeless reflection of rational structures. They radically dehistoricized the question of the origin of language and tried to show the necessity of, and to justify linguistic forms based on, transcendental categories.[126] In his *Philosophy of Art* (1802), for example, F. W. J. Schelling explained the genesis of language by the intrinsic necessity that drives the idea to provide itself with a body in which to fulfill itself; historical tongues were a manifestation of the idea of language in the real. Being of an ideal essence, language had to be considered an spontaneous, autonomous organism, which most closely resembled its underlying idea in its earliest forms.[127] The notion that language existed first as an idea reversed the notion that primitive man was a beast driven by his needs and passions to substitute abstract signs for grunts. The Romantics believed language degenerated from a state of perfection; a divine force spontaneously bestowed upon humans the rational capacity for language and with it the conditions of their humanity.

Fichte's notion of the "idea of language" endowed words with a new type of constructive power, one the Romantics associated less with cognition than with the aesthetic forms of human culture. As James Stam has observed, Fichte seemed to imply that "language lives and acts by its own independent rules and dynamics, almost as though language would exist even if there were no speakers of it."[128] At the turn of the century, language as an idea acquired the same spontaneity of any other self-determining idealist subject. Novalis, for example, who studied Fichte's essay in the two years after it was published, described poetry as "language enthusiasm." He believed that "Sanskrit would speak in order to speak because speaking would be its pleasure and its nature." The poet credited words with having a life of their own, seemingly independent of the will and personality of speakers: "The essential idiosyncrasy of language, that language only cares about itself—this nobody knows. . . . [Words] make up a world for themselves—they simply play with themselves, express nothing other than their own wonderful natures, and it is for exactly this reason that they are so expressive."[129] Other early Romantic poets, such as S. T. Coleridge, the spokesperson of idealist philosophy in Britain, likewise depicted words as "living powers," autonomous agents free to constitute the world in and through themselves.[130]

Fichte's essay likewise indicates that within an idealist framework, the cognitive role of language was reduced to the representation of thoughts once they left the realm of pure reason. In this view, language was not a precondition for thought. "I do not intend to prove here," he wrote, "that man cannot think or have general, abstract concepts without language. He certainly can do so through the images that his fantasy creates for itself. Language, in my opinion, has been considered far too important, when one believed that without it no use at all of reason could have taken place."[131] For Fichte all language arose out of the natural need for one human being to communicate his rationality to another. The original idea of language had been "to indicate our thoughts to each other using arbitrary signs."[132] Its very possibility presupposed self-reflection in the form of an intention to communicate one's thoughts and to be recognized as rational. For Fichte the act of self-reflection had a determinate structure that was not derived from a particular linguistic formulation or from specific content. This was the *Grundsatz* or the scientific foundation around which he hoped to systematize Kant's philosophy and construct a unified "theory of knowledge" or *Wissenschaftslehre.* His recourse to a language-independent act of self-conscious reflection merely bypassed the concerns of the *Metakritiker,* however, and was an uncertain foundation for defending transcendental philosophy against a living, willful language.[133]

Following the publication of Herder's *Metacritique* in 1799, August Ferdinand Bernhardi, considered to be the expert on linguistic matters among the early German Romantics, attempted to reinscribe language into Fichte's *Wissenschaftslehre.* A teacher and rector at the Friedrichs-Gymnasium in Berlin, Bernhardi had studied classical philology and linguistic theory with F. A. Wolf at the University of Halle and was a close personal friend of Fichte after he moved to the Prussian capital. In 1800 Bernhardi reviewed Herder's essay in the journal *Atheneum* and later expanded his defense of Kant into a two-volume *Theory of Language* (*Sprachlehre*). Bernhardi's *Theory of Language* (1801–3) attempted to create a new type of universal grammar that supported the transcendental categories of Kantian philosophy.[134] As such, the two volumes represent the only serious response to Herder's demand that transcendental philosophy be grounded in *Sprachkritik.* Its publication coincided with the bitter break-up of Bernhardi's marriage to Sophie Tieck, however, and its impact was overshadowed by that event's role in dissolving the circle of Berlin Romantics.[135]

The *Theory of Language* argued for the central role of language in mental representations, cautioning that a universal theory of grammar and syntax must be part of any critical philosophy. In contrast to Fichte, Bernhardi believed that the structure of self-conscious reflection could not be developed independently of linguistic matters. He insisted instead that transcendental philosophy had to be built upon "the fundamental principles of language," the *Sprach-Grundsätze* that mediated between the understanding and sense impressions.[136] The bulk of Bernhardi's two volumes was dedicated to reducing "the various types of presentation which occur in language . . . to a universal grammatical schema."[137] He argued that the various parts of speech, grammar, and syntax matched the transcendental scheme that Kant presented. For Bernhardi the languages of ordinary life manifested the same qualities and criteria required of philosophical thought. In every national tongue, for example, nouns embodied the Kantian category of quantity, adjectives corresponded to quality, and verbs to modality.[138] Language, he concluded, must necessarily have a formal structure supporting the human capacity for intersubjective communication and representation.

Bernhardi's transcendental grammar suggested to its first reviewer the outlines of an empirical project that combined critical philosophy with a rigorous analysis of the way national tongues mediated pure reason. August Wilhelm Schlegel concurred in 1803 that questions regarding the origin of language had only been obscured by anecdotal "observations of actual languages" and by "travelers' reports about primitive peoples." He affirmed Fichte's precept that the idea of language could only be deduced "from the organism of human mental activities." In addition, Schlegel's review proposed relating "the specialized grammars of individual languages" to the "universal theory of language." Following Herder, Schlegel believed that national tongues "expresse[d] the inner organism" or soul of those who spoke them; "comparative grammar" allowed philologists to determine "what is most characteristic" among national groups. But he suggested that comparative language studies could also delineate how the structures of diverse national tongues related to "the law-governed organism of language in general."[139] The demands of the project were technically too ambitious for the state of comparative linguistics at the time. In the decades that followed, however, Wilhelm von Humboldt applied the new insights of comparative philologists to a philosophical survey of the diverse transcendental thought structures enabled by national tongues.

Wilhelm von Humboldt's Philosophy of Language

Wilhelm von Humboldt took active part in the early Romantic reaction to Kant, translating the philosophical concerns of his followers into a concrete and influential research agenda for language scholars. Reason, for Humboldt, may have been a spontaneous product of the creative mind, but it was also conditioned by the organic, historical development of particular national tongues. His attempt to reconcile these two positions produced empirical analyses of the relative effectiveness with which historical languages fostered mental activity. Humboldt's work is often recognized as the forerunner of the so-called linguistic relativity thesis. This phrase is taken from the work of two twentieth-century American linguists, Edward Sapir and his student Benjamin Lee Whorf, who argued that the words, grammatical structures, and habitual language practices associated with individual national tongues condition the worldview of their speakers.[140] The constructivist aspects of Humboldt's linguistic philosophy fall just as much within the tradition of German idealism, as they emanate from the legacy of French thought. Therefore, it is misleading to assume that nineteenth-century German linguists excluded issues relating national tongues to the mind and representation. The attempt to reinsert language into Kantian philosophy gave rise to a particular type of *Erkenntniskritik* or epistemological critique that followers of Wilhelm von Humboldt carried through to the late nineteenth century.

Friedrich Heinrich Jacobi was a close personal friend of Humboldt and introduced him to the problem of mediating between reason and sensibility in 1788.[141] When Humboldt moved to Jena in search of an intellectual vocation, he had thus already confronted the difficulty of reconciling the spontaneity of human reason with the receptivity of sensibility. Fichte also took up residence in the center of German classicism in the spring of 1794, and it was under his tutelage that Humboldt's appreciation of Kant turned to linguistic matters. Fichte's lectures and his essays on language had such a profound impact on Humboldt's intellectual development that he later found himself defending Kant against the disciples of Condillac in Paris. The ideologues, as Humboldt explained in his notebooks, wrongly stressed the receptivity of the mind, assuming that sensibility alone conditioned language. Kant asserted that free mental activity generated representations, and human cognition depended on the spontaneity of the subject. In Humboldt's view, empiricist conceptions of language could not sufficiently account for creative acts of the mind. Only a transcendental approach to language could successfully depict words as free, constructive subjects, while recalling that they were also objectively conditioned by historical existence.[142]

Language thus enjoyed a liminal status for Humboldt, existing between the subjective and objective realms of experience. It was for him what the synthesis of judgment was for Kant.[143] Words and grammatical structures acted as the filter through which the mind perceived and represented the external world. "No thought, not even the most pure," Humboldt argued in "On Speaking and Thinking" (1794–95), "can occur without the help of the general forms of our sensibility."[144] Humboldt agreed with Kant that perception resulted from an individual interacting with an object of experience. For him, however, only the active application of language to sensation could bridge the gap between a priori concepts and intuitions. Language served Humboldt as an "intermediate world" (*Zwischenwelt*);[145] it was "the great point of crossing from subjectivity to objectivity."[146]

Humboldt's conception of language resembled Fichte's in that both derived the idea of language from rational structures already present in the human mind. Much of Humboldt's empirical research was dedicated to cataloging the universal qualities required for representation in the form of a general grammar. As he stated in the *Principles of the General Linguistic Type* (1824), "the basic determinations of grammar are already contained in the universal rules of thought. . . . In this area universal grammar falls together with logic to a certain extent."[147] Like A. F. Bernhardi, Humboldt applied the Port-Royal tradition of general grammar to support the universality of Kant's categories of perception and understanding. He had read Bernhardi's *Sprachlehre* immediately upon its publication in 1801; the two were acquainted in Berlin, and Humboldt readily acknowledged his debt to his predecessor: "I am accustomed to follow Bernhardi's linguistic principles in dealing with concepts of general grammar."[148] For example, he concluded with Bernhardi that Kantian categories were most apparent in the four grammatical cases, the nominative, dative, genitive, and accusative.[149]

As a trained philologist, however, Humboldt analyzed the grammatical structures of individual national tongues to determine how each fulfilled its representational function. Empirical research was to establish how national tongues articulated the inborn capacity humans had for language (*Sprachvermögen*) while responding to the historical world they inhabited.[150] Upon retiring from public life in 1819, Humboldt wrote extensively on the diversity of human language construction and its cultural and philosophical implications. The essays proposed a hierarchy of national tongues based on how effectively the grammatical forms of each approximated Kantian categories. Did some languages come closer to embodying the ideals of a universal, transcendental grammar? Because Humboldt believed nationality conditioned the historical existence of language, it is advisable first to examine his views on this relationship before turning to his linguistic findings.

Humboldt's early essays on classical antiquity presupposed a conventional reciprocity of language and nationality. Like Herder and the early Romantics, he cited language, poetry, philosophy, and literature as contributing factors in the formation of national groups.[151] Later, Humboldt focused on the specific relationship between nationality and the structure of language. There is an ambivalence in these writings as to whether national character determined the forms of language or whether language itself affected how a nation thought. His essay "On the National Character of Languages" (1821/22) suggested that it was historically impossible to determine what priority should be given to language as a cause of national diversity. The "individuality of nations and epochs is so entwined with that of languages" that empirical research could never restore the "the beginning of such a progression."[152]

In the decade that followed, Humboldt gravitated to the position that national character existed prior to and itself molded the so-called inner form of language.[153] By his account, national character existed as a "living force" (*Kraft*). It was an elusive energy, impulse, or vitality that produced in all people of a nation a common emotional orientation or instinctive mood.[154] When evaluating how the "mental individuality of a people" related to the "shape of its language," Humboldt explained, "we must see the real principle of explanation and true determining ground in the mental power of nations, since this alone stands independently living before us."[155] Feelings and desires internal to the mind were active, prelinguistic forces that shaped what Humboldt termed the "inner form" of language. The particular way a language denoted the relations between the parts of a sentence originated in the depths of the nation that spoke it. Humboldt rejected the notion that race, skin color, physical build, or physiognomy had an impact on the development of national tongues. Nevertheless, Jeffrey Grossman and others have seen a racialist dimension in Humboldt's notion that an inborn national character could be an original cause of linguistic variation.[156]

The assumption that some mental activity occurred prior to language testifies to the impact John Locke had on Humboldt. But Humboldt also claimed that "to regard words as mere signs," as the empirical tradition had done, was the "basic error that destroys all linguistics and all correct evaluation of language."[157] For him, all thought that involved judgment or awareness depended on speech.[158] As Humboldt stated in the *Principles:* "language [is] not only a designation for thoughts that are formed independently; rather, it is the creative organ of thought itself."[159] Language had a constructive role in the processes of concept formation and perception. It was, in this sense, a transcendental precondition for constituting objects.[160] "Intellectual activity," Humboldt concluded,

> spiritual and internal throughout, and to a certain extent passing without a trace, becomes, by the tone of discourse, externalized and perceptible for the senses. . . . Intellectual

> activity and language are therefore one and inseparable; one cannot merely regard the former as that which produces the latter and the latter as that which is produced. Intellectual activity is connected to the necessity of entering into a connection with a tone; thinking cannot otherwise attain clarity, the representation [*Vorstellung*] cannot become a concept [*Begriff*].[161]

Language, for Humboldt, was more than a means of communication or a mechanism of sociability. "Speech," he agreed with Herder, was "a necessary condition for the thought of a sole person in solitary isolation."[162]

The constitutive role language had in thought implied that the forms of language also structured the subjective life of speakers.[163] In 1811–12 Humboldt had suggested that "language is an independent being, guiding and controlling man, even as it is produced by him."[164] Vitalist metaphors in biology, as well as the Romantic aesthetic theory of A. W. Schlegel, in which poetry was a creative force, contributed to this view of language.[165] Humboldt likewise based the autonomy of language on its status as an organic, historical being. In his view, each national tongue was an "organic totality." It lived and changed over time, vicariously altering the concepts through which the understanding mediated experience. He explained in *On the Diversity of Human Language Construction and Its Influence on the Mental Development of the Human Species* (1830–35) that "we must look upon language, not as a dead product, but far more as producing. . . . It is not a product [*ergon*], but an activity [*energeia*]. Its definition can therefore only be a genetic one."[166] Historicizing language as a living organism endowed national tongues with autonomous, constructive powers that molded the thought of the speaking subject.

Humboldt specifically held language responsible for creating the unique worldview (*Weltansicht*) that shaped how a people thought and experienced the sensual world. "Thinking," he suggested in 1820, "is not merely dependent on language in general, but also, to a certain extent, it is determined by each individual language." The constructivist aspects of Humboldt's linguistic theory are most apparent in his discussions of the different conceptual worlds generated by the diversity of historical languages. What members of a nation could think was determined and confined to the total conceptual possibilities available to their national tongue at different moments in history. "Each language," Humboldt elaborated, "carries at every point of its existence the expression of all concepts which at that time can be developed in the nation. Further, each is at every point in its life exactly equal to the conceptual range of the nation at that time. Each ultimately, in each of its states, develops the totality of a worldview, in that it contains expressions for all representations that the nation makes about the world, and for all the sensations the world brings forth in it."[167] On these grounds, Humboldt concluded that each language drew a closed conceptual "circle" around the nation that spoke it. Individuals could only reach beyond the limits of their mental horizons by switching languages. Learning a foreign tongue enabled, according to Humboldt, the "acquisition of a new standpoint in the previous worldview."[168]

The three-volume Kawi work that Humboldt assembled in the last years of his life detailed what the empirical study of language revealed about various national capacities for intellectual and cultural development. The book-length introduction proposed that classifying languages into types would help researchers order nations based on how well various grammatical structures fostered "the growth of man's mental powers."[169] The Kawi language was to provide a common link through which the world's tongues could be related and opposed. Humboldt had begun studying South Pacific languages in 1827, focusing on Malaysian tongues. Kawi, the courtly language of Java, was intriguing because it mixed "Sanscritic" languages and what are now known as Western and Central Austronesian tongues.[170] These had a wide dispersal throughout the Pacific Rim and thus allowed for integrating other language families as well. By analyzing their "organic structure" and their "method of constructing language," Humboldt expected to discover the possibilities for thought, expression, and intellectual development built into a broad swath of language types.[171]

The hierarchy of national tongues that Humboldt proposed distinguished three types of language based on how they designated grammatical relationships in a sentence: inflection, agglutination, and incorporation. These terms did not represent absolute principles of classification; any given language could mix grammatical methods.[172] But Humboldt maintained, as Friedrich Schlegel had before him, a clear distinction between organic and mechanical schemes. Sanskrit and other inflectional languages, which included Hebrew, were, in his view, the only ones to achieve a truly organic unity of designation. By definition, these languages signified the grammatical function of words by fusing onto a radical affixes that had no intrinsic meaning beyond their role in clarifying syntax.[173] The use of "meaningless" symbols to designate grammar was for Humboldt preferable to employing independently meaningful words or affixes.[174] He believed inflectional languages to be "more excellent" and "perfect," "correct," and "happy"; they were the "most natural and most suitable" and distinguished by a "completeness and purity" of structure.[175] Humboldt drew a continuum between two "extreme" linguistic types: Sanskrit, the form in which "the mental cultivation of mankind has evolved most happily"; and Chinese, which departed "furthest from the natural demands of language."[176] The advantage of inflection was that it supposedly represented most completely the universal laws of cognition that could be derived from the rational structures of the mind. According to Martin Manchester, Humboldt held that this language type better maintained at the symbolic, linguistic level distinctions that supposedly existed at the level of concept formation and perception.[177]

Wilhelm von Humboldt's synthesis of transcendental philosophy and empirical language study was not easily replicated. A. F. Bernhardi himself had insisted on separating the "philosophical approach" from the "historical approach" to language.[178] And the early nineteenth century witnessed a growing breach between empirical philologists who pursued comparative-historical studies and more speculative generalists interested the philosophy of language.[179] It is testimony to the legacy of Kant that later German idealists largely dismissed the epistemological concern for language that intrigued the Romantics. There is nevertheless a forgotten chapter of German linguistic philosophy that carried Humboldt's work into the twentieth century.[180] After 1850 figures such as Heymann Steinthal, Moritz Lazarus, and Gustav Gerber rekindled Humboldt's ambitious philosophical project. Under the influence of J. F. Herbart's psychology, they reopened questions of how language structured patterns of representation and cognition. It is to them that Humboldt's posthumous reputation as a language theorist is due. And, as chapter 6 shows, it is through Humboldt that the viability of using language to critique metaphysics and the autonomy of the subject was preserved.

Philology and the Philosophy of Language

The professional nineteenth-century German philologists whose institutional standing Wilhelm von Humboldt helped secure largely avoided philosophical consideration of the role national tongues played in cognition. The generation of language scholars who came of age after 1800 confined their research to empirical analysis of specific national tongues and the history of the communities that spoke them. The metaphysical critique of Hamann, Herder, and Humboldt was of little use in this endeavor. Still, the intimate connection this trio drew between words and national cultures redefined the discipline of philology as it had been practiced to date. For most of the eighteenth century, philology—primarily the study of Latin, Greek, and Hebrew—had existed as a supplemental field subsumed within theological and law faculties. Scholars of language tended to the epistemological needs of their host disciplines by exploring the sign systems of their respective discourses. Through recitation, disputation, and formal textual reconstruction, students of language learned ideal rhetorical strategies for transmitting knowledge of the material and metaphysical world. Familiarity with classical rhetoric and grammar, for example, prepared lawyers for reading legal texts and trained future ministers in the skills of biblical criticism. Philologists provided a largely pedagogical service, relaying mastery of a style of eloquence and erudition required of the educated elite.[181]

Herder's critique of Enlightenment semiotics helped transform philology into a discipline in which language was central to a historicizing and secularizing program of cultural studies. His characterization of language as a historical being entwined in the construction of culture and community enabled classicists in the late eighteenth century to redefine the intellectual terrain of traditional philology and establish themselves as specialists and professionals in a highly regarded, independent field of cultural studies. The transformation of *Altphilologie* into a genuinely critical and interpretive discipline has been well documented by Robert Leventhal and requires only a brief summary here. In the 1770s the founder of the prestigious philological seminar in Göttingen, Christian Gottlob Heyne (1729–1812), reconceived the task of philological study in response to Herder's claim that words themselves embodied historically particular modes of giving meaning to the world. His cohort of influential classicists asserted the importance of philology as a tool for reconstructing the historical and cultural totality of the ancient world, demonstrating at the same time the importance of linguistic inquiry and a self-reflective reading of texts to other disciplines in the humanities.[182] Humboldt himself served as head of the newly created Department of Culture in the Prussian Interior Ministry from 1809 to 1810, and he institutionalized language study as the mainstay of humanistic inquiry.

Classical philology thus stood at the fore as the German universities evolved from pedagogical institutions and schools of professional training to modern, research-oriented institutions. Friedrich August Wolf, the first in 1777 to matriculate as a student of philology, excluded pedagogical and rhetorical training from the curriculum of the seminar in classical studies he established in Halle in 1787, dismissing with disdain the narrow pedantry and empty formalism of older forms of language studies. In the early 1790s, a series of pedagogical and educational reforms that placed a new premium on expertise, research, and disciplinary specialization further devalued the contributions traditional *Altphilologie* made to German intellectual life. Teachers of Latin and Greek responded by asserting the exclusive prerogative of philologists to teach the interpretive skills necessary for the new humanistic sciences and by forging classical philology into the modern professionalized field of *Altertumswissenschaft* (classical studies).[183]

As the following chapters show, classicists quickly lost their monopoly on the study of language despite the continued prestige of their textual and historical methods. Experts in ancient Greek and Latin shied away from the comparative and historical studies that formed the avant-garde of the language sciences in the nineteenth century. Faith in the universal aesthetic forms of Greek language and culture kept classicists from embracing a relativist landscape of nations and situating the Hellenes within the larger "physiognomy of nations" that Herder envisioned. Only after the Napoleonic invasions did a younger generation of Orientalists and Germanists fulfill the historical ambitions he and Humboldt had for comparative philology.

Constructivist theories of language and the particular perspective of German idealism informed the empirical agenda of comparative philology. The field's characteristic veneration of origins and primordial linguistic forms arose from an attempt to recover the original "idea of language" in pure form. Fichte and the early Romantics tended to displace historical discussions of the origin of language onto Adam and Eve and an empirically unverifiable period of human history.[184] At the start of the nineteenth century, new empirical techniques promised to recover that Golden Age when the world's languages most closely approximated their underlying, divine idea. Origins retained a generative capacity and were granted the power of setting the patterns by which organic structures evolved. The legacy of the late Enlightenment is likewise manifest in the constructive role nineteenth-century philologists attributed to language in the formation of culture and community. Organic metaphors continued to credit languages with molding the souls and spirits of national groups.

By 1800, words had come alive in an odd mixture of Protestant theology and an idealist veneration of the creative, divine idea. According to late eighteenth-century theorists, linguistic forms structured the possibilities for self-expression, identity formation, and being in the world with slight regard for individual speakers. Wilhelm von Humboldt and his contemporaries had begun to doubt that a truth existed outside the structures of language and to investigate whether words themselves did not produce the reality they were intended to represent. In so doing, these scholars introduced a characteristically conflicted modern understanding of language. Words were regarded as both the expression of the subjective will of those who spoke them and as set pieces in an evolving grammatical grid that structured meaning independently of the speaker. Comparative-historical philologists welcomed this tension between the expressive and constructive aspects of language as a dynamic explanation for the formation of national communities. Later scholars of language would lose their reverence for the past as they translated a radical historicization of language into an appreciation of the confines that fixed grammatical structures imposed on a faltering subject.

2

Urheimat Asien

German Nationhood and the "Indo-Germanic" Language Family, 1770–1830

On January 11, 1809, the German Orientalist Heinrich Julius von Klaproth (1783–1835) returned to Saint Petersburg, suffering from a high fever that had killed his travel companions in the Caucasus mountains. For over a year, Klaproth and his assistants had plodded through "deep and unsound snow" to reach remote mountain villages in the provinces stretching between Baku and the Volga-Don line. The Russian Academy of Sciences had engaged them to complete a geographic and ethnographic survey of those northern areas recently brought under Czar Alexander's control and those further south still being contested militarily. But the twenty-five-year-old Klaproth was most interested in taking linguistic samples of the myriad little-known tongues spoken in Georgia, Armenia, and Azerbaijan. He was drawn by the prospect of finding surviving evidence of early Medo-Germans he believed had once inhabited the Caucasus or traversed the region during their prehistoric migrations westward into Europe. Klaproth was not disappointed. His memoirs recall encountering speakers of the Ossetian language not far from the Inguri and Terek Rivers. To his delight the members of this group appeared to use root words similar to those in German and Farsi and had curiously blue eyes and blond or red hair.[1] Based on his findings, Klaproth proposed the term "Indo-Germanic" in 1823 to designate those tongues and peoples he believed had descended from a common central Asian homeland or *Urheimat*.[2]

Julius Klaproth was one in a long line of German Orientalists whose linguistic talents served the Russian Empire. His concern for the prehistoric ties early Germans may have had to the East also exemplifies a key preoccupation of nineteenth-century German language scholars. Was the cultural starting point of the German nation to be found in central Asia? Russian imperial expansion into the Persian and Ottoman Empires provided Klaproth with the opportunity to seek first-hand evidence of Germanic migration across the so-called "bridge of nations from Asia to Europe."[3] His research falls within a tradition of German language study that aided colonization of the Russian borderlands. It also points to an overwhelmingly positive national identification that German scholars cultivated with central Asia as a possible primordial homeland. Since the publication of Edward Said's *Orientalism* (1978), there have been numerous attempts to identify an "Orient" that was the particular preserve of German scholarship and to characterize the relationship between knowledge and power among Orientalists trained in states without colonies.[4] Early nineteenth-century German philologists were particularly interested in central Asia. Their efforts suggest possible connections between linguistic research and colonial expansion, but they also highlight the significance of comparative philology for the definition of German nationhood.

This chapter reconstructs the first of three national genealogies that German language scholars created in the early nineteenth century. As Klaproth indicates, the Orientalist model of German national origins relied heavily on perceived linguistic ties between modern German, Farsi, and Sanskrit. Philologists drew ethnological implications from the invention of the "Indo-Germanic" language family, tracing lines of linguistic descent back to a primordial Germanic past. The chapter suggests why words were considered the key to discovering the national origins and ethnic affiliations of the world's peoples. Orientalist attempts to pinpoint the German *Urheimat* grew out of a long-standing desire to locate a terrestrial paradise or Garden of Eden in Asia. The prospect that the first Germans were migrants from the East drew its initial authority from traditional biblical narratives of the dispersal of nations after Babel. Language had been the key to the genealogy of nations offered in Genesis, and it continued to inform German efforts to reconstruct new lines of cultural origin and descent in the nineteenth century.

German Orientalists revised the traditional biblical framework in which much ethnographic work had been structured to date. Comparative philology enabled a new type of comparative cultural history that rewrote the genealogical table presented in the Old Testament, questioning its monogenetic view of human origins and seeking other models for the emergence of cultural diversity than the story of Genesis. The chapter begins with a brief account of how biblical scholarship informed comparative-historical philology in the late eighteenth century. It then shows how deeply philological narratives of national origin were embedded in theological debates. The historicization of Indo-European and, especially, Semitic languages had substantial implications for biblical criticism, as it did for the German national self-understanding. Only with the gradual institutional separation of linguistics from Oriental philology did religion retreat behind the mask of disinterested scholarship.

Mosaic Ethnology and the Persian Impasse

Since the writing of the Old Testament and in all the Jewish, Christian, and Muslim traditions that drew on this source, language has been interpreted as an indication of the genealogical relations among human communities. Genesis suggests that Noah's three sons, Shem, Ham, and Japheth, were responsible for spreading the diverse national tongues across the globe, and for centuries researchers tried to align existing languages and peoples with biblical figures. Medieval scholars, for example, compiled lists of the supposed seventy-two world languages and aligned them with the seventy-two descendents of Noah's sons named in Genesis.[5] Thomas Trautmann has aptly described this tradition of classifying nations and peoples based on the book of Genesis as "Mosaic ethnology,"[6] and it is within this Christian context that the German relationship to the East was viewed in the late eighteenth century. The descriptive study of human communities was tied especially in this period to the legacy of Georg Wilhelm Leibniz (1646–1716) and authors of universal history (*Universalgeschichte*).[7]

Writing in the political chaos that followed the Thirty Years War, Leibniz recognized the central role of linguistic homogeneity in the formation of nations and was a chief advocate of strengthening the "*teutsche Nation*" through devotion to the vernacular. As the founder and first president of the learned society that evolved into the Prussian Academy of Sciences, Leibniz proposed compiling a comprehensive historical dictionary of German and its respective dialects.[8] German, he believed, was equally as ancient as Hebrew and likely, in a more archaic form, had once reigned over much of Asia and Europe.[9] Leibniz likewise demonstrated how the study of individual tongues could be used to establish genealogical relationships and historical descent among nations. Words, in his view, were "the oldest monuments of peoples" and "best indicate[d] their origins, kinships and migrations." He himself classified the world's languages into two "species," the northern Japhetic family and the Aramaic of the south; he was the first to suspect historical ties between Finnish and Hungarian and to use archaic river and place names in tracing the migrations of peoples, especially the Basques.[10]

Leibniz's linguistic initiative directly inspired the emergence of ethnology as a field in late eighteenth-century Germany. In 1713 he had written to Peter the Great encouraging him to survey the many non-European languages found in the expanding Russian Empire. Half a century later, the Göttingen Orientalist and historian August Ludwig Schlözer (1735–1809) undertook to classify the peoples inhabiting the region that stretched from Iceland to Kamchatka based on the word lists that the German scholars had subsequently assembled in the reign of Catherine the Great. His *General History of the North* (1771) coined the terms "*Ethnographie*" and "*Völkerkunde*" and explained how Leibniz's proposition "to infer from uniformities in language and descent . . . that nations share in the same customs and fate" made possible a new "science of peoples": "In this I consult no history or travel books, rather I examine the languages themselves based on the available grammars, dictionaries, and Bible translations. . . . Then I classify these languages according to the main tongues and vernaculars and determine from them classes of people along with their subdivisions."[11] On the basis of language, Schlözer believed he had identified the five main peoples living west of the Ural mountains (Finns, Latvians, Slavs, Germans, and Samoyeds) and the twenty-two primary linguistic groups of the Asian north.

Schlözer's work is significant for the priority it assigned to language in the identification of ethnic groups. He outlined three defining features that helped constitute a *Volk:* geographical proximity, common descent, and membership in a political community; all were "derived from the use of language whose force neither history nor philosophy can overcome."[12] But Schlözer lacked a sufficiently historical view of language that might have enabled him to turn his essentially static or Linnaean system of northern peoples into a historicizing narrative of common descent. As soon as he integrated linguistic communities into larger historical continuities, Schlözer ceased to regard them on their own terms, characterizing peoples solely based on their position within the progress and development of "the human species" in its totality.[13] Although he longed to reconstruct a genealogy of peoples that led from Adam and the Old Testament to the current inhabitants of the north, Schlözer feared that the necessary "middle links" between languages spoken by followers of Noah's sons and his own subjects could never be recovered.[14] Until the nineteenth century, etymology was largely a speculative science. Comparativists lacked adequate tools for bridging the historical distance between recorded languages and those prehistoric tongues alluded to in the Jewish Bible.

Nevertheless, Europeans speculated on the likely location of the Garden of Eden. The philosophical cultural histories of late Enlightenment scholars such as J. G. Herder presumed central Asia, specifically the region around Kashmir, to be the cradle of humanity and by extension the ultimate point of origin of all Europeans.[15] The German connection to central Asia could not be confirmed by concrete historical or linguistic evidence, however. In the late eighteenth century, genealogies of language aimed primarily at identifying the relative progress with which individual idioms allowed for the exercise of reason and not at reconstructing the history of human communities.[16] Even those scholars with a historical interest in language, such as the preeminent German comparativist Johann Christoph Adelung (1732–1806), had to conclude that "Noah's ark is a sealed bastion, and the ruins of Babylon lie still before me."[17] The gap between languages of historical record and the time of Babel was impassable without methods for reconstructing prehistoric linguistic states. Late eighteenth-century comparativists could only trace the actual ancestry of modern Germans as far east and "back in time" as Iran.

As the lingua franca of south and central Asia and the language in which East India Company officials were trained, Farsi was well known to European scholars, and its connections to German were readily apparent.[18] Scholars intrigued by possible German ties to the East thus focused on the similarities between their mother tongue and Farsi, drawing on a tradition of language comparison that dated to the sixteenth century and relied primarily on lexical items.[19] Similar sounding words in German and Farsi (such as *Bruder* und *barâdar*) could be shown to have equivalent meanings (in this case, "brother"), from which the researcher could conclude that the two languages were related. This approach to comparative linguistics invested instances of lexical convergence with genealogical significance but without sophisticated mechanisms for tracing lineage or linking such ties to affinities in the collective consciousness of speakers.

Adelung's *Ancient History of the Germans* (1806) explored the German-Farsi connection in depth, concluding that similarities between the root syllables of the two tongues were so compelling that they could not be explained by borrowing or mixing but only by "an original derivation" of the languages and peoples from each other.[20] In his view, the Goths had enjoyed a "long sojourn" on the Black Sea from where they had penetrated parts of Iran and lived in close proximity with its inhabitants. These tribes adopted so much of the local language that, according to Adelung, German must be seen as a "very deteriorated descendent of Parsi, the original language of the southern provinces."[21] Notably, Adelung refused to pinpoint the exact location in Asia from which the Goths had swept into Iran, leaving open the question of the ultimate origins of Germans and humankind. He recognized the great age of Sanskrit but neglected to connect it directly to German, grouping ancient Indic together with such unrelated languages as Hebrew, Syrian, and Turkish.[22] Adelung later speculated that the cradle of civilization where "the honorable ancestors of all . . . peoples and languages" once resided likely lay somewhere in the eastern part of Kashmir, near Tibet. This region he described as an Asian "paradise" akin to the Garden of Eden: the first human couple was at home here, and the most simple monosyllabic languages from which all others derived flourished in its protective embraces.[23] But Adelung could not connect Farsi to the language of Adam.

It was a better understanding of how to reconstruct archaic states of a language as a basis for determining the proximity of linguistic groups that enabled Sir William Jones to see connections between Sanskrit, Slavic, German, and the classical European tongues in 1786. His "discovery" of the Indo-European language family is often depicted as a decisive break from speculative biblical narrative, but his realization that Farsi was related to ancient Indic initially did little more than bring European scholars closer to Eden and push European ancestry deeper into Asia. In his presidential address to the Royal Asiatick Society of

Bengal, Jones observed that Sanskrit bore to Greek and Latin "a stronger affinity both in the roots of verbs and in the forms of grammar, than could possibly have been produced by accident; so strong indeed that no philologer could examine them all three, without believing them to have sprung from some common source."[24] These words inaugurated modern scientific philological discourse. Jones demonstrated the greater reliability of grammatical rather than lexical comparisons and identified most major branches of what became known as the Indo-European language family; he also suspected the existence of a common mother tongue, more ancient than Sanskrit itself, which has now been reconstructed as Proto-Indo-European.

In its eighteenth-century form, however, the Indo-European thesis was little more than an attempt to practice Mosaic ethnology. Jones was reluctant to consider himself a linguist per se and never questioned the premodern assumption that language was a perfectible instrument of knowledge and not an object of study itself. His comparisons were intended to show the common origin of what was believed to be the five main Asian nations (Persia, Chaldea, Turkey, India, and China) and ultimately to recover the lost common language of Noah and Adam. For this reason he included the unrelated languages of Egypt, China, Japan, Java, and Myanmar, as well as those of the Incas and Aztecs, in the same family as Sanskrit. Indeed, it was the possibility raised by the mythologist Jacob Byrant that Greeks and Indians were related to Egyptians as common descendents of Ham (not Japheth) that allowed Jones to see ties across the family. He never intended to separate Indo-European and Semitic languages and only inadvertently discovered that Sanskrit bore no resemblances in words or structures to Arabic.[25] Nevertheless, Jones's approach to etymology and historical grammar opened a new avenue for reconstructing the early history of languages and peoples that could theoretically reach back to Babel while challenging the genealogical table of the Pentateuch on purely linguistic authority.

Before Babel: India and the Romantic Search for Origins

Nineteenth-century German scholars of Indo-European languages owe a great debt to William Jones, but the popularity of the comparative method is due largely to German efforts. German Indologists quickly surpassed their British colleagues in both the quality and quantity of their scholarship.[26] Until Friedrich Max Müller (1823–1900) advocated instruction in Sanskrit for civil service candidates, British universities neglected the field. Colonists tended to agree with Thomas Babington Macaulay's remark to parliament in 1835 that a single row of books in a European library was more valuable than Asian literature in its entirety. The eager reception of comparative philology in Germany and its rapid decline across the channel can be attributed to more than the sobering effects of Britain's colonial encounter, however. Differing conceptions of language and its perceived role in defining human communities were a factor as well. The legacy of the language theorist Horne Tooke rendered British scholars indifferent to the comparative-historical techniques introduced by Jones. Until 1830 British scholars persisted in regarding language as a reflection of the rational structures of the human mind.[27]

J. G. Herder and his mentor, J. G. Hamann, were seminal figures in the transfer of Indian studies from Britain to Germany. In the last decade of the eighteenth century, Georg Foster (1754–94) and Friedrich Majer (1772–1818) published the first German renditions of the Sanskrit works Jones had translated into English. Fascinated by the religious and philosophical teachings of the Brahmans, especially as found in the mythology of the *Law Book of Manu*, these two introduced Herder, J. W. von Goethe, and Friedrich Schiller to the *Sakuntala*. Herder's commentaries on the drama set the template for the mythical image of India that long fascinated the Romantics.[28] Before this time, however, Hamann and Herder had already introduced the early Romantics to the notion that the first languages and human communities had developed in India.[29] In their view, the poetic forms of Eastern languages recalled the divine word of revelation and contained hidden religious symbolism. Knowledge of Sanskrit promised to unlock the mysteries of a primordial and deeply authentic mythology.

The geographic reorientation of German Orientalists toward India did not eliminate interest in Iran. Well into the 1820s, a number of German Orientalists still viewed Avestan (or Zend, the ancient Iranian language of the sacred Zoroastrian books) as the *Ursprache* from which modern German derived. Before his "conversion" to Sanskrit, the then professor of philosophy in Bamburg Othmar Frank (1770–1840) found "the light of primordial German nationality still burning" in the ancient religious teachings of Iran. His works *On the Persian Language and its Origins* (1806) and *The Light from the Orient* (1808) recommended founding a "Philosophical-Persian Academy" in Germany, dedicated to the "oldest wisdom of the Orient and the German nation."[30] Heinrich Friedrich Link (1767–1851) argued that Avestan was the mother of Sanskrit and of all languages related to it, concluding in 1821 that the earliest Germans had once inhabited the mountains of Media, Armenia, and Georgia.[31] Bernhard Dorn (1805–81) likewise followed Adelung in emphasizing the German-Farsi connection.[32]

Ancient India began to eclipse the importance of Iran within the cultural imagination of nineteenth-century Germans after the publication of Friedrich Schlegel's *On the Language and Wisdom of the Indians* (1808). Schlegel believed that he had finally pinpointed the actual location of the elusive terrestrial paradise that Adelung and Herder had cautiously placed in Kashmir. The craze for India that developed among the German Romantics relates to this, as well as to a growing disillusionment with what was perceived as a rational and mechanical post-Enlightenment European culture.[33] Schlegel hoped to reverse the apparent degeneration of Christianity in the modern world by returning to "the source of all languages, all thought, and all poetry of the human spirit."[34] Inspired by the work of Sir William Jones, Schlegel had traveled to Paris in 1802 where he was introduced to Farsi by Antoine-Léonard de Chézy and received private lessons in Sanskrit from Alexander Hamilton, an English marine officer who was the only one on the continent who knew the language. Previous work in comparative Indian, Greek, and Germanic mythology had led Schlegel to expect he would find evidence of a primordial religion (*Urreligion*) in India whose principles would reconcile apparent deviations in the diversity of later accounts of the divine.

On the Language and Wisdom of the Indians falls at a transitional moment in Schlegel's development. In the year of its publication he converted to Catholicism, repudiated his early Romantic sympathies for pantheism, and joined Metternich's imperial court, where he embraced conservative, pro-Austrian German nationalism.[35] The text thus reflects an odd mixture of Catholic apologetics and nationalist ambitions. Schlegel's search for the divine in India aimed to reverse the process of rationalizing religion and naturalizing God that supposedly began with the Protestant Reformation.[36] In his view, ancient Indians had preserved traces of original revelation, but the force of reason within Indian religion and philosophy had wildly distorted God's word until it culminated in pantheism.[37] By equating the pantheism of ancient India with that pantheism of which contemporary Protestant theology was accused after the Spinoza controversy, *On the Language and Wisdom of the Indians* upheld Catholicism as the religion maintaining the truest ties to original revelation. Recourse to India likewise allowed Schlegel to resuscitate the ancient Germanic tribes as worthy rivals of the classical Greeks, rather than primitive, nomadic inhabitants of the northern forests.[38] For Schlegel not only revered India as the original source of religious inspiration. He suspected India to be the most likely *Urheimat* of Germans in Asia and offered evidence in his work that the earliest German speakers had migrated westward from this land. His joint association of India with divine revelation and the German homeland set a precedent for sacralizing the nation and for regarding German speakers as a people chosen by God.

The narrative of German descent from India that Schlegel elaborated in the book's third section, titled "Historical Ideas," followed traditional biblical notions of the emergence of cultural difference. By this account, German speakers and related linguistic groups originated from a sacred homeland in the East that had also been the site of the "first revelation." Humanity had experienced its first religious awakening and been introduced to the idea of the true God in a terrestrial Indian paradise. Sanskrit, in Schlegel's analysis, was the "oldest descendent," the most proximate historical language of the lost "*Ursprache*" or divine first language of revelation.[39] At the same time, Schlegel drew on affinities in language, mythology, law, and architecture to conclude that "the greatest empires and most noble nations" of antiquity, including the Egyptians and Hebrews, were "colonies" founded by Indian priests. He distinguished the first Germans as one of several "descended nations" or emigrant groups, including the Persians, who had left Asia during a period of religious strife and civil war that followed disagreement over the meaning of God's word. In his analysis, religious motives compelled the Germanic tribes to leave Turkistan along the Gihon for the north side of the Caspian Sea, from where they crossed the Caucasus and headed north into Scandinavia.[40] Only later did a second wave of migration found the civilizations of Greece and Rome.[41]

Schlegel, however, altered the Christian narrative of Asian descent by claiming only one people to have been witness to God's word. In 1808 he contrasted those populations whose languages pointed to a "common descent" from Sanskrit with those for whom "no original kinship" could be determined. In his view, Latin, Greek, Farsi, and

German could all be "derived from Indic and understood based on her composition." He based this assumption initially on the affinity of root words common to them all, such as the names for mother, father, brother, and sister, but extended his analysis into their "innermost structure and grammar," suggesting that "comparative grammar" promised new insights into the genealogy of languages.[42] Schlegel discerned that the above idioms followed a similar "structural law" according to which grammatical relationships were expressed within a sentence. He detected in all "a shared principle by which all relationships and subtleties of meaning are signified not by appended particles or helping verbs, but rather by *inflection,* that is by modification to the root." In other words, those languages that derived from Sanskrit were united by their common use of changes to the roots of words to signify grammatical functions such as number or tense. In his analysis, Sanskrit and its cognates were "organic" and flexional; the root was a "living seed" that expressed its grammatical function through "inner change."[43]

The conglomeration of languages to which Schlegel attributed Indian origins was set apart from a more varied second group, including Chinese, Hebrew, Arabic, and American Indian languages, that had a "diametrically opposed grammar." He characterized these lesser tongues as "mechanical" rather than "organic" because they made use "only of *affixa* rather than inflection" and expressed grammatical relationships with the help of an "added word."[44] Schlegel denied that inflectional forms could have been obtained by affixing previously independent words; thus these types were radically incommensurate. This second group supposedly evolved from the languages of primitive "natives" (*Urbewohner*) who lived in areas outside of India and had not been privileged by the word of God, developing their speech instead from simple cries and sounds found in nature. These "wilder peoples," in his view, tended to be "isolated" and "uncultivated" and had contributed little to the "moral development" of humanity.[45]

In his *Lectures on Universal History* (1805–6), Schlegel had based this hierarchical distinction on a polygenetic view of human origins; only the "honorable" and "cultured" nations of Asia and Europe were said to have their roots in India.[46] Having resolved to convert to Catholicism while writing his 1808 essay on India, Schlegel later associated this division of humanity with the biblical story of Cain and Abel.[47] Explaining human "degeneration" through the metaphor of a fallen brother enabled the author to reconcile his distinction between cultured and barbaric peoples with a monogenetic Christian philosophy of history.[48] It also allowed Schlegel to privilege German speakers as a chosen people destined to recreate the lost religious knowledge of divine revelation following an enlightened return to the paradise from which they had been expelled. Significantly, he believed the first Germans had left India in search of the holy mountain Meru, celebrated in ancient legend, and were drawn toward Scandinavia by "a wonderful notion of the great dignity and splendor of the north."[49]

Schlegel's admonition that further research into Indian antiquity was "very important for our fatherland" invited scholars with more directly nationalist concerns to turn eastward.[50] His work initially had a mixed reception during the Napoleonic period due to his conservative nationalism.[51] But it found a host of welcome readers among Bavarians, including Othmar Frank (1770–1840), Franz Bopp (1791–1867), and the poet-Orientalist Friedrich Rückert (1788–1866). Rückert, in particular, followed Schlegel in associating India jointly with the origins of the German nation and with a Golden Age before Babel in which the divine had been revealed in language. The celebrated author of the patriotic *Fiery Sonnets* (1814) reworked Schlegel's expectations of finding religious revival in the East into salvationist national narratives that promised the resurrection of spiritual harmony as the basis of German national unity. This fusion of Christian and national narratives resulted in an enduring conception of German national culture that anticipated a kind of millenarian fulfillment in which German speakers emerged as a people chosen by God.

Comparative Grammar: Franz Bopp

Comparative philology as a field distinct from the Romantic longing for India emerged under the auspices of Franz Bopp, the first Professor of General Linguistics and Oriental Literature in Berlin. Bopp established comparative grammar as a distinct school within German Indological scholarship, separate from textual analysis and historical criticism, as well as from the comparative study of religion. As such, his career marks the initial separation of linguistics from other philologies and theology. The conditions of his appointment relieved Bopp from teaching exegesis of the Holy Scriptures; in fact, Bopp was given preference over an incumbent theologian who was already teaching Sanskrit in Berlin. That linguistics took root as a secular science in Prussia reflects the extent Wilhelm von Humboldt had already emancipated philology from theology and helped secularize academics.[52] In this capacity, Bopp historicized Sanskrit as one of several natural tongues that had descended from an unknown, more ancient mother. Nevertheless, the Romantic quest for the Indo-European *Ursprache* and *Urheimat* maintained a spell over the field until the 1870s; only then did comparative philologists who did not specialize in Sanskrit receive chairs in general linguistics.[53] The salvationist rhetoric and millenarian expectations introduced by Friedrich Schlegel continued to shape notions of German descent from Asia even as they were enshrined in scientific terms.

Bopp's own path to comparative philology reflects a broader reorientation of Indology from Catholic-Romantic apologetics to Enlightenment trends in the human sciences, especially in relation to Humboldt.[54] Born a Catholic in Mainz in 1791, Franz Bopp was the youngest son of six children, his father a civil servant at the court of Elector Friedrich Karl von Erthal. When French revolutionary troops captured the city, the Bopp family fled with the government to Aschaffenburg. Several faculties of the local university likewise transferred, so that Bopp was able to attend Karl Joseph Windischmann's lectures on philosophy and natural history. A follower of F. W. J. Schelling, Windischmann combined an interest in mysticism and aesthetics with a fascination for the languages and literatures of the East. Like Friedrich Schlegel, J. J. Görres, and G. F. Creuzer, Windischmann was full of enthusiasm for Indian wisdom and philosophy, and he imparted this to an eager Franz Bopp.[55]

Bopp initially squeezed enough support from the Bavarian Academy of Sciences to pursue Sanskrit studies abroad. From 1812 to 1815, he resided in Paris, enjoying the company of Sylvestre de Sacy, A. L. Chézy, L. M. Langlès, and Alexander Hamilton. Here Bopp dedicated himself to studying and translating the Indian epics *Bhagavad Gita, Ramayana,* and *Mahabharata*. His ambition was to translate the Vedas so that he might uncover hidden truths behind Indian myths. "I will later free myself from the myths and contemplate pure truth," Bopp wrote, "Indeed, these myths, honorable poetry, are not without real, philosophical value. The truth is shrouded in them so that they do not blind the profane."[56] Shortly before the publication of *On the Conjugation System of Sanskrit* (1816), Bopp shifted his attention from myth and philosophy to language itself. In a letter to Windischmann, he explained that he intended to "make the study of language philo-

Franz Bopp

Franz Bopp, professor of general linguistics and Oriental literature in Berlin, demurely displaying the Order Pour le Mérite for Sciences and Arts that King Friedrich Wilhelm IV bestowed upon him in 1842 as a member of the first civilian class.

sophical and historical and not to be satisfied with understanding what is written in a language."[57] Schlegel advised comparing the grammatical structures of languages rather than just items of shared vocabulary, and Bopp discovered that investigating verb conjugation systems was more rewarding than studying declension.[58]

Grammar proved to be the intellectual bedrock upon which the emerging field of comparative-historical philology rested. Bopp asserted that every language had an internal mechanism of growth that determined its evolution over time and space. Borrowing terminology from botany and comparative anatomy, he characterized languages as "organic, natural bodies formed according to definite laws, having a life-giving principle within; they develop and gradually die out after losing consciousness of their true nature and throwing aside or mutilating or misusing . . . their members or forms."[59] One could construct a genealogy of languages by identifying this "linguistic organism" (*Sprachorganismus*), discovering its original form, and comparing it to others.[60] Bopp ascribed mental activity to language as if it were an independent thinking being. Language also assumed a life of its own in his hands, posing to later scholars the question of whether historical change was regulated by autonomous inner laws or external intervening factors. He likewise assumed scholars encountered language already in a state of decline and mutilation.[61] This view encouraged a concern for prehistoric states of linguistic development and a reverence for the supposed youth, vitality, and purity of language.

On the Conjugation System of Sanskrit demonstrated how similarities in the verb conjugation patterns of Greek, Latin, German, and Farsi could be used to prove that the languages in question were related and of shared historical origin. Here Bopp adopted Schlegel's notion of inflection, but denied that Sanskrit was the oldest tongue in the family: "in all languages that descend from Sanskrit *or with it from a common mother*, no grammatical relationship is expressed through an inflection not shared with this original language [*Ursprache*]."[62] The "truly organic way" in which Indo-European verbs inflected and took shape in a sentence was not, according to Bopp, replicated in other families such as Semitic or Chinese.[63] He showed that the root form of the verb in Sanskrit, Greek, Latin, German, and Farsi underwent a similar series of modifications or inflections when conjugated in a sentence. The inflection of a verb determines its grammatical function by assigning number, tense, voice, and mood to the root. In the verb "to eat," for example, the past tense "ate" is formed or inflected by a change in the initial vowel of the stem; the third person singular, indicative, present tense ("eats") is formed by appending the inflection "-s" to the stem.[64] Bopp discovered that "as in the conjugation of ancient Indic verbs," the grammatical relationships in all related languages "are expressed through corresponding modifications to the roots."[65] Without detailing these modifications, suffice it to say that the success of his comparative method derived in part from the frequency and precision of the agreement among Indo-European languages in the particulars of their morphology.[66]

Bopp's ability to convince contemporaries of the basic structural identity of Indo-European languages was also a result of his not following the Indic grammatical tradition in his treatment of Sanskrit. He disassociated what he saw as the essential structure of the language from the system presented in native and missionary grammars he encountered in Paris.[67] The structure of Sanskrit could only be made visible, in his mind, by transferring to it the apparatus of Greek grammar. This move made Bopp's work accessible to a broad range of European-trained scholars. The fact that his study drew exclusively on two English grammars of Sanskrit and he neglected to conduct independent research in ancient texts was later criticized by a rival school of more philologically traditional Indologists in Bonn who branded Bopp "a Grimm without Ulphilas."[68] Bopp's lack of formal university training generally made him a ready target for colleagues who feared Oriental studies would not earn adequate recognition within the neohumanist universities.

In 1816, Bopp unsuccessfully sought academic employment in Bavaria. Crown Prince Ludwig instead bestowed five hundred gulden on him for a research trip to London, where Bopp became acquainted with Sir Charles Wilkins and H. T. Colebrooke. Bopp also met and gave Sanskrit lessons to Wilhelm von Humboldt, who was then Prussian ambassador to the court of Saint James. During this time, Bopp continued to publish critical editions and Latin translations of episodes from the *Mahabharata,* including *Nala and Damayanti* (1819). He also published an "Analytical Comparison of the Sanskrit, Greek, Latin, and Teutonic Languages" in the *Annals of Oriental Literature* (1820), which extended to all parts of grammar what his first book had done to the verb alone. As Peter K. J. Park has shown, this essay marks a gradual distancing of Bopp from both Schlegel's scholarly precepts and his own Catholicism.[69] Based on a new understanding of verbal and pronominal roots, Bopp denied that Indo-European languages displayed inflection as their dominant principle. In his view, original Indo-European roots had been monosyllabic and thus incapable of inward inflection and alteration; they relied on foreign additions to express grammatical notions. Within Sanskrit, the only possible forms of inflection in Schlegel's sense were certain vowel changes and reduplication.[70]

Despite these achievements, Bopp was denied the first German post in Indology that opened at the newly founded University of Bonn. August Wilhelm Schlegel, Friedrich's older brother, received this honor in 1818.[71] A. W. Schlegel only came to Sanskrit studies at the age of forty-eight, and it was Bopp who instructed him in Paris. However, Schlegel's classical training in Göttingen under C. G. Heyne and his promise to apply "the principles of classical philology" to Sanskrit literature "and indeed with the most scientific of precision," made him the more attractive candidate.[72] Under his leadership Bonn emerged as the center of research on the literature, history, art, religion, and philosophy of India, drawing such renowned students as Christian Lassen and Heinrich Heine. Schlegel's critical editions of Sanskrit texts and his impeccable Latin translations and commentaries garnered the respect of classical philologists, the most notable of these being his *Bhagavad-Gita* (1823) and selections from the *Ramayana* (1829–38). He harshly criticized Franz Bopp for his faulty Latin and his errors in issuing fragmentary, rather than intact, segments of Indian epics.[73] By the 1830s Sanskrit studies were divided into two mutually opposing schools of Berlin linguists and Bonn philologists.[74]

Bopp lacked the prestige of more traditional, literary philologists. He also departed from the mold of the typical German Orientalist who served theological faculties. Thus, in 1820 the University of Würzburg denied him a post as an Orientalist. The theologians there declared they needed no additional instructors in Oriental languages; one Professor K. J. Fischer already offered Hebrew, Aramaic, Syriac, and Arabic. The philosophical faculty added that Sanskrit was a "literary luxury." Instruction in Sanskrit and Farsi was appropriate for "capital cities and academies" and had no place at a provincial university.[75] Only through the assistance of Wilhelm von Humboldt did Bopp obtain a position at the Friedrich Wilhelm University in Berlin. In 1821 he was appointed to a chair in Comparative Grammar and Oriental Literature, and one year later he was elected a member of the Royal Prussian Academy.

Bopp rarely applied his theories of linguistic relations to the cultural history of the groups that spoke them. Nor was he interested in speculating on the philosophical significance of Indo-European grammatical forms.[76] Subsequent linguists have even criticized Bopp for a lack of methodology: his work did not offer a theory or systematic method for linguistic science.[77] Rather, Bopp's empirical studies grouped languages into families by isolating their dominant linguistic principles and then tracing these back to a few distinct points of origin. He was particularly interested in the "organism" shared by what he referred to as the "Indo-Classical" languages, researching not only the "physical and mechanical laws" that united them, but also speculating on the "origins of the forms that signify grammatical relationships."[78] This was the main preoccupation of the *Comparative Grammar of the Sanskrit, Zend, Greek, Latin, Lithuanian, Gothic, German, and Slavonic Languages* (1833–52). Here Bopp defined as inorganic all grammatical principles that could not be derived from the original structures of Indo-European languages, detaching the term completely from its association with inflection.[79]

The tripartite division of languages presented in the *Comparative Grammar* confirmed Bopp's repudiation of Friedrich Schlegel's tutelage. Languages in the first class of Bopp's scheme, including Chinese, were "without proper roots and the capacity for compositions and hence without organism, without grammar."[80] Indo-European tongues and all others that did not fit into classes one or three were characterized by monosyllabic roots capable of composition. According to Bopp, they "create their organism, their grammar almost exclusively" through composition. The third class made up of the Semitic languages had disyllabic verb roots with three consonants; languages of this type created grammatical forms both through composition and "inner modification of the root."[81] Bopp justified his classification of Semitic tongues as inflectional by the fact that they "indicated subordinate grammatical notions through the mere inner transformation of roots." By contrast, the roots of Indo-European languages formed "an almost unchangeable, sealed kernel that surrounded itself with foreign syllables . . . whose function is to express subordinate grammatical notions, which the roots themselves cannot express." The vowel(s) found in Indo-European roots formed part of the base meaning and could only be lengthened or intensified, a process that did not signify grammatical relationships.[82] Here Bopp recognized reduplication, or the repetition of radical consonants, as the only inflectional form originally found in Indo-European roots.[83]

This reclassification of languages did not alter the high esteem in which Bopp held the original forms of Indo-European tongues, nor his differentiating them fundamentally from those of Semitic languages. The "great advantage" the Indo-European family held over the Semitic lay, for Bopp, in the "richness of the grammatically truly significant . . . attachments" appended to their roots: "in the reflective, meaningful selection and use of these, and the precise and clear designation of the most varied relationships made possible by them; finally in the beautiful integration of these attachments to a harmonious whole that resembles an organic body."[84] Bopp never challenged the monogenetic origins of humankind, although his typology may have encouraged polygenecism in Bopp's students, such as F. A. Pott. As Bopp explained to the Berlin Academy in 1823, he followed the theologian Wilhelm Gesenius in accepting the possibility that the current condition of Semitic roots "could have evolved from an earlier period" when the law of disyllabic roots had not yet been established.[85] The plausibility of this early affinity was heatedly debated throughout the nineteenth century.

The rival Indologists in Bonn mounted a feeble attempt to reverse Bopp's classificatory scheme. Compelled to defend the family honor and the organic interpretation of inflection upon which Bopp's theory quickly gained, A. W. Schlegel planned (but never completed) his own comparative grammar. As an insult of sorts, his student Christian Lassen labeled Bopp's notion that composition was the origin of inflecting forms in Indo-European agglutination or composition theory. However, their efforts could offer nothing positive to replace Bopp's typology. Schlegel and Lassen's opposition was gradually forgotten, leaving Bopp in undisputed possession of the new field in comparative grammar.[86] His followers were left to supplement and make more precise Bopp's principles of comparison, while fleshing out the cultural and philosophical implications of his work.

The First Indo-Germans: Julius Klaproth

Denying that any of the presumed *Ursprachen* (Sanskrit, Avestan, ancient Greek, or Hebrew) was the truly most ancient mother tongue complicated the search for the exact geographical location of the Indo-European homeland in Asia. Following William Jones and Franz Bopp, German Orientalists searched for a new Asian homeland outside of

India where presumably the common ancestors of all Indo-European speakers had resided. Some language scholars literally traveled east on a quest to identify the linguistic communities from which modern Germans descended and to which they were related by exclusive ethnic and cultural ties. They spatialized and territorialized Schlegel's narrative of expulsion from paradise as they mapped out the likely location of this *Urheimat* and identified the migration roots the first Germanic tribes reputedly took from central Asia into Europe.

The first comparativist to situate the German homeland outside of India and to map out the early diffusion of linguistic groups in central Asia was Julius Klaproth (1783–1835). His extensive comparisons of Asian and European languages were based almost exclusively on the correspondence of root words and meanings, and they only superficially took account of grammatical structure. For this reason, his contributions to the early history of Indo-European linguistics have been undervalued by disciplinary historians. In 1832 August Friedrich Pott criticized Klaproth's comparative charts as "a shabby last resort, . . . by which only insufficient, often very misleading conclusions about linguistic relations can be drawn."[87] His combative personality and the scandals associated with Klaproth also distanced him from the profession. Klaproth was rumored to have left Saint Petersburg in haste under suspicion of having stolen valuable manuscripts from the local library in 1810; later in Paris he was suspected of being a Prussian spy.[88] Despite his maverick status, Klaproth's term "Indo-Germanic" was widely accepted as the German-language designation for the extended family of languages and peoples he, Bopp, and others perceived to be united by linguistic ties and a common early history.[89] He had a founding role in the study of central and east Asian languages, helping to edit the *Fundgruben des Orients* and the *Journal asiatique*. In 1811 Friedrich Wilhelm III appointed Klaproth professor of Asian languages and literatures in Bonn, paid his salary, and supported the publication of his works, although Klaproth resided in Paris from 1815 until his early death in 1835.

Asia Polyglotta (1823), Klaproth's major work, laid out a comprehensive "system of Asian peoples and languages" that purportedly established the linguistic and historical relations among more than fifty Asian tongues and offered a new explanation for the dispersal of so-called *Indo-Germanen*. His narrative rejected the story of Babel as an explanation for cultural diversity but persisted in assigning a pivotal role

The adventurous Julius Klaproth preferred the term *indogermanisch* over Indo-European. (Courtesy Brown University Library)

to the biblical tale of the flood in its conception of human prehistory. In Klaproth's view similar sounding words with equivalent meanings could be found in the languages of the most diverse, unrelated peoples. This "general" linguistic correspondence resulted from the partial survival of remnants from an *Ursprache* that had survived the flood. Of greater interest to Klaproth, however, were similarities among lan-

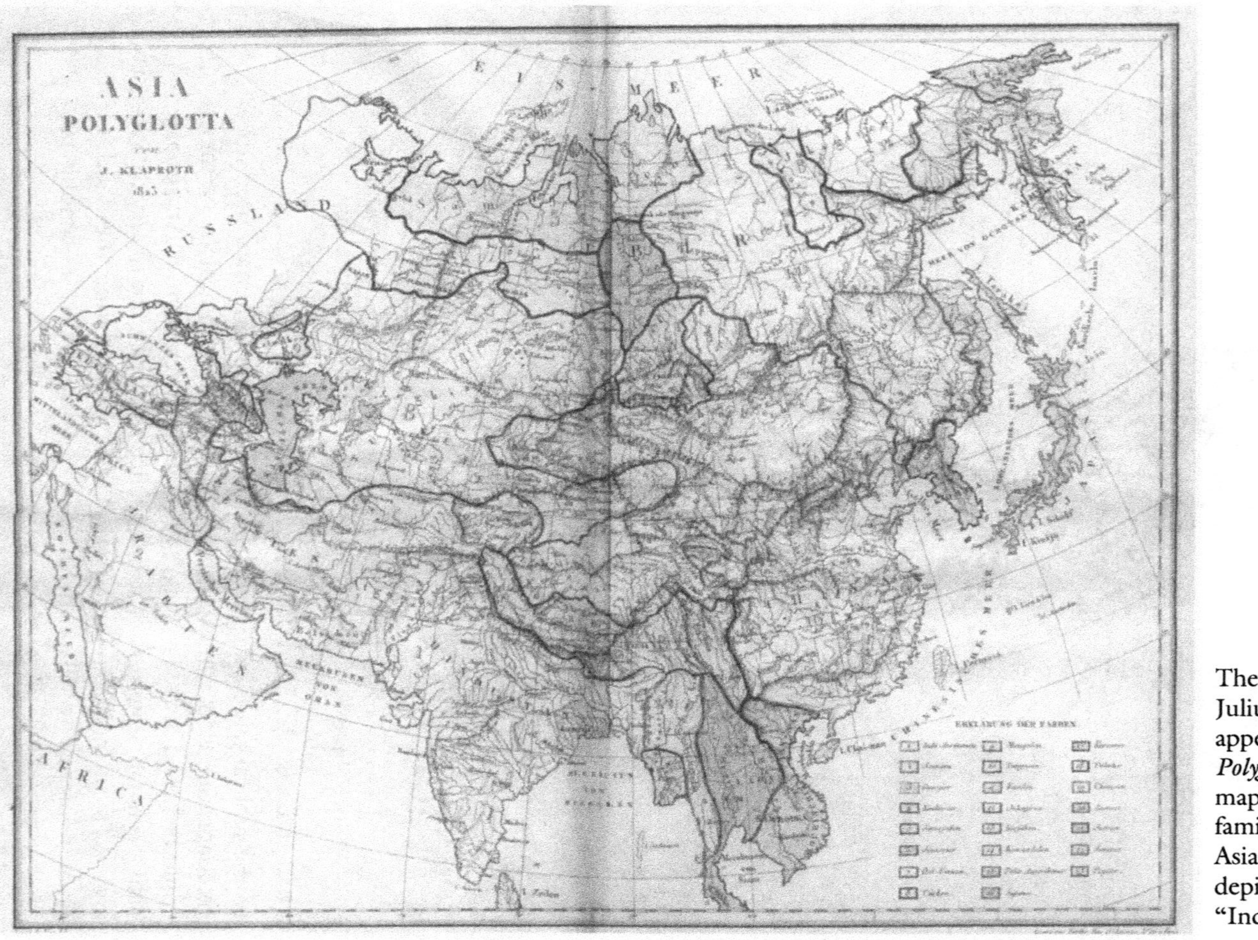

The linguistic atlas Julius Klaproth appended to *Asia Polyglotta* (1823), mapping the language families of central Asia. The first division depicts the lands of "Indo-Germans."

guages of groups whose affinity was also documented "through history or physical uniformity."[90]

In making this distinction, Klaproth pushed the original division of the first mother tongue back into a period of prehistory inaccessible to philologists and effectively adopted a polygenetic model for explaining the origin of linguistic diversity. The spread of distinct national tribes and language families across the globe, he claimed, was antediluvian. When high waters covered the earth, certain individuals had found refuge on the mountain peaks of India and America, as well as on Mount Ararat, and had independently preserved elements of their unique languages. These survivors formed the core of the "main tribes" (*Stammvölker*), their languages the basis of the "core languages" (*Stammsprachen*) from which Klaproth derived thirteen separate language families, naming the mountain peaks from which their earliest speakers likely descended. According to Klaproth's scheme, early speakers of "Indo-Germanic" had migrated into the plains of Europe and into southern Asia from two separate mountain chains, the Himalayas and the Caucasus, a fact that explained the physical differences among the family's speakers. Ancient Indians, he believed, had traveled south from the Himalayas and quickly mixed with "brown or Negro-like natives" who themselves had retreated to the hills of Malabar. The Goths, on the other hand, left the Himalayas for the north and entered Europe through Scandinavia. The other Germanic tribes (Medo-Germans) had wandered from the Caucasus to the shores of the Caspian Sea, through Persia and into Europe from the south.[91]

Klaproth's findings had the result of relocating the geographical origins of the German nation from the Ganges, as specified by Schlegel and Rückert, to the northern Himalayas and the Caucasus. It was "absurd," Klaproth insisted, to derive "the German people [*das deutsche Volk*] from the Hindu" since both nations grew independently out of a few surviving speakers of Indo-Germanic.[92] At the latest, speakers of Sanskrit, he believed, had lost contact with the European branch of the Indo-Germanic language family "on the meridonal slopes of the Himalayas," a conclusion supported by the fact that the birch was the only tree whose name was shared by all members of the family. Sanskrit names for trees growing in more southern, Indian climates had been borrowed from unrelated languages native to the south of the subcontinent.[93]

Subsequent comparativists concurred with his interpretation. In an 1840 entry on the Indo-Germanic language family in Ersch and Gruber's encyclopedia, August Friedrich Pott reported scholarly consensus that the mountainous region that is the source of the Amu-Darya and Syrdarya rivers in central Asia was the German *Urheimat.*[94] This change made the prospect of an Asian homeland more attractive by disassociating Proto-Germans from the colonial subjects of India, as well as from the mystical visions of the early Romantics and controversial mythologists such as Friedrich Creuzer. It also had the advantage of distancing the first German migrants from the "black natives" of India whose languages had displaced Indo-European elements. The first Germans did not originate in India but in an exclusive enclave that lay across the Hindu Kush.

Empire and Ethnic Identity in the Caucasus and Central Asia

Starting in the 1820s, German Orientalists set out to scour the borderlands of the Russian Empire for evidence of an Indo-Germanic *Urheimat.* The Caucasus Mountains and beyond them central Asia became the focus of intensive German fieldwork sponsored by the Russian Academy of Sciences, which had a strategic interest in mapping the linguistic and ethnographic landscape of the Empire's borderlands. German Orientalists flocked to the Russian Empire, enticed by the possibility of a salary and by the prospect of tracing the westward path taken by Indo-Germans. Scholars such as Christian Martin Frähn, Bernhard Dorn, Issac Jacob Schmidt, and Julius Klaproth struggled to sort out the linguistic affiliations of the Caucasian tribes and the nomadic peoples of the central Asian steppes, debating which aspects of their speech were Turkish and which Indo-European.[95] In the process, the Indo-Germanic language family was defined in reference to linguistic groups on its eastern borders. Scholars also began to see a correlation between language and the likely physical characteristics of ethnic groups.

Traveling to Russia was a wise career choice given the obstacles hindering the pursuit of Oriental studies in the German states in the early nineteenth century. Colonial powers such as England and France were far better equipped to stock their national libraries with manuscript collections and rare reference works. In 1837 the Arabist and scholar of Hebrew Heinrich Ewald regretted that Germany still suffered from a "dismal lack of material and resources."[96] Aspiring German scholars regularly made pilgrimages to colonial metropoles where the royal library in Paris or London's East India Company offered more vibrant intellectual communities. Although increasing in the 1820s, the number of university posts available to Orientalists was also limited. In 1826 alone important university positions went to Friedrich Rückert in Erlangen, the Indologist Peter von Bohlen in Königsberg, and to Othmar Frank at the newly founded Ludwig-Maximillian University in Munich. This raised the number of salaried scholars in Oriental languages and literature to a half dozen. At a time when prominent Germanists, such as Jacob and Wilhelm Grimm, still served as librarians, the institutionalization of Oriental studies was notable, but hardly sufficient for an internationally recognized group of scholars.

The imperial ambitions of the Russian czars created a demand for language specialists which Germans readily filled. In the early nineteenth century, Russia was progressively pushing its southernmost border through the Caucasus, annexing territory from Persia and the Ottoman Empire, and exploring the steppes of Kazakhstan and Turkmenistan. German linguists, such as Julius Klaproth, were invaluable aids in this process. Klaproth had taught himself Chinese while attending the Joachimsthal Gymnasium in Berlin. His knowledge of the language so attracted the Russian diplomat Jan Potocki that he appointed Klaproth professor of Asian languages and literature in Saint Petersburg in 1804. From 1805 to 1807 Klaproth accompanied a Russian diplomatic mission through Mongolia to the Chinese border, where he studied local languages and collected manuscripts that were eventually sold to the Berlin Academy. The return trip took Klaproth through Kyrgyzstan, Kazakhstan, and the Lake Baikal region. One year later he was dispatched on the ill-fated mission to the Caucasus mountains.[97] Klaproth subsequently helped author an influential plea by the future Minister of Education Sergei Uvarov for the establishment of an Asian Academy in Russia, developing for the purpose a detailed series of courses on Oriental languages and literature.[98] For his services the German scholar was made a member of the Russian Academy of Sciences and was knighted into the order of Vladimir.[99]

The development of Oriental studies in the reign of Czar Alexander I (1801–25) was part of a larger project of the Europeanization of Russia and generally relied on foreign scholars.[100] The recognized founder of the modern discipline in Russia was the Arabist Christian Martin Frähn (1782–1851), a German scholar enticed to enter Russian service by the cultural spoils of its wars. Frähn had studied theology and Oriental languages in Rostock, where he habilitated in 1806 under O. G. Tychsen with an interpretation of the prophet Nahum. Here he also held lectures on Arabic grammar and numismatics. In 1807 Frähn accepted one of the first Russian professorships of Oriental literature in Kasan with title of privy councilor. The Arabist applied his talents to writing early histories of Russia and the eastern Arabic empire. After Tychsen's death in 1817, Frähn was offered the open post in Rostock, which he intended to accept. But en route to Germany he stopped in Saint Petersburg to catalogue coins in possession of the Russian Academy of Science and remained indefinitely. The Russian emperor named Frähn a member of the academy and its head librarian; Frähn also became the director of the affiliated Asian Museum and an honorary librarian of the royal collection. For German scholars interested in the linguistic history of Asia, Russian colonial activity produced a wealth of source material. In the words of C. M. Frähn, "Their last campaigns against the Persians and Turks were once again honored by a series of conquests in the realm of science; their generals not only brought back guns and enemy flags as trophies of their brilliant victories, but also entire libraries of manuscripts; and as before our religious mission in Peking and our traveling scholars have using peaceful means acquired immense quantities of precious Chinese and Mongolian literary works."[101] The German states could offer no such advantages to their fledgling Orientalists.[102]

Frähn brought other German Orientalists to Russia, including Bernhard Dorn (1805–81), who had a specific interest in Indo-European tongues. After receiving degrees in theology and philology in Saxony, the native Bavarian spent several years perusing Iranian manuscripts in London. In 1827 his research led him to conclude that German and Farsi were like two rivers in which "One blood flows"; they either "pour forth from a common source, that is, were originally one, or they mutually arise and receive their life from rivers that stem from this original source."[103] These similarities convinced Dorn, as they did Klaproth, that the Caucasus "held in the midst of their arms a people in whom perhaps the same blood flows as in us."[104] Dorn accepted a position as professor of Oriental languages at the University of Kharkov in 1829, building a career in Russia that was dedicated to studying Farsi, the Pashto dialect of Afghanistan, and Caucasian tongues.[105] In 1835 he joined the Institute for Oriental Languages established by the Russian foreign ministry in Saint Petersburg, and he later replaced Frähn as the director of both the Asian Museum and the academy library. His major works included multivolume histories of the peoples bordering the Caspian Sea and those inhabiting the Caucasus, regions he visited in the early 1860s.

Fieldwork in the Caucasus mountains led Orientalists such as Dorn and Klaproth to link the linguistic forms of the Indo-European family to certain characteristic physical attributes. Klaproth's reflections on Ossetian, a member of the northeastern Iranian branch of Indo-European languages spoken in the northern Caucasus, are a case in point. Despite his conviction that the Caucasus had been the original homeland of Medo-Germans, the majority of local languages were unique and indigenous; only Ossetian, Armenian, and three Turkish tongues have ties to larger language families. Thus, when Klaproth braved war and the plague to visit isolated speakers of the Ossetian language, he was enticed by the prospect that they were the remains of an ancient Medo-German colony. In *Asia Polyglotta,* Klaproth cited patterns in "the formation of the cranium"[106] as evidence that apparent lexical convergences were not indications of shared ethnic ties; linguistic affinities could only be confirmed, in his mind, through "physical uniformity."[107] The Ossetes, he reported, distinguished themselves "in language and facial structure from all others in the Caucasus."[108] The tribe was a "well-built people" whose "physiognomy" resembled "that of Europeans";[109] the members had "blue eyes and blond or red-brown hair . . . truly back hair almost never."[110] This suggested to Klaproth that Ossetian was the lost fifth branch of the Indo-Germanic language family.

Other German Orientalists identified tribes in the eastern reaches of central Asia. The debate Klaproth and his rival Isaac Jacob Schmidt (1779–1847) held over the ethnic affiliations of the ancient Uighurs, inhabitants of Chinese Turkistan, for example, was part of an attempt to discover how far the Indo-European language family extended into Tibet, Mongolia, and western China. It was clear that Indo-Germans had migrated to the furthest reaches of western Europe, but what was their relationship to the ancient inhabitants of the Eurasian plateaus? Schmidt was the leading early nineteenth-century scholar on the Mongolian and Tibetan languages, publishing in the course of the 1830s grammars of both, a Mongolian dictionary, and an extended work on the religion and literature of the two peoples. His interest in the region was varied, emanating, on the one hand, from a practical desire to further Russian trade and industry by documenting the customs and traditions of their neighbors.[111] Schmidt was also intrigued by the origins of the tribal migrations that had reshaped the ethnic landscape of Europe in the early medieval period. "Such national movements that were aroused in inner Asia without a doubt extended their influence deep into Europe long before our time period and probably populated our part of the earth," he explained in 1824, "but we know neither the ancient history of the same nor of the largest part of Asia; really we know the history of the tribal migrations of the fourth century alone in their effects, not in their cause."[112]

Born the son of a salesman in Amsterdam, I. J. Schmidt received his only formal education from the Moravian Brethren in Neuwied between 1785 and 1791. When his father was compelled for financial reasons to take a post as a civil servant in Java in 1798, the nineteen-year-old Schmidt was sent to Sarepta on the Volga River to fill a post in the trade business of the Brethren. In neighboring regions Schmidt learned Kalmyk, a Mongolian language spoken by Buddhists in the region of Dzungaria. From 1804 to 1806 he resided with various nomadic tribes, learning their languages and customs, and traveled across the steppes stretching between the Volga, the Don, and the Caucasus mountains. Schmidt remained in Russia working in the trade offices of the Moravian Brethren in Moscow and Saint Petersburg. As the head of the Russian Bible Society he translated the New Testament and other religious works into Kalmyk and Mongolian; in 1843 he published the first Tibetan book in Europe, *The Wise Man and the Fool,* in the original language and in German translation. The University of Rostock bestowed a doctorate on him in 1827 and Schmidt was eventually accepted into the Saint Petersburg Academy of Science before he went blind in 1842.

Schmidt's research was concerned with establishing the nature of the cultural connections between ancient India, China, and the mountainous regions that lay between them. Like Wilhelm von Humboldt, who researched the languages of southeast Asia, Schmidt was intrigued by the spread of Sanskrit forms. He likely came to Mongolian and Tibetan in an effort to learn more about the religious teachings of ancient India. According to Schmidt, "the central Asian people, the true guardians" had preserved aspects of otherwise extinct "ancient religious teachings" that had once been widespread in "Hindustan."[113] Schmidt and the few German Sinologists of the period believed that

India had exerted extensive influence on the development of Chinese culture through a shared history in the Himalayan Mountains. He regarded the Chinese people as "originally perhaps nothing more . . . , than a bastard nation arising from a mix of Indian and high-Asian blood." The inhabitants of India and their *Bildung*, he asserted, were "far older" than those of China, who "certainly had no other nation in the same degree as the Indians to thank" for their early development.[114]

The belief that the inhabitants of central Asia had ties to Sanskrit-speaking India led to the classification of certain languages as "Indo-Chinese." While they testified to the degree that Indian cultural influence extended eastward, these languages also marked the limits of Indo-Germanic expansion in Asia. Under the rubric of Indo-Chinese were included languages such as Burmese, Thai, and Vietnamese that, according to the Sinologist Wilhelm Schott (1807–89), both demonstrated a "spiritual kinship with Chinese" and were "permeated with words from the Sanskrit family." While none of these was considered to be a "connecting link between Chinese and Indian," language families contemporary linguists now distinguish from each other, their coexistence "from time immemorial in a land that stretches from anterior India to south China" seemed to point to substantial cultural ties between speakers of Chinese and early Indo-European languages.[115]

Despite these attractions, German research on Chinese languages was scant in the first half of the nineteenth century and reflects a reluctance to identify early German speakers with east Asian civilization. When Wilhelm Schott disparaged in the mid-1820s that "in this area very little has been achieved in our fatherland" and "in part the most adventurous and perverted views of the Chinese . . . still circulate,"[116] he was not mistaken. Schott and Carl Friedrich Neumann (1807–89), a Sinologist at the University of Munich, were two of only three German philologists who specialized in the language. Schott hoped that Chinese might one day be held "approximately in the same regard" as Sanskrit was for the study of Indian languages and Arabic was for Islamic history, given its importance in the Far East and its ties to Annamese, Korean, and Japanese.[117] However, his immersion in the Chinese language was not equal to the demands of fellow philologists. Schott's sources for learning Chinese were, according to Klaproth, inadequate—a three-year acquaintance with two native speakers in Europe whom Klaproth derided as "two common fellows from villages in the administrative district of Canton . . . , one of whom worked as a cook, both of whom had forced themselves on a prospector in order to show themselves for money like wild animals in Europe."[118]

The negative associations with the study of Chinese in Germany suggest that the German national identification with the East, while it extended to the central Asian peoples who had supposedly sparked the tribal migrations, broke down at the Chinese border. Not being an inflectional language, Chinese was not so amenable to the techniques of comparative-historical philology as Indo-European tongues and was quickly stigmatized as a primitive, underdeveloped language. Friedrich Schlegel believed Chinese to be of the lowest rank in the hierarchy of affixional languages;[119] Jacob Grimm thought primordial speech would have resembled Chinese—more advanced tongues developed inflections and richer syntax;[120] Wilhelm von Humboldt counted Chinese among the "less perfected languages," the one most distinct from Sanskrit.[121] C. F. Neumann feared that Chinese speakers had never reached a crucial third stage in evolution of writing; they "never . . . broke down or dissolved the word into its simplest elements; they never progressed to the most perfect medium of representation, to the letter alphabet."[122]

Nevertheless, when C. M. Frähn invited the Sinologist Wilhelm Schott to accept a position at the university of Saint Petersburg in 1840, he opted to remain in Berlin. Schott's decision reflects both the development of Oriental studies in Germany and the limits of Russia's scholarly attractions. In the early 1820s, Schott had hoped to train in Paris under the Sinologist Jean Pierre Abel Rémusat (1788–1832). Financial considerations compelled him to restrict his travels to Berlin, where he was hired to catalogue Chinese books at the royal library. In 1838 Schott was made professor of Chinese, Tartar, and east Asian languages and no longer felt a compunction to venture abroad. By midcentury newly acquired reference materials and library collections had made language acquisition less laborious for German Orientalists; publishers in Bonn, Berlin, and Munich had come into possession of the Sanskrit type necessary to print affordable editions of Indian works.[123] (German scholars active in central Asia found it "absolutely necessary" to publish in Germany due, in Klaproth's words, to the "difficulty of circulating a book published in Russia in the rest of the world.")[124] The technical acumen of the comparative-historical techniques inaugurated by Bopp and Jacob Grimm had likewise made Germany a recognized center for philological study in Europe.[125]

BIBLICAL CRITICISM AND THE HISTORICIZATION OF HEBREW

If German Orientalists reached consensus on Chinese marking the eastern border of the Indo-Germanic language family, languages that A. L. Schlözer had termed "Semitic" in 1804 presented the discipline with more of a dilemma.[126] The theological faculties of German universities had long revered Hebrew as a sacred language that supposedly gave privileged access to ontological truth and was the most likely immediate descendent of the divine *Ursprache* spoken before Babel. In the 1820s and 1830s the study of Hebrew began to emerge from within theological faculties and became subject to the critical standards of comparative-historical philology. But the theological training of the leading Semitic philologists made the radical historicization of the language within its immediate family slow and contentious. At stake, on the one hand, was the unsettling application of comparative philology within liberal Protestant biblical criticism. More precise knowledge of Hebrew and related tongues enabled scholars of the Old Testament to challenge traditional ideas about authorship, for example, or the history of the Israelite religion.[127] Language scholars contributed to a long assault on the Protestant dream of an orthodox church founded on biblical authority, frequently disrupting more traditional readings of scripture.

On the other hand, the historicization of Semitic languages raised larger questions regarding the perceived cultural affinities and historical relations between Christian and Jewish Germans. Protestant scholars of Hebrew, including Wilhelm Gesenius (1786–1842), Heinrich Ewald, Julius Fürst, and Franz Wüllner, tried to prove that the Indo-European and Semitic language families were more closely related than at first believed. They developed a theory of the languages' "root word affinity" (*Wurzelverwandtschaft*) that rested on the assumption that the earliest ancestors of these language families had once lived in close proximity to another and that the verb roots typical of both languages were similar. Their efforts were part of an attempt to show that comparative linguistics could support biblical history and that the origins of humanity were monogenetic.[128] Such an approach stood in conflict with some comparative-historical philologists, still a minority, who insisted on a greater distinction between Indo-European and Semitic tongues and on a polygenetic view of human beginnings.

Wilhelm Gesenius, the first scholar to approach the Semitic language family with new comparative and historical methods, did so in his capacity as theologian. Born in Nordhausen, Thuringia, in 1786, Gesenius studied philosophy and theology at the University of Helmstedt, later transferring to Göttingen where he worked under J. G. Eichhorn and T. C. Tychsen. By the age of twenty-five, he had obtained a chair at the University of Halle. Gesenius insisted that that "a secure basis" for the historical-critical exegesis of the Old Testament could only be established "through precise and certain knowledge of language."[129] He argued that his fellow theologians were mistaken when "the majority" regarded Hebrew as the closest descendent of the "originary, universal" tongue and tried to prove this with linguistic evidence.[130] Gesenius's *Hebrew-German Dictionary* (1812) and his influential *Hebrew Grammar* (1813) leveled all distinctions in the treatment of biblical tongues, situating Hebrew historically in relation to other Semitic languages such as Arabic, Syriac, Aramaic, Samaritan Hebrew, and Maltese.

The implications that historicizing Hebrew had for biblical criticism Gesenius articulated in his *History of the Hebrew Language and Script* (1815). The text broadly distinguished two periods in the history of Hebrew, with the Babylonian exile marking a point of transition.[131] More significantly, Gesenius argued that the language of the Pentateuch did not date to the time of Moses. It coincided, rather, with other historical books, generally believed to have been written one thousand years later. In his view, either Moses did not compose the Pentateuch, or Hebrew's lack of change over time was an event "unequalled in the history of language, namely that the living language of a people and their circle of ideas had remained unchanged."[132] He suggested that the Mosaic texts tried to imitate an older style, but that the various compilers were not able to withstand "the pressure of a living language."[133] Priests, for example, had compiled the books of Chronicles using material from the earlier books of Samuel and Kings. Even documents contained in the Pentateuch that might have been very ancient were probably rewritten in a later language. Gesenius based this interpretation not on contextual clues, but on "language in the narrow sense, that is, the linguistic inventory, its particular forms and appearances."[134] The compilers had anachronistically substituted later words for earlier ones, while adding grammatical glosses, explanations, and supposed improvements.[135]

The scandals associated with another liberal theologian, Wilhelm Martin Leberecht de Wette (1780–1849), indicate just how contentious these claims were. In his *Critical and Historical Introduction to the Canonical Scriptures of the Old Testament* (1806–7), de Wette applied a concept of myth derived from early Romanticism to claim that the five books of Moses were useless as a chronology of events. In his view, they should be regarded instead as a Hebrew national epic that mirrored the spirit and mentality of Hebrew theocracy.[136] According to the Old Testament, Moses gave the Israelites a fully fledged legal system, sacrificial cult, and priesthood. De Wette countered that the laws and sacrifices attributed to Moses actually dated to the reigns of David and Solomon. The Pentateuch had been written hundreds of years after the fact in order to legitimate religious practices that emerged only after the Babylonian exile.[137] Politically, as George Williamson has shown, de Wette equated Protestantism with obedience to conscience and the defense of individual and national autonomy. This required distancing Protestantism from the myths of Judaism and Roman Catholicism. It also brought de Wette into conflict with Prussian authorities. After the murder of August von Kotzebue in 1819, de Wette was branded a radical democrat and demagogue, was suspended from his teaching position in Berlin, and was eventually replaced by the conservative theologian Ernst von Hengstenberg (1802–69).[138]

Gesenius himself fell victim for supporting de Wette's position on philological grounds. In 1830 an anonymous article published in Hengstenberg's *Evangelische Kirchenzeitung,* a strictly orthodox journal, charged Gesenius with "rationalism" and undermining the teachings of the church, as well as with inciting his students to laughter during lectures. According to his opponent, Gesenius's approach to the Old Testament undercut its "authority as a font of divine revelation."[139] The accusations gave rise to the famed "*Hallischer Streit,*" in which Gesenius's students protested in his support. The Prussian minister Karl von Altenstein convened a commission to investigate the charges, which King Friedrich Wilhelm eventually dropped after a reprimand that Gesenius remain solemn in class.[140] It is likely that Gesenius was not a convinced rationalist of the theological kind, but rather that his historical sense merely evoked mistrust of anything miraculous and supernatural.[141]

Not all students of Semitic languages followed the example of Gesenius. His great rival, Heinrich Ewald, opposed the path de Wette charted, although not for reasons of orthodoxy. Born the son of a linen weaver in Göttingen in 1803, Ewald combined liberal politics and language scholarship. For most of his career he held a position in Oriental philology and Old Testament exegesis in the town of his birth, where he helped reform the Hanoverian church. When he joined the "Göttingen Seven" in protest of King Ernst August's revocation of Hannover's liberal constitution in 1837, Ewald was forced to enter eleven years of exile in Tübingen until the constitution was restored. When Göttingen became Prussian in the wake of the war with Austria, he refused to take a new oath of loyalty to King Wilhelm I and was forced into retirement in 1867. Ewald applied Bopp's method of linguistic criticism to the language structures and historical evolution of Semitic tongues. He opposed what he perceived as the superficiality of the empirical knowledge upon which comparative grammar rested in the 1830s and 1840s, however, and sought to elevate it to more than a technique.[142]

Ewald's eight-volume *History of Israel* (1843–52) was more positive about the Mosaic texts than Gesenius, finding pieces of authentic history in the narratives of the patriarchs. Ewald applied to the Old Testament the same method used by B. G. Niehbuhr and K. O. Müller, who uncovered a solid basis for history in classical legends and myths.[143] The introduction to the first volume presented a complex theory of literary composition. In Ewald's view large amounts of material in the Old Testament had been rewritten before assuming their extant form, but precise historical dating could identify truly archaic passages. Ewald first established that the Hebrews possessed the art of writing at the time of Moses. "Investigation into the Semitic languages," he argued, proved that an early version of Hebrew characters was "first employed by an unknown primitive Semitic people." From them, all the "Asiatic members" of the "Semitic nations" received writing, along with a common name for God.[144] Ewald then ordered his sources into three chronological groupings based on "rare and archaic peculiarities in the usage of words":[145] the Great Book of Origins, including the Pentateuch and Joshua; the Great Book of Kings; and the Great Book of universal history to Greek times. In his view the descriptions of Israel's religion in the early monarchy were more than a fantasy of the post-exilic period.[146]

For the duration of the nineteenth century, there was residual resistance to philological attempts to historicize and contextualize the Old Testament based on language. Ewald's most prominent student, for example, Julius Wellhausen, declared that his mentor long prevented the correct insight into the development of Israelite history from taking hold.[147] An analysis of how philology, as an interpretive practice, shaped Protestant biblical criticism in the nineteenth century is beyond the scope of this study; most exegetes were not linguists, and their arguments revolve around the use, not the history, of language. But language scholars provided the tools necessary for theologians to date scripture and discuss authorship. The synoptic gospel debate, sparked by Christian Hermann Weisse's *The Gospel History Critically and Philosophically Treated* (1838) is a case in point. Theologians had long had difficulty explaining textual similarities and differences among the Gospels of Mark, Matthew, and Luke. The dating of language enabled Weisse to argue that the Gospel of Mark was an earlier source upon which Matthew and Luke had built, along with a lost collection of Jesus's sayings. For decades, Weisse stood isolated against the accepted Tübingen school, which favored the Griesbach hypothesis; its notion that Mark was a synthesis of Matthew and the later Luke was more amenable to the prevailing Hegelian philosophy.[148] Only with the publication of Heinrich Julius Holtzmann's *The Synoptic Gospels: Their Origin and Historical Character* (1863) did a revised version of the (now largely accepted) two-source hypothesis prevail.

Debates over Mosaic history extended beyond issues of scriptural authority to address the historical relationship between Christianity and Judaism. Language scholarship contributed to reducing the significance of Jews to the faith of Christ. Julius Wellhausen (1844–1918), for example, advanced in 1876 his well-known Documentary Hypothesis. His *History of Israel* divided passages from the Pentateuch into three historical groupings. Their progression revealed the institutionalization of the Israelite religion and its supposed process of degeneration. In the first stage, inferred from the Yahwistic history (J) and the related Elohistic source (E), the religion of Israel was a natural faith, free from law and compulsion; documents in the Deuteronomic strand (D) revealed that the festivals were increasingly detached from nature; the dates of their celebration were mathematically determined, and the priesthood was exclusively Levitical; the Priestly source (P) testified to a religion with a centralized cult, fixed festivals, and a priesthood limited to the clan of Aaron. Wellhausen implied that "Judaism" was the religion of Israel after it had died; the spiritual religion of Israel had devolved into the ghost he called "Judaism." For Wellhausen, the injunctive elements of the Torah, the commandments, defined Judaism, but the book merely represented "the ghost of a life which is closed." Similarly, the Pharisees of Jesus's time were Jews in the extreme: narrow, legalistic, exclusivistic, compulsive, and hypocritical.[149] The assurance that the Law was later than the rest of the Old Testament enabled Wellhausen to argue that Christ's restoration of righteousness without the Torah represented a return to the pure faith of Abraham's day.[150]

Language factored into biblical critics' attempts to understand the contributions neighboring peoples made to the early history of Judaism as well. Semitic tongues tend to vary more with place than with time. Hebrew texts written before and after the Babylonian exile are thus not as distinct as parts of the Old Testament composed in Babylonia, Palestine, and the Southern and Northern Kingdoms. Theodor Benfey lamented in 1869 that there still was no comparative grammar of Semitic languages equivalent to those for the Indo-European family. Yet the list of Hebrew scholars working on Aramaic, Syriac, Arabic, Samaritan, and Ethiopian is considerable.[151]

Starting in the 1840s, comparative philologists tackled Assyrian with a view to the influence the language of ancient Babylonia had exerted on Hebrew. In 1857 the German Orientalist Julius Oppert (1825–1905) was one of four men to decipher the cuneiform script found on the Michaux Stone brought from Mesopotamia to Paris in 1800. Oppert had joined a French archaeological expedition to Babylon from 1851 to 1854 and was later appointed Professor of Assyriology at the Collège de France. The Berlin Semitist and founder of German Assyriology Eberhard Schrader (1836–1908) began applying the language to the study of scripture in *The Cuneiform Inscriptions and the Old Testament* (1872), suggesting that elements of the Hebrew Bible had been borrowed from the Babylonian religion.[152] In the same year, the *London Times* carried the announcement that the Assyriologist George Smith (1840–76) had discovered close parallels in cuneiform tablets between the Gilgamesh epic and the biblical stories of Creation and the Deluge. Friedrich Delitzsch later advocated revising the interpretation of Hebrew favored by Wilhelm Gesenius in *The Hebrew Language Viewed in Light of Assyrian Research* (1883). According to

Delitzsch, the Assyrian language, "which embodies a world of ancient Semitic thought and speech, disclosed an entirely new foundation for the understanding of the sacred language of the Old Testament."[153] Specifically, he believed that Hebrew etymology should no longer be derived from the supposedly original meanings found in Arabic roots. These were often too recent, and scholars should instead rely on the ancient language of Babylon.

Conservative Protestants rallied against the derivation of the Old Testament from Assyrian precedents following the three notorious *Babel-und-die-Bibel* lectures that Delitzsch held at the German Oriental Society from 1902 to 1905. Son of the theologian Franz Delitzsch, Friedrich served as professor of Semitic Languages and Assyriology in Leipzig and Breslau before joining the Friedrich Wilhelm University in Berlin in 1899. He published dictionaries and grammars of Assyrian and Sumerian, as well as his interpretation of Hebrew based on Assyrian research. With Kaiser Wilhelm II present, Delitzsch proclaimed that the Hebrews borrowed the stories of the Creation, the Fall, and the Deluge from Babylonia, where they had originated in pure form. A public outcry followed his presentations, and the Kaiser was forced to distance himself from Delitzsch's notions.

Minimizing the importance of the ancient Hebrews within the history of Christianity had clear anti-Semitic overtones. As Maurice Olender has noted, this is typical of much comparative philological scholarship. Detailed knowledge of grammar and etymology helped dissolve biblical narrative within a broader history of the nonbiblical East. Oriental studies, as Suzanne L. Marchand argues, disrupted the biblical foundations of European identity, as well the nineteenth century's idealization of classical Greece.[154] The historicization of sacred languages was a key moment in the unsettling of theological orthodoxy. The study of Semitic languages and New Testament Greek therefore remained ensconced in the traditional environment of biblical scholarship long after comparative philology earned independent status as a discipline.

The Other Orient: Jews and Indo-Germans

Research on Hebrew and its affiliates had more than religious urgency. The presence of a linguistic minority in the German states that was associated with Hebrew and whose nationality was being questioned as part of the reaction against the emancipation edicts of the Napoleonic period raised questions about the likely proximity of the Indo-European and Semitic language families. The emancipation of German Jews had not been made on the basis of natural rights; rather, arguments for easing restrictions on occupation, residence, and excessive taxation had relied on the notion that German Jews would be "regenerated" under the supervision of a tutelary bureaucratic state. Jews were expected to break out of their supposedly autonomous communities and become fully integrated in society by, among other things, adopting the German language.[155] During the first half of the nineteenth century, the everyday language of most of the Ashkenazi Jewish community living in central Europe was still Yiddish. But the period from 1806 to 1819 was one of language acculturation in which German increasingly became the dominant language of the Jewish public sphere. At a time when other German dialects were gaining new cultural prestige, Yiddish lost its standing as a language in its own right and came to be despised as bad or corrupt German.[156]

Despite, or perhaps, as a result of these efforts, there was an often repeated perception in mainstream society that Jews were imitating, not mastering, the German language. "*Mauscheln*"—speaking German as Moses might have—was the derogatory term applied to the Jewish dialect. The success of language acculturation depended on factors such as social mobility, urbanization, and gender so that poorer Jewish immigrants from eastern Europe or new arrivals in the towns tended to retain their distinctive dialects; second- and third-generation speakers of German preserved the vocabulary of insular subcultures, especially words relating to trade and commerce, as well as their own distinctive gestures, rhythms, and intonations. Even university educated Jews speaking faultless High German, Jacob Toury has suggested, appeared to have artificial language skills because they could not slip into a local "German" dialect as their peers did in informal settings.[157]

Anti-Semitic works from the post-Napoleonic period cited the artificiality of Jewish German as evidence that Jews had not earned the right to full participation in the national community and, in fact, were not capable of ever fully acquiring the language that defined one's Germanness. One critic claimed in 1816 that because "nationality and youthful impressions can never be fully eradicated, these problems confront . . . even the most educated Jews. And even if they are successful in adopting certain linguistic forms . . . to a point of deception, some time or other a mistaken national tone [*nationaler Mißlaut*] will surprise them . . . and then arouse a very odd sensation."[158] In the late eighteenth century, Yiddish had been perceived as a jargon of crooks and robbers, a secret language binding together Jews engaged in commerce and business.[159] After emancipation, the continued use of Hebrew and Yiddish was thought to undermine bourgeois ideals of social respectability. Jewish religious services and schools were branded sites of "irreverence and undignified behavior" and were seen as such a threat to the social order that the rulers of some German states ordered prayers to be said in German and forbade noise, merriment, and the moving about during religious services.[160]

Given the expressive theory of language favored by comparative-historical philologists and the perceived centrality of German to membership in the nation, debates over the affinities between Indo-European and Semitic tongues became debates over the limits of Jewish acculturation, emancipation, and cultural regeneration. If the two language families evolved from a common ancestor, then speakers of German and Yiddish could be shown to have common historical roots and to share aspects of the same linguistic organism thought to shape a people's intellect and nationality. If the perceived points of origin for German and Yiddish speakers were irreconcilable, then preserving the integrity of German national culture would mandate a much higher degree of Jewish integration.

The theological background of many Orientalists encouraged several prominent students of Hebrew to search for bridging mechanisms that linked the Semitic and Indo-European language families in a shared prehistoric union. Following Friedrich Schlegel, the majority of strict comparative-historical philologists distinguished Hebrew by the dissyllabic character of its verb roots. In their written form the roots of Hebrew verbs are made up of three consonants, forming two syllables rather than one as is the case in Sanskrit. Contemporary linguists no longer consider the number of root syllables to be decisive in classifying languages, as the unity of the syllable itself has been cast into doubt.[161] But theologically minded philologists attempted to derive Hebrew roots from simpler forms so as to show their affinity with Sanskrit and thereby light the way to a common, primordial homeland.

Heinrich Ewald's *Hebrew Grammar* (1828), for example, argued that Hebrew roots consisting of three consonants were actually based on a shorter root form composed of a radical that either doubled itself or added a soft consonant on the end. Because he believed these shorter radicals to be closer to the "shortest original roots" (*Urwurzeln*), Ewald concluded that Hebrew occupied a level of language development that was midway between Chinese, "which had remained truest to primordial times," and the "Indo-Germanic language family which had matured to manhood," a supposition that assumed the original unity of language types. Similarly, Gesenius remarked in the 1830 edition of his *Hebrew Grammar* that Semitic and Indo-European languages showed an affinity in large numbers of their root words. He concluded based on this evidence that the two families must have developed their roots together before branching off; Indo-European patterns of inflection had arisen later and were therefore unique to that family.[162]

These efforts to reconcile the grammatical structures of Semitic and Indo-European were part of a campaign to preserve the original unity of language and humanity despite the secularizing effects of comparative philology. Well into the nineteenth century theologically inspired Hebraists tried geographically to locate the likely Garden of Eden where the common ancestor of both families had resided. Julius Fürst (1805–73), a student of Gesenius who had broken off his rabbinical training in order to pursue a career in Semitic philology, argued in 1835 that the Semitic and Sanskrit language families had once been united in an "original northern residence" somewhere in southwest Asia. His *Collection of Aramaic Idioms with Reference to the Indo-Germanic Languages* (1835) intended "to bring Semitic closer to the familial band of Indo-European languages" by presenting evidence of a "formal original unity" of language.[163] In 1862 Heinrich Ewald likewise argued that there was a "higher connection" among the most diverse of language families. Turkish, Indo-Germanic, Semitic, and Coptic showed evidence of "a primordial identity" that, in his view, could only be explained by "their separation from a common last source." According to Ewald, language had developed fully among an "original people" (*Urvolke*) before splitting into separate families, and "humanity's first tribe" had been at home in "northern Asia."[164]

The Indologist Theodor Benfey (1809–81) likewise stressed the ties linking Semitic and Indo-Germanic antiquity, but without the compulsion of theology. Born the son of a small-town Jewish merchant in the state of Hannover, Benfey was a precocious student of languages. As a four-year-old boy he learned Hebrew from his father; older brothers taught him to conjugate and decline Latin long before he could read the alphabet. When his father requested that Benfey defer studying medicine due to the young age at which he entered the University of Göttingen, he chose classical philology instead. Benfey acquired formal training in Hebrew, Greek, and Latin from K. O. Müller and G. L. Dissen, spending a semester with Heinrich Ewald and Friedrich Thiersch in Munich. He shared their commitment to liberal nationalism, attending the Hambach Festival in 1832 and later welcoming Prussia's efforts to unify Germany. These political sympathies, however, do not explain why Benfey struggled to find a salaried university position. He labored as an unpaid lecturer in Göttingen for nine years, postponing his marriage to Fanny Wallerstein, and then only obtaining a meager salary in 1843 after winning the prestigious Volney prize for a lexicon of Greek roots. Despite a splendid career he was repeatedly denied promotion and lodged British students to supplement his income. According to Benfey's daughter Meta, the impossibility of a Jew pursuing a career in comparative Indo-European philology forced him to convert in 1848.[165]

An accidental wager encouraged Theodor Benfey to learn Sanskrit in 1830. Friends bet that four weeks were too few for him to review a book in an unknown language. Benfey proved them wrong and increasingly dedicated his energies to Indology.[166] Like A. W. Schlegel he approached the field from a foundation in classical philology, applying his critical and textual skills to editing the Vedas and placing Vedic Sanskrit in historical and comparative perspective. The publication of a 356-page article on India in Ersch and Gruber's 1840 encyclopedia first earned him success in the field. Critical editions and translations of the *Sama Veda* (1848), ancient Vedic religious chants, and the *Panchatantra* (1859), a collection of Indian animal fables, as well as Benfey's Sanskrit grammars and dictionaries solidified his reputation. Benfey likewise edited inscriptions in Old Persian, rightly arguing for a close connection between Vedic Sanskrit and Old Avestan, the language of the sacred Zoroastrian hymns or Gathas.[167]

Hebrew and other Semitic languages also received Benfey's attentions, so that contemporaries held him in awe for his mastery of both Indian and Hebrew antiquity.[168] His two main works in the field both foregrounded moments of cultural contact between speakers of Indo-European and Semitic languages. His treatise *On the Month Names of Some Ancient Peoples* (1836), for example, argued that Hebrew names for the months had been adopted from Farsi during the Babylonian

Theodor Benfey, scholar of Indo-European and Semitic antiquity.

exile; the later expansion of the Persian Empire into Syria and Palestine reinforced the borrowed terms.[169] Similarly, the introduction to Benfey's *Pantschatantra* stressed the importance of Arabic and Jewish translators in the transmission of Indian fairy tales and animal fables to Europe.[170] More significantly, Benfey proposed in *On the Egyptian's Relationship to the Semitic Language Family* (1844) that Semitic tongues were related to Coptic, the variant of ancient Egyptian spoken circa 200–1100 and the liturgical language of Coptic Christianity. He successfully linked Semitic, Berber, and Cushitic (Ethiopian) languages, helping to classify what is today known as the Afro-Asiatic language family. Baron Christian Karl Josias von Bunsen had earlier proposed that Coptic arose in a union of Semitic and Indo-European languages.[171] And Benfey acknowledged a possible affinity in the root words of both families, while partaking in Bopp's skepticism of their sharing inflective forms.[172]

Benfey's main contribution to linguistics challenged, albeit unsuccessfully, Bopp's understanding of the original monosyllabic elements that had composed Proto-Indo-European. His theory of "primary verbs" made more likely the prospect of finding evidence that Semitic and Indo-European forms had descended from the same source. Bopp assumed the existence of two primordial classes of Indo-European roots. Verbal roots had evolved into verbs and nouns; pronominal roots gave form to pronouns, conjunctions, particles, and prepositions.[173] By 1837 Benfey had rejected the term "root" on the grounds that the most primitive elements of Indo-European languages had not been roots, but a primordial type of monosyllabic verb.[174] These primary verbs had produced nouns and all other grammatical forms.[175] A new theory of suffixes supported this hypothesis. Within the Indo-European family, Bopp assumed that noun forms originated from the affixing of a case-sign to a root. Most such nouns had an element between the root and the case-sign, known as stem-forming suffixes. Bopp believed that all stem-forming suffixes derived from a collection of pronouns. In Benfey's view, these suffixes were originally the same and derived from the verbal form *ant*, which appears in the present active participle of Sanskrit.[176]

According to Benfey, the search for primary monosyllabic verbs took the linguist back to an earlier moment in the evolution of Indo-European languages before roots had formed. Primary verbs "preceded [roots] by many stages of linguistic development."[177] He accepted, furthermore, the "possibility of a common origin for all languages." "Languages for which no connection can be proven," Benfey argued, could "have sprouted from a common stock and have distanced themselves more than others from it." Unfortunately, he feared, the evidence taken from various languages in support of this thesis was still "incapable" of withstanding "a critical gaze." Knowledge of how roots emerged within the Semitic languages was "still in the deepest obscurity," and linguists only stood "at the beginning" for other tongues.[178] Nevertheless, discovering monosyllabic primary verbs made it more conceivable that the different root types found in Indo-European and in Semitic languages could have emerged from a common source or *Urform*.

A number of comparativists differentiated strictly between Indo-European and Semitic languages and rejected the principles upon which their supposed affinity was based. Taking Franz Wüllner to task, Friedrich August Pott, for example, launched a diatribe against the type of "lumping languages together" (*Sprachmengerei*) that was based exclusively on lexical comparisons of words, roots, and syllables. Gesenius, Ewald, and Fürst had supported their arguments for the original unity of humanity and language with the theory that grammatical comparisons were not necessary as a criterion of relationship if similarities in root words could be proven.[179] Pott dismissed such "heroes of pseudo-etymologies," calling their work a "shameful horror" and the "death of true science."[180] Similarly, the Bonn Indologist August Wilhelm Schlegel insisted that the Semitic languages were "distinct" from the Indo-Germanic family: "no etymological *tour de force* can bring them back to a common origin."[181] Schlegel, like Pott, believed in "pluralistic human beginnings" and in an "original diversity . . . of foreign language families."[182]

Theories of the radical otherness and inferiority of Hebrew, the language thought to be what defined the Semitic family, initially built off of Friedrich Schlegel's mistaken belief that it was not an inflectional language like Sanskrit. According to Konrad Koerner, the triconsonantal base of Hebrew and Arabic would actually have qualified them as inflectional languages.[183] In 1808, however, this grammatical particularity was not recognized. Schlegel, who maintained functionally polygeneticist views and saw no correspondence between basic linguistic types, classified Hebrew as a language in which "declensions are formed by supplementary particles, instead of inflections of the root" rather than as an organic language related to Sanskrit.[184] He denied that dissyllabic languages were truly philosophical; as the ancient Hebrews had lived under "Oriental" climatic conditions, he believed their literature to be the product of the uncontrolled imagination that prevailed in hot climates and therefore to be lacking in refinement.[185]

Hebrew's perceived distance from Sanskrit assumed larger cultural significance in early nineteenth-century Germany given the emphasis placed on language and origins in German ideas of nationhood. Wilhelm von Humboldt's essay *On the Diversity of Human Language Construction and Its Influence on the Mental Development of the Human Species* (1830–35), for example, argued that language was a creative power or *energeia* that governed the cognition and worldview of its speakers. Words were responsible for "shaping the mental power of the nation," so that one could discern the degree and type of a given people's "intellectuality" based on the linguistic principles of their native tongue. In Humboldt's view the peculiarities of the Semitic languages did not just point to an alternative cultural starting point from the Indo-European family; they reflected the different mental energies of the "nations" that spoke them. Hebrew, in his analysis, belonged to those languages that possessed an "imperfect organism" and deviated from "the natural build" of the Indo-European family. The triconsonantal base of Hebrew verbs resulted, Humboldt explained, in "a constrained word formation to which the freedom of other languages, especially of the Sanskrit family, is justly preferable."[186] He acknowledged that Hebrew made use of inflections, but believed them to be of an inferior kind; in his interpretation, declensions and pronouns in Hebrew were expressed through additional particles.[187] For these reasons, Humboldt concluded, one had "to count the Semitic languages among those that deviate from the most acceptable path of mental development."[188]

This view did not necessarily translate into political anti-Semitism. Humboldt was an important advocate of the 1812 Prussian act of emancipation and favored granting equal legal status to Jews on the basis of natural rights alone.[189] Yet he expected a process of emancipation and reeducation (*Bildung*) to create a culturally and linguistically homogeneous community in which the Jewish subculture was completely dissolved.[190] The Romantic ideology of the Christian state and the continued Christian character of the German university system during the Restoration reinforced the notion that Jews must acquire the cultural, religious, and political traditions of mainstream German society before becoming members of the nation.[191] Even when German nationalism did not directly include devotion to the Christian faith, nationalist goals were often identified with the content and significance of Christianity.[192] Fears that the Jewish minority formed a "state within a state" refusing to submit to bureaucratic authority evolved into a negative depiction of Jews as a distinct *Volk,* especially as the mechanical view of the state typical of the eighteenth century gave way to an organic conception of nationhood.

Comparative philologists aided in this process of cultural segregation by "Orientalizing" the ancient Hebrews and excluding Jews from the sacred drama of salvation being carried out by a chosen Indo-European people. The Orientalization of European Jews has a history prior to the nineteenth century. Enlightenment Pietists, for example, wishing to purge ceremonial and ritual "Jewish" elements from their religion of pure ethics, had already tried to detach Christianity from its "Oriental" origins.[193] Insisting on the disparate origins of the Semitic and Indo-European language families once again threatened to rob the ancient Hebrews of religious significance. As Maurice Olender has observed, nineteenth-century philologists were willing to accept that the ancient Semites held the secret of monotheism but denied them any role in universal historical progress. Science, art, and the mastery over nature were portrayed as achievements of Aryan antiquity; the Semites were depicted as being immobile and in need of the dynastic and migratory abilities of the Indo-Europeans to spread the word of God.[194] In his view, Hebrews were identified with an invariable truth that excluded them from historical change and as such were in need of being rescued from the timeless paradise to which they had been relegated.[195]

Comparative philologists such as Johann Heinrich Kalthoff (1803–39) devalued the contributions ancient Hebrews had made to religion and cultural progress.[196] A student of A. W. Schlegel, he combined comparative philology and archaeology in his *Handbook of Hebraic Antiquities* (1840). According to Kalthoff, "ancient Jewish life . . . found in religion its entire definition." However, he understood the religiosity of the Hebrews within the larger context of a mystical, religious Orient.[197] The only thing unique about the Hebrews was that unlike the Chinese, for example, they were able to differentiate God and nature and recognized the true creator and Lord. The "outward cultural state" of the Hebrews revealed to Kalthoff their failure to progress. Despite an intense inner life and "all their true high *Bildung,*" the Hebrews were "only to be regarded as barbarians." In Kalthoff's estimation, they did not possess adequate knowledge in science and art, or the capacity in industry and trade, "to be counted amongst the cultured, civilized nations." He calculated the "cultural level" of the Hebrews to be above "the utterly uneducated and truly barbarian peoples of Asia, Africa, and Europe," but it was "still far behind many other Oriental peoples such as the Egyptians, Phoenicians, Babylonians, and Indians." The "overall character" of Hebrews lay "in diametrical opposition" to peoples who earn "the title of Hellenic-European *Bildung*."[198]

The distinction comparative-historical philologists drew between the Indo-European and the Semitic cultural inheritance was by no means set in stone in the first half of the nineteenth century. The desire to find in language evidence supporting the monogenetic Christian account of human origins led philologists to search for bridging mechanisms between Sanskrit and Hebrew. Lingering notions of an *Ursprache* and of Old Testament notions of cultural difference endured despite the secularizing effects of comparative-historical philology. The characteristic features of the Indo-European language family and its defining language, Sanskrit, continued to be associated with the qualities of the divine first language or *Ursprache* once thought to have been in existence before Babel. But these biblical references were increasingly being put to use in a new cultural and ethnic understanding of modern Germans' descent from an Indo-European homeland, however, that emphasized exclusive linguistic communities and a polygenetic model of human dispersal. As German Orientalists narrowed their understanding of the exclusive original population and homeland of their ancestors, their notion of German nationhood assumed a new focus on ethnicity and shared historical descent. By 1830 scholars had proclaimed the existence of an exclusive "Indo-Germanic" language family whose members were distinguished from unrelated speakers of Chinese and Semitic languages. The superior cultural forms of this chosen people were depicted in opposition to an internal, Orientalized other who lacked the cultural and religious traditions to become full members of the German nation.

With the articulation of distinct Indo-European and Semitic language families, the implications that a comparative-historical approach to Oriental studies would have for German conceptions of nationhood had not yet run their course. After 1830 the term "Aryan" took hold within the discipline as an alternative designation for "Indo-Germanic," and the role of language in defining cultural difference expanded to include a racialist element that linked language, nationality, and human communities in more rigidly hierarchical formations. The idea that Germans were a chosen people and a nation acting out the historical drama of salvation was tied more closely to notions of racial purity, territorial expansion, and cultural superiority. Before the transformation of Indo-Germans into Aryans can be examined, though, two competing notions of the German national heritage—one Germanic and one Hellenic—need to be situated in relation to the Orientalist model.

3

Urvolk Germania

Historicizing Language and the Nation in German Philology, 1806–72

In the dismal winter of 1807–8, the idealist philosopher Johann Gottlieb Fichte (1762–1814) delivered several lectures in a series called *Addresses to the German Nation* to sparse noontime audiences in the aula of the Berlin Academy. The city had been occupied by Napoleon's soldiers, Prussian king Friedrich Wilhelm III had fled to Köngisberg, and Fichte had been compelled to reconcile a new Francophobia with the otherwise universalistic aspirations of his theory of knowledge. His lectures presented plans for a German national education based on J. G. Herder's assumption that the "sum total of the sensuous and mental life of the nation" was "deposited in language." Germans would persevere and be resilient in the face of French aggression, Fichte assured his audience, because they were an "*Urvolk,*" a primordial people, distinguished even within the larger family of *Germanen* by the "greater purity of their descent." In contrast to "Neo-Latin peoples" such as the French, Germans still spoke "the original language of the ancestral stock" and resided in the "original fatherland." Romance languages, conversely, were "dead at the root" because the introduction of Latin had severed their speakers' ties to the distant past. For Fichte, the strength of German culture and philosophy derived from the superiority of a language "whose life extends back to the first moment it issued from the force of nature," and he urged the nation to rally around its most precious possession.[1]

Historicizing the German nation as an *Urvolk* whose youthful language preserved pure cultural ties to antiquity was a rhetorical strategy common to patriots of the Napoleonic period. During the French occupation language acquired new significance as a marker of nationality and political allegiance. Ernst Moritz Arndt, Friedrich Ludwig Jahn, Friedrich Schleiermacher, and Heinrich Luden all publicized the notion that the nation's vitality lay in its stalwart mother tongue and that cultural education in its literary expressions and history was crucial to strengthening German nationhood. Their emphasis on the autonomous historical development of the German language propagated anti-French sentiment by evoking a genealogy distinct from that of Romance-speaking peoples. Since German humanists rediscovered Tacitus's *Germania* in 1457 and with it the heroic tale of Hermann the Cherusker defeating the legions of Quinctilius Varus in the Teutoburg Forest in 9 AD, recourse to a specifically Germanic past had been used to shield northern Europe from perceived waves of Roman culture. By the late eighteenth century, a number of resurrected literary works and forgotten myths had succeeded in breaking the Mediterranean monopoly on antiquity and in elevating the prestige of what appeared to be a deep and noble northern past.[2] Jordanes's *History of the Goths* suggested to Danish scholars that Europe had been populated from the north, and late eighteenth-century translations of the Old Norse *Edda*s convinced J. G. Herder and others that Scandinavia offered the German genius a "treasure trove" that was "more appropriate than the mythology of the Romans."[3]

This chapter outlines a second model of German linguistic nationhood, one built on a new valuation of the Germanic past over and against classical antiquity. It shows how the process of historicizing the German language enabled philologists to resurrect the primordial past of a German *Urvolk*, while giving nostalgic witness to its dissolution through time. The techniques of historical grammar developed by Jacob Grimm (1785–1865) helped identify the cultural starting point of the first *Ur*-German speakers and trace their subsequent division into different tribes and dialect groups. The diversity and political fragmentation of contemporary Germans, let alone speakers of more broadly Germanic tongues, compelled these scholars to reconcile an ideal of original linguistic unity with a reality of provincialism. And the chapter explores the different ways Protestant Germans from the north and Catholics from the south, especially Johann Andreas Schmeller (1785–1852), interpreted the relative authenticity and cultural value of linguistic expressions that differed by region, confession, and class, as well as those particular to women and rural populations. Reflections on the antiquity and historical character of standard written High German and German dialects responded to conflicts and differences within the German states and in turn set expectations for how different linguistic groups could participate in the nation.

For most of the nineteenth century, scholarship on the German language took place within the broader literary field of German philology—itself nominally distinct from, but closely entwined with, the study of German law and history or Germanics.[4] The success with which German philology established itself as a university discipline depended on the degree to which the German states were willing to tolerate and then themselves mobilize nationalism as a political force. Until the 1860s German language scholars maintained a largely oppositional stance to local princes as representatives of bureaucratic state interests rather than the nation. The liberal-nationalist convictions of German philologists slowed the creation of university chairs in the field, as well as reforms at the secondary school level that would have produced a greater demand for academically trained teachers of German. This chapter examines the intersection of German language scholarship and the nationalist movement, tracing the gradual conversion of the field to a relatively conservative defender of Prussian interests in the years prior to unification in 1871.

The chapter likewise analyzes what impact a focus on the origins and historical descent of the German language had for how the community of the nation was imagined. The historicization of language in the early nineteenth century, it will be seen, changed the conditions of linguistic community as they had been imagined by the language purists and patriots of the eighteenth century. Rather than represent speakers' ability to participate in a pragmatic network of communication and exchange, the German mother tongue came to symbolize common descent from a northern homeland. Recourse to a common set of origins appealed to nationalists at a time when their educated middle-class audiences suffered from regional and professional fragmentation. Language provided a semblance of historical continuity that gave credence to the new cultural memories and narratives of national origin that defined the national elite. Yet celebrating a prehistoric *Urvolk* failed to address the very real problems nationalists faced in forging dialogue and unity among diverse regional populations who literally had trouble communicating across confessional and class lines. A historical approach to language tended to emphasize the autonomy of language as a being shaped by its formative origins, rather than its malleability as a system of signs under the direction of free linguistic agents.

Grimm's Law and the First *Germanen*

Early attempts to historicize the German language transpired within a larger antiquarian movement to document and preserve the national past.[5] Inconsistent philological methods, however, hampered the process of historical recovery. One of the brightest beacons illuminating the Germanic past in the early nineteenth century was the *Nibelungenlied,* a southern German saga composed around 1200. Historical interest in the text erupted in a brief euphoria in the 1770s after Johann Jakob Bodmer (1698–1783) and Johann Jakob Breitinger (1701–76) published a newly discovered manuscript. The Swiss philologists claimed the heroic Hohenstaufen period had been comparable to Homeric Greece in its cultural production and impact on the German national consciousness.[6] The exploits of Siegfried and Kriemhild offered Protestant intellectuals a source of pre-Christian German religious beliefs from which to construct an explicitly national mode of worship, while feeding the early Romantic appetite for the German Middle Ages.[7] Often derided as amateur achievements by later philologists, reproductions of the saga aimed to reach a popular audience. Early Germanists such as Friedrich Heinrich von der Hagen (1780–1856), who published the first of his five editions of the *Nibelungenlied* in 1805, rendered the epic's Middle High German into an odd mixture of contemporary and archaic expressions. Antiquated language preserved the historical ambience of the epic, in his view, yet threatened the success of a modern transmission. Hagen indulged in a "free reproduction," loosely transcribing incomprehensible passages while preserving the marks of the epic's alterity.[8] These efforts earned him the first position in German antiquities at the newly founded university in Berlin in 1810.

Scholarship on the German language provided an important venue for the expression of nationalism in the Napoleonic period.

Friedrich Ludwig Jahn (1778–1852), for example, *Turnvater* to the highly politicized gymnastic movement was also a founding member of the Berlin Society for the German Language; his influential *Deutsches Volksthum* (1810) recommended the study of language as a basis for German cultural reconstruction; the purity and authenticity of language offered an ideal foundation for nation building.[9] These organizations offered a "northern" alternative to the classical ideal of *Bildung*, recapturing physical aspects of Greek education ignored by neohumanists, while celebrating Germanic military heroes such as the valiant Hermann or the Swiss martyr Winkelried. After 1810 members of Jahn's nationalist circle attended Friedrich Heinrich von der Hagen's lectures on the *Nibelungenlied*. Later academic Germanists, such as J. G. G. Büsching, Joseph Görres, Hans Ferdinand Maßmann, the Grimms, and Heinrich Hoffmann von Fallersleben likewise understood their studies to be in service of the fatherland. Many wore patriotic "old German" dress: a long back overcoat with white collar, berets, beards, and long hair parted down the middle. A "tent-and-field" edition of the *Nibelungenlied* strengthened the resolve of volunteer soldiers during the Wars of Liberation; the brothers Jacob and Wilhelm Grimm likewise dedicated the proceeds from their edition of a twelfth-century Swabian epic to Hessian troops.

As German philology acquired disciplinary rigor, von der Hagen fell victim to a new vanguard of scholars. His pseudohistorical transcriptions of the *Nibelungenlied* were, in the eyes of one 1823 critic, nothing more than "glaring pretense . . . and ostentation . . . laziness and the vague guesswork of a dilettante."[10] Hagen pursued no systematic study of language or grammar and knew Old German and Old Norse only sufficiently enough to enable a basic understanding of the literature.[11] His renditions, for example, replaced such sequences as "*harte balde*" with "*viel balde*" (literally "much soon") which is understandable but incorrect. A more consistent translation would have substituted the contemporary word "*sehr*" (very) for "*harte*."[12] For his part, however, the early Germanist showed open condescension toward those "renowned persons, even famous linguists" whose erudition was "too much for them to handle."[13] Such sticklers, he believed, suffered from a "fixed idea that language was stuck in time and specific to a province," and sacrificed poetic finesse for linguistic accuracy.[14]

Hagen's disregard for the historicity of language is not surprising given the conventions of late eighteenth-century grammar. An antiquarian interest in Gothic and Old German was already present among northern humanists such as Franciscus Junius (1589–1677); German language scholars compiled rudimentary dictionaries and grammars through the mid-eighteenth century, although without adequate attention to issues of sound change. By the last decades of the century, an interest in practical and philosophical grammar had overshadowed this historical approach. The primary concern of Enlightenment grammarians, including Johann Christoph Gottsched (1700–1766) and Johann Christoph Adelung, was to establish German as a language of academic discourse equivalent to Latin. Their largely prescriptive works developed key terminology for classifying contemporary German and set grammatical, lexical, and orthographic norms that standardized the language.[15] Although Adelung, in particular, believed grammatical principles had to be understood in their historical evolution, there was among early Germanists little attempt to reconstruct specific historical states of the mother tongue.

German philology earned greater recognition at the university by applying the critical methodology of classicists to the interpretation and critical editing of medieval German texts. In 1805 Georg Friedrich Benecke (1762–1844), a student of the classicist C. G. Heyne, procured the first post in German philology at the University of Göttingen, promising to expend equal philological rigor on the literature of the fatherland. Benecke argued that university instruction in German should extend beyond the scant practical training in rhetoric, style, and aesthetics that had been available in the eighteenth century, offering courses in the history of medieval German literature. Karl Lachmann (1793–1851), his prodigy, similarly impressed the neohumanist establishment in 1816 by adapting to the *Nibelungenlied* the epic theory and textual criticism exemplified in F. A. Wolf's *Prolegomena ad Homerum* (1795). One of two joint chairs in classical and German philology, the Berlin professor set the standards for the critical, historical interpretation of German literature and for the editing of Middle High German texts. His disciplined editions and equally demanding personality banished from the field perceived dilettantes such as von der Hagen, whose questionable "modernizations" of the *Nibelungenlied* contributed as much to the saga's popularity as to the lowly reputation suffered by early Germanists.

The invention of historical grammar—which was the most dramatic achievement of early German language scholars—responded, however, to precedents within comparative philology. German language study tailored itself more closely to the methods and concerns of Orientalists than to the techniques of classical scholars. The two fields shared a concern for origins and early history that students of Greek dismissed as insignificant on aesthetic and moral grounds. Comparativists likewise legitimated the study of "barbarian" antiquity by depriving ancient Greek of its pretensions to being the ideal or primordial language. As Jacob Grimm recalled in 1854, Greek once loomed over all other tongues "as an unattainable ideal." But once confronted with Sanskrit, philologists had to recognize that language as a "still more perfect paragon of language, perhaps the purest, of the highest antiquity."[16] German was placed on more equal footing with the classical languages once Orientalists deemed its archaic forms to be equivalent in age to ancient Greek and perhaps more proximate to the common Indo-European mother than its southern neighbor.

Having read Franz Bopp and Friedrich Schlegel, Jacob Grimm likewise acknowledged that the first Europeans had likely migrated westward from Asia into Scandinavia. Grimm, in fact, confided in the preface to the *German Grammar* (1819) that he would have preferred to have written a comparative history that included all members of the Indo-European family. Citing his inadequate knowledge of the languages involved, Grimm relinquished this project to the Danish Germanist Christian Rasmus Rask (1787–1832), who was at the time making his way through eastern Russia on an extended trip to India.[17] Nevertheless, the desire to discover when the first *Germanen* broke off from the larger Indo-European family and to identify what distinguished them from the neighboring Slavs, Franks, Greeks, and Lithuanians permeates Grimm's most important linguistic study. Published in four volumes from 1819 to 1837, the *German Grammar* established the framework for historical linguistics in a way that Bopp's *On the Conjugation System of Sanskrit* (1816) had done for comparativism. It recounted a history of the grammatical changes that shaped the Germanic languages from their first appearance to the present, arguing for their original unity and setting standards for judging the relative antiquity of documented linguistic forms.

The experience of Napoleonic occupation motivated Grimm's historical sensibility, as it did his devotion to the language, literature, and popular culture of the German *Volk*. When French troops entered his home city of Kassel, the tradition of Roman law that he had pursued as a student of Friedrich Karl von Savigny now seemed tainted by foreign influence.[18] Grimm left a post in the legal profession and dove into the study of Old German literature and folklife. Having procured a position as the private librarian of King Jérome Bonaparte, he published with his brother Wilhelm the *Altdeutsche Wälder* (1813–15). In the tradition of other Romantic collections such as *Des Knaben Wunderhorn,* the serial offered excepts and short commentaries on German folk poetry, fairy tales, epics, and folk songs. In the wake of the French Revolution, conservative thinkers such as Friedrich Schlegel, Ludwig Tieck, Novalis, and W. H. Wackenroder had sought to revive the spiritual integrity and political stability of the Holy Roman Empire.[19] Their medievalism celebrated the Catholic church and its artistic expressions as a means of resurrecting the ethical, religious, and social ideals attacked by rationalist thinkers of the Enlightenment. The feudal structures and paternal government of the medieval Hapsburg monarch appeared to be the only institutions capable of checking the revolutionary spirit and guaranteeing the return of Germany's greatness.

For Protestant scholars of the Napoleonic era, the model of national life offered by the High Medieval period verged too closely on an acceptance of Catholic Austria and absolutist political structures. The early Germanic tribes offered a tradition of political freedom, austere virtue, and participatory government that was older and therefore presumably more authentic than Hapsburg imperial rule. Protestant intellectuals likewise regarded the recovery of a "native" pre-Christian mythology as central to the reassertion of a German *Volk.*[20] For Friedrich Schlegel, the discovery of a primordial revelation in India had reinforced a commitment to Catholicism and conservative nationalism. Research on Norse and Germanic mythology linked the pagan faith of the earliest Germanic tribes to the "German" Christianity of the Reformation. Uniquely German heroes, myths, and legends provided Protestant Germans with a native religious imagery not dependent on the "foreign" myths of the Bible or the superstition of Roman Catholicism.[21] For this reason, the search for a primordial German *Ursprache* was largely the preserve of liberal-nationalists and Protestants.

While collecting material for a volume of *Fairy Tales* (1812) and a history of the German saga (1816), Jacob and his brother Wilhelm thought they had uncovered remnants of a pre-Christian primordial faith or *Urmythus.* Similarities in the narrative core of these stories and the repetition of poetic motifs across time and space pointed, in their minds, to a shared primordial revelation. The Grimms undertook comparative studies of mythology that drew in such diverse sources as the *Arabian Nights* and Hindu legends in an attempt to ascertain an original theme that dated to the dawn of time. There were alluring parallels, the brothers observed, between the diffusion of religious beliefs and the spread of languages described by Friedrich Schlegel.[22] When August Wilhelm Schlegel sharply reprimanded the brothers that identical poetic motifs could appear independently without their having derived from an *Urmythus,* Jacob turned to language as the only sure foundation for reconstructing prehistoric genealogies.

The choice of language as a conduit into the Germanic past responded to Grimm's disillusionment with the failure of the Congress of Vienna to give cultural and political form to the recovered historical memory of an authentic German national identity. After returning from the deliberations in Austria, Grimm, as John E. Toews has shown, devised a theory of cultural development that purported to explain the historical distance separating the present from an authentic, yet alienated native past, while at the same time holding out a lifeline linking contemporaries to a pure moment of national origin. The German language in its historical evolution seemed to reveal the deep structures of German identity and yet to bear the telling marks of the type of cultural transformation and change that contingent historical events could inflict on an original essence.[23] Language also appealed to Grimm as the cultural form with the most intimate connection to a preexisting national spirit; in his view, other cultural expressions such as literature, folktales, and myth all built upon the structures of the language in which they took shape.[24]

Actual research into archaic forms of language was made possible by Grimm's extensive study of medieval manuscripts. That Grimm served as served as a librarian for thirty years of his life, turning down numerous university positions before accepting an offer at Göttingen in 1829, indicates how important the availability of medieval sources was to acquiring a historical appreciation of language. The majority of Germanists active between 1800 and 1850 served as librarians at some point in their careers, undertaking extended trips in search of manuscripts and collecting them privately.[25] The critical editions issued in the late eighteenth century and radically improved in the next decades under the influence of classical philology's exacting textual methods were a necessary basis for reconstructing earlier stages of the

German language. Correctly discerning the end rhymes of Old German verses, for example, enabled researchers to document archaic words with more precision. Grimm's own editions of medieval texts, his prose transcriptions, and the historical view of legal terminology he gained while working on "Concerning Poetry in Law" (1816), made possible the observations offered in the *German Grammar.*

Nevertheless, until 1816 Jacob Grimm had only vague notions of the development of German linguistic forms and engaged in a speculative type of etymology whose validity had been made obsolete by advances in the new field of comparative philology. The prior existence of an *Ursprache* (or universal language) that lived on in all national tongues, Grimm once believed, justified using any words from any language to explain others that sounded alike.[26] Two events combined to change this perspective. In his critical review of the *Altdeutsche Wälder,* August Wilhelm Schlegel accused the brothers of replicating the "chaos of Babel" in their studies. "Whoever brings such etymologies to light," he insisted, "[is] still a foreigner to even the most basic principles of linguistic research." He advised Grimm that it would be impossible to achieve an adequate understanding of ancient Germanic texts "without knowledge of grammar,"[27] a reproof that the recipient took painfully to heart. The discovery of the so-called *i-Umlaut* in Middle High German likewise gave Jacob confidence in the regularities of grammatical structure and showed him the importance of sound in language. In 1816 Grimm observed a specific change in the development of certain words over time, namely that the vowel "a" becomes an "e" in the root syllable of words, if in Old High German or Old Saxon an "i" or a "j" followed in the end syllable.[28] Knowing how to track regular changes in linguistic forms hastened the completion of the *German Grammar* two years later.[29]

A historical approach to language had already facilitated the comparison of languages in other contexts by uncovering obscured elements certain tongues once held in common. Friedrich Schlegel, for example, drew on "old monuments of the Germanic language" such as Gothic, Old Saxon, and Icelandic to prove the similarity of case endings in modern German and Sanskrit.[30] Rasmus Rask's prize essay on Icelandic, *A Grammar of the Icelandic or Old Norse Tongue* (1811), had a more immediate impact on Grimm. The Danish Academy of Sciences had held a competition aimed at establishing the linguistic forms of proto-Nordic. In an entry that Grimm reviewed in 1811 Rask insisted that a defensible prehistoric stage of language could be reconstructed. This prospect likely inspired Grimm to break with earlier German grammars, such as the one compiled by Johann Christoph Adelung in 1781, that erected an edifice of norms and rules to codify contemporary forms of the language.

As Bopp had done for the Indo-European language family, Grimm uncovered the "linguistic organism" that united Germanic tongues. While Bopp's work was primarily comparative and assumed that the grammatical structure of language had a certain independence from historical change, Grimm's analysis was in the first instance genetic. "The grammatical structures of the present can only be established historically," Grimm insisted, "every word has its own history and lives its own life."[31] The *German Grammar* established that "the branches of the Germanic language family" shared a common set of grammatical principles that pointed to their mutual evolution from a single, prehistoric tongue.[32] Grimm used the word "*deutsch*" in the sense in which Germanic (or Teutonic) is used today and included in his study Gothic, the Nordic languages, Low German languages such as Saxon, Angle, and Frisian, as well as Old and Middle High German.[33] The choice of this terminology in the grammar and subsequent works was designed to recall that New High German was of the same origin as related tongues and correctly reflects the central importance of the language in Grimm's definition of the family. It was an affront to Rasmus Rask, however, who feared the term "*deutsch*" diminished the importance of Scandinavian languages and himself preferred "*gotisk*," which Grimm rejected as too narrow.[34]

The "fundamental and exclusive characteristic" that defined membership in the Germanic language family was for Grimm a series of regular vowel modifications in the syllables of words as they are built up and assume grammatical function in a sentence.[35] In his view, the Germanic languages were distinguished from other Indo-European tongues by their use of the *Ablaut* and *Umlaut* in the inflection of words. Grimm introduced these designations into German grammar and distinguished between so-called strong and weak verb declensions, conventions still followed in language instruction today.[36] The term *Ablaut* refers to a series of regular vowel changes that Grimm derived from the conjugation of strong verbs but that also extend into other aspects of the Germanic languages. Among the strong verbs, changes in the vowel are used to signify tense. For example, the infinitive "*binden*" (to bind) inflects to assume the form "*band*" in the past and "*gebunden*" in the past participle. This *Ablaut* is the defining feature of strong verbs; according to Grimm, it was their "soul." But similar changes can also be seen in the formation of derivative nouns, in this case in the variations "*die Binde*" (the bandage), "*das Band*" (the bond or tie), and "*der Bund*" (the bundle).[37]

Grimm proposed that those verbs distinguished by their regular use of internal vowel modification to signify tense were constitutive of the family and not, as commonly assumed, peculiar exceptions to the more prevalent form of conjugation in New High German. The defining feature of the more common weak verbs is their appension of regular inflectional endings to the stem to form the past tense, as in the infinitive "*hoffen*" (to hope) which inflects as "*hoffte*" in the past and "*gehofft*" in the past participle. Grimm believed that the strong verbs "directly reveal[ed] . . . the profound, pensive order of the linguistic spirit [*Sprachgeist*]," and he revered the *Ablaut* as the living force behind the language.[38] In his analysis, systematic vowel changes lay at "the foundation of all Germanic word formation," the *Umlaut* being another modification typical of the Germanic languages.[39]

This association of vowel inflection with the authentically Germanic was reinforced by Grimm's discovery of the archaic, primordial nature of this grammatical form. Grimm interpreted the *Ablaut* as being characteristic of "the truly oldest form of conjugation," having evolved in a historical period before the first writers.[40] In his view, strong verbs were relics of older, more organic linguistic forms and could be used as a measure for tracking the gradual degeneration of language. Grimm identified three "gradations" of the Germanic languages based on the decreasing frequency with which the *Ablaut* designated grammatical function.[41]

The question of when Germanic speakers emerged as a *Volk* distinct from their Indo-European neighbors was not broached until the second edition of the *Grammar*, published in 1822.[42] The new 596-page section "On Letters" detailed the separation of the Germanic languages from the larger Indo-European family with reference to sound changes that evolved historically in a particular series of consonants. Grimm discerned in the composition of Germanic root words a "double sound shift that has important consequences for the history of the language and for the stringency of etymology." Since 1837 this has been known as "Grimm's Law." It specified that "just as Old High

German has sunk down a level in all three grades from Gothic, so did Gothic itself sink down a level from Latin (Greek, Indic)."[43] Grimm took those consonants appearing in the roots of Greek, Sanskrit, and Latin words to exemplify constructions shared by the common ancestor of all Indo-European languages and showed that in the first Germanic languages roots of similar meaning were built using an alternative series of consonants. Secondly, he demonstrated that consonants in Old High German had undergone a second series of modifications that distinguished the language from what is now known as Proto-Germanic.[44]

To show the systematic nature of these consonant shifts, Grimm devised several tables.[45] In each case, those sounds typical of the common ancestor of western Indo-European languages are shown to evolve into an alternative set first in Proto-Germanic and then again in Old High German:

Table 1

Greek	P.	B.	F.	T.	D.	TH.	K.	G.	CH.
Gothic	F.	P.	B.	TH.	T.	D.	. .	K.	G.
Old High German	B(V)	F.	P.	D.	Z.	T.	G.	CH.	K.

A secondary table showed changes in guttural consonants as they appeared in Latin:

Table 2

Latin	c	g	h
Gothic	h, g	k	g
Old High German	h, g	ch	k

When contextualized in the written word, these sound changes are more comprehensible. For example, the evolution of the word for "you" which in Latin is "tu," in Gothic "Þ," and in Old High German "dû," shows the progressive shift in T to TH to D; as it evolves from Latin "ego" to Gothic "ik" to New High German "ich" the word for "I" reveals the change in G to K to CH.[46]

The first Germanic sound shift indicated to Grimm that the earliest Germans had broken off from the other western branches of the Indo-European family and emerged as a "nation" some time before the Christian era. The second or High German sound shift was believed to have taken place between the first and eighth centuries AD and to have separated speakers of the West Germanic languages into a High and Low German group. Practically, Grimm's observations enabled philologists to use etymology more accurately when tracing the historical development of linguistic forms. In his words, it was no longer a question of demonstrating the "equivalence or affinity of generally related consonants" but of recognizing "historical levels of gradation that cannot be displaced or reversed."[47] Etymology evolved from being more or less subjective guesswork to a science that enabled a precise genealogy of language. For example, after Grimm's *Grammar*, the New High German word for "head" (*Kopf*) could no longer be derived from the Latin "*caput*" despite the similarities in their sound and meaning. Rather, the German word "*Haupt*" must be seen as the true derivative of the Latin having gone through the C–H,G–H,G transition in its Gothic and Old High German forms.[48]

As presented in the *German Grammar*, Grimm's sound shifts attributed to language an autonomous internal principle of organic growth that itself defined communities of speakers. For Grimm, the inner life of language consisted in a subjective agent embodying itself in external forms.[49] This implied that the type of community formation at work in the emergence of the German nation transpired almost as a function of language itself. According to Grimm, language change charted a path of progressive decline through history, its forms appearing "more noble" and "purer" the further they reached back toward Gothic in the pre-Christian era.[50] He imagined the linguistic perfection found at the moment of origin to consist in language merging with the world so that virtually no gap existed between words and things.[51] As language matured, it acquired more mediated, abstract, and conceptual forms, mirroring the evolution of *Natur-* to *Kunstpoesie*. This raised the prospect of modern speakers self-consciously manipulating the observed gap between language and the world, as that between a lost national essence and the present. According to Toews, Grimm was not prepared in the 1820s to envision integrating more authentic linguistic forms into the structures of modern High German. Rather, as his subsequent work *German Legal Antiquities* (1828) indicates, a native tradition of German law appeared to offer a more appropriate social and political form for unifying the linguistic community.[52] Nevertheless, the continued presence in language of an original moment of cultural formation theoretically had the power to unite modern Germans in a shared linguistic community once this continuity was recognized.

Grimm's grammar notably celebrated New High German as the most authentic and original of the existing Germanic languages by revealing that it had participated to a much lesser degree in the general shift from synthetic to analytic structures than other members of the family. Contemporary scholars still describe German as being linguistically conservative because it retained more of the grammatical complexities of Proto-Germanic than English or Dutch.[53] Grimm interpreted the relative youth of standard written High German as a sign of the nation's vitality and strength. German developed its written norms late, according to Grimm, and was therefore still young and vital when ancient Greek and Latin crystallized into fixed literary forms. No other nation, in his view, had a two-thousand-year linguistic history in which to take pride, nor could another people match the "raw but healthy power of Germans" who had brought the Roman Empire to its knees.[54]

Defining the linguistic community based on its members' shared historical descent from a pure *Urvolk* represented a break with the importance Enlightenment scholars placed on creating a democratic discursive order of exchange. Eighteenth-century language purists advocated standardizing the spoken vernacular in an attempt to democratize social and political discourse; the literary public sphere was to be open to all who mastered the rules of engagement. For nineteenth-century nationalists, the vernacular no longer signified the possibility of mutual intelligibility among social groups who mastered its forms, but an exclusive ancestry and cultural legacy. In Grimm's conception, the unifying power of language no longer lay in the efficacy with which words and grammatical forms promoted mutual understanding or a pragmatic network of communicative relationships. Rather, the binding force of language derived from its evoking memories of a collective, primordial origin. Speakers of Germanic tongues were drawn together by the common experience of breaking away from the Indo-European language family. They were to recognize their affinity in the unique linguistic structures that resulted from this separation and were still preserved in each of the Germanic tongues.

Regionalism and Dialects: J. A. Schmeller

Imagining a national community self-consciously united by awareness of its shared linguistic descent was little more than wishful thinking in 1822. The decade between the Wars of Liberation and the Hambach Festival of 1832 marks a lull in the nationalist movement. German nationalism had limited popular appeal in the first half of the nineteenth century due to the strength of other loyalties and identities, whether confessional, regional, occupational, or state-based.[55] The diversity of languages and dialects spoken across the German Confederation, Scandinavia, and the Low Countries literally prevented the supposed descendents of Grimm's Germanic *Urvolk* from communicating across state lines. If a national language is a dialect with an army and a navy, modern German had neither before 1871. Even educated speakers of standard written High German retained such strong regional variations in pronunciation that understanding traveling theater groups could be difficult.[56] Nineteenth-century Germanists needed mechanisms to reconcile a broad definition of the linguistic community with the reality of local populations who had little affinity for standardized written or spoken tongues.

Local dialects brought the actual diversity and fragmentation of the German linguistic community into sharp contrast with a historical ideal of unity. Jacob Grimm himself appreciated that dialects had preserved the contact between language and concrete forms of life.[57] But they also seemed to divide German speakers with the result that neither of the Grimm brothers studied dialects formally. "Only by virtue of our written language do we Germans feel the bond of our descent and community to be alive," Grimm cautioned in the *German Grammar*, "and no tribe can believe to have paid too high a price for such an advantage."[58] Jacob welcomed that in the sixteenth century a standard written form of New High German supposedly vanquished "all signs of earlier tribal difference."[59] To mitigate linguistic divisions, he even proposed redistributing local expressions in dialect throughout German-speaking Europe.[60] Grimm considered independent national tongues, such as Dutch or Swedish, to be mere "dialects within the greater Germanic family."[61] The terms *Dialekt* and *Mundart* (idiom) could also refer to much smaller regional vernaculars, such as Swabian, rural or urban idioms, or slang peculiar to a social class. The Grimms spoke High German at home, although with a provincial intonation, and the

The Bavarian dialectologist Johann Andreas Schmeller in 1849.

brothers lacked sufficient knowledge to speak or edit even the local Hessian dialect.[62]

The founder of modern dialectology in Germany, Johann Andreas Schmeller, a contemporary and colleague of Grimm, likewise embraced as "altogether good and praiseworthy" that through standardized High German "all provinces of Germany are more or less united by one single shared language."[63] Along with Karl Lachmann, the two make up the trinity of German philology's founding fathers and pioneered the historical approach to grammar that dominated language study through midcentury. But, as the fourth child of rural Bavarian basket weavers and a speaker of dialect himself, Schmeller had a much more sympathetic and practical approach to the difficulties vernacular idioms posed toward national integration. His work, not surprisingly, also emphasized problems of sound change and phonetics that Grimm had neglected in favor of the written word.

Schmeller and Grimm are interesting foils in the linguistic definition of nationhood because of their differing notions of community. Grimm was rooted in Protestant northern Germany and turned to the Nordic lands as a beacon of cultural rebirth. Schmeller was one of a small minority of Germanists active outside of Prussia and the middle German states. A Catholic with ties to the artisan class, he located the nation's heart in a southern linguistic community that extended into Austria and across the Alps. Schmeller's work on Bavarian idioms aimed, moreover, at democratizing and making more inclusive the discursive community that defined the nation. He translated a historical view of language into an argument for the particular cultural contributions that dialect speakers made to the nation.

Schmeller's unique perspective stemmed from an untimely intellectual trajectory that took a windy detour around Romanticism and its adoration of the *Volk*. The association of peasants with origins and the nation's creative soul could hold few illusions for a poor upstart who joined Spanish mercenary troops in 1804 because his home village of Rimberg bei Pfaffenhofen offered few prospects. Talent and parental initiative had enabled Schmeller to attend the Lyceum in Munich. He never completed formal university education, but as a young man he enjoyed the attention of the school's director, Cajetan Weiller. A leading figure of the Munich Enlightenment, Weiller instilled in his student a practical pedagogical concern for improving the lot of disadvantaged social groups, a calling that Schmeller understood in linguistic terms.

Already as an eighteen-year-old, Schmeller reflected on the relationship between the spoken and written word and devised strategies for alleviating the social disadvantages faced by speakers of dialect. His essay "On Writing and Its Instruction" (1803) was an unsuccessful attempt to enter the ranks of Bavarian literati, but it presented the innovative argument that spoken dialects should not be considered deviant forms of the standard written language to be dismissed with "ridicule or . . . despite." Rather, they should be approached as independent languages in their own right. Schmeller's plea was based on the new notion that the prestige associated with the written word was a social and historical "convention" with no linguistic foundation.[64] Writing, he claimed, was simply "the art of making spoken language visible using an alphabet"; language itself consisted of a system of sounds that existed independently of any text.[65] This insight enabled Schmeller to perceive laws of linguistic change not apparent in written form. Even at this early juncture, he recognized that the forms of the standard written language were not sufficient to express the spoken word. When transcribed, Schmeller feared, dialects "may assume the appearance of a depraved written language, which in principle they are not."[66]

The vernacular initially presented Schmeller with a pedagogical problem. His essay suggested to teachers how they might break down the barriers between the vernacular and the standard written language and, in so doing, integrate speakers of nonstandard German into a broader linguistic community. Schmeller did not wish to extinguish the vernacular, but rather to acquaint students with standard High German by relating it to the dialect with which they were familiar. His views contradicted those of the majority of language teachers and researchers still working within a seventeenth-century tradition that taught standard High German independently of the vernacular, and are surprisingly modern in their approach.[67]

During the Wars of Liberation, Schmeller's interest in vernacular German took the same historical and nationalist turn that largely deprived the word *Volk* of its sociological dimensions among the Romantics. By his own explanation, this change resulted from an expatriate recognizing the German language as the only common bond uniting his fatherland at a moment of crisis. When Bavaria joined the coalition against Napoleon in 1813, Schmeller returned to enroll as a lieutenant in a voluntary riflery battalion. He later recalled not being able to conceal his "joyful amazement" to hear "so many sounds and expressions in the cottages of the homeland" whose "tones had grown foreign to my ear."[68] Remaining on active military duty after a triumphant march to Paris, Schmeller devised a plan in consultation with the Munich librarian Josef Scherer to compile a Bavarian dialectical dictionary similar to what Franz Josef Stalder had published for Switzerland in 1805.[69] "Language generally expresses the external and inner life of a nation," he argued to the Munich Academy of Sciences in 1816, but "the language of books" only captures the life of those "estates [*Stände*] who move in higher, studied forms." In his view the "natural life of the people" was "only expressed in the vernacular [*Volkssprache*]."[70] His petition for funds to research Bavarian idioms was granted, and Schmeller dedicated the next twenty-one years of his life to assembling material for a Bavarian grammar (1821) and dictionary (1827–37).

Studies of local customs, histories, and antiquities contributed in the early nineteenth century to a new set of narratives concerning regional contributions individual German states made to the nation.[71] Schmeller's project was thus commensurate with broader nationalist aspirations. "If Germany is my fatherland, Bavaria is so, as well,"[72] Schmeller noted in May 1813; he felt bound by loyalties to both his "narrow" and the "common German fatherland."[73] The scholar's ability to bridge provincial reality with a national agenda was at the same time compromised by the service the grammar was to render the Bavarian state. The decision to fund the project was one of several measures the newly independent monarchy undertook to strengthen regional loyalties after the collapse of the Holy Roman Empire. For this reason, the scope of the Bavarian grammar and dictionary was artificially limited to the political boundaries of the Wittelsbach kingdom. Neither study covered the entire region where Bavarian was spoken; this would have extended beyond *Altbayern* to Austria and parts of Upper Palatinate and Bohemia. Schmeller ignored the dialects of Austria and Tyrol, except those spoken around Salzburg, which was Bavarian during the time of his research, but included treatment of the unrelated Alemanic, Swabian, and Franconian dialects because such speakers lived within the borders of the state.

The Bavarian Vernaculars built from the provincial to the national by documenting the historical proximity of the Bavarian dialects to archaic and thus "authentic" German linguistic forms. Schmeller had begun studying older versions of German while abroad and upon his return was struck that spoken Bavarian "vividly reminded me of the

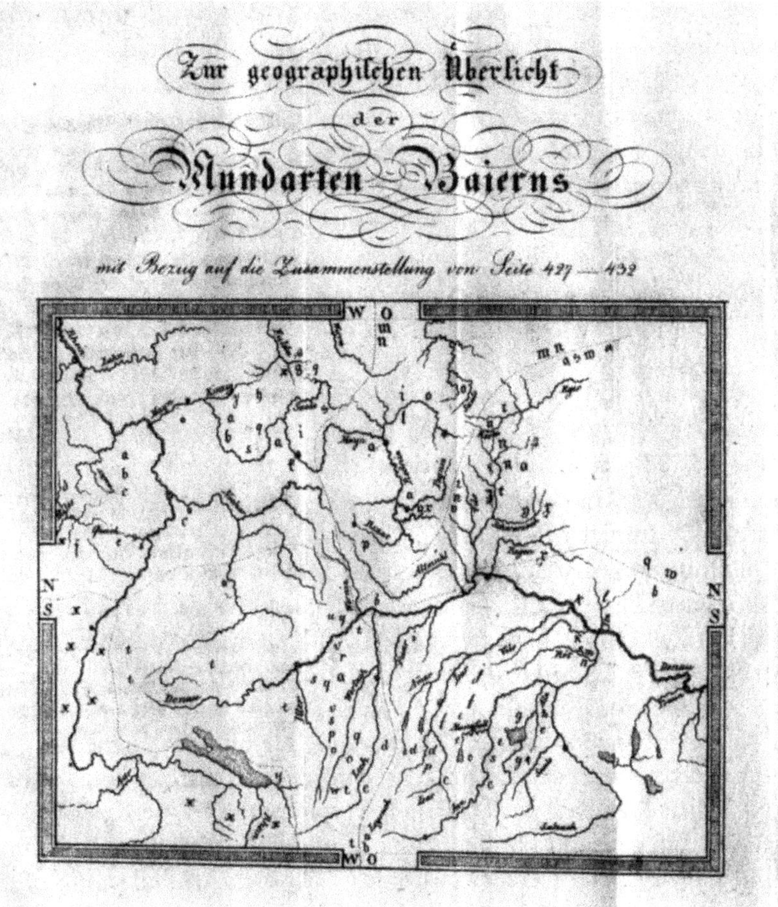

J. A. Schmeller's mapping of the Bavarian dialects in *Die Mundarten Bayerns* (1821).

language of German antiquity."[74] "Only the common man," he observed, "especially in the country, and preferably in remote forested or mountainous regions has preserved pure and vividly most of the above mentioned analogies in pronunciation."[75] In emulation of Grimm's work, Schmeller's grammar structured the presentation of declension and conjugation around phonological and sound changes. By strictly separating written letters from their spoken values, something Grimm failed to do, Schmeller proved that dialects developed in regular patterns from older versions of a language, yet evolved independently of its written forms. He showed, for example, that some Bavarian verbs retained the use of vowel modification (the *Ablaut*) when conjugated, although the standard written language had long since resorted to appending auxiliary particles. The past participle of the verb "*deuten*" (to explain or signify), he noted, sometimes appeared in dialect as "*geditten*" instead of "*gedeutet*." This was evidence that "here, too, . . . the dialects have preserved something originary."[76]

Linguistic historians debate the extent to which Schmeller's corpus departed from the rationalist tradition of the eighteenth century; the grammar displays certain synchronic tendencies characteristic of general grammar.[77] This resulted from the author's trying to create a standardized written form of the Bavarian dialects and to gain recognition of their equality with Latin and other European languages.[78] Nevertheless, Schmeller demonstrated that German dialects could be used to illuminate earlier linguistic periods and to reconstruct prehistory. Philologists, he believed, could deduce "reliable traces in the living present" of "what may have happened in the Germanic world and about which history has little to disclose."[79] The idiomatic pronunciation of place names, for example, tended to resemble their older forms more closely than current written designations. He also maintained that dialect speakers had a special ability to comprehend the meanings of older roots that he referred to as "living folk-etymology." Whereas the philologist had to research the derivation of unusual words, persons familiar with the vernacular were "accustomed to knowing the meaning of certain parts of words and word formations that a language upholds . . . from century to century."[80]

Similar observations had been made about the antiquity of Swiss German by Bodmer in the eighteenth century, and the grammarian J. C. Adelung claimed the language of peasants still resembled Old High German.[81] Similarly to J. A. Schmeller, the Grimm brothers associated regional German identities with more intimate ties to the Germanic past. Six hundred years ago, Jacob Grimm wrote, "every common peasant knew the perfection and elegance of the German language, that is, he practiced them daily."[82] Even today, Grimm believed, the meanings of root words were "preserved more truly by the folk than in the written language."[83] Archaic languages were, in Grimm's view, generally superior to living tongues because they displayed a greater variety of inflections, a richness of vowels and simple roots, and a synthetic structure since lost to the present. Grimm nevertheless detected in "the language of the common man a certain rawness and unruliness."[84] Dialects had undergone a more drastic degeneration without the mediating effect of poets and writers who added to the spiritual and intellectual power of High German.

Dialects likewise had value for Grimm because they preserved the regional specificity of the *Heimat* or homeland. The *German Grammar,* for example, assumed an original identity of dialects and Germanic tribes. Fears that Prussia might engulf Saxony as part of the settlement agreed to at the Congress of Vienna (1815) had awakened in Jacob Grimm the particular concern that the smaller Middle German states could be sacrificed to their larger neighbors. In Grimm's view the destruction of their individuality would not aid the unification process, but would rather detract from the vitality of the nation. As Jacob Grimm confided to Savigny in 1814: "We feel ourselves to be Hessians and want to stay so, and are in this way better Germans."[85] He believed that history and the *Volksgeist* were most alive in Middle Germany: the ancient division of the German nation into tribes was still visible here, and geographically this region had been the center of the Old Reich.[86]

Nevertheless, the fidelity with which dialects preserved the archaic past and regional diversity was offset by their affiliation with the lower social classes. Grimm's ambivalence toward dialects thus suggests the limits of his professed populism. The *German Grammar* suggested that as one tribe had gained dominance over another, it had imposed its language on the subjugated people. Only "the noble part" of the population adopted the new dialect of a conquering tribe, while the "native vernacular flees among the masses," "sinks and becomes common."[87] With time there emerged a few select, standard written languages now shared by the educated descendents of the victorious Germanic tribes: New High German, Dutch, English, Swedish, and Danish. The remaining tongues had been condemned to the underclasses. For Grimm, dialects were thus comparable to "a comfortable house dress in which one does not go out."[88]

Grimm's rejection of the German dialects suggests that the social groups associated with vernacular idioms should literally not to come into play as independent political actors in the nation. Grimm conceded that the folk maintained closer ties to the Germanic past than the educated classes. In his mind peasants and artisans possessed originality, authenticity, and certain creative powers that were essential to the formation of a national consciousness and public opinion. The creators of fairy tales and sagas, Grimm suspected, had an inborn love for the *Heimat,* a healthy sense for family and the patriarchal order, respect for religion, as well as a natural feel for what is right and just.[89] But he did not believe that all people should share in the governing process. For Grimm the state was principally a paternalistic apparatus of administration and government that, while it served the interests of the nation, was independent of it. The historical sensibilities of the folk did not justify bestowing political sovereignty on the people.

The community of German speakers that Johann Andreas Schmeller envisioned was united by a more inclusive discursive order of exchange. As a scholar and teacher, Schmeller considered it his duty to involve underrepresented populations in the elite social and political life of the nation. He dedicated the grammar to "everyone who wishes to have contact with the common man"; it was intended to help school teachers, priests, judges, and civil servants "lift the masses higher and understand them."[90] Their right to participate was not dictated by a special connection to the cultural starting point of the German nation, but by the goal of promoting mutual understanding and communication. "I have not entirely lived for nothing," Schmeller reflected, "even if out of the law giver, world reformer, poet, etc. of my youthful dreams, only a culler of words and a pedant has emerged. But it is noteworthy to have made something out of nothing or at least out of the lowest of the low, and to have brought the language of the Bavarian farmer into the chambers of the very learned on the North and Baltic Seas, yes even into the elegant chambers of important men." He credited himself with having earned "certain honors" for the only possession in which the rural inhabitants of Bavaria could take pride: their native language. Soon, he hoped, one would consider it "atrocious . . . to disinherit them of all the other goods of life."[91]

At a time when the diversity of German speakers and the sovereign powers of the states severely compromised the nationalist movement, Schmeller's linguistic history from below may have offered a more useful model for communal integration than the prospect of shared historical descent. Basing national unity on the written bond of standardized High German held little attraction for the manifold speakers of German dialects. Schmeller's grammar forged ties between the actual mother tongue of Bavarians and the High German spoken by the educated elite. The conditions he outlined for the formation of linguistic community, mutual comprehension, and participation in a democratic discursive order of exchange were, however, Enlightenment concepts that were increasingly sidelined by the importance Grimm and other German philologists attributed to shared historical descent from a Germanic *Urvolk*.

German Families and the Mother Tongue

The close supervision of German universities during the Restoration posed a difficult environment for the establishment of German philology as an academic field. By 1830 there were only six university professorships in German language and literature.[92] The suppression of political dissent enabled by the Karlsbad Decrees (1819) targeted nationalist gymnastic associations such as those founded by the Germanist Hans Ferdinand Maßmann in Jena and Breslau. Having stood trial for initiating the burning of un-German books at the Wartburg festival, Maßmann was arrested again in 1819 and 1823, and his papers were confiscated by the Prussian Ministry of the Interior. Like other potentially subversive instructors, he was banned from further teaching and entered into exile. One fourth of all Germanists active in the first half of the nineteenth century suffered similar political or legal persecution.[93] The secondary schools likewise failed to offer a venue for cultivating nationalism.[94] German instruction at the gymnasium level had few ties to the more politicized, nationalistic field of university Germanics. The university course of study was not designed to prepare future teachers, and recipients of advanced degrees in German did not seek employment in secondary schools.

Under these circumstances, language scholars often imagined the nation taking form in upper-middle-class homes, publicizing their historical reconstructions in literary collections and reference works designed for private use. The bourgeois household was an important social space for the construction of German nationhood given limitations on middle-class participation in economic and political life.[95] Members of the bourgeoisie distinguished themselves by upholding certain values and cultural models of behavior; the social signs and symbolic language cultivated in discussions of literature or art provided cohesion at a time when the middle class was regionally and professionally still quite diverse.[96] The Grimms' *Fairy Tales* is only the best known of the texts that presented families with images of "authentic" German traditions and folklife, while reinforcing bourgeois notions of domesticity and gendered social roles. Anniversary celebrations of historical events or the lives of "great" poets also strengthened the national consciousness of the elite by creating shared memories of a collective past.[97] During this period, moreover, the nation often appeared as a "folk family," in which men and women assumed roles parallel to those they filled in the patriarchic home.[98] As the carriers of early German nationalism, members of the educated bourgeoisie imposed their own conceptions of gender and sexual difference on the nation.[99]

Gendered conceptions of the nation and family overlapped with the gendering of language in German philology. For one, the historical trajectory carved by the German language followed gendered patterns. The earliest stages of language Jacob Grimm associated with a primal maternal power that was expressed in vowel sounds and verbs; he saw this reflected in the prevalence of three "*Ur*-vowels" (a, i, u) in ancient Indian words.[100] Malleable and soft, vowels represented an illusive creative energy. The masculine and acculturating forces of consonants and grammar were needed to give it form in words.[101] Women's influence on the development of language was likewise restricted to the beginning of time. Women had created separate feminine and masculine declensions by "cultivating their own customs and stating positions that were independent of men."[102] This gendering of language represented for Grimm the extension of a natural order onto cultural forms. The division of nouns into masculine, feminine, and neuter originated in a "fantastical extension of natural relations onto all other objects."[103] Masculine nouns were "the more lively, powerful, and primordial"; feminine words were "later, more nimble, busy, malleable, and reproductive."[104] Even personal names for men and women, Grimm suspected, derived respectively from terms applied to animals and plants.[105]

A shifting balance in the internal gender composition of language signaled the historical transformation of language from a primordial force of nature to a cerebral tool of mankind. According to Grimm, Old German had once been "corporal, sensuous, full of innocence," but with time the language had "gradually sought to suspend her nature." "The corporal decline" of language was not an absolute loss, though.[106] Rather, Grimm discerned a parallel "spiritual ascent" of language that followed the progressive "education of mankind." The language of the present, he surmised, "is working toward being more spiritual and abstract; it sees pretense and ambiguity in words, which it tries to avoid at all costs . . . ; its expressions are becoming clearer, more conscious and more precise."[107] Language, in other words, was maturing "with honor to manhood."[108] If in an earlier period German was closer to nature and the sensual, it was now ripe for the abstract and conceptual thought of men. He praised, in particular, Luther's translation of the Bible for giving High German "male bearing and force."[109]

The language spoken by women did not participate in this historical trajectory. Women remained incapable of self-consciously wielding the power of words. Like the folk, women supposedly retained the instinctive relationship to language that characterized the historical period of *Naturpoesie*. In their daily speech, women made unconscious use of grammatical principles and displayed knowledge of archaic roots that had otherwise been lost. They embodied their "own, living grammar" and for that reason had no use for teachers or the scientific study of language.[110] Domestic areas were thus ideal sites of cultural transmission. The entire realm of the feminine—women, children, the home, and also the folk—was believed to have maintained more authentic connections to an original, unadulterated form of Germanic culture, one not directly accessible to educated men.

The gendering of language and linguistic ability literally assigned women the task of giving their children "speech with the mother's milk." It was the responsibility of mothers to transmit the "instinctive secret" that Grimm believed "intuned our vocal organs for the characteristic sounds of the fatherland, its declensions, idioms, severities, or softness." In teaching young children to talk, women were the first to evoke in German speakers "that indestructible feeling of longing" that resonated among members of the nation when they encountered artifacts of the German past.[111] As such, women's participation in the nation was limited to the family, providing raw cultural material that men then mastered. Katerina Viehmann (1755–1815), the model storyteller from whom the Grimm brothers collected the majority of their fairy tales, represented this ideal of feminine cultural transmission. She was, however, not a peasant transmitter of oral folk tradition, but a literate member of a large Huguenot community settled near Kassel.[112]

The preface to the *German Dictionary* (1854) offered a snapshot of the ideal gendered use of language within domestic life, as Grimm imagined it. Despite its scholarly apparatus, Grimm expected this "sacred monument to the German people" to become a "household necessity" that educated families read aloud "with devotion" like the

Bible. "[W]hy should the father not select a few words," he wondered, "and, going through them with his boys in the evening, test their knowledge of the language while he refreshes his own?" "[T]he mother," Grimm added, "would gladly listen in." He elaborated: "with their healthy mother's wit and their memory for good maxims, women often carry with them a true desire to exercise their unspoiled feeling for language." Women, he believed, would most often return to the pages of the book in the course of the day as they lyrically rhymed a known word with one less familiar and endeavored to fill gaps in their knowledge. In this way, the dictionary would instill in literate German men and women a more vital understanding of the "worth and . . . superiority" of their mother tongue. The literary references cited in each definition would likewise awaken readers' "love for native literature" and introduce them to a common body of great German works.[113]

Even during the politically restrictive Restoration, myths of cultural origin and descent reached an educated audience and prepared the middle class to conceive of a national community that extended beyond state borders and warranted a formal constitution.[114] The home, not the public school, was initially the space where the ideology of a national mother tongue spread. German language instruction was slow to establish itself at the gymnasium level during the *Vormärz*. No mandatory testing of German teachers existed until 1831, when the Kingdom of Hannover required candidates for secondary school posts to have historical knowledge of German.[115] German lessons were most often entrusted to masters of Greek and Latin, and former students recalled their instruction as unmethodological and unorganized.[116] Not until the 1840s did the study of German include composition and literary analysis, skills generally relayed by classicists.[117] Members of the bourgeoisie resisted training in the mother tongue because they associated it with the polytechnic, practical municipal schools of the artisan and working classes.[118] This aversion hindered the development of university Germanics, while confining the nationalist sentiments of the field to elite circles.

Linguistic Nations in the North and South

The linguistic genealogies created by nineteenth-century philologists bear traces of the same regional fault lines that divided the German nationalist movement. Until delegates to the Frankfurt national assembly reluctantly voted for a small-German (*kleindeutsch*) solution to unification in 1848, excluding Austria and eventually offering an imperial crown to Prussian king Friedrich Wilhelm IV, nationalists often assumed the linguistic community encompassed German speakers living throughout and even beyond the German Confederation.[119] The breadth of this vision, however, should not obscure the fact that most nationalists followed the Grimm brothers in placing the geographic heart of the nation in the Protestant north and tracing its cultural starting point to the Goths and the Nordic lands. This emphasis reflects the regional origins of the vast majority of Germanists, as well as the actual concentration of antiquities in the north. The earliest textual artifact of the German language was a fourth-century Gothic translation of the Bible; runic inscriptions, archaeological remains, and early medieval manuscripts were more abundant in Scandinavia than in more southern parts of the continent. Confessional boundaries and alternate political orientations toward Prussia and Austria reinforced the north-south divide. Political discourse was replete with confessional language in the first half of the nineteenth century, and Protestant nationalists feared Catholic subservience to Rome.[120]

For students of language, the most fundamental breach in the nationalist movement was accentuated by the historical separation of the Germanic languages into High and Low German groups and by the southern dialects' affinities with Austrian vernaculars. Linguistically, New High German evolved from dialects spoken in the south; the Low German languages common to the north became the basis for modern Dutch. Martin Luther's importance for the standardization of written High German and the dominance of conventional northern pronunciations in its spoken form, however, resulted in most nationalists crediting the north with provenance over the national tongue. The idea that High German was spoken with greatest perfection in the region surrounding the coastal city of Hamburg does not reflect its historical roots. Rather there was a greater disparity there between local vernaculars and the standard written language. The acquisition of High German in the north depended most heavily on its textual representation, so distinctions in the sounds of spoken consonants were rendered more true to linguistic form.[121] Austria's reactionary politics and Metternich's success in halting the spread of nationalist organizations into Habsburg territory likewise limited the opportunity for southern Germans to reclaim the mother tongue as a historical outgrowth of the south.

Despite a tradition of conservative, Christian Germanism that looked to Austria to restore a quasi-feudal political order, there was, nonetheless, a progressive southern German vision of the linguistic nation that existed alongside the dominant northern perspective. Johann Andreas Schmeller imagined a German cultural community that was rooted in the southern states and extended into Austria. For him, this region was united by its common ancestry. The tribe from which modern Bavarians supposedly descended had once occupied a swath of territory that spanned the Danube River from its source as far east as Hungary.[122] As he wrote to Franz von Heheneider in November, 1817: "Tyroleans, Bavarians, and Austrians are of the same flesh and blood, as much as politics might have picked and teased at this. Language attests to it, she makes a nation out of them. . . . Thus I dream sometimes of the dark history of our forefathers and see them all descending from the mountains."[123] Schmeller's convictions arose less from a confessional identification with fellow Catholics than from the linguistic knowledge that "two branches grew out laterally from the trunk of the Germanic language family—one toward the north and the Scandinavian lands . . . , the other toward the south and the valleys of the Alps."[124] He had an ambivalent relationship to Catholicism, recognizing its significance for the cultural life of Bavaria, but skeptical of its doctrines and political uses. As a librarian in Munich, a post he received in 1829, Schmeller catalogued vast numbers of medieval manuscripts whose survival he attributed to the secularization of 150 Bavarian and Swabian cloisters in 1803.[125]

Schmeller's *Bavarian Dictionary*, published in installments from 1827 to 1837, drew on linguistic evidence to reconstruct the shared cultural history of southern Germans just as Jacob Grimm was completing histories of Germanic law and myth. Schmeller looked deep into the Alps for the heart of the southern German community. In 1833 he traveled to the mountains near Venice to research an isolated people living in northern Italy who spoke a Tyrolean-Bavarian dialect, later publishing a dictionary (1855) and several academy lectures on his findings.[126] But like the grammar, the dictionary accepted the political boundaries of Bavaria as the limits of its linguistic purview and specifically aimed to further the "mutual understanding and respect" of those persons subject to the Bavarian king and constitution regardless of their actual linguistic affiliations.[127] Language left him "little doubt as to their tribal unity" with Austria, but Metternich's reactionary politics opened "much patriotic dissent as to where the actual core of the tribe can be found.[128] Ludwig I, crown prince and later king of Bavaria, earned Schmeller's political loyalties, having made him Professor of Old German Literature and Language in 1828. The appointment was temporarily suspended until 1830 while it went to the senior, but politically suspect, Hans Ferdinand Maßmann. Bavaria's support for the Greek War of Independence and Ludwig's own interest in the Germanic past, already manifest in plans to build Walhalla, rendered the state relatively receptive to the gymnastic movement.[129]

Dedicated to the young Ludwig, the dictionary documented cultural continuity in Bavarian folklife from archaic times to the present. It was, by Schmeller's account, an "essay on the language, manners, and customs of His people" as they were revealed in spoken language and provincial literature[130] To this effect it united a collection of "expressions appearing in living dialects" with those "found in older writings and documents."[131] Each definition included historical documentation of the word's use and full morphological information on its construction.[132] The entries were not sorted alphabetically by the first letter, but according to an "etymological-alphabetical arrangement" that followed the series of consonants that made up the stem syllable of the word.[133] Thus, to find the word "*Garten*" (garden), the reader followed the alphabetical sequence "g-r-t," giving only secondary attention to the intermediary vowels. It could be found between "*Gersten*" and "*Gerten*."

The construction of the dictionary rendered it of primary use for professional philologists with an interest in the historical evolution of German linguistic forms. But Schmeller also hoped his work would serve as "a portrait gallery of the versatile life of the folk as it is expressed in language."[134] He planned (but ultimately neglected) to append a thematic index of terms related, for example, to religious and domestic customs, agriculture, or trade that would assist readers who "think more of the things [*Sachen*] than of the words."[135] As is commensurate with his sociological understanding of "the folk," however, the dictionary entries do not romanticize or try to define what is authentically German in Bavarian popular culture. Rather, it drew attention to the poor living conditions of less educated speakers of vernacular. Schmeller sought to correct, for example, idealized contemporary images of rural life by offering critical commentary on the living conditions of small farmers, on their treatment by landowners, and on their daily work.[136]

Jacob Grimm praised the *Bavarian Dictionary* for highlighting the "living connection" language maintained to custom and tradition. The two had since met twice in person, and Grimm's own *German Dictionary* (1854) aspired to mesh language and cultural history in a similar fashion. In a dismissive move that reflects Grimm's northern German bias, however, he criticized the focus on the Bavarian vernacular. The true national tongue, New High German, was for him a "Protestant dialect . . . whose freedom-loving nature has long since overpowered poets and writers of the Catholic faith."[137] Lutheranism was often championed in defense of princely authority; in the early modern period its view of the state as a moral community was cited in support bureaucratic absolutism. For the Romantics, however, Luther symbolized a type of a patriotism based on the free pursuit of ideas and the struggle against the spiritual tyranny of Catholicism.[138] Grimm's crediting of Protestants with the creation of a national tongue conformed to his denominational upbringing while slighting the authority of Austria and its repressive legislation.

The Reformation symbolized for Grimm a revolutionary moment when Germans escaped the tyranny of Roman culture and recovered lost aspects of their own prehistory. Grimm blamed Roman Christianity for having destroyed early Germanic folk beliefs and endeavored, in the *German Mythology* (1835), to reach back to what he thought were the "seeds" of a purer faith. "Christianity was not of the people," he recalled, "it came from abroad and sought to displace time-honored, native gods" who were "part and parcel of the people's traditions, customs, and constitution."[139] In their "slavish subjection to distant Rome," missionaries had inflicted "multiple injuries on the national consciousness."[140] Luther supposedly reversed much of this damage. "Lifting the burden of the Roman ban," Grimm observed, the Reformation "rendered our faith at once freer, more inward, and more indigenous. God is near us everywhere and He blesses each fatherland from which fixing our gaze beyond the Alps would alienate us."[141] It was inevitable, he argued, that "the Reformation happened directly in Germany": "just like language and mythology, the inclination of a people's faith is something that cannot be erased."[142]

The migration paths of the Germanic tribes also seemed to support the northern emphasis of Grimm's conception of the linguistic community. The ancient historian Jordanes and later Scandinavian scholars believed the first *Germanen* had entered Europe from the east and north so that the earliest and richest evidence of German culture was to be found in Scandinavia and Saxony. Gothic and Old Icelandic were as important for Germanists as Greek and Latin were for students of classical antiquity because, in Grimm's words, the earliest myths, sagas, and legal texts "flow[ed] freely in Scandinavia but sparingly in Germany."[143] The wave of Christianization and Romanization that had destroyed many Germanic traditions had broken from the south, leaving barbarian culture intact later and in more complete form among inhabitants of Iceland and the far north. Jacob Grimm drew extensively on Nordic and Anglo-Saxon sources in his histories of ancient Germanic mythology and law, convinced that the lands that withstood Christianity and Roman rule the longest retained "many precious advantages in the common life of the folk."[144] His faith in the unity of continental German and Norse mythology resided foremost in language and the success with which contemporary German languages had been tied in descent to a common *Ursprache.*[145]

As a student of Danish runes, Wilhelm Grimm was more familiar with Nordic prehistory than his brother.[146] He, too, insisted in 1820 that "the Germanic element of our *Bildung* . . . was preserved and developed more purely and with less disruption in the isolated north. . . . Nordic antiquity relates to Germanic antiquity like the languages of people living in isolated valleys and mountains to the languages of those living in cities." Although no runes had of date been uncovered in Germany, Wilhelm Grimm rightly surmised the existence of German runes based on extent literary evidence. The Germans, he argued, had like the Norsemen "brought the first foundations of a letter alphabet with them from the Asian homeland."[147] Germanic tribes such as the Saxons living in the north near the Danish border had, in his view, used this ancient alphabet, and one need only study their northern neighbors to reconstruct an early chapter of German national history.[148]

Until the emergence of the so-called *Deutschkatholiken* in 1844, Catholics played only a minor role in the German nationalist movement. The influence the church maintained over gymnasial and university education outside of Prussia, where an independent ministry of culture had been instituted in 1817, kept the study of German language and literature centered at the Protestant universities in Berlin, Göttingen, Halle, Jena, Breslau, and Leipzig. Even here the local focus of liberal and nationalist politics hampered the coordination of a "large German" nation that included the south. Two years following the publication of the *German Mythology,* Jacob and Wilhelm themselves were dismissed from their professorships in Göttingen for having protested King Ernst August's revocation of Hannover's 1833 constitution. Along with five of their colleagues, they were left without employment and forced to leave the state. Not until Friedrich Wilhelm IV assumed the throne in 1840 did the Grimms join the Royal Prussian Academy of Sciences as full members working on the *German Dictionary* project, though still lacking civil service appointments at the university.

Prussia and Pan-Germanism in the *Vormärz*

Upon their arrival in Berlin, the Grimm brothers were uncertain whether Prussia would be able to overcome its particularist ambitions as a territorial state and give form to the nation. The pair had previously resisted several calls to the capital, suspicious of Prussia's claims to represent German national identity. As Toews argues, however, Jacob Grimm increasingly felt at home in the court of Friedrich Wilhelm IV, finding a niche within the officially sanctioned ideology of post-Romantic historicism that rose to prominence in the 1840s.[149] Grimm demonstrated to the Prussian elite that his research into the Germanic past could contribute to the creation of a new national public culture. Under a regime that itself aspired to national cultural leadership, his resurrection of a national cultural identity lost its oppositional character.[150] This commitment to Prussia should not obscure, though, the degree to which Grimm's vision of the nation resisted the confines of state structures. Defining the linguistic community by shared historical descent verged on Pan-Germanism. And especially following the failed revolutions of 1848–49, Grimm tended to privilege bonds of ethnicity over a conscious commitment of loyalty to the state.

Grimm's call to Berlin coincided with a substantial growth in German nationalist institutions. A threatened French occupation of the Rhine in 1840 renewed patriotic sentiment in the form of Heinrich Hoffmann von Fallersleben's "Deutschlandslied" and Max Schneckenburger's "Wacht am Rhein." A series of national festivals and public memorials erected to great Germans such as Gutenberg and Schiller likewise popularized a movement once dominated by intellectuals. In 1842 alone Walhalla, Ludwig I's temple to Germanic heroes, opened outside Munich, construction began to complete the medieval Cologne Cathedral in neo-Gothic style, and the monument to commemorate Hermann's victory over the Roman legions was well under way. Not only had the idea of the "nation" expanded beyond a narrow reading public in the 1840s, but nationalists had developed a sustainable network of communication that enabled coordinated political action among the middle class.

German language scholars participated in these developments at annual academic conferences where Germanists discussed nationalist issues while avoiding the ban on suspect gatherings imposed by the German Confederation in 1832.[151] At the inaugural meeting in Frankfurt in 1846 Jacob Grimm served as the organization's first president. His opening address posed the provocative question "What is a nation [*Volk*]?" Grimm's response cited the spread of language as the only limitation on the territorial growth of a people. "A nation," Grimm replied, "is the embodiment of people who speak the same language. that is for us Germans the most innocent but also the proudest definition because it . . . turns our gaze to the . . . near future when all barriers fall and the natural law will be acknowledged that neither rivers nor mountains divide nations but that language alone can set boundaries around a people that has pushed past mountains and streams."[152] These words were a specific commentary on the two main political issues facing the conference: the current crisis of succession in Holstein and the continued emigration of large numbers of German speakers to the United States. The presence of a German-speaking majority in that northern province and in the neighboring Danish territory of Schleswig suggested to Grimm that both should be part of the confederation. Grimm also expected German emigrants overseas to retain ties to the fatherland and "reinforce" their native language so that it would "live forever forth" in the New World.[153]

Besides work on the *German Dictionary,* the major piece of linguistic scholarship that Grimm undertook in Berlin was a two-volume *History of the German Language* completed in 1848 as the March revolutions struck the capital city. The work wove a broader cultural narrative around the linguistic events sketched in the *German Grammar.* Dedicated to a fellow member of the Göttingen Seven from Frankfurt in June 1848, it was, in Grimm's words, "political through and through," arising out of the "duties and dangers of the fatherland."[154] The *History* publicized what he termed "the inner bonds of a people" in expectation of overcoming the fatherland's "unjust partition by princes."[155] In what was criticized as an overly "speculative manner,"[156] Grimm argued for the original affinity of the languages once spoken by the ten main European tribes as they migrated westward. His main goal was to establish, using etymology and lexical considerations, the "identity of the Goths and Getae,"[157] a tribe now believed to be related to the Celts that inhabited Thrace, a province between the Balkans and the Carpathian mountains. Grimm also argued for the probability of more extensive contacts between the Goths and the Daci, supposed ancestors of the Danes. These links between north and south were, for Grimm, evidence of original affinity among present-day speakers of Germanic tongues. Comparativists criticized his almost complete lack of attention to Sanskrit and other related languages, and his main thesis of Gothic-Getic identity ultimately failed despite the popularity of the book.[158]

Nevertheless, Grimm successfully demonstrated how the recovery of language could aid in reconstructing material and cultural history. The two volumes aspired to "reach from the words to the things,"[159] inaugurating the so-called "*Wörter-und-Sachen*" approach to prehistory and anthropology.[160] "There is more vital evidence for nations than bones, weapons, and graves," Grimm explained, "and that is their languages . . . when all other sources run dry or the existing remains leave us uncertain and in doubt, nothing can be more conclusive for ancient history than careful research on the kinship or deviations of every language and vernacular unto their finest veins or fibers."[161] Words, Grimm demonstrated, revealed new affinities in the "faith, law, and customs" of the prehistoric Germanic tribes as they abandoned a nomadic lifestyle for sedentary agriculture.[162] The *History* contained material intended for a history of German custom and mores, and for linguists its most valuable contribution was examining the vocabulary of material culture as related, for example, to metals, livestock, or grain, in early Germanic languages.[163]

A new conception of language and its role in the formation of communities distinguishes this account of the Germanic tongues from the *German Grammar.* The greater confidence Grimm amassed as an insider to the Prussian project of translating the historical recovery of a national past into official public memory lessened the autonomy Grimm attributed to the evolution of language as an organism. As Toews indicates, Grimm's discussion of the two Germanic sound shifts now stressed that the historical forms of language were motivated by more than a formative point of origin. The inner laws governing the linguistic organism alone could not explain the sound shifts. Rather, language also had to be approached as a sign system that responded to an external reality; grammatical structures now demonstrated that cultural existence was also historical in a contingent sense.[164] Grimm believed that the rapid advance of the Germanic tribes in their westward migration destabilized inherited linguistic forms and forced those in the lead to adapt their language to a new reality. Significantly, the sound shifts had only occurred among certain groups of German speakers possessing the greatest pride and ambition.[165]

Despite this recognition, the political institutions of Prussia did not seem adequate to the task of reconstituting a national linguistic community. The historical model of Germanic unity that the Goths provided was expansive and Pan-Germanic. Gothic, in Grimm's analysis, most closely resembled proto-Germanic of all extant languages, and he confirmed that its speakers formed the "earliest ranks of the German nation."[166] The *History,* moreover, emphasized the expanse of their dominion in early medieval Europe. The various Gothic tribes, he noted, extended their rule over the Pyrenees into Spain, over the Alps into Italy, south and east through Thrace, Macedonia, and Greece, and up to the border with Byzantium. "If the strength of the Goths had remained intact" he lamented, "and if their rule in the east had been secured like that of the Franks in the West, then the fate of Germany and the German language would have taken another direction."[167] As it was, the second Germanic sound shift divided Gothic speakers into High Germans, Low Germans, and Scandinavians. But readers should not forget that "all Germanic languages, however far their branches and boughs may have grown apart, clearly stem from the same trunk . . . ; the further back one reaches, the more similar appear the Goths, High Germans, Low Germans, and Scandinavians. All are of the same origin."[168]

Gothic unity in the early medieval period resembled a Pan-Germanic empire that looked beyond specific political organizations to encompass related speakers throughout Europe. Grimm presented a new theory of dialect change in the *History* that foresaw a reversal of the Germanic dialects' tendency to drift apart. High and Low German, Anglo-Saxon, Frisian, and Nordic all evolved, Grimm suggested, during a period of political crisis when the Lombards, the Franks, and the Arabs threatened the Goths. Today, however, a "vividly awakened desire for a closer union" could convince the five dominant Germanic tribes to reverse the process of fragmentation and merge their respective "dialects" into a new mother tongue. "I hold a conversion of the Dutch to High German, of the Danes to Swedish not only for likely in the next centuries," Grimm observed, "but also for beneficial for all Germanic peoples."[169] "Before many generations have passed, only three peoples will share in the dominion of Europe: Romans, Germans, Slavs."[170] In his correspondence with Danish and Norwegian scholars, Grimm spoke of a "great alliance" between the German states and Scandinavia that "recall[ed] the primordial tribal union" with a certain degree of political expectation.[171] Other Germanists, such as Heinrich Hoffmann von Fallersleben, sympathized with the fate of Flemish speakers in the newly founded kingdom of Belgium. Fallersleben's twelve-volume study of Belgian literature (1830) responded to the pain of observing "this land being torn away from the greater German tribe (*Volksstamm*)" as French became the official state language.[172]

As the *History of the German Language* went to press, Jacob Grimm served as a representative to the Frankfurt parliament charged with drafting a national constitution for Germany. The delegates deliberated for close to a year on the most suitable form for German unification, finally admitting that the paltry state of the nationalist movement in Austria prevented the inclusion of Habsburg territory.[173] Their debates dismissed the apparent historical necessities of language and ethnicity in favor of treating citizenship rights independently of cultural background.[174] Like the majority of delegates, Grimm favored a small Germany led by a hereditary Prussian emperor for practical reasons, expecting that the other Germanic peoples would gradually join the union. Johann Andreas Schmeller likewise resigned himself to excluding Austria at this time, awaiting the spread of liberal reform to the monarchy and wary of its imperial structure.[175] He, too, had been voted into the professor-parliament in the Paulskirche but had been unable to attend due to injuries incurred crossing the Jaufen mountain pass.[176]

In September 1848 Grimm himself quit the assembly in protest of the generous peace treaty Prussia had signed with Denmark. He feared that Prussia had once again demonstrated that it valued its own interests as a state above its national responsibility to unite German-speakers everywhere.[177] Friedrich Wilhelm IV's rejection of the imperial crown and the violent suppression of the revolution by Prussian troops in the spring of 1849 did little to dispel this view. A practical concession to small-German plans for unification was no longer necessary; political avenues of nation building were closed for a second time since the Napoleonic invasions.

In his speech "On the Origin of Language" to the Prussian Academy in 1851, Grimm again confirmed that language, not princes or armies, was the driving force behind the consolidation of the German nation. Language is "our history, our heritage," he argued. "The power of language" "builds nations and holds them together, without such a bond they would burst apart; the wealth of a people's thought is principally that which secures its dominion in the world."[178] The essay attributed an explicitly ethnic dimension to the German cultural community, associating the successful transmission of national tongues with the inheritance of a particular physical body. An abandoned newborn of French or Russian parentage who was "taken in and reared in the middle of Germany" would naturally speak German like the other children around him.[179] But "some of our German sounds," Grimm suggested, would always "seem hard" to him. Language, Grimm explained, had an "underlying basis which is necessarily conditioned by the created body." The "voice instruments" that produced sound were, in his mind, "inherited" and particular to national groups.[180] "Already present in the throats of children," he concluded, was "the inherent tendency towards the expression of appropriate sound modifications." Slavs, for example, were conditioned to use "strong sibilant combinations" or "harsh gutturals." The study of anatomy, he predicted, would soon enable scholars to distinguish even the "linguistic instruments" of a northern German and an Alpine shepherd.[181]

For Grimm in 1851 lines of ethnic descent qualified a child's ability to master German as a native tongue. Joining the German linguistic community through a process of voluntary self-identification would necessarily leave a mark of difference. There were clear limits to the degree language as a historical form could be mobilized by free linguistic agents in a self-determining community. For Grimm, the cultural integrity of the nation ultimately depended on the historically necessary bonds imposed by shared descent from a common cultural starting point. As Toews concludes, Jacob Grimm never did regard politics as a forum where individuals could freely adapt and recreate historical identities.[182] Even as German unification under Prussian leadership became increasingly probable in the 1860s, the perceived evolution of the German language maintained a substantial degree of independence from the control and direction of speakers. Deeply rooted ethnic continuities likewise appeared to withstand the contingencies of historical existence.

German Philology and Linguistics: Wilhelm Scherer

After midcentury, research on the German language increasingly fell to the purview of scholars trained in comparative linguistics. Jacob Grimm had left unresolved the implications comparative grammar had for analyzing Germanic tongues. Wilhelm Scherer (1841–86), the star of post-Grimm Germanics, pursued both German and comparative Indo-European philology in Vienna before writing his own *On the History of the German Language* in 1868. Several of Franz Bopp's students developed concentrations in Germanic tongues, including Albert Hoefer (1812–83), professor of Comparative Linguistics and Old German Philology in Greifswald. Ferdinand Justi, F. L. K. Weigand, and Rudolf von Raumer likewise combined the fields; Marburg professor Franz Dietrich specialized in Germanic and Semitic languages. Knowledge of Sanskrit enabled this generation to study the historical evolution of Germanic vowels, which Grimm found impossible given their considerable deviation from original Indo-European forms. The cohort emerging in the 1850s likewise endeavored to supplement Grimm's understanding of sound change with attention to the distinction between written and oral forms.[183]

The integration of German language study into the field of linguistics initially worked to the benefit of Germanists. Comparative linguists gave impetus to the secondary school reforms that in the 1860s substantially increased the number of university chairs in German philology. In 1857, for example, Albert Hoefer, member of the Greifswald committee examining candidates for German language posts at the gymnasium level, sent an invective to the Prussian minister of culture titled "German Philology and Linguistics and Their Demands on the Present." In his view, teachers of German could not possibly fulfill their duties without training in "Sanskrit and comparative linguistics, in Gothic, Old and Middle High German."[184] Academic knowledge of the mother tongue required both comparative and historical literacy by the 1850s. A Prussian regulation passed in 1866 set the first high standards for secondary school German teachers. In addition to familiarity with the style and history of German literature and the ability to make aesthetic judgments, the teaching candidate either needed to demonstrate "enough knowledge of the historical development of language that he can read and interpret texts in Old and Middle High German" or have training in philosophy.[185]

The 1860s mark the consolidation of German philology as a full-fledged university discipline. The number of chairs grew from thirteen to twenty.[186] Rudolf von Raumer arranged for Germanists to be accepted in 1861 as a special section of the annual meetings of classical philologists, school masters, and Orientalists; the more rigorous training of secondary school teachers had improved the reputation of Germanics in the eyes of classicists.[187] These developments coincided with a closer orientation of the field toward the Prussia of Otto von Bismarck. Wilhelm Scherer famously depicted German philology as "the daughter of national enthusiasm," a field motivated by "love of the nation."[188] The wars of German unification and the founding of a North German Confederation made apparent that Prussia was ascending to national leadership. As the resolution to the constitutional crisis of 1862 indicates, many German liberals were willing to sacrifice their political convictions for national unity, and so, it appears, were academics in the field of German philology.

Born in Lower Austria to family of civil servants, Wilhelm Scherer is a case in point. Scherer completed his secondary education in Vienna during the period of reaction that Emperor Franz Joseph instituted after 1848. For two years he studied German philology with Franz Pfeiffer, as well as comparative linguistics, at the University of Vienna. The repression of nationalism and liberalism in Austria and a conflict with Pfeiffer over the interpretation of the *Nibelungenlied,* however, brought Scherer to Berlin, where he attended Jacob Grimm's lectures and studied text-historical methods with Karl Müllenhoff. In a debate over the authorship of that saga, Pfeiffer meshed criticism of Prussia with his opposition to Müllenhoff's northern German philological school. Scherer opted to bestow his nationalist ambitions and political loyalties on Prussia even after its crushing defeat of the Austrians in 1866.[189] Scherer launched his academic career as an assistant to Müllenhoff, editing early medieval poetry and prose. But when offered a position in Vienna in 1864, he returned to his native city. During his eight-year tenure at the university, Scherer repeatedly faced reprimand for his support of Prussia and German national unification.[190] Although he imagined the German nation expanding beyond state borders to include native speakers in Austria, Scherer never sympathized with the idea of a *Großdeutschland.*

Scherer's linguistic interests precede his better known work in the history of German literature.[191] Yet, as late as 1873 he considered language to be "the truest mark of nationality," one that enabled "deep gazes into the thoughts and feelings of nations."[192] His monograph *On the History of the German Language* shed light on the "origin of our nation"[193] by revisiting from the perspective of phonetics the sound shifts that produced Proto-Germanic and Old High German. Rejecting Grimm's focus on written form, Scherer examined primarily sound properties. He also extended Grimm's historical trajectory in both directions, incorporating evidence from early Indo-European tongues, as well as observations of speech factors in the living languages and dialects of his time.[194] According to Scherer, the historical evolution of language could not be divided into a period of growth followed by decline. He borrowed from geology the notion of uniformitarianism, arguing that the conditions of language change remained consistent over time; there was "only development, only history" in language.[195] Scherer assumed linguistics to be a historical science. In his view, however, it was closely related to the natural sciences because processes observed in the present could be projected onto the past as an explanation for historical change. The scientific method best identified regular features in the uniform development of language.[196]

Evoking images from Prussia's wars of unification, Scherer asserted that similar power relations governed the "life of language" and "the life of nations and states." Roots behaved like "independent historical powers." Some "expanded their territory" and achieved "extensive sovereignty," while others "went under." The *History* appeared two years after Prussia's 1866 victory over Austria, which enabled King Wilhelm I to consolidate his control over the north German states. For Scherer, the process of German unification was visible in language as well. Certain words rose to the top, in a way resembling "power changes on the . . . world historical scene." Specifically, Scherer argued that the "two reoccurring processes" of "transference" and "differentiation" explained the declining number of roots in Germanic languages and the increase in *composita*, or words that expressed meaning by adding prepositions. One verb expanded to cover the meanings of other roots, forcing their disappearance; the meaning of old roots was transferred to the victors, which then added prepositions to differentiate among the various meanings they represented.[197]

Theories of sound physiology and acoustics, taken from Viennese physiologist Ernst Brücke, helped Scherer explain the "causality"[198] behind the sound shifts that Grimm had observed. He assumed that uniform tendencies in the workings of German linguistic muscles and organs across time had distinguished the language spoken by the earliest members of the nation; physiological laws at work in contemporary Bavarian dialects, for example, could be used to explain why the German vowels *î* and *û* evolved into *ai* and *au*.[199] Three processes "easing the formation of consonants" had produced the first sound shift and separated Proto-Germanic (*germanische Grundsprache*) from Indo-European. Physiologically, this entailed, for example, "a mere contraction of the vocal cords rather than a complete closing of the glottis in voice-stop consonants." Scherer speculated that the fine "hearing of our Germanic forefathers" had allowed them to transform "sonorous Aryan stops into whispered voice-stop consonants."[200] The second sound shift distinguishing Old High German involved select tribes "preserving the original power" and increasing the relative importance of the secondary accent in root syllables or the "low tone." Speakers of Nordic languages and Low German emphasized the main accent of roots words "at the expense of the low tone."[201]

A deep psychological fusion of inborn German bellicosity and the spirit of Roman antiquity provided the broader context for the linguistic changes that produced High German, and thus the nation. According to Scherer the particularly lively intonation in Old German pronunciation derived from Germans being "filled with an all-powerful desire" and an "active potency" that expressed itself in an eternal love for war. War, he argued, had been the "greatest desire" and the "ideal of German existence." This aristocratic trait was "most deep and lasting," and Scherer wondered what possibilities it might bring for the future.[202] At the same time, "direct and lasting contact" with Roman antiquity had also shaped the second sound shift. An early separation of future Germans from the mass of migrating peoples and their rapid forward advance exposed them to the sounds of Latin poetry. Scherer concluded that the uniqueness of the German language had also been wrought by the "transformation in the spirit of our nation that the conditions of social life after the occupation of Germany" had instilled.[203] As Franz Greß notes, Scherer and his generation of Germanists still honored neohumanist cultural ideals and did not accept what Scherer denigrated as "the narrow concept of mere blood relations."[204]

The implications of this are varied. Did Germans have to fear that cultural contact with speakers of Romance languages might once again fracture the nation? Was war with France necessary to guarantee German unity? Either way, Scherer assumed the existence of an essential, deeply rooted German "psychology"[205] that acted in concert with physiological mechanisms to produce the language that united the nation. The national tongue, in turn, shaped the mentality and outward cultural forms that drew together speakers of German. Historical contingencies had only a slight impact on the regular and consistent laws governing the inner life of language. As holds true for earlier Germanists, Scherer attributed a powerful explanatory potential to the interpretation of origins. Deciphering an act of emergence allowed the linguist to pinpoint a national essence and trace its continued impact on generations of German speakers.

The linguists who came to prominence in Germany in the 1870s owed a substantial debt to Scherer. According to Hermann Paul, Scherer taught the Neogrammarians (*Neugrammatiker*) the importance of sound physiology, the exceptionless nature of linguistic laws, and how to explain sound change based on the principle of false analogy. Four of the founding members, including Paul, specialized in Germanic tongues and likewise credited Scherer with revealing the importance of Old High German in determining Proto-Germanic forms. However, the Neogrammarians also dealt Scherer devastating blows for lacking a sound empirical basis and for his hastily drawn conclusions.[206] Scherer's search for a deep psychological explanation for language change ran counter to their more stringent form of positivism. Scherer was quickly discarded as a mentor and his linguistic studies tapered off by the later 1870s. The center of German language study had shifted away from the discipline of German philology.

In 1872, following the Franco-Prussian war, Scherer himself eagerly accepted a chair at the new imperial university in the recently occupied Alsatian city of Strassburg. His self-proclaimed mission was to invest local students with a sense of their German cultural inheritance and thus earn their loyalty for the new *Kaiserreich*. Scherer's expectations far exceeded the reality of nation building, however. Shunned by the Alsatians, the German professors remained isolated among themselves, finding their only contact with soldiers.[207] Scherer remained in the post at the personal request of Bismarck until 1877, when he rejoined his former colleagues in Berlin as the first chair in the History of German Literature.

After the *Reichsgründung*, the field of Germanics increasingly served the ideological needs of the new nation-state, having lost the liberal and oppositional overtones of the Restoration and *Vormärz* periods. A conservative nationalism infused the institutionalization of university seminars in Germanics after 1871, as well as German instruction at the secondary schools.[208] The *Kaiserreich* pursued a conscious policy of promoting the field, as German language, literature, and history occupied a central place in its national-cultural agenda. Comparative linguistics profited, as well, by virtue of its association with the history of the German language, gaining both prestige and an expansion in academic chairs.[209] Not until the 1890s, however, could Germanics truly compete with classical studies as a *Brotwissenschaft* or bread-and-butter discipline.[210] Kaiser Wilhelm II declared to a conference of school reformers in December 1890 that "Our school system lacks at present, above all, its national basis. We must take German for the foundation of our gymnasia. We want to educate our pupils into young Germans, not young Greeks or Romans."[211] For most of the nineteenth century, scholars of Greek and Latin held sway over the German cultural imagination, even as a comparative and historical approach to language stuck a thorn in their idealization of classical antiquity.

4

Urbild Hellas

Language, Classical Philology, and the Ancient Greeks, 1806–66

In 1807 the director of the prestigious philological seminar at the University of Halle asserted the cultural value of classical studies by denigrating the "barbarians" of antiquity. Friedrich August Wolf (1759–1824), who with C. G. Heyne had helped found the new discipline in the 1780s, argued in his *Classical Scholarship: A Survey (Darstellung der Altertumswissenschaft)* that the Egyptians, Hebrews, Persians, and "other nations of the Orient" should not be studied along with the Greeks and Romans. His distinction between cultures was not based on patterns of historical contact, but on aesthetic and moral judgments. Only the Greeks had reached that level of "civic stability [*Policirung*] or civilization" capable of fostering "a truly higher intellectual culture." Like Friedrich Schiller in his "Letters on the Aesthetic Education of Man" (1794), Wolf idealized the ancient Greeks as a universal model for cultural development. No antique people before the Hellenes had attained such a "high spiritual or literary culture," nor had another nation yet matched the originality of the organic Greek cultural synthesis. Hellenic antiquity embodied "the cultivation of pure humanity" for Wolf, and he hoped the modern Germans would soon emulate its ideal.[1]

The Oriental Renaissance questioned such assumptions. In 1808 the comparativist Friedrich Schlegel made a plea for recognizing the importance of Indian antiquity. "May the study of India," he wished, "find a few settlers and patrons like those who . . . extol[ed] the study of Greece in Italy and Germany during the fifteenth and sixteenth centuries." Schlegel believed that the "poetic beauty and philosophical depth" of Indian epics rivaled the cultural and intellectual achievements of the Greeks. India, too, promised to "change and rejuvenate" the European world.[2] Schlegel assured his readers that the "art, philosophy, and poetry of the Greeks" would remain "very much a necessary preparation . . . for profound erudition." But just as Latin had clarified the transmission of ancient Greek traditions to the Germanic Middle Ages, knowledge of Sanskrit would now "illuminate yet entirely unknown areas of earliest antiquity."[3]

Classicists initially regarded comparative philology with disdain, and the friction between the fields is not hard to fathom. Schlegel predicted that the cultural significance of Oriental studies would eclipse that of classical philology. He also identified India's source of the leverage over classical antiquity—its presumed originality. If the Hellenic past had to be interpreted with reference to earlier Eastern traditions, then the Mediterranean could no longer be considered the autonomous cradle of European civilization. Comparative philologists, for their part, dismissed the old guard, declining to defer to their knowledge of language and the example of Hellenic antiquity. "Classical philology, the old leader of the dance, has been truly outflanked," the comparativist August Friedrich Pott sneered in 1833, "May it collapse upon itself; the minuets are out of fashion . . . a science that worships two or three peoples like idols and scorns the others as barbarians or wild men."[4]

Disputes over language lay at the heart of the comparativist-classicist divide. At stake was provenance over language study and its role in the historical appreciation of antiquity. Until the rise of comparative-historical philology, students of Greek and Latin held a virtual monopoly over general linguistics and the study of grammar and etymology. The linguistic structures of Greek and Latin were presumed, moreover, to mirror in exemplary fashion universal laws of logic and rationality. Yet students of Greek gradually lost their authority as linguists. The transformation of *Altphilologie* into *Altertumswissenschaft* undermined the philosophical justification for venerating the pure forms of Greek grammar. Classicists began to approach Greek and Latin texts as one of antiquity's many cultural artifacts and a contextually specific object of historical criticism. Comparative philologists created linguistic genealogies that illuminated the earliest points in a nation's history. This practice was of little use to classicists who wished to assert the normative value of the Greek language and culture and to defend the autonomy of Hellas's Golden Age.

This chapter investigates how comparative-historical philology altered the way classical scholars approached language, as well as the impact it had on the neohumanist German veneration of ancient Greece. It shows that classicists were initially reluctant to embrace the new techniques of their colleagues because a comparative perspective questioned the prevailing view that classical Hellas was the *Urbild* or the primordial, ideal model of cultural development and nationhood that modern Germans should emulate. Ancient Greek had once rivaled Hebrew as the possible *Ursprache* or divine language of revelation. Some classicists still believed that the graceful style and structures of Greek most accurately represented the material world; others considered its presumed universality and transparency evidence that Greek was the medium best equipped to express metaphysical truth. The presumed proximity between ancient Greek and the modern German language further appealed to German speakers who styled themselves as the most adept interpreters and custodians of the Hellenic legacy, having been, they claimed, the only Europeans to have escaped the imprint of Latin.

Comparative philology encouraged classicists to inquire into the origins and broader historical context of the Greek ideal. Perhaps not the timeless embodiment of universal human values, ancient Greece had to be reconceived within a view of world history that derived all things from the East. Was Hellas merely derivative of Indian or Egyptian traditions? Was the national affinity that appeared to bind modern Germans to ancient Greeks less compelling in light of new theories of Indo-European descent? Classicists eventually adapted to a comparative perspective, linking Greece to the story of the Indo-European language family in a manner similar to Germanists. Bracketing the question of ultimate origins, they defended the autonomy, integrity, and universal cultural significance of the ancient Greek language, as well as the literature, mythology, art forms, and philosophy of its speakers.

The chapter opens by considering the role of philosophical grammar within the aesthetic idealization of Greece, detailing the emergence of a specifically national identification with the Hellenes after the Napoleonic invasions of 1806. It follows the progressive historicization of the Hellenic ideal under the leadership of Wolf's most prominent student, the Berlin classicist August Boeckh (1785–1867). Material philologists (*Sachphilologen*) or "realists," such as Boeckh, diminished the importance of language study within the German reception of Hellenic antiquity, reducing words to one of many historical expressions of the Greek spirit. Boeckh and his students also reconsidered the normative value of Hellenic antiquity, opening discussion of the likely origins of Greek culture. Comparativists challenged classicists to situate ancient Greece within a larger genealogy of human development that began in the East. The Greek War of Independence against the Ottoman Turks and its political implications for Germany inspired them, in turn, to "de-Orientalize" Greece. The philhellenist Friedrich Thiersch (1784–1860) expected modern Germans, as the current representatives of the Hellenic spirit, to return Greek independence and learning to classical soil after centuries of Turkish occupation. Karl Otfried Müller (1797–1840) and Friedrich Gottlieb Welcker (1784–1868) likewise defended the cultural autonomy of ancient Greece against Orientalists who insisted on deriving European culture from a common Asian homeland. By midcentury, however, these scholars and figures such as Georg Curtius (1820–85) had learned to appropriate tenants from comparative-historical philology itself to argue for the cultural significance of ancient Greece to Germany.

Philosophical Grammar and the Hellenic Ideal

The normative authority Hellenic antiquity wielded over German culture rested, as F. A. Wolf stipulated, on a moral and aesthetic vision. As a pedagogical alternative to the utilitarian rationalism of the Enlightenment and the Latin learning of the church, German neohumanism promised to cultivate the inner life of the self-realizing, moral subject. The philological seminars of G. F. Heyne in Göttingen and F. A. Wolf in Halle venerated Hellas less as an actual historical achievement than as a model of personal wholeness, social responsibility, and natural freedom. The self-reflective and interpretive practices required of classical scholarship aided the self-cultivation of ethical individuals and rewarded achievement and merit over the precedence of birth.[5] The specialized research ethos of the discipline and the esoteric knowledge produced by professional classicists often contradicted the ideal of resurrecting moral freedom through aesthetic integrity.[6] But for early classicists the forms of Greek culture expressed a pure humanity that offered a holistic antidote to the fragmentation of an overspecialized modern world. The prestige of the educated bourgeoisie in Germany depended on the academic professions, and classical philology was the choice discipline for ambitious members of the Protestant middle class. The type of *Bildung* imparted through contemplation of the Greek language and literature allowed graduates of philological seminars to claim for themselves a disinterested, universal, and public vision of cultivation that extended beyond the narrow interests of traditional forms of privilege.[7]

For this reason, classical studies tended to attract moderate liberal nationalists and Protestants, such as the Bonn philologist Friedrich Gottlieb Welcker, brother of the liberal activist Theodor. Classicists assumed that ability and education warranted an expansion of political representation to their ranks—male members of the upper middle class. Welcker, for example, was fired from his post in Gießen in 1816 for publishing an article, "On the Constitution of the Estates and Germany's Future," that demanded a national constitution. His repeated struggles to gain and retain employment despite being one of Germany's foremost classicists are one extreme case of the republican pillars informing Hellenism. The classical polis exemplified an ideal of civic and intellectual freedom that supported middle-class constitutionalism.[8] Most classical philologists, however, came to enjoy a closer partnership with the state than the more radically politicized and oppositional Germanists.

Language helped resurrect the Hellenic past in several ways. On the one hand, Wolf regarded ancient Greek as an "instrument" or "tool" that "acquainted" the philologist with "historical things."[9] Texts were the primary window on the past, and critical interpretation and exegesis required solid grammatical knowledge. Wolf listed grammar and language studies as the first pillar of philology; mastery of Greek and Latin was necessary before attempting hermeneutics, political history, or the study of mythology. On the other hand, his *Classical Scholarship: A Survey* presumed language to be "a large storehouse of ideas . . . that a *Volk* has."[10] Wolf followed Herder in claiming the native tongue to be "the measure of a nation's culture."[11] Language represented the spirit of the Hellenes "as well as morals and customs." It therefore comprised part of the totality that classicists investigated. "Does one learn language to explore the history and fate of ancient nations, or just as language?" Wolf debated. "What is the means, what are the ends?"[12] Students of material culture largely adopted the first perspective, seeing in language a practical vehicle for research. Grammarians held to the second.

The neohumanist veneration of Hellas relied, moreover, on the profoundly ahistorical perspective of general grammar. As rhetoricians serving theological and law faculties, philologists had traditionally regarded language aesthetically. Greek and Latin supposedly offered ideal cognitive models for expressing ideas with precision and elegance. Wolf assumed words were "signs" for communicating ideas, as well as for "making one aware of his own thoughts and recalling them."[13] His vision of classical studies likewise maintained an intrinsic connection between ancient languages and the ideal forms of thought. "Philosophical or general grammar" was the first and most important discipline that had to be mastered before learning Greek and Latin. Students needed familiarity with "the general principles and rules upon which human languages are built."[14] For Wolf knowledge of universal rules facilitated language acquisition, even among school children.[15] Grammar, more importantly, had philosophical import. Similar to logic, it made apparent the universal "laws of human thought."[16] "Because human language is designed in the same way as thought," he explained in 1810, "the general rules that bind all languages can be derived very easily from the nature of the human spirit." Each tongue emerged "analogically" to the rational structures that governed the universe; their diversity was caused by "anomaly" or an inevitable process of mistaken deviation from the norm.[17] Studying the Greek language thus offered Wolf "a means to perfect our concepts and clarify thought." He assumed ancient Greek to be "an excellently designed language" with inherent intellectual advantages.[18]

The most prominent Greek grammarians of the early nineteenth century upheld a rationalist approach to language. "Verbalists," classical scholars who made the text, including questions of grammar, meter, and style, the main object of their analysis, tended to idealize the cognitive advantages of Greek. Gottfried Hermann (1772–1848), professor of eloquence and poetry in Leipzig, headed the grammatical and critical school of the classicists. Born the son of a prominent German lawyer in Leipzig and a French mother, Hermann received his degrees from the university in his native city. In 1794 he briefly studied Kantian philosophy in Jena.[19] His mentor, K. L. Reinhold, argued that the universal categories of the understanding could be found mirrored in language. Hermann, who lectured on logic and Kant's *Critique of Judg-*

ment upon returning to Leipzig, himself advocated a rationalist approach to grammar. His *De emendanda ratione Graecae Grammaticae* (1801) derived Greek structures and forms systematically and logically rather than reconstructing them from historical evidence. Language, Hermann insisted, was a reflection of the human mind. He sought to identify the strict laws governing thought while honoring the free expression of artistry made possible by rhetoric.[20] Accordingly, Hermann's textual criticism proceeded "prophetically." He sought to perfect places where literary works appeared corrupt or dissolute, correcting what the author "meant" to say based on his knowledge of rhythm and poetic form.[21]

Several tensions characterize the nineteenth-century German reception of antiquity, including a contradictory vision of Greece as a historically particular, yet universally human culture. Latent nationalist rhetoric also pervaded the German appreciation of ancient European languages despite Hermann's universalizing assumptions. The idealization of Greece was often couched in nationalist terms that gave German classicists sole provenance over the legacy of the Greeks. In his *History of Ancient Art* (1764), for example, the art historian Johann Joachim Winckelmann upheld the sublime aesthetic embodied in the statues of Periclean Athens as an antidote to the baroque, aristocratic tastes and values of the old regime. In his view, Greek art embodied man's true, uncorrupted nature freed from the artificial social distinctions of the court and the overspecialized modern world. Of all national styles it referred least to the historical context of its production and was most likely to draw agreement on its being beautiful.[22] Winckelmann's preference for Greece was, at the same time, an overt criticism of the extent to which French classicism celebrated imperial Rome, in particular of the parallels Charles Perrault drew between the reign of Augustus and the absolutist *siècle* of Louis XIV.[23]

The years of the Napoleonic occupation increased the emphasis classicists placed on the national attributes of classical antiquity. According to Manfred Fuhrmann, the eighteenth-century *querelle* over the respective virtues of the ancients and moderns was reformulated in this period into a new comparison of the national characteristics of the Greeks, the Germans, and the Romance countries of Europe.[24] The French regime equated its political might with that of imperial Rome; Germans identified with the vanquished Greeks of the second century BC. Although politically fragmented and subject to a foreign power, they could rely on cultural and spiritual ties to sustain the nation. During the Wars of Liberation publicists exploited the neohumanist affinity for Greece, depicting German resistance as an effort to escape from the political tyranny of Roman culture. In occupied Germany, where the national spirit was believed to have taken refuge in cultural and educational institutions, the philological seminars of such universities as Berlin readily assumed patriotic tones.[25] A highly politicized program of neohumanist pedagogical reform that began in Prussia and gradually spread to the other German states likewise made public the nationalist reception of Greek antiquity.

The Prussian statesman and educational reformer Wilhelm von Humboldt, likewise a student of C. G. Heyne, exemplifies the transition of neohumanism from an antiaristocratic, eighteenth-century movement to a moderately nationalist state-sponsored program. For a brief period between February 1809 and July 1810 Humboldt served as the head of newly created Sektion für Kultus und Unterricht of the Prussian Interior Ministry. As part of the wide-ranging series of reforms begun by Karl von Hardenberg and Karl Freiherr vom Stein, he established classical studies as the backbone of German education. Humboldt restricted university admissions to graduates of classical schools or gymnasia who had passed the *Abitur*, an exam requiring extensive translations of Greek texts, as well as testing in Latin. Humboldt likewise designed the model university of Berlin, the first working and research university in Germany, around F. A. Wolf's philological seminar. This institutionalized the cultural leadership of classical philologists in the universities and secondary schools, affirming the importance of neohumanism to the state and public sphere.[26] Philological seminars became the training grounds for future bureaucrats in the expanding administration of the territorial states, as well as for ecclesiastics in the Lutheran state churches.[27]

For Humboldt, Hellenic antiquity offered foremost a *Bildungsideal* that could be applied to the cultivation of the self. As he explained in "Latium and Hellas: Observations on Classical Antiquity," an essay written in 1806 while Humboldt was serving as the Prussian ambassador to the Holy See in Rome, the pedagogical value of Greek antiquity lay in its embodying the ideal in all aspects of human life. Only the Hellenes "allude[d] to the ideal in everything" and demonstrated in art, poetry, religion, morality, and public life how one can achieve a "bridge from the individual to the ideal."[28] Humboldt's neohumanist reforms were founded on the principle that studying Greek language and literature provided students with the best insight into the ideal of human development, civic responsibility, and moral freedom that the Greeks exemplified.[29] Immersion in the Greek past supposedly liberated the individual from regulated society and emancipated one spiritually from the one-sidedness and compartmentalization of the modern world. Humboldt aspired to create loyal, self-willed, and ethical citizens who honored merit and achievement over birth as criteria for social advance.[30]

Humboldt idealized ancient Greece in largely ahistorical terms and tended to value the cosmopolitan world citizen over the patriot. The origins of "Greekness," he conceded, were "difficult to determine historically, and the causes that contributed to its development . . . primarily internal." One could not easily specify why humanity evolved to such perfection in ancient Greece: "It was because it was."[31] His essay significantly omitted all reference to ancient Rome and neglected to draw an explicit connection between the German national character and the ability to resurrect the Greek ideal. Rather, in a brief comparison of the ancient Hellenes and "most cultivated nations after them," Humboldt proposed that the main strains of the Greek character had been split and jointly inherited by the French and Germans. The affinity of both nations to the Greeks was, in his view, "only incomplete"; their respective virtues were "almost equally far removed from the Greek." Humboldt only hinted that Germans approached something that is "closer to the meaning of the Greek."[32] He revered Greece as the foundation for building an individual, ethical, and civic ideal that stood above national loyalties and did not rely on a specifically German inheritance of the classical past.

The collapse of the Holy Roman Empire brought Humboldt back to Prussia to care for his family estates in Tegel near Berlin. German defeat to the French likewise inspired him to depict the Greek-German connection in more assertively nationalist terms that insisted on the special historical ties between modern Germans and the Hellenes. Humboldt's *History of the Fall of the Free Greek States* (1807) thus compared the political fate of occupied Germany with that of the Greek city-states under the Roman Empire. Germany, in his view, displayed "in language, in the versatility of its endeavors, in the simplicity of its temper, in its federalist constitution, and in its most recent fate, an undeniable similarity with Greece." The northern fatherland, he hoped, would likewise survive by virtue of its cultural strength. Humboldt now emphasized German speakers' exclusive ability to emulate the ideal forms of Greek culture, grounding this claim in the linguistic affinities that existed between the two tongues. "The Germans deserve the uncontested merit," he explained, "of being the first to comprehend Greek *Bildung* truthfully and to have felt it deeply . . . other nations have never been as fortuitous in this."[33] Because the Romance countries of Europe had adopted so much Latin into their native languages, their direct connection to the ancient Greeks had been broken.

The nationalization of Hellenic antiquity altered the perceived significance of language studies. Classicists had once justified their monopoly on teaching rhetoric, grammar, and syntax by asserting that fluency in Latin and Greek had inherent intellectual merits. In the early nineteenth century the circle of classicists surrounding the gymnasial reformer Friedrich Immanuel Niethammer (1766–1848) in Bavaria and the other main representative of south-German neohumanism, Friedrich Jacobs, demonstrated the national importance of studying ancient Greek, while still drawing on older theories of general grammar. Friedrich Ast (1778–1841) and Franz Passow (1786–1833) embraced Hellenic antiquity as the foundation of a specifically German national *Bildung* during a period of political crisis. Greece for them was an "emblem of national virtue,"[34] a paragon of strength and cultural authenticity that would transform schoolchildren into patriotic Germans.

The special affinity these classicists felt for Hellas relied on a vision of ancient Greek as the oldest and most perfected language. Johann Arnold Kanne (1773–1824) had already pointed out the lexical similarities between Greek and German roots, speculating in 1804 that the two tribes might once have lived together in northern Europe or that modern Germans were the direct descendents of the ancient Greeks.[35] Friedrich Ast, who had joined the Bavarian university of Landshut in 1805, explored the significance of this connection more thoroughly in his essay *On the Spirit of Antiquity and Its Meaning for Our Age* (1805). Ast had studied speculative philosophy with the Jena Romantics J. G. Fichte, F. W. J. Schelling, and Friedrich Schlegel, and he considered language "to be the most original and true revelation of the human spirit, the *Ur*-poetry of a people."[36] Greek, according to Ast, was "the prototype [*Urbild*] of all languages," the primordial ancestor to which all European languages traced their roots but also the universal "ideal of language generally."[37] There was, moreover, a historical basis for "the unmistaken kinship of Germanic and Greek." As Romance languages, the other European tongues had been "mediated first through the Latin language."[38]

The historical ties Ast extended from Greek to German were not genealogical in the way that Friedrich Schlegel linked his mother tongue to Sanskrit. Ast tended to conflate historical distance by equating in dialectical fashion the present day with an idealized moment in the Greek past. The Hellenes, in his view, had coalesced as a "harmonious living state" in which each individual faithfully encapsulated the spirit of the whole.[39] His teleology of world history attributed to the ancient Greeks a youthful stage of humanity, one blessed with vitality and beauty, but unselfconscious and unaware of its significance for the development of culture. Modern Germans were philosophically more attuned to the historical progress of the human spirit, but they also suffered from this inwardness. When one compared the "public and national life" of the ancients, Ast feared, Germans appeared as "barbarians against the Greeks." Ast hoped they would model their public life on classical antiquity, thus completing the spiraled development of culture that began in Greece.[40]

An instructor at the Conradinium in Jenkau bei Danzig, Franz Passow had more concrete, pedagogical expectations for the study of ancient Greek. "The Importance of the Greek Language in Educating German Youth" (1812) was one of two articles he published in the 1812 *Archive for German National Education,* delineating the benefits that familiarity with Greek grammar had for strengthening the German national consciousness. The journal, of which he was coeditor, had solicited contributions discussing curriculum for a "national school" in Germany. Studying ancient Greek was for Passow "a national [goal]"[41] because it helped the younger generation "achieve higher *Bildung* and nationality."[42] He acknowledged the need for instruction in the mother tongue, "the noble, vigorous, rich, patriotic language" that the aristocracy had banished "with criminal indiscretion." But Greek was an essential first foundation. It was "most analogous to the German language" and due to its "innermost affinity" with German could best clarify the grammatical principles and root meanings of words in the mother tongue. Greek was also "the most perfect, the nearest reflection of the ideal"[43]—an indication of the "general cultural state of a nation."[44]

Wilhelm von Humboldt envisioned an even broader role for language study. His essay "Latium and Hellas" made a case for a textually based historical appreciation of classical antiquity by characterizing language as a reflection of an external reality, but one that was molded by the idealizing impulses of the Greek mind. The word, in Humboldt's analysis, was both a "picture of the thing" that it describes and an indication of how the external world was "thought with reason or imagined with fantasy."[45] Thus, by studying language, "an expedient between fact and idea," classicists could decipher how ideal Greek cultural forms had evolved from within the imperfect, historical world. According to Humboldt, language also revealed the Greek national character. Geography, climate, religion, and the polity were, in his mind, more or less coincidental to the formation of the spirit of the nation (*Volksgeist*). Language, by contrast, "not only offers a means for comparing several nations but also a handy mark for tracking the influence of one nation on another."[46] Classical philologists ultimately declined to follow Humboldt's suggestion that the study of linguistic structures themselves, as opposed to the textual meaning embodied in them, could help negotiate between the ideal and historical aspects of Hellenic antiquity. And Humboldt himself slowly gravitated to the comparativist camp, eventually favoring Sanskrit over Greek after meeting Franz Bopp in London in the early 1820s.

Not surprisingly, classicists shunned the new methods of comparative philology long after they had set the scientific standard for language study in other fields. Gottfried Hermann and his students Christian A. Lobeck (1781–1860) and Karl Wilhelm Krüger (1796–1871), reacted with cool indifference, suspicion, and even open hostility to the newcomers' attempts to interpret the classical languages.[47] In the *Acta Societatis Graecae* of 1830, Hermann mocked those who "without mastery or refined reading, hoped that light would come from the regions where the sun rises, while only contemplating the aurora borealis. They . . . try to explain the meaning found in vestiges of Greek and Latin verbs without sufficient knowledge of the languages."[48] Jacob Grimm had shown comparative-historical linguistics to be useful for research on individual languages in 1819, but with a few exceptions classicists preferred to retain older principles of grammatical criticism in their treatment of Greek and Latin. This reaction was partly an effort to protect the status of classical studies as the model philological discipline; its representatives feared a leveling of the institutional distinctions still maintained between the fields.[49] But the obstinacy of classicists was also a response to the uncertainty and experimental nature of comparative-historical linguistics, whose practitioners often displayed severe deficits in their knowledge of individual languages.[50] The necessity of producing Greek and Latin school grammars likewise encouraged classicists to seek strict and simplified rules with which to codify these tongues, rather than to explore otherwise revealing deviations from the norm.[51]

Not until the mid-1830s did the first Greek grammars using the comparative method begin to appear, such as that by Theodor Benfey (1834) or Georg Curtius (1852). Others followed that examined Greek roots and particles or sketched brief histories of the Greek language.[52] Their treatment of Greek phonology and morphology was so rudimentary, however, that as late as 1869 the comparativist Theodor Benfey (1809–81) described as the "doubtlessly most glaring gap in Indo-Germanic linguistics" that there was still no satisfactory comprehensive grammar of Greek.[53] Classicists generally did not encourage a genealogical approach to the ancient European tongues and studied neither modern Greek nor such dialects as Doric, Aeolic, and Ionic, preferring to focus on the standardized Attic language of the late fifth century BC.[54] Even New Testament or Koine Greek (Common Greek), the vernacular dialect spoken in the first-century Roman provinces of the eastern Mediterranean, had received, according to Benfey, "very unsatisfactory" attention.[55] The apparent ambivalence of classicists led one perturbed comparativist to assert in 1841 that his colleagues had achieved more for language studies in the past twenty years than all the classicists leading up to Gottfried Hermann in the previous two hundred.[56]

Historicizing the Greek Ideal: August Boeckh

Nationalist rhetoric often elided the historical distance separating ancient Greeks and modern Germans by emphasizing their elective affinities. Friedrich Ast, for example, placed little importance on the historical specificity of thought or action; in his view, the classicist needed to be a philosopher and aesthete so that he could establish the identity between the timeless spirit of ancients and moderns.[57] Classicists did not emphasize problems of genealogy and origins as did Germanists or Orientalists. Rather, two definitions of antiquity permeated classical studies: one that idealized Hellas as a literary, artistic, pedagogical, and ethical norm, and one that subjected the Greek past to more rigorous historical scrutiny. Nevertheless, when considering how classicists interpreted language, it is insufficient to claim that historicism made "little headway" against normative claims to Greece's aesthetic superiority[58] or that aestheticism remained the "dominant strain"[59] in the German reception of Greek antiquity in the years after the Wars of Liberation.

An increasingly historical approach to Hellas is visible in the way classicists such as August Boeckh regarded language. Born in Karlsruhe, the capital city of Baden, Boeckh studied with F. A. Wolf in Halle before, at the young age of twenty-five, he assumed leadership of the philological seminar at the newly founded university in Berlin. In 1814 he was elected member of the Academy of Sciences, serving for many years as its secretary. Boeckh's own work exemplifies the tension in classical studies between humanism and historicism. Boeckh suggested that the Greek past was "particularly worth knowing."[60] Its pedagogical value lay in ancient Greece's offering a model of individuality[61] and teaching "true political freedom and the lasting principles of the same."[62] A moderate liberal, Boeckh compared the Greco-Persian wars to the German struggle against Napoleonic France, for example, and often related Berlin to Athens.[63] Nevertheless, he set aside considerations of general linguistics and largely limited the study of language to analyzing syntax, word-formation, and meter, techniques that aided classicists in textual criticism.[64] Boeckh's break with the tradition of rationalist grammar helped unravel the largely ahistorical adoration of Hellas that dominated the field in the 1810s. Rather than merely uphold the Greek past as a normative ideal, Boeckh introduced a new approach to classical philology that raised questions about the origins of Hellenic culture.

Boeckh's efforts to historicize classical antiquity unfolded in his posthumously published *Encyclopedia and Methodology of the Philological Sciences,* a series of lectures first held in Heidelberg in 1809 and repeated twenty-six times before Boeckh's retirement in 1865. Classical philology, in his view, took as its domain "the entire historical manifestation" of Greek and to a lesser degree Roman antiquity.[65] More than any other of his students, Boeckh carried out Wolf's encyclopedic program for *Altertumswissenschaft* by including previously untouched areas of Hellenic life within the scope of philological study. He divided classical antiquity into four main spheres of activity: the state, private life, art and religion, and science or knowledge (*Wissen*). Boechk's own work covered such topics as the financial system of Athenians, mining in antiquity, and weights and measures.[66]

The task of the philologist was, in Boeckh's well-known formulation, to gain "knowledge of what the human spirit has produced, that is, knowledge of what was produced by other minds,"[67] and then through analysis and translation to reconstruct the "totality of this knowledge." For this reason, Boeckh believed his definition of philology fell "together with that of history in the broadest sense." Philology as a discipline was "purely historical," and history also had to proceed "philologically" because it drew on written sources. Boeckh held the only difference between the two fields to be one of scope. History concentrated on political life, while philology considered "the rest of cultural life in connection with the state."[68] He preferred the designation "classical philology" over Wolf's term, "classical studies." The study of Greek and Roman antiquity was for Boeckh only one area of the larger historical field of philology, which included textually based research on any epoch.[69]

The critical techniques developed within classical philology (and later adopted by the Roman historian B. G. Niehbuhr) helped establish the tradition of idealist historiography in Germany; through his student J. G. Droysen, August Boeckh played a key transitional role in the emergence of German historicism.[70] Historical phenomena were, in his view, concrete manifestations of eternal ideas that needed the interpretive tools of philosophy to be comprehended in full. Philology, Boeckh explained in the *Encyclopedia and Methodology,* "proceeds historically, not from concepts; but . . . philology cannot reproduce the totality of a people's knowledge without working philosophically on this construction."[71] The act of interpretation transpired, in Boeckh's view, as an ever-building spiral driven by the tension between the formal and material elements of antiquity. The particular in the historical life of the Greeks only had meaning when it was "conceived within a whole" and related to "the idea of antiquity in itself." Boeckh stressed that this general principle was "admittedly only an ideal that can never be fully reached because it is impossible to unite all the individualities under a totalizing perspective."[72] This hesitation to complete the hermeneutical circle marks Boeckh's distance from the speculative philology of Friedrich Ast who thought classicists capable of smoothly resolving the relationship between the general and particular.[73]

Boeckh's redefinition of classical philology encountered resistance within the discipline, not least from the ranks of the "verbalists" or *Wortphilologen.* Under the leadership of the aging Leipzig classicist

Gottfried Hermann, these scholars sought to preserve an exclusive focus on the study of language and literature and thereby to uphold the normative status of Hellenic antiquity. Classical philology as practiced by Boeckh's most vocal critic was restricted to the art of understanding, interpreting, and reproducing a literary tradition that was held to be exemplary. Boeckh expanded the program of classicists to encompass all cultural phenomena and their function in relation to the cultural and social system of antiquity.[74]

In 1819 a debate over the direction the field of classical philology should take gathered force following a critique Hermann published of Boeckh's work on metric theory in Pindar. At stake were the implications of historicizing Greek antiquity and the importance of language study within the German reception of classical antiquity. The antagonisms escalated in the years after the 1825 publication of the first volume of the *Corpus Inscriptionum Graecarum,* a substantial collection of Greek inscriptions undertaken by Prussian Academy of Sciences at Boeckh's request shortly after he was made a member. Until 1835 most classical philologists felt compelled to state their position in the quarrel, although it was often not a case of taking one side or another but of assessing the benefits and disadvantages of each position. Ultimately, the realists who focused on "things" instead of words prevailed, but the tenacity of Hermann's vision suggests the extent to which scholars still looked to the Greek language as an ideal of self-cultivation.

At the heart of the controversy lay "two very different conceptions" of language, which Gottfried Hermann clarified in 1826. Working within the rationalist tradition of the Enlightenment, Hermann believed that language was a reflection of the human mind. He objected to Boeckh's assumption that the ancient tongues were "merely a medium and do not need to be the object of knowledge."[75] For Hermann, language was the "most important and excellent thing [*Sache*]" of classical antiquity. On the one hand, the mother tongue of ancient Greeks was "in itself . . . the vital image of their spirit" because "it best characterized their essence or being."[76] On the other hand, he held language to be "first and most indispensable because only through it can everything else be understood."[77] Hermann insisted on the priority of words even when studying the "things" of antiquity. Thorough knowledge of language was already knowledge of the material world, in his view; the philologist could grasp the essence of archaic objects by studying their representation in language. Texts, moreover, best illustrated the ideal nature of the Greek past. Hermann still had faith that the eternal qualities of the rational mind were expressed in the timeless classicism of ancient Greek literature.

In an 1827 article published in the *Rheinisches Museum*, Boeckh affirmed that language was important to understanding the ancient Greeks but challenged the significance the senior scholar attributed to the pursuit of grammar. Philology, he suggested, was not a generalized study of human reason but a scientific, historical examination of the "life and work" of "a particular people during a relatively restricted period." As a form of thought, language should be considered one of the "things" of antiquity comparable with religion, political life, or household practices. It, too, gave insight into the national character of the Greeks, but, in his view, should not be privileged above other aspects of ancient life. Language was most important for Boeckh as the "means to recognize almost all the other creations of antiquity." Precise knowledge of Greek was essential to researching other areas of classical life, but he insisted that philology present the facts and ideas of antiquity based on "the monuments of language, but without getting stuck on the interpretation of language itself."[78]

Linguistics proper was condemned to an ancillary role within Boeckh's model of classical philology. The field, Boeckh insisted, was not "identical with the study of language."[79] The *Encyclopedia and Methodology* treated language as part of a larger section on science and knowledge, giving a brief history of ancient Greek following other historical sketches of geography, political life, religion, art, and literature. He described language as "the general organon of knowledge," while rejecting the rationalism of Hermann. The Greek national tongue was "the pure expression of all understanding, not only of reason."[80] Therefore philology must explore its forms as part of a larger historical appreciation of classical antiquity. Boeckh deemed it impossible to compose a universal grammar. Ancient Greek had to be presented "in its development through time and space"[81] in order to complement a greater cultural complex. At the same time, Boeckh rejected the proposition that language determined the content of cognition. The Greeks, in fact, were the first to establish "dominion over the natural side of language,"[82] regulating variations in sound and abstracting words whose first meanings were bound to concrete, material artifacts. Language existed for Boeckh as a "system of signs that change according to the ideas signified."[83] It was merely an instrument for larger cultural articulations and thus no more than an artifact of Greek historical life.

The one midcentury classicist to make linguistics central to his research on antiquity, while denying the normative claims of rationalists like Hermann, worked outside of Germany. Johan Nicolai Madvig (1804–86), an internationally renowned Danish Latinist, introduced Wolfian-style *Altertumswissenschaft* to Denmark. He likewise resembled other classicists of the period in that he rejected the emphasis Bopp, Grimm, Humboldt, and Pott placed on linguistic genealogy. Philology, in his view, was a historical science designed to replicate great currents in the development of ancient civilization. Language study, in the form of hermeneutics and textual criticism, was an essential tool of historical inquiry. Madvig's *Encyclopedia of Philology*, compiled from the lecture notes of students at the University of Copenhagen, argued that general linguistics should be the foundation for Greek and Latin studies. But grammar had a significance of its own that could not be derived from the rational structures of thought.

The language theory Madvig outlined in academy speeches and essays published in the 1830s and 1840s represents an interesting transitional phase between general grammar and the structuralist theories developed by Meilleit, Bréal, and Ferdinand de Saussure in the late nineteenth century.[84] Like earlier Enlightenment figures, Madvig viewed language primarily as a practical means of communication that emerged within a specific social and cultural context. Signs were arbitrary and conventional; the meaning of words depended on the agreement of the community and the continuous sanction of its members. Reconstructing how a society attributed meaning to signs would assist the classical philologist in drawing together the many cultural manifestations of antiquity into a unified whole. Madvig advocated a synchronic, structural approach to Greek and Latin that focused on problems of syntax and signification, rather than phonology and morphology.

Madvig's reconciliation of classical philology and linguistics found little support on the continent. A rationalist approach to language had failed among the German classicists who historicized the idealized vision of Hellas passed down by Wolf and Hermann. Their reception of antiquity relegated language to one among many cultural artifacts, while acknowledging the methodological necessity of skilled textual criticism. Classicists likely avoided linguistic theory because the search for pure and original forms dominated it so heavily in Germany. And a genealogical appreciation of Greek and Latin threatened to embed Hellas within cultural traditions that originated in a more ancient East.

(De-)Orientalizing Greece: Friedrich Thiersch

In the 1820s German classicists, nevertheless, inquired into the historical origins of ancient Greek culture, a sensitive topic first broached in *The Histories* of Herodotus and debated throughout the eighteenth century.[85] The Munich classicist Friedrich Thiersch and several of Boeckh's students asked how and why "Greekness" arose at the time it did. Their findings confirmed that the classical Greek aesthetic of the fifth-century BC was neither timeless nor had it graced Greek soil since time immemorial. Rather, Hellenic culture appeared to derive from precisely those Middle Eastern and Asian sources that Wolf had dismissed as insignificant. The Romantic mythologist Friedrich Creuzer (1771–1858) helped raise these issues. His *Symbolism and Mythology of the Ancient Peoples, Especially of the Greeks* (1810–12) linked Greek religious symbolism to an Asian homeland and sparked a heated dispute with such classicists as Hermann, Lobeck, and K. O. Müller.[86] The Greek War of Liberation, which began in 1821, also raised new concerns by highlighting Greece's liminal status between Europe and the Ottoman Empire; it set Greece at the center of debates around national self-determination and liberal political reform as well. At a time when the restoration of monarchical authority troubled many classicists and German university professors, a despotic "Orient" loomed over the perceived cradle of European civilization.

Deriving Greek culture from Asia had for Friedrich Creuzer been a conservative statement compatible with reactionary politics. As George Williamson argues, his assault on the humanist image of ancient Greece and his emphasis on the "oriental" heritage of Christianity undercut a Protestant ideal of "freedom" in favor of Catholic "authority."[87] A decade later, Thiersch modified this position to support a liberal political agenda, albeit one that appealed to the Bavarian court. As a philhellenist, Thiersch campaigned to drive the Turks from the Peloponnesian peninsula and "return" classical learning to its rightful homeland. He conceded the Egyptian and "Oriental" roots of Greek culture, but insisted on the uniquely Hellenic ability to elevate inherited wisdom to ideal forms. This disgruntled classicists, such as K. O. Müller, who insisted on the local authenticity of Hellenic culture and on Greece's independence from Eastern influences.

Born the son of a baker and small Protestant landholder in Thuringia, the young Thiersch earned a scholarship to the prestigious Schulpforta boarding school where he received a classical education. He began studying theology in Leipzig with Gottfried Hermann. The degree Thiersch took in philology came from the University of Göttingen, where he met August Boeckh. An unusual set of circumstances brought Thiersch to Munich as a professor at the local gymnasium in 1809. Princess Caroline of Baden, second wife of the then Elector Maximilian IV of Bavaria, was a Protestant. Her influence convinced Maximilian to solicit Protestant scholars to the Bavarian Academy of Sciences, including F. I. Niethammer, who procured Thiersch's post. The classicist enjoyed close ties to the House of Wittelsbach, first as the tutor of Caroline's four daughters, then as advisor to Crown Prince Ludwig, a philhellene in his own right. After ascending to the throne, Ludwig charged Thiersch with restructuring Bavaria's schools on the humanistic model; in 1829, he passed a bill requiring classical languages for gymnasium students, just as Wilhelm von Humboldt had done for Prussia.[88]

During the French occupation, Thiersch initially encountered considerable opposition in Bavaria as a liberal nationalist from northern Germany. Catholic supporters of Napoleon, including Baron Johann Christoph von Aretin, hoped the French armies would secure a victory for the Roman church over Protestantism. Von Aretin's sympathizers declared Bavarians to be Celtic, not German and, as such, natural partners of the Gauls; Napoleon from this perspective stood poised to resurrect a Bavarian-Celtic kingdom. In 1809 von Aretin published a pamphlet targeting German nationalists, including Thiersch, Friedrich Heinrich Jacobi, and Anselm Feuerbach. At stake in the quarrel was also his defense of Enlightenment educational ideals over and against Romantic neohumanism.[89] Thiersch responded with a pamphlet on the differences between northern and southern Germans and with a sermon at the Protestant court chapel. On the last night of Carnival in 1811, an attempt was made on his life. Thiersch survived the stab wound to his neck. The assailant was never caught, but Thiersch blamed his Catholic opponents.

Thiersch's *On the Periodization of the Fine Arts among the Greeks,* first published in 1826 but presented earlier as a series of three academy lectures, addressed the problem of Greek origins. The piece took issue with the art historical interpretation of Greek sculpture J. J. Winckelmann had outlined in *On the History of Ancient Art* (1764). According to Thiersch, Winckelmann was mistaken in believing that Greek art was "independent of foreign influence, having sprouted from native soil"[90] and wrong in seeking its origins "in Greece alone."[91] Thiersch likewise objected to how his predecessor periodized the developmental stages of Greek art, denying that Greek sculpture had consistently and rapidly evolved "from its first origins in progressive development to its greatest blossoming."[92] Previous scholars had dated the beginnings of Greek art too late, Thiersch asserted, "so that they could hide the fact that it had progressed for over one thousand years without achieving success."[93] Rather than document the idealized forms of Greek art as they materialized in Periclean Athens, Thiersch chose to focus on a less spectacular early period of Greek culture whose value lay primarily in explaining the historical circumstances that enabled the subsequent rise of more magnificent forms.

Thiersch's argument was simple. He held that the Greek islands and peninsula had once been a tabula rasa; the Pelasgians and other peoples who had inhabited the area before the Greek-speaking migrations were without "images of the gods even without those works out of which art first strove to develop." Rather, they symbolized their nameless and undifferentiated divinities with a "raw stone."[94] Thiersch did not venture to assert where the original homeland of Greek-speaking population lay, maintaining only that art had been introduced to Greece at the time its inhabitants began to build cities. Following Herodotus, Thiersch argued that the Greek religious cult came from Egypt, concluding that the first sculptures on Greek soil had been attempts to depict these new gods.[95] Thiersch acknowledged the likely cultural contributions of all the peoples bordering on Greek waters, including the Thracians, Phoenicians, and Libyans. But he honored Egypt "if not as the actual mother, than as the oldest and most efficacious guardian of ancient Greek art."[96] Under the impression that the gods did not want their images to be changed, the Greeks based their aesthetic sensibilities on Egyptian traditions until almost a century before the dawn of the golden age, displaying little individual freedom and complacently relying on fixed types.

This legacy was less disturbing for Thiersch than the Turkish yoke the Ottoman Empire had since inflicted on the modern descendents of the Hellenes. Since the fall of Constantinople in 1453 the Greek-speaking peninsula and islands had been subject to Turkish rule, and many early nineteenth-century observers feared that the Balkan peninsula had been irretrievably "Orientalized."[97] Historians have interpreted central European involvement into the failing Ottoman Empire as a form of "surrogate" imperialism.[98] Austria, in particular, has been labeled a colonial power due to the history of its incursions into the region.[99] Another German state, the Kingdom of Bavaria, likewise tied its dynastic ambitions to establishing a presence on Ottoman soil. Johannes Irmscher's suggestion that "Bavarian expansion to the south" (*Drang nach dem Süden*) is comparable to the Prussian "expansion to the east" (*Drang nach dem Osten*) overestimates the magnitude and duration of Bavaria's involvement in Greece.[100] But following the Greek War of Independence, the House of Wittelsbach ruled over the new state. During the three decades leading up to the expulsion of the German regime from Athens in 1862, Bavaria acted as a colonizing power in one part of the "Orient," inviting settlers and attempting to resurrect the glory of the ancients with the assistance of its most noted classical philologist.

Friedrich Thiersch's interest in the fate of the modern Greeks dates to a trip to Vienna in 1814 where he met the future Greek president, Ioannis Kapodistiras, who solicited the classicist's support in efforts to free the Greek homeland. Thiersch joined the Philomusen Hetàrie, a society founded in Athens and dedicated to the preservation of antiquities and the establishment of new schools, a library, and a national museum in Greece. He later opened an Athenaeum in his Munich home that, under the auspices of the Academy of Sciences, prepared young Greeks to study at German universities and enabled them to attend the lyceum where Thiersch directed the philological seminar. When news of Alexander Ypsilanti's revolt against the Turks reached Germany in 1821, Thiersch published the first series of numerous articles in the *Augsburger Allgemeine Zeitung*, predicting the immanent spiritual rebirth of Greece and pleading for European intervention on behalf of the revolutionaries.[101]

The universities in the 1820s were a center of German philhellenism, a movement that supported Greek independence in a thinly veiled critique of Metternich's conservative policies. As Christoph Hauser has documented for the southwest, where philhellenic societies were most active, the Greek cause offered liberal nationalists the opportunity to assert their right to political participation.[102] By 1822 the realities of war had dampened the initial enthusiasm of the approximately three hundred German military recruits sent to Greece. The idealistic philhellenic vision collapsed not least from the fact that unlike German liberals who envisioned the restoration of Hellenic culture and the ancient political system, Greek nationalists aspired to the so-called Megáli Idéa of Greece: the restoration of the Byzantine Empire with an eastern capital at Constantinople.[103]

Bavaria's King Maximillian I initially joined the other European royal houses in condemning the revolution's assault on the monarchical principle. Thiersch attempted to solicit state support for the Greek cause as the private tutor of the royal children and an advisor to the crown prince's architect Leo von Klenze. Thiersch was forced to publicly retract his plan for building a Greek-German army, however, and to refrain from further philhellenic activity until October 1825. In this year Ludwig I assumed the Bavarian throne. The rapid Egyptian conquest of Athens and Missolunghi, where the English Romantic poet Lord Byron lost his life, also convinced the major European powers to reverse their policy of nonintervention. Ludwig himself donated significant sums of money to the Greek cause and sent officers from his army to fight in Greece. The London Protocol of 1830 established Greece's independence from the Ottoman Empire and offered the Greek throne to a neutral party that would maintain the European balance of power. Bavarian Prince Leopold von Koburg rejected the title when offered to him. On Thiersch's urging, however, Ludwig accepted the Greek throne for his second son, Otto von Wittelsbach.

Bavarian aspirations in Greece were largely dynastic. Ludwig envisioned his kingdom emerging as a great European power by breaking the confines of a German *Mittelstaat* and expanding through Greece across the Aegean Sea.[104] The massive Bavarian investment in postwar Greece, which threatened to bankrupt the state and forced Ludwig's abdication in 1848, also stemmed from Ludwig's personal infatuation with Hellas as a cultural model for the kingdom on the Isar. Ludwig declared he would not rest "until Munich looks like Athens," and his placement of his son at the heart of Hellenic antiquity was intended to solidify the spiritual union between Bavaria and the ancient Greeks. His official court architect, Leo von Klenze, who designed classical monuments around the Königsplatz in Munich, restored the classical appearance of the Greek capital Athens and halted military use of the Acropolis.[105]

In August 1831 Thiersch himself traveled to Greece on behalf of the publisher Cotta, nominally to build a network of correspondents and to procure art treasures for Ludwig's Glyptothek. Financing the voyage himself through the sale of a ring, he hoped to explore the major cities of Greek antiquity but was quickly embroiled in the political turmoil that ensued following Kapodistrias's execution in 1831. The two-volume work he published upon his return, *The Current State of Greece and the Means to Achieve Its Restoration,* argued that continued Bavarian rule was necessary to reacquaint the Greeks with classical traditions and to sustain the geopolitical significance of Greece as a European outpost bordering the Ottoman Empire. In Thiersch's view, Ottoman rule had Orientalized the modern Greeks. He drew a disturbing portrait of "the state of dejection"[106] in which the moderns languished, suffering from habits of corruption and intrigue. Yet Thiersch claimed to find linguistic evidence that the Greek people had maintained the core of the Hellenic character despite centuries of Turkish domination.[107]

Returning the traditions of classical antiquity to Greece, as they had been preserved by German neohumanists, was for Thiersch the only way to ensure Greece "enter[ed] into the large family of civilized Europe."[108] His report suggested to fellow classicists "the measures to take to restore to Greek soil letters, sciences, and the arts that had their origins there long ago and there attained their perfection."[109] He proposed, for example, creating elementary "Hellenic" schools, neohumanist gymnasia, and an Otto University in Athens based on the German model, as well as a national academy of science. "The sacred land of antiquity," he proclaimed, has been "called once again to be the cradle of a civilization." "Having left the Orient and matured under Hellenic skies and having passed through the nations of the north," classical civilization is "returning in this moment to the banks of the Ilisse, to spread out over the shores of Asia, of Syria, Palestine, and Egypt, who assisted in its birth."[110] For Thiersch Greek learning had originated in the Middle East, flowered in classical Hellas, taken a detour into Germany, from whence it would now return to its cultural starting point. Following the revolution of 1843, which imposed a national constitution on the monarchy, the Bavarians lost all significant political influence within Greece. Two years after Thiersch's death in 1860 Otto and Amalia were driven back to Bavaria after uprisings in several Greek cities. Classicists, however, had shown that like Orientalists working for

The philhellenist Friedrich Thiersch shortly after his second excursion to Greece under the Bavarian King Otto I in 1852.

the Russian Empire in central Asia, their scholarship on antiquity could have imperial implications.

The Problem of Greek Origins: K. O. Müller

Karl Otfried Müller, chair of classical philology at the University of Göttingen, also defended the cultural autonomy of the Hellenes, but he did so by reclaiming their historical specificity within the larger family of Indo-European peoples. Müller's conception of the early Greek past, as well as his understanding of language, reflect the influence of comparative philology. Müller was one of the first to integrate insights from the field into classical studies. He accepted Europe's Asian origins. As a student of August Boeckh, the young Müller once sympathized with the Romantic approach Creuzer took toward mythology. But Müller ultimately defended the autonomy of Greek religion in a way that reflects his moderate liberal nationalism. He preserved the idea of Greek independence, refusing to admit that the Greeks could have succumbed to Egyptian authority in what George Williamson describes as an anticolonial impetus.[111] Müller's accommodation of comparativism and classicism helped diffuse the nagging threat of Oriental studies, while encouraging comparativists to maintain a special regard for the unique forms of the Greek language.

Müller accepted Winckelmann's proposal that Greek art and mythology were local creations, but offered an alternative interpretation of why the Greeks had successfully maintained their cultural independence. In his view, the magnificence of Hellenic culture was not a response to the unique natural surroundings in which artists worked. Rather, it expressed the superiority and strength of the Greek national character. Müller first broached the topic of Greek prehistory in a review of Thiersch's academy lectures but constructed an ever more complex defense of the cultural autonomy of the Hellenes in the wake of the so-called Creuzer affair of the early 1820s. Friedrich Creuzer had used Egypt as an intermediary point of contact when deriving all things Greek from India. Friedrich Schlegel, too, had suggested in 1806 that the kingdom of Egypt was founded as an Indian colony, a line of argument pursued, though not undisputed, through the 1830s.[112] Rather than dismiss comparative-historical philology, as most classicists had done, Karl Otfried Müller made use of the new Indo-European genealogies that excluded Semitic languages and also Egyptian from the family to which Greek speakers belonged. He argued for Greece's autonomy within a model of northern Indo-European descent and evoked new historical narratives to sustain the German-Greek connection.

"On the Presumed Egyptian Origin of Greek Art" (1820) took Friedrich Thiersch to task, countering that Egypt was neither the source of Greek art nor an earlier stage of it, as Winckelmann had believed. Müller's argument that each culture had evolved independently was based on the supposition that visual art was determined "by nationality" and belonged "essentially to the nation [*Volk*]." Scholars, he cautioned, should be wary of assuming that any given tradition was "implanted from abroad" unless they could prove that the nation in question had been conquered, subdued, or "spiritually deadened" by another.[113] In his view, Egyptian art had been caught "forever in an involuntary striving to imitate nature"; their sacred buildings followed the basic form of the mountain. By contrast, "inner laws of order and accordance" had guided Doric architecture, which achieved harmony and stark, majestic beauty.[114] Müller concluded that the strength of the Greek national character and the superiority of Greek artistic forms would have prevented African traditions from taking root on the other side of the Mediterranean despite extensive contact with Egypt.[115] "In every higher spiritual activity," he wrote, "the feeble and cowardly Egyptians lagged far behind the youthful Hellenic *Volk*, just as a noble race always triumphs over the ignoble one."[116]

Central to Müller's argument for Greek cultural autonomy was a distinction among the three main Greek-speaking tribes of antiquity. The Dorians, inhabitants of the southern and eastern Peloponnesian peninsula loyal to the city of Sparta, represented for Müller the true core of Hellenic antiquity. He admired the tribe inordinately, a reflection, Josine Blok has argued, of his Protestant and conservative ideals.[117] This dialect group was honored in antiquity for its discipline, sobriety, and military qualities, and Müller gave the Dorians an unmistakable Prussian flavor: Dorian architecture aspired to "harmony and stark beauty"; the Dorian character opposed "everything immoderate, irregular, erratic."[118] Much different, in his view, were the Ionians who lived on the west coast of Asia minor bordering the Aegean sea and had been subject periodically to Persian rule. This tribe lacked national integrity. Their "restless longing for the outer world and lively interest in everything foreign" was for Müller reflected in lax morality and a luxurious way of life. Ties to Persia had softened and feminized these Greeks so that Ionian architecture displayed less majesty and more grace. Instead of "manly strength" the Ionians idealized "female daintiness," instead of "quiet simplicity, colorful diversity."[119]

Orchomenos and the Minyans (1821), the first volume of Müller's *History and Antiquities of the Doric Race* expanded his crusade against the derivation of Greek culture from the East. The book denounced comparative mythologists such as Creuzer and Josef Görres who turned "their eyes perpetually and only to Egypt, Phoenicia, and the most distant Orient." Müller regarded with suspicion their attempts "to drive the Hellenic as much as possible out of Hellenic ways and tie them via tangled webs of mythical ideas to ancient Indian wisdom or to the turbid and dismal religions of the Near East and Egypt."[120] His argument that these traditions were based "in separate particularities and authentic truths each for itself"[121] focused on the Minyans, who once controlled significant parts of Boetia. from the city of Ochomenos. What Martin Bernal calls the "ancient model" of Greek prehistory stipulated that Greek culture arose after Egyptians and Phoenicians colonized the northern Mediterranean circa 1500 BC. Following the Greek historian Herodotus, nineteenth-century scholars such as August Boeckh held that the Minyans had originally enjoyed close relations with Egypt. Müller sought to debunk this view by questioning those Greek myths that supported the theory of the Egyptian and Phoenician colonization of Boetia.

In volume two of his history titled *The Dorians* (1824), Müller offered an alternative account of Greek origins that omitted all reference to Asia. The Dorians, he maintained, should be considered the heart of the Greek nation; their history and no other provided the best insight into the earliest attestable traces of Hellenic culture. Moreover, the homeland of the Doric tribe, Müller argued, lay in northern Europe in "regions in the North where the Greek nation borders on very diverse and widely diffused barbarian tribes."[122] In his view, the mountain range stretching from Olympus to the Acroceraunian peaks in the West divided the Greeks from the neighboring Illyrians, who spoke a different language and had other customs. It was impossible, Müller believed, to discover from whence Greek speakers had moved into this region; there was not the "faintest glimmer of a tradition" that could tie them to Asia.[123] Historical evidence revealed, however, that the Dorians migrated south around the first millennium BC, conquering ever greater sections of what was to become Greece. The Greek nation thus existed for Müller as far back as philologists could legitimately track its prehistory, and it had greater affinities with northern Europe than Africa and the East. The Doric dialect, for example, appeared to him to have a "northern character," one similar to German.[124]

Müller's account of Greek origins fit easily into Orientalist narratives of westward cultural transmission. Like Jacob Grimm, he solicited comparative-historical philology to assert the autonomy of one group of supposed Indo-European descendents, claiming the Greek nation proper, like the first Germans, emerged as an independent entity after reaching Europe. During the mid-1820s, Müller took a greater interest in language as an indication of nationality and cultural descent, a new focus that is apparent in a second review Müller published criticizing Thiersch in 1826.[125] Here Müller identified language, not religion or art, as the most originary expression of Greek national culture. "As long as you cannot show us an Egyptian or Phoenician Homer," he cautioned the "Oriental party," "from which the Greek Homer learned and borrowed . . . the artistry of his plan, the grace of his narrative, and the sense for beauty in his treatment of language, all of your derivations of Greek culture from the Orient remain unproductive—you see mosquitoes and swallow elephants." Centuries before the Greeks had expressed themselves so eloquently in the visual arts, they had shown their mastery "over the material of language," a "miracle" that cannot be explained, Müller believed, "by any kind of Oriental influences and initiatives."[126]

The reviews of Greek grammars that Müller published in the 1830s reveal an exceptional fluency in comparative-historical philology that reflects his close friendship with the Grimm brothers, who moved to Göttingen in 1829.[127] Himself familiar with Sanskrit, Hebrew, and Arabic, Müller rebuked Greek grammarians for not applying the new philology to classical tongues in an 1836 review of Gottfried Hermann's *Acta Societatis Graecae*. "The original state of most roots, many derivative forms, and almost all inflections [can] only be . . . determined . . . by comparative linguistics," he advised his colleagues.[128] Classical philology had no choice but to honor the new linguistic principles: "Philology [must] either give in completely to a historical understanding of the development of language, of etymological research on the shape of roots and the organism of grammatical forms or trust in comparative linguistics as a guide and advisor in these areas."[129] Müller did not, as Martin Bernal has suggested, express reservations about etymology as a tool for interpreting Greek myths.[130] Rather, he only questioned that type of "speculative etymologizing"[131] that was not based in the new strict rules of linguistic correspondence and change that Franz Bopp and Jacob Grimm identified.

A rapprochement between classicists and comparativists is evidenced in Müller's concluding his review of Hermann with the remark that languages were "the most eloquent witnesses for the spiritual life of nations" when treated comparatively and historically. Religion he now only held to be "the second product of the spirit of these peoples," followed in declining importance by their political life, literature, fine arts, and sciences.[132] "Common to all languages of a family" such as Indo-European, he postulated, was "a primordial image, a feeling . . . for the meaning of the sounds present in the minds of the peoples during the period in which the language developed." But this was less significant than the differences separating the related languages of a family. "The original diversity of the physical and spiritual condition of nations modifies," he explained, "the realization of the language-idea." Ancient Greek may have derived from Sanskrit, but like German it assumed particular forms once it broke away from the primordial mother.[133]

While welcoming Indo-European narratives of descent, Müller continued to assert the normative superiority of Greek culture. The *History of Greek Literature* (1841), which appeared one year after Müller's death from sunstroke at an excavation in Delphi, declared that any "impartial linguist" would recognize the Indo-European language family as the "most accomplished." "In this richness of grammatical forms and in the fine nuances of thought connected with it," he asserted, "[lies] an ability to observe and a capacity for judgment . . . that we take as irrefutable proof of the correctness and delicacy of the ways these people think."[134] This status was confirmed by the great territorial expansion of the family and by its having the most members of any language group. A higher aptitude for culture and for developing language," he concluded, "[was] in prehistory closely tied to greater physical and spiritual energy, in short to all the characteristics upon which finer enrichments and the growth of peoples . . . depend."[135]

Greek stood out against all other Indo-European languages for Müller. It had preserved its grammatical richness from Homer until the emergence of the Attic dialect and did not suffer from the general degeneration of grammatical forms. Sanskrit could take pride in certain consonant combinations lacking in Greek, which, he added, "it was almost impossible for a European mouth . . . to pronounce and mimic." Yet Sanskrit was plagued by the frequent repetition of the short "a" vowel, which "tires our ear to the greatest degree." The use of short vowels in Greek was more pleasing, Müller felt, especially considering how harmoniously they were interspersed with consonants. He considered Egyptian to be related to Semitic languages; its reliance on "external sequences" distanced the tongue "even further form the inner, organic richness of Greek."[136]

What were the implications for Germany? Scattered throughout Müller's work are infrequent but significant references to the affinity between modern Germans and the ancient Greeks. He noted that both nations were composed of different tribes loosely affiliated by language, customs, and physical attributes. Even before the various Greek tribes were united in a state or under a common name, they had existed as a cultural nation, just as, Müller added, the Goths, Saxons, and Franks had done.[137] Their respective languages displayed a northern character and were distinguished among other Indo-European tongues by more autonomous development. In places, Müller also compared the influence Rome had on the Germanic tribes with what the Egyptians had over Greece. In both cases, two peoples of opposing character bordered on each other and cultural exchange between them only ensued in the wake of military conquest. A strong national character was able to develop only as long as the purity of the local culture was maintained. "Did not that part of the Germanic people, which kept itself pure and isolated," Müller asked, "always show the most spiritual versatility and force in the treatment of foreign cultural material?"[138] The European peoples had been strong enough to resist foreign cultural influences. Modern Germans, it followed, should cease searching for a primordial homeland in the East and direct their attention instead to the true cradle of European civilization.

When applying the broader perspective of comparative philology to his field of specialty, K. O. Müller evaded the problem of ultimate origins. No reliable connection linked the Dorians to a primordial Asian homeland, thus the likelihood of Asian descent did not threaten the cultural autonomy of the Greeks. Rather, reference to the Indo-European language family assisted Müller in endowing the Greeks with a distinctly northern cultural heritage. His approach to Greek origins redirected attention away from the eastern Mediterranean, Egypt, and Phoenicia. Müller, to this extent, shared with Indo-Europeanists a troublesome tendency to limit the perceived impact that Semitic peoples had had on European culture.

Greek and Comparative Philology: Georg Curtius and Adolf Deissmann

By the 1840s comparative philology no longer wore on the sensibilities of classicists as it had in decades past. Despite the growing prestige of linguistics, classical philology readily achieved peaceful coexistence with the field. One external observer remarked in 1841 that Orientalism and medievalism threatened to overwhelm a traditional reverence for European antiquity. In a chapter titled "De la Renaissance Orientale," Edgar Quinet spoke favorably of a new humanism in Germany that focused on the revival of Oriental texts.[139] Classical philologists were less apprehensive of this intrusion than they were of other perceived threats to the discipline. What was perceived as the waning cultural authority of neohumanism was a topic of frequent discussion at the annual conferences of classical philologists and secondary schoolmasters that met from 1838 to 1848. Called to order by Friedrich Thiersch, the philological association defended the value of classical studies against new demands for training in practical and natural scientific fields. Comparative philology was more of an ally in this effort than an opponent.

The talk the Bonn classicist Friedrich Gottlieb Welcker prepared for the 1841 conference in his home city (but which was read by Friedrich Ritschl due to Welcker's absence in Greece) is indicative. In the opening to his paper "On the Meaning of Philology," Welcker acknowledged "some anxiety" about the future of philological studies, referring to those "fly-by-night spirits" who declared that classical philology should be incorporated within "general linguistics." He urged his colleagues not to be alarmed by the current "furor" caused by the new field. Even if practiced by a small number of loyal supporters, classical studies would still retain an "inner value" and an "inner life" lacking in profane fields. Oriental studies and Germanics were "our colonies," he suggested, uncharted territories that could still reap a profit for the "motherland."[140] Welcker's preference for classical antiquity drew on two conventional neohumanist arguments: the "eternal exemplariness" of Greek antiquity and its national affinity with Germany. "Particularly our national people," he recalled, "displays through language, through its originally free social arrangements, through patriotic feelings, poetic and speculative talents and through a most ancient religion, an especially close affinity with the Hellenes."[141] Nevertheless, the distinction linguists drew between Semitic and "Aryan peoples" proved useful to Welcker as he debunked "the misconceived derivation of Greek gods from Egypt" in his *Greek Mythology* (1857–63), published when the then blind author was seventy-three.[142]

Three years after Welcker's speech, the association welcomed German Orientalists as a "special section" of the society. The newcomers held separate sessions whose minutes did not form part of the official report. As the statutes of the classicists allowed the conference to expand to include language study as a whole, the Orientalists' 1843 petition to join was accepted. In 1850 August Boeckh, serving as president of the meeting in Berlin, opened the conference by declaring the study of Greek and Latin grammar can "no longer dismiss its ties to comparative grammar and the Indo-Germanic languages." The new principles of linguistics were essential for a full appreciation of classical antiquity. Setting aside the "controversy" over the influence the Levant and especially Egypt had had on early Greece, Boeckh recalled that knowledge of Asia was essential to understanding Greece's later history, especially in light of Persian rule in the Mediterranean. He expressed hope that in the future a "comparative cultural history of all antiquity" would emerge in the spirit of "comparative linguistics."[143]

The first student of classical languages fully to adopt comparative techniques was the Leipzig professor Georg Curtius, younger brother to Ernst Curtius, the well-known archaeologist and historian who accompanied K. O. Müller to Delphi. Born in Lübeck in 1820, Georg Curtius straddled in his training the best of two worlds. As a student in Bonn and Berlin, he worked under Friedrich Wilhelm Ritschl (1806–76), Welcker, Lachmann, and Boeckh. Curtius simultaneously pursued comparative philology with Lassen, A. W. Schlegel, and Franz Bopp. After receiving advanced degrees in the classics, he joined the linguist August Schleicher as a professor of classical philology in Prague, from whence he eventually reunited with Ritschl in Leipzig in 1861. Curtius announced in his inaugural lecture "that I have made it the scholarly mission of my life to set classical philology . . . in vital interaction with general linguistics."[144] And Leipzig was the city in which to do so. In his twenty-five years there Curtius's followers included Friedrich Nietzsche, as well as Hermann Osthoff, Karl Brugmann, and Ferdinand de Saussure. He maintained friendships with the Sanskritists Albrecht Weber, Adalbert Kuhn, and Ernst Windisch, and lived long enough to criticize the controversial practices of the local Neogrammarians.[145]

Curtius's scholarly achievements include examining the classical languages from a comparative perspective, as well as introducing Greek scholars to the methods of general linguistics. His reflections in *The Results of Comparative Philology in Reference to Classical Scholarship* (1845) chided the field for "the prejudice which it bore against its young rival."[146] Many colleagues, he noted, had been "scared from Comparative Philology by the notion that the object of the science is to reduce the magnificent forms of the Greek and Latin languages to some oriental originals, and to exhibit them in the light of mere abortions or mutilated remains of these eastern perfections."[147] In an effort to convert classical philologists into linguists, Curtius drew parallels between old copies of a lost original manuscript and the genealogical tree of Indo-European languages.[148] The Indo-European language family, he admitted, did "dispel the deceitful illusion that in Greece everything had a Greek beginning."[149] Still, comparison and the historical method were necessary to appreciate classical tongues individually and with scientific rigor. Curtius himself developed a theory of the "more intimate union"[150] between Greek and Latin within the larger Indo-European family. He likewise showed how linguistics could clarify the etymology and morphology of Greek, as well as conjugation patterns and laws of sound change.

Comparative philologists excelled for Curtius in a new type of "philosophical grammar." As a strictly historical science, he feared, the field of classics had yet to investigate the first operations of thought as they were manifest in language. Linguists alone realized that the human mind was most gloriously expressed in language.[151] Curtius rejected the attempt his Leipzig predecessor, Gottfried Hermann, had made to identify universal rational structures in grammar. "No longer can one get away with explaining language," he stated, "as the product of clever invention or even consensus or wish to derive linguistic forms from logical categories and schematics."[152] Rather, comparativists advanced "another perspective on the nature of language" that revealed national tongues emerging "from the natural or instinctive life of a people, just like religion, custom, and law." Classicists would remain masters in exploring the "cultural side of language," especially its contributions to literature. But they must learn how linguists tackled the "natural side," documenting how grammatical forms themselves shaped the thought and spirit of a people.[153]

The classicist and comparative philologist Georg Curtius.

Friedrich Nietzsche realized Curtius's expectation that classicists embrace the new philosophical concerns of German language scholars. This student of Curtius combined training in classical philology with linguistics as he developed his epistemological concern for language. Already in 1862, however, Curtius observed that "the importance of comparative linguistics for philology has entered the consciousness of classicists . . . after a long enduring battle with ingrained habits and persistent prejudices."[154] Classical philologists adapted readily to the new view of European prehistory presented by Indo-Europeanists. Their continued idealization of the Hellenes as the paragon of the good, the true, and the beautiful guaranteed a place of honor for ancient Greece within the Indo-European language family. Even comparativists themselves recognized the exemplary status of Greek; their work aimed in part to explain this language more fully.[155]

A comparative-historical approach to New Testament Greek proved more contentious than historicizing the classical Attic dialect. Spoken around the Mediterranean world from the conquests of Alexander to the founding of the Byzantine Empire, Koine, or "common" Greek, differed substantially in its grammar, lexicon, and phonology from its classical predecessor. Although the learned elite attempted to "Atticize" Hellenistic texts, this form of Greek contained clear traces of Egyptian, Persian, and Semitic languages. Classical philologists largely ignored it, believing New Testament Greek less beautiful than the Attic dialect. Theologians likewise neglected to historicize Hellenistic Greek, revering it as a sacred tongue through which the word of God had reached first-century Christians. Both parties balked when the Berlin theologian Adolf Deissmann (1866–1937) attempted to historicize and desacralize New Testament Greek in the 1890s. Archaeological finds of Egyptian papyri and stone inscriptions enabled Deissmann to contextualize the language of scriptures within the everyday language of Hellenistic speakers. He transformed what had once been regarded as an "isolated linguistic phenomenon"[156] into a bone of contention for theologians.

The two volumes of Deissmann's *Bible Studies* (1895–97) criticized both theologians and philologists for their "dogmatism" regarding New Testament Greek. On the one hand, the former had advanced a "doctrine of verbal Inspiration" in which the Holy Spirit merely "used the Apostles as a pen."[157] As an example of this approach Deissmann cited the influential Pietist and supernaturalist Richard Rothe (1799–1867). Born in Posen, Rothe studied theology under Friedrich Schleiermacher, G. W. F. Hegel, and Friedrich Creuzer before in 1823 being appointed chaplain to the Prussian embassy in Rome, where he developed a friendship with Baron von Bunsen. His work *On Dogmatics* (1863) presented a speculative theosophy in which Rothe derived everything in the world from the idea of God.[158] The third section, on Holy Scripture, claimed one could "speak intelligibly of a language of the Holy Ghost." "The divine spirit," Rothe wrote, "created from the language of the people who lived in the place a very peculiar religious language. . . . The Greek of the New Testament demonstrates this fact most clearly."[159] This perspective entered into more formal linguistic studies. The introduction to Hermann Cremer's *Biblio-Theological Lexicon of New Testament Greek* (1866) cited Rothe as a legitimate authority on the language of scripture.[160]

Philologists, on the other hand, had been equally irresponsible in declaring the language of the New Testament to be a special dialect used by Jews who lived among Greek speakers. The ubiquity of Hebraicisms in Hellenistic Greek suggested to Georg Benedikt Winer (1789–1858), for example, and briefly to Julius Wellhausen, that the language was a blend of two tongues, comparable to contemporary Yiddish. A Protestant theologian in Leipzig, Winer in 1821 applied the rationalist approach of his colleague Gottfried Hermann to Hellenistic Greek grammar. His influential *Treatise on the Grammar of New Testament Greek: Regarded as a Sure Basis for New Testament Exegesis* proposed that New Testament Greek was a "mixture of the (later) Greek with the national (Jewish)." Winer proposed to "investigate scientifically the laws according to which the Jewish writers of the N.T. wrote the Greek of their time." He noted the influence of a "foreign tongue (the Hebrew-Aramaean)" and awaited the moment when New Testament Greek could be compared to the Koine of gentiles.[161]

Deissmann did just this, concluding that the real language of the New Testament was a popular, colloquial Egyptian Greek dating to the Ptolomaic kings. In his view, Hellenistic Jews had spoken Greek as their native tongue and only learned Aramaic as a second language; it had not been a dialect comprehensible only to the elite.[162] Deissmann's evidence was the language used by state officials on stone inscriptions and the vernacular descriptions of private life preserved on papyrus documents. Secular Greek from the period of the Septuagint translation of the Old Testament was, Deismann argued, identical to the "sacred" Greek of scripture. The "Semitisms" that distinguished the Greek of the New Testament were common to the vernacular of all Alexandrians. This suggested that earliest Christianity, especially as represented by Paul, had been a movement of the nonliterary classes.

As was the case with Hebrew, the historicization of New Testament Greek opened new perspectives on religious history. Early twentieth-century exegetes used a new appreciation of the language to evaluate, for example, whether the Gospels had been translated from Aramaic; the Semitic expressions that so indicated proved to be present throughout Koine Greek. Analysis of language likewise shed light on whether early Christians, such as Mark and Paul, were bilingual, or whether the Greek written in individual books was schooled or colloquial.[163] The historicization of sacred Greek extended the reevaluation of scripture that biblical philologists initiated in the early modern period. Comparative-historical treatment of New Testament Greek contributed to a drawn-out process by which scripture lost its status as the direct word of God. The messages of the Old and New Testaments appeared constrained by the historical languages used by their authors and compilers.

Biblical philologists and classicists traveled in different intellectual circles. By the end of the nineteenth century, however, theology and classical studies had faced the implications of historicizing Greek along the model of comparative-historical philology. Classicists retained their appreciation of ancient Greece as a cultural and historical ideal, able to subsume comparative philology into their idealization of the Hellenes. The special status of New Testament Greek as a sacred language made comparative-historical philology more disruptive to theologians. Nevertheless, a contingent of classicists and biblical philologists shared with comparative philologists an interest in limiting the perceived influence of Semitic peoples on the ancient Indo-Europeans. K. O. Müller diverted the Greek ancestry to northern Europe, just as scholars of language began questioning how important the ancient Hebrews had been for the history of Christian monotheism.

5

Comparative Linguistics

Race, Religion, and Historical Agency, 1830–80

On September 8, 1854, Arthur Comte de Gobineau wrote a second letter to Germany's foremost comparative philologist, the Halle professor August Friedrich Pott (1802–87). With reverent words he inquired why Pott had ignored his first epistle and had still not endorsed his work. In June the nineteenth century's most notorious racial theorist had sent Pott his *Essay on the Inequality of the Human Races* (1853), asking for an appraisal. Gobineau reported that he held Pott's linguistic achievements in "high esteem." The *Essay,* he confessed, had been "born of roots . . . entirely German." Gobineau believed that there was an "exact correspondence . . . between language and racial type." In his view, comparative philology could provide a "scientific foundation" for his racist history of humanity. He hoped Pott would submit the publication to "the examination and critique of German science." Pott's approval was "precious" to Gobineau because German language scholars claimed the authority to classify human communities and explain their historical development. Linguistics, by this time, had established itself as a field of study in its own right, and Gobineau wanted confirmation for his pernicious racial doctrine. Pott's silence unsettled the French author, who repeatedly solicited his correspondence over the next two years.[1]

Gobineau was not entirely amiss in expecting a rave review. His *Essay* cited Pott's research on the Indo-European family and drew heavily on the writings of Pott's late mentor, Wilhelm von Humboldt. "With regard to the special character of races," Gobineau asserted, "philology confirms all the facts of physiology and history." In his view, linguistic changes occurred "in exact proportion to the successive modification in the people's blood." Grammatical structures were likewise the best measure of the relative "intelligence" and "mental stages" of races. It was a "universal axiom," Gobineau claimed, that "the hierarchy of languages is in strict correspondence with the hierarchy of races."[2]

When Pott did respond, he cautioned Gobineau not be alarmed by what would certainly be "a candid contradiction" of his racial determinism.[3] Pott was so incensed by the causal connections Gobineau drew between language, race, and intellectual ability that he could not confine his objections to the pages of the journal he edited for the German Oriental Society. It took Pott two years to publish a dense monograph titled *The Inequality of the Human Races from the Perspective of Linguistics* (1856), which offered an alternative "survey of the relationships among peoples."[4] The book comprised one of the harshest contemporary responses to Gobineau's treatise.[5] Pott emphatically refuted the conflation of language and race proposed by his adversary. Language, in his view, pointed to clear cultural hierarchies, but these had no material foundation in the body.

Had Gobineau so badly misinterpreted the claims of comparative philology? Was there a precedent for his asserting that the diversity of languages mirrored racial hierarchies and divisions? This chapter investigates the uneasy association of language, race, and religion in the mid-nineteenth century. It identifies the contribution language scholars made to the German invention of race, especially to the formulation of the so-called Aryan myth.[6] The Bonn Indologist Christian Lassen and his mentors, Friedrich and August Wilhelm Schlegel, helped transform Indo-Germans into Aryans. This chapter tracks the progressive association of the term with the physical characteristics of linguistic groups. It likewise follows the expansion of comparative-historical philology to France and England. Ernest Renan (1823–92) and Friedrich Max Müller (1823–1900), both Orientalists and scholars of religion, contributed to the field's growing international reputation at midcentury, while popularizing the racialist distinction German comparativists drew between Aryans and Semites. As Maurice Oldender has shown, discussions of race within nineteenth-century language scholarship closely intersected debates on the early history of Christianity. The distinction between "Aryan" and "Semitic" language families was part of a larger theological effort to minimize the importance of the ancient Hebrews in the emergence of monotheism. This endeavor, however troubling, grew out of an Enlightenment, liberal tradition of applying philology to critique theological orthodoxy.

The attempt to place the respective histories of language, race, and religion within meaningful, interrelated constellations necessarily raised questions of mutual influence and priority. Did the material conditions of the body explain how and why languages evolved and branched out into distinct national tongues? To what extent were grammatical structures responsible for shaping particular perceptions of the divine? At stake were the very mechanisms and limits of linguistic determinism, as well as larger questions of historical agency. What drove language change over time? Was it a preexisting national spirit, a hidden racial essence, the physical qualities of linguistic organs, the willful intervention of speakers, chance historical events, or the laws governing a self-determining linguistic organism? Comparative philologists tended to view the pairing of language and race as a threatening attempt to favor the body over words in the classification of human communities. Starting in the 1850s, turf battles with the emerging field of physical anthropology caused language scholars across Europe to disavow an earlier, overtly racialized conception of the linguistic community. Some urged a new form of linguistic determinism, defending language as a uniquely human trait and reaffirming the extent to which words shaped cultural practices. Others confronted the materialism of their competitors on the latter's terms. August Schleicher (1821–68) and his followers declared the autonomy of "linguistics" as its own natural science, repudiating the humanism and historicist hermeneutics of traditional philology.

The introduction of materialist concerns to comparative philology did not solidify race as an analytical category. Rather, as the case of August Schleicher will show, a natural scientific approach reinforced the perceived autonomy of language vis-à-vis human communities. Schleicher's attempt to derive the diversity of languages from the material conditions of the body actually detached words further from the willful control of speakers. He insisted that the world's tongues were natural organisms that evolved independently of conscious human intervention. This perspective eliminated race and the *Volksgeist* as possible causes of linguistic diversity, but it also begged the question of historical agency. If the soul of a people did not guide the evolution of national tongues, what did? In the 1870s the Leipzig school of Neogrammarians began to formulate exceptionless laws of linguistic change to describe the growth of national tongues. Yet its main representatives were unable to explain why language evolved so regularly despite their situating words in relation to the physiological and psychological mechanisms of the body. Associating language with the material conditions of its production eventually forced a dehistoricization of language. A new interest in the structural and performative aspects of language began to pierce German linguistics in the late nineteenth century, a field that by then had distanced itself from more radically historicizing forms of philology.

From Indo-Germans to Aryans: Christian Lassen

German philologists very early equated linguistic affinity with similarities of biological descent. For Friedrich Schlegel, the presence of shared grammatical structures implied that Persians and most Europeans hailed from India; the diffusion of national tongues indicated migration and the separation of human communities. Disagreement existed only over names and historical narrative. Since the publication of Franz Bopp's study *On the Conjugation System of Sanskrit* (1816), various designations had been applied to this new conglomeration of related peoples and tongues, including Japhetic, Sanskritic, Indo-Celtic, and Indo-Classical. "Indo-European" was an invention of the Englishman Thomas Young, and despite Bopp's approval it never gained currency in German-speaking Europe. Julius Klaproth's term "Indo-Germanic" became the accepted name for the family in 1823, likely because it celebrated the supposed inclination of the western members of the group to expand geographically. *Asia Polyglotta* proclaimed the Indo-Germans to be the "most widely dispersed tribe in the world." And as August Friedrich Pott recounted: "the name seeks to unite the eastern and western ends of the tribe in order to indicate in some measure the geographical expansion of the latter."[7]

Orientalists, moreover, interpreted the branching genealogy of Indo-European languages as evidence for the rapid imperial expansion of the nations that spoke them. Pott believed a propensity for territorial expansion was apparent in the prehistoric migrations of Indo-Germans, as well as in the colonial conquests of modern Europeans. He remarked in 1840 that the westernmost branch of the tribe "now rules over three regions of the world almost in their entirety." Its emissaries had returned to "monstrous and mighty Asia, their own motherland" and successfully expanded into Africa and the Americas. Driving this mobility was thought to be the unique grammatical structures of early Indo-European languages, which were interpreted variously as inflective or compositing. Pott thus speculated that Indo-European dominance was guaranteed "by the exquisite word bestowed upon them, queen over all language families, a wonderful, agile, and adaptive organ, and the true likeness of their very spirit.[8] The unique character of Indo-European verbs supposedly preconditioned speakers' minds for activity, exploration, innovation, and the spread of their culture and traditions. In other languages, the root form of the verb was thought to remain solid and stable, hampering both cultural progress and military conquest.

When introduced to language scholars in 1819, the term "Aryan" grafted these migration narratives onto biblical stories of a chosen people destined to spread the word of God. Friedrich Schlegel evoked the label while trying to reconcile Old Testament notions of divine revelation with the secular history of human origins that J. G. Rhode had constructed from passages in the *Zend-Avesta*. The German word *Arier* was a creation of the 1770s and a translation of Anqueitel Duperron's French term *Ariens*, which he had derived from ancient Indic and Persian sources. The bards in the *Rig Veda*, a collection of sacred Hindu verses, apparently described their gods and themselves with the root form "Aryá." In the founding religious text of the Zoroastrians, the *Zend-Avesta*, the same root is applied to the legendary, primordial homeland of early migrants into Iran and northern India, to these tribes themselves, and to the regions they came to inhabit.[9] Schlegel ventured that Asian Aryans had been witness to God's primordial revelation. The word of God had been imparted in an "Aryan language"[10] that was closely related to Avestan and Sanskrit.[11] The ancient people (*Stammvolk*) chosen to receive it were likewise called "Aryans" and lived in the mountainous heights between Iran and India.[12] This suggested to comparative mythologists that the most ancient roots of Christianity lay in the Aryan past, not in Hebrew antiquity. For Schlegel, the revelation of the Old Testament was a lesser derivative of a primordial faith still manifest in the *Zend-Avesta* and the *Vedas*.

Questionable etymologies enabled Schlegel to attribute particularly close ties between modern Germans and the Aryans of antiquity. "Our German ancestors," he wrote, had been known by the "name of the Aryans" while still in Asia and they had been a "warlike, heroic people." Schlegel interpreted the Sanskrit root *Ari* as meaning "splendid and excellent, famous" and related it to the German word for honor, *Ehre*. The frequency with which it appeared in archaic German names for heroes pointed, in his mind, to the close historical ties between modern German speakers and the privileged witnesses to revelation.[13]

Only after 1830 did the term "Aryan" gain widespread acceptance among philologists. In a footnote to an article published in the *Indische Bibliothek,* the Bonn Indologist Christian Lassen urged scholars to use the label instead of "Indo-Germanic" because it gave a better sense of the shared historical descent and subsequent geographical expansion of the people. Concerned that conventional designations were "unhistorical," the Norwegian-born student of A. W. Schlegel recommended "Aryan" as the "common name" for the family of Indo-European languages, as well as for the people (*Volk*) that spoke them.[14] Lassen likewise prided Germans on their close connections to the homeland. Drawing on instances where the Roman historian Tacitus referred to an ancient Germanic tribe as "Arii," he suggested that even among "the warlike Germans," the term "Aryan" was "not unworthy of its honorable meaning."[15]

During the 1830s the association between language, territorial expansion, and cultural superiority broadened to include a more prominent racial dimension. German studies of Indian prehistory racialized the term Aryan while trying to reconcile the presence of dark-skinned Indians on the subcontinent with notions of Aryan cultural superiority. In an article "On the Origin of the Hindous" (1834), August Wilhelm Schlegel proposed that the Indian "nation" was a compilation of two "distinct races" (*races différentes*). Indigenous Indians had been "black savages"; they were badly armed and lived "in vast primitive forests."[16] Those Indians with ties to Indo-European speakers were members of "the white race"[17] and had introduced the natives to the "first rudiments of civilization."[18] The relocation of the Aryan homeland outside of India enabled this distinction. Schlegel concluded that the "fertile motherland" of the Hindus lay "in the interior of the great continent, in the area around and east of the Caspian Sea." Migrating tribes had entered India through the Punjab region, eventually conquering the basins of the Ganges and mixing with the local population.[19]

Christian Lassen's *Indian Antiquities* (1847) expanded this two-race theory of India with a more detailed study of the "original ethnographic conditions of India."[20] The "sharp contrast in the physical appearance of the two races"[21] derived from the fact that "old inhabitants distinct from the Aryans" once inhabited the continent.[22] These natives had a "very black skin color with curly almost wooly hair and their own non-Sanskrit language."[23] They belonged to what Lassen termed "the black Asian race," a "raw, wild," and "uncivilized stock."[24] Since the Aryan invasions, this "black race" had numbered among the "defeated races," like "the Australian Negroes . . . and the red men of America."[25] Aryan Indians, by contrast, were "a more lightly colored people" with a "physiognomy different from the neighbors." Their "corporal structure and facial expressions"[26] proved them members of the "Caucasian race."[27] According to Lassen, the Aryans represented "the more perfectly organized, entrepreneurial and creative nation." They always proved to be "the dominant, victorious race," successfully driving away the "weaker, yielding" natives.[28]

Lassen defined the cultural and spiritual proclivities of Aryans in relation to speakers of Semitic tongues. In his view, Aryans and Semites were members of the same race; they shared a "a higher capacity for self-reliant cultivation" and had lived in close proximity in antiquity. Yet Lassen insisted that language revealed an "original spiritual gift" that Aryans only shared with other members of the language family. A "genius instilled at creation"[29] had endowed them with "higher provisions from which sprouted everything great they accomplished." This meant for Lassen that Aryans had "surpassed all others" in the discovery of the practical arts, in instituting laws, civil society, and the state, and in perfecting the fine arts and sciences.[30] "In their ceaseless activity," he concluded, the Aryans "envelop the external world and the realm of the spirit; their aspiration is to dominate the entire globe."[31]

Lassen's *Indian Antiquities* also characterized speakers of Semitic tongues based on a set of deficiencies later echoed by Ernest Renan. According to Lassen, subjectivity was the essential Semitic trait. It rendered Semitic speakers incapable of philosophy or epic poetry and drew them toward monotheism. Lassen claimed the Hebrew religion to be "selfish and exclusive," denying "every other god a moment of truth." Semitic religious practices were also "intolerant," tending toward "fanaticism, as to a rigid devotion to religious law." The Hebrews had been unable to spread their religion to other peoples because they lacked the "tolerance . . . and freedom of thought" characteristic of the mobile Aryans.[32]

In the first half of the nineteenth century, German philologists did not equate the consolidation of national unity with the recovery of the racial purity thought to have existed in a primordial Aryan homeland. Neither Christian Lassen nor the Schlegel brothers directly contrasted the "tarnished" identity of Indian Aryans who had mixed with a darker native people with a Germanic ideal of racial integrity. The differences separating Aryans and Semites were cultural not racial, and subsequent philologists would be more concerned about the families' respective contributions to the history of religious thought than with their bodies. Nevertheless, already by the mid-1840s several major components of "Aryan theory" as it was adopted by later racial theorists, including Joseph Arthur Comte de Gobineau, had been articulated. Aryans were a territorially expansive white race who were competing with Semites for world hegemony. Modern Germans represented the westernmost branch of the family, and language suggested that they had maintained particularly close ties to the primordial ancestors in Asia.

The "Linguistic Physiology" of August Friedrich Pott

Lassen's racialization of the Aryan language family raised the possibility that words had a material foundation in the body. Could the diversity of national tongues be explained by physical differences in the linguistic organs of speakers? Such considerations were inimical to German idealism but had a long history in the language sciences. Since antiquity, speech had been studied in relation to the body. Aristotle located the production of all animal voices in the lungs and windpipe and sought to explain why human tongues alone could articulate words. Epicurus of Samos (341–270 BC) considered the problem of linguistic diversity, suggesting that the exhalation of voice took a different form based on the *ethnos* of speakers.[33] In the early modern period, behaviorist models of linguistic performance likewise explained speech pathologies such as stuttering or aphasia. The literature of medicine and natural philosophy attributed phonetic disturbances to the movement of the larynx and speech organs.[34]

The mind-body dichotomy proposed by René Descartes relegated the corporal aspects of language to a trivialized subfield of mechanics. He was concerned with providing a physical account of mental operations and their connections with the body.[35] Yet, for Descartes, the unique status of human beings depended on the separation of language from the natural order. In the fifth *Discourse on Methods* (1637), he proclaimed speech to be the sole feature distinguishing humans from automata. A mechanical monkey would be identical to its real counterpart, but a true human would stand out through the ability to declare his or her thoughts to others and to act based on reasoned reflections. Language was both the symptom and the criterion of having a soul and a rational mind. To locate the language faculty in the body would for Descartes have denied its divine origins and threatened the distinction between human and animal.

Favoring the body over the soul, eighteenth-century theorists investigated the physiological mechanisms that produced the spoken word. Materialists, such as Charles de Brosse in his *Treatise on the Mechanical Formation of Language* (1765), encouraged physical explanations of disordered verbal behavior. The physician Denis Dodart and other French anatomists studied the organs that gave voice to language, comparing the human body to a musical instrument. By the 1740s, experiments conducted on human and animal larynxes had clarified the mechanisms of voice production. French doctors linked impaired speech and language deficits to anatomical defects. Physiologists did not converse with grammarians, however. French philologists presumed the source of linguistic diversity lay in the passions or characters of nations, not in the otherwise universal operations of the body.[36] Climate and environment were the only factors thought to influence linguistic difference. Warm temperatures loosened the mouth, producing soft vowels; the cold made for terse tongues and heavy consonants.[37]

In the early nineteenth century, differences in body type were thus not held responsible for Babel. Each language was thought to embody its own underlying idea, which gradually came to full self-realization in the material world. Toward midcentury, comparativists nevertheless faced a methodological quandary over how to relate language, cultural development, and the physical bodies of speakers. Comparativists such as August Friedrich Pott were unsettled by the "contradictions and uncertainties"[38] that surrounded the concept of race. Pott considered himself a strict "ethnographer and linguist" and established what he believed to be a secure foundation for systematically relating the physical and spiritual life of a nation.[39] Like many of his contemporaries, though, Pott eventually retreated from the type of materialist determinism that the racial classification of human communities entailed. His attempt to negotiate the intersection of words and bodies ultimately ran afoul of his liberal political views, and Pott lashed out against all who overtly conflated language and race.

As a student of Franz Bopp, Pott helped define the first generation of self-professed German linguists, Orientalists who institutionally and intellectually distanced themselves from textual philologists and theologians. "General linguistics" (*allgemeine Sprachwissenschaft*), Pott argued in 1849, must "distinguish itself from its sister, philology." The field's particular mission was to investigate the "nature and origin of language generally as a characteristic of man from both the physical and psychological perspective." Based on the results, linguists should "group together or separate humanity into . . . orders of relation based on race, nation [*Volk*], and language."[40] Pott, in other words, set on scientific footing the genealogical project of ordering languages and nations. Perceiving the biblical account of national genealogies to be a threat still worthy of response in 1863, he lashed out against the notion that the Mosaic tables contained divine inspiration. Theologians such as Franz Kaulen who speculated on the language that Adam and Eve spoke in paradise were guilty of "unauthorized involvement in matters that are ours."[41] Moses was no linguist, according to Pott, and any vision of the past based on scripture must appear "strangely displaced and distorted."[42]

Born into a family of Lutheran clerics in the Kingdom of Hannover, Pott lost his father at age nine and later received a stipend to pursue theological studies in Göttingen. He turned to philology after taking lectures in classical languages from G. L. Dissen and K. O. Müller and absorbing the legacy of Michaelis's biblical criticism. Franz Bopp oversaw the completion of his training and, along with Wilhelm von Humboldt, helped him obtain a chair, which Pott himself termed General Linguistics at the University of Halle. Here Pott had ties to the Young Hegelians, especially to Arnold Ruge. He contributed to Ruge's *Hallesche Jahrbücher für deutsche Wissenschaft und Kunst*, which Marx continued as the *Deustch-Französische Jahrbücher* in Paris.[43] In the polarized atmosphere of the University of Halle, where

The comparative philologist August Friedrich Pott.

theological orthodoxy battled its rationalist detractors, Pott suffered a reputation as antitheological, rationalist, and democratic.

The introduction to Pott's most influential work, *Etymological Studies of Indo-Germanic Languages* (1833) outlined a comparative method that took into consideration the bodies of speakers. The book expanded Bopp's *Comparative Grammar*, adding a lexical component to his analysis of verb roots. As Grimm had done for the Germanic tongues, Pott examined similarities in the morphological structures of five Indo-European languages, establishing their affinity through shared sound changes. Phonetics was the key to etymology for Pott. He contributed to the establishment of fixed laws of phonetic change and developed the first comparative phonetic tables, setting an example for later Neogrammarians.[44]

Pott termed his comparative method "linguistic physiology" (*Sprachphysiologie*) to emphasize that language was "dependent on [man] . . . as a spiritual and corporal being of nature."[45] In his view, national tongues differed in part due to "the physical language apparatus of man."[46] This required that comparative philology be subdivided into three areas of study: the philosophical, the physical, and the historical. "What else," Pott asked, "except the study of language, craniums, and customs [*Sprachen-, Schädel-, und Sittenstudium*] will ever disentangle the web of nations that entwines the globe?"[47] According to his scheme, philologists should first dissect the "anatomy" of language as if it were an "organic natural object."[48] Pott sorted languages by their "genus" and "species," measuring formal similarities in grammar and phonology to elucidate the "structure and linguistic character" of each.[49] Secondly, the philologist needed familiarity with the "physical habitat" of a language's speakers and their bodies. Finally, Pott suggested, national groups should also be viewed in light of political, religious, and legal history, as language "retained in its faithful memory the timbre and many tones of their collective fate."[50]

Indo-European speakers, in his view, constituted a community of shared parentage. "Across Orient and Occident," he wrote in 1833, "from the breasts of Bengal to the Atlantic Ocean, there extends one, rarely broken chain of kindred peoples."[51] According to Pott, speakers of Indo-European tongues had left a primordial Asian homeland, which had also been cradle to the "first corporal and spiritual powers of humanity": "Ex oriente lux! . . . the flow of culture has for the most always followed the sun. The nations of Europe once lay on Asia's breasts, and she, the mother, embraced them as children."[52] Pott himself restricted the term "Aryan" to only one of the five recognized branches of the Indo-European language family, the Medo-Persian tongues.[53] He likewise insisted on the disparate origins of Semitic and Indo-European peoples. Yet Pott was the first comparativist to include the Sinti and Roma within the family of Indo-European speakers. The "gypsies" actually have a much closer connection to India than the descendents of the Goths, having left the Punjab region at the end of the first millennium AD. In 1844 Pott defended Romany's status as a "real national language," denying that it was "thieves' Latin" used as a secret idiom for organizing swindles and robbery. In his view, the language descended from "the already degenerate forms of popular Indian dialects."[54] Despite its "exceeding bastardization and depravity," it could take pride in "having blood relations with splendid Sanskrit."[55]

For many comparativists the decision of whether to apply the term "Aryan" to the entire family of Indo-European languages or merely to the Iranian branch hinged on the frequency with which derivatives of the root "arya" appeared in related languages. The Genevan scholar Adolphe Pictet, for example, derived the name Ireland from "arya" and embraced the broader designation in *The Origins of the Indo-Europeans or the Primitive Aryans* (1859). August Schleicher and K. J. Windischmann likewise cited Tacitus's references to the Germanic tribe *Arii* to justify calling the entire family "Aryan," while Friedrich Rückert's student Paul Lagarde preferred the restricted meaning.[56] German comparativists directed their attention almost exclusively to the "superior" languages of the Indo-European family. They rarely found it worthwhile to draw Semitic languages into the comparison or to examine other language families in detail. By 1890 German linguistics had virtually ceased to use the term Aryan except to refer to Indo-Iranian tongues. This restriction was a defensive measure to protect the language sciences from new fields such as anthropology, comparative law, and religion, as well as racial theory, which had appropriated the term from philologists and expanded its applicability beyond words and grammar.[57]

By the 1840s actual physiologists had located the general faculty of language in specialized lobes of the brain. Based on the placement of lesions in patients who experienced loss of speech, phrenologists outlined the anatomy of the central nervous system in its supposed relation to the production of language and intelligence.[58] German anatomists suggested that such findings aided the classification of tongues. The anatomist and early anthropologist Adolf Bastian asserted that languages differed according to the "physiological racial type" of speakers. The "racial formation of the vocal tools" determined how sounds for given objects were produced.[59] In 1851 the zoologist Carl Vogt suggested that the shape of the cranium was responsible for linguistic diversity. In his view, highly developed "frontal hemisphere lobes" produced languages "rich in expressions for abstract concepts," the opposite encouraged "a material wealth in sounds, roots, and grammatical movement." People with receding foreheads and jaws that jutted out thus lacked the faculty for abstract reasoning. Karl Penka later claimed to have located the source of Indo-European inflection in the shape of speakers' skulls. Physical differences among conquered tribes explained for him the diffusion of an original Aryan *Ursprache;* a physical cause lay behind the Germanic sound shifts.[60] In 1876 the Austrian linguist Friedrich Müller derived the world's language families from three different hair types, wooly, straight, and curled.[61]

Pott's linguistic physiology had no room for such considerations. The limits of his flirtation with materialism were already apparent in 1833. Pott assumed language embodied the subjective character of its speakers. Words were not inert products of the body. Rather, each national tongue possessed its own "spirit" (*Sprachgeist*). This Pott compared to a "heavenly flame that lives and flutters in the letter."[62] His ambitions were just as much philosophical as they were ethnographic. According to Pott, "if you wish to get to know humanity and its reason, then learn the languages of humanity."[63]

In his review of Gobineau, Pott defended in rather tortured prose his liberal and idealist principles. *The Inequality of the Human Races* apparently aroused Richard Wagner's interest in racial doctrine, yet Pott denounced Gobineau's "chemistry of nations" in no uncertain terms. Pott's argument against racial determinism built on a traditional humanist faith in the perfectibility of man as a rational, free being. Gobineau had falsely equated humans with the "sedate matter . . . of the chemist," which was "eternally condemned to follow set and unchanging laws." Gobineau's vision of "insurmountable racial necessity as set by nature" contradicted Pott's confidence in the individual as a "free personality capable of self-determination." For Pott, the fate of nations was not predetermined by "ethnic gifts presented in the cradle."[64] Man had the ability to make of himself what he willed, a conviction related to Pott's liberal politics. He reproached Gobineau for being "no democrat," insisting that the ideal state was not pregiven, but "a creation of freedom and human self-determination."[65] Gobineau's second sin was to deny clear evidence of human progress through history. Pott objected to the notion that racial mixing necessarily resulted in "degeneration and inescapable social corruption."[66] Nations that Gobineau condemned to "moral and intellectual degeneration" were for Pott nothing less than "underdeveloped children" who could still redeem themselves.[67]

Language study, in Pott's view, presented a more precise method for classifying human communities because it highlighted the "spiritual dividing lines" between nations.[68] Language, not race, was "the truly characteristic and tangible lineament that distinguishes nations, to some extent almost the only one."[69] It was, moreover, the "barometer of intellectual development." Pott hesitated to equate the structure of a language with the cultural achievements of its speakers; the "instrumental value" of a language did not exactly parallel the "level of a people's culture." He conceded, for example, that Africa was "irrefutably of all corners of the world the most unwieldy, a truly unarticulated and dismembered stump." But Pott recalled that not a single one-syllable language had been found there, as had been found in China and India.[70] Along with the Hebraicist Heinrich Ewald, he was one of the first comparativists to study Bantu languages,[71] and much of Pott's critique drew on African and Native American examples.[72]

Comparativists, such as Pott, who correlated national tongues, mental ability, and the physical body, tended to prioritize language as exerting the most powerful influence on cultural production and the worldview of speakers. Nevertheless, Pott did subscribe in muted form to an ideal of racial, national, and linguistic unity. Racial theory was not off-limits to progressive liberals.[73] Many midcentury philologists instead redefined race to accommodate a form of linguistic, rather than biological, determinism. Racialist discourse thoroughly permeated research on the Indo-European and Semitic language families, as the cases of Friedrich Max Müller and Ernst Renan indicate, even if most comparativists rejected a reduction of linguistic diversity to biology.

Phonology vs. Ethnology: Friedrich Max Müller

The growing tension between philology and ethnology is exemplified in the work of Friedrich Max Müller, a prolific Orientalist who introduced German notions of Aryan antiquity to Britain. While hardly the first representative of the field abroad, Max Müller solidified the fame and interdisciplinary appeal of comparative philology outside the German states. Few did more than Max Müller to popularize the image of an "Aryan race" or more than Ernest Renan to stigmatize so-called Semites. Race entered their linguistic work in the context of an admittedly liberal approach to the comparative history of religion and mythology. Philologists since the Enlightenment had drawn upon linguistic and historical evidence to challenge biblical orthodoxy. Like other mythographers Max Müller expected his research on the Aryan past to reconfigure Christian religious narratives without relying on the Bible and thereby to renew contemporary religious consciousness.[74] His and Renan's attempts to "Aryanize" the origins of Christianity drew on a quasi-racial form of linguistic determinism in which grammatical structures shaped culturally specific perceptions of the divine.

Comparative-historical philology arrived in Britain well before Max Müller. And as in Germany, the field spawned the related disciplines of ethnology and prehistory. In the 1810s James Cowles Prichard (1786–1848), a doctor in Bristol, learned German and introduced himself to comparative methods. A newly converted Anglican of Quaker descent, Prichard used philology to both defend monogenicism and illuminate the cultural origins of contemporary Britons. His *Researches into the Physical History of Man* (1813) advanced the controversial thesis that Sanskrit had descended from Hebrew. Celtic, in his view, was a missing link between the two language families.[75] Prichard's *Eastern Origins of the Celtic Nations* (1831) likewise traced the Celtic ancestry to an Asian homeland. The author sought to free the Irish from the contempt in which the Celts were held by proving that the Saxons had been less civilized than the Indo-European ancestors of the Irish themselves.[76]

In 1843 Prichard introduced British audiences to the German term "ethnology," presenting a field aimed at tracing the historical roots of linguistic communities. His presentation to the British Association for the Advancement of Science explained how "ethnological philology" used language to classify the world's peoples.[77] For Prichard the study of physical features was subordinate to the dictates of phonology and grammar. Bodily features and structures were studied but remained subsidiary to linguistic concerns.[78] This approach to human communities was paradigmatic of British ethnology in the first half of the century and lent authority to comparative philologists who proclaimed language the quintessential human trait.[79]

Despite the precedent of William Jones, neither comparative philology nor Oriental studies made significant inroads in early nineteenth-century Britain. The politics of deriving national ancestry from a south Asian homeland were far more risky across the channel than in the German states, given the reality of British imperialism. Not until 1832 did a British university create a chair in Oriental languages. The newly founded University of London hired Friedrich August Rosen, who had studied under Franz Bopp in Berlin. Even then the position was the result of a private endowment and intended to promote the translation of the Bible into Sanskrit. Similarly, the type of historical research that culminated in the Oxford English Dictionary lagged behind in Britain. Not until the 1830s did two Old-English scholars, Benjamin Thorpe (1782–1870) and John Mitchell Kemble (1807–57), who had studied abroad with Rasmus Rask and Jacob Grimm, approach Anglo-Saxon historically.[80]

A German émigré, not surprisingly, introduced British audiences to the term "Aryan" and popularized narratives of shared Asian descent. Born in Dessau, Friedrich Max Müller studied philology with Gottfried Hermann in Leipzig and with Bopp and Friedrich Rückert in Berlin before moving to England in 1846 to secure funding and prepare an edition of the *Rig Veda*. Through Baron Christian von Bunsen, Prussian minister at Victoria's court and a proficient Egyptologist in his own right, Max Müller acquired a professorship of modern languages at Oxford in 1851 and eventually received the first British chair in comparative philology in 1868. From 1861 to 1863 he entertained a captivated London public with his brilliantly delivered Lectures on the Science of Language. At the Royal Institution Max Müller spoke to full halls on topics ranging from the supposed Aryan and Turanian language families to comparative mythology and Kantian philosophy.

Max Müller shared similar expectations with Bunsen regarding the contributions comparative philology could make to ethnology and the history of religion. In a terse exchange that started their friendship, Ernest Renan accused Max Müller of pilfering Bunsen's unreliable term "Turanian" to refer to tongues not included in either the Indo-European or Semitic families. Max Müller, like Bunsen, assumed that language and religion offered the clearest evidence of humanity's earliest state of consciousness. Philology could also unlock the sacred books of the world's religions and reveal parallels in the development of language and thought. Bunsen's *Outlines of the Philosophy of Universal History Applied to Language and Religion* (1854) argued for Christianity's continuity with the ancient religions of India and Egypt. Max Müller pursued a similar argument in relation to the Vedas, seeking in the sacred texts clues to every aspect of Aryan antiquity.[81]

As the oldest book of humanity, the *Rig Veda*, according to Max Müller, provided a rare glimpse of the "primitive and undivided family of the Aryan nations."[82] He found evidence in the epic of a racial kinship linking Britons and Aryans in Asia. At a special session of the British Association for the Advancement of Science, Max Müller for this reason criticized British scholars who denied Sanskrit's influence on modern Bengali.[83] This ignorance wrongly separated Britain's colonial subjects from a glorious Aryan past and obscured for Max Müller "the ethnographic and linguistic relations" of contemporary Indians.[84] Following Christian Lassen, Max Müller presented a "two-race" theory of Indian civilization.[85] Scholars were wrong who assumed all Indians belonged "one great branch of the Caucasian race."[86] Language proved otherwise. Modern Indian dialects were divided into "two great classes." The northern languages had "strong claims to an Indo-Germanic origin," while those in the south were "more closely connected with the language of aboriginal and non-Brahminical inhabitants of India."[87] The Vedas "put it beyond all doubt" that the former could be traced to a "Brahmanical people . . . of Arian origin" who had immigrated into India from Iran.[88] This people had "crushed and extinguished" the "savage and despised" masses of aboriginal inhabitants, who fled to the forests and mountains or were enslaved.[89]

On the one hand, this narrative suggested to Max Müller continuity between British colonizers and the Aryan conquerors of antiquity. He depicted the "English armies" who were occupied in subduing hostile Indian groups as "descendents of the same race, to which the first conquerors and masters of India belonged." The British had "return[ed] . . . to their primordial soil, to accomplish the glorious work of civilization, which had been left unfinished by their Arian brethren."[90] On the other hand, Max Müller concluded that language proved the racial identity of Englishmen and elite Indians. "No authority" besides comparative philology, he wrote in 1854, could "convince the English soldier that the same blood was running in his veins, as in the veins of the dark Bengalese. . . . And yet there is not an English jury now-a-days, which, after examining the hoary documents of language, would reject the claim of a common descent and a legitimate relationship between Hindu, Greek and Teuton."[91] As the biographer Nirad Chaudhuri has noted, Max Müller's notion of a common Aryan family fanned Hindu nationalism and the self-conscious Aryanism of Indians who demanded greater self-determination based on their presumed affinity with Europeans.[92] His later disavowal of language as an indication of racial affinity likely stemmed from the discomfort this vision of kinship presented to the British.

Friedrich Max Müller spent the remainder of his career disentangling this conflation of words and bodies. He retained the term "race" as a general designation for Aryans and other linguistic communities, but distinguished "ethnological race" from "phonological race." In his *Letter to Chevalier Bunsen on the Classification of the Turanian Languages* (1853), Max Müller proposed that the relationship between ethnology and philology should be no more than "mutual advise and suggestion." Bunsen had earlier proposed classifying all of mankind according to language. Max Müller countered that the two fields were "not commensurate," and no compromise should obscure the "glaring contradictions" between them. The student of physiology, he wrote, should pursue his own science, "unconcerned about language": "Let him see how far the skulls, or the hair, or the colour, or the skin of different tribes admit of classification; but to the sound of their words his ear should be as deaf as that of the ornithologist's to the notes of caged birds." This rebuttal established if not "a complete divorce, at least . . . a judicial separation between the study of Philology and the study of Ethnology."[93] As Thomas Trautmann has noted, Max Müller on occasion violated his own principles, searching, for example, for historic traces of Aryan noses in Sanskrit texts.[94] But the Indologist continually stressed the impossibility of speaking of "an Aryan race, of Aryan blood, or Aryan skulls, and to attempt ethnological classification on purely linguistic grounds."[95]

The emergence in Britain of a physical anthropological approach to race undercut the priority Prichard and Max Müller once claimed for language as an indication of genealogical descent. Starting in the 1850s comparative philology began recanting its authority to pass judgment on race as a physical category, deferring to natural scientists who measured skulls and skin pigments. Speaking to British anthropologists, Max Müller, for example, denied that the three main skull types (dolichocephalic, orthognathic, and euthycomic) could ever correspond to his scheme of Aryan, Semitic, and Turanian tongues. "Who, then would dare at present to lift up a skull and say that this skull must have spoken an Aryan language," he asked, "or lift up a language and say this language must have been spoken by a dolichocephalic skull?" This reluctance resulted from the realization that language study could never take the researcher back to the origins of human beings as a distinct biological species. As George Stocking has noted, the discovery of skeletal remains vastly expanded the short biblical chronology for human history. Racial differences were assumed to have emerged over vastly longer time periods, far earlier than the first appearance of Indo-European languages.[96]

After midcentury, Max Müller and other Orientalists focused their efforts instead on reconstructing the cultural life of the first Aryans before their departure from an Asian homeland. The German scholar Adalbert Kuhn, a friend of Max Müller's from Berlin, announced this intention in 1855. As Jacob Grimm did in the *History of the German Language* (1848), Kuhn assumed that words found in two or more related languages "extend beyond the history of only one of the family's nations and must illuminate the history of the *Urvolk*."[97] In 1859 Adolphe Pictet coined the term "linguistic paleontology" to describe the historical research of philologists. Like Max Müller, these authors agreed that the original Indo-Europeans had inhabited a temperate climate with mountains and waterways. They also concurred on the supposedly high level Indo-Germanic culture. The *Urvolk* had presided over a highly structured system of family, state, and regional organization; it had developed agriculture and possessed almost all domesticated animals; and the earliest Indo-Europeans knew how to mine and work the most important metals.[98]

Max Müller's contribution to this research was to explain how the structures of Indo-European languages shaped thought and religious beliefs. Philology, in his view, could distill continuities in the thought patterns of linguistic groups. "There is no Aryan race in blood," he announced in *Biographies of Words and the Home of the Aryas* (1887), but whoever has received "the Aryan blessing" belongs to that "unbroken spiritual succession" that united "the first apostles of that noble speech" with "the present day."[99] Max Müller took the cultural continuity language provided quite literally, suggesting in the foreword to his English translation of *The Critique of Pure Reason* (1881): "While in the Veda we may study the childhood, we may study in Kant's critique the perfect manhood of the aryan mind."[100] Having studied Kantian philosophy at the University of Leipzig, Max Müller envisioned himself extending Hamann's, Herder's, and Humboldt's attempts to integrate language into a theory of the mind.[101] His *Science of Thought* (1887) thus proposed that there was "No Reason without Language, No Language without Reason." Meaning and articulate sound were, for Max Müller, "two sides" of an indivisible entity such as a coin or an orange and its peel.[102]

Philologists, by implication, could deduce from historical tongues how the speakers of each had reasoned at a given moment in time. Language offered Max Müller an "archives" or "annals" in which the "historical development of the human mind" was preserved.[103] Thus, he hoped to interpret Indian mythology by reducing "every thought that crossed the Indian mind" to the "offspring" of some 120 "mother-ideas," simple concepts or root forms.[104] According to Max Müller, the original roots of human speech had neither been imitations of natural sounds (the "bow-wow" theory) nor involuntary interjections (the "pooh-pooh" theory). Rather, they reflected "inward mental phases."[105] The *Biographies of Words* purportedly identified the basic 800 roots of Sanskrit, just as Ernest Renan isolated 500 original roots in Hebrew.

Transferring linguistic categories to religion was justified, according to Max Müller, by the historical role words and metaphors had played in the emergence of belief. One of the first comparative mythologists, he assumed that humans had been driven by their natural perception of the infinite in the historical world to name and give voice to the divine. The growth of words and concepts documented a dialectical struggle on the part of the mind to transcend the materiality of linguistic expression. As a result, the primary elements of religion were for Max Müller not rituals, customs, or sacrifices, but words and texts whose true meaning only etymology could divulge. In his view, for example, the tripartite division of languages warranted a parallel classification of religious practices. Semitic speakers supposedly presented God in history; Aryans saw the divine in nature; and the ambiguous Turanian family worshiped natural and ancestral spirits.[106]

Mythology, the first stage of religion, was in Max Müller's famous formulation a "disease of language."[107] The original meaning of roots had been material, in his view, derived from the impressions speakers had of their surroundings. But names had a tenuous relationship to the objects they represented. Each designated an object based on a sensible attribute; these could be numerous and imprecise. The original bond between a word and its object was also quickly forgotten, as metaphors expanded this primitive, sensual vocabulary. According to Max Müller, myths and stories of divine personalities emerged from misinterpretations of a word's original meaning. Phonetic decay and the invention of false etymologies likewise blurred the history of signs.[108] Max Müller believed that terms for the sun and other solar phenomena were the sources of Aryan mythology. Both he and Renan took from Eugène Burnouf the notion that names (*nomina*) became divine powers (*numina*). The idols and various divinities of all heathen religions emerged from the multiplicity of names used in liturgy.

Philology peeled back the layers of confusion surrounding the origin of religious thought, according to Max Müller, and indicated that the Aryans of Vedic India had experienced an original form of monotheism. Christianity, in Max Müller's view, was the culmination of all religion, the first faith to give voice to the idea of the true God. Its roots, however, extended further back than Hebrew antiquity. Contradicting Ernest Renan, Max Müller denied that the "Semitic instinct" had given birth to monotheism. In his view, both Aryans and Semites had experienced a "primitive intuition of God" that could only have resulted from an original divine revelation.[109] The expression of this feeling merely differed according to the peculiarities of national tongues. Aryans tended toward polytheism because they were "less fettered" in their linguistic expression; the roots of their first language referred to activities rather than sedate states. Semitic speakers called on God in "adjectives only" or in words that conveyed a predicative meaning. They thus had the benefit of a language that expressed the "abstract qualities of the deity."[110]

This linguistic sleight of hand enabled Max Müller to undermine the ancient Hebrews in the one area they threatened to surpass the Aryans: the invention of monotheism. "Our forefathers," he reported, discovered "the wisdom of Him who is not the God of the Jews."[111] Religion and civilization had spread westward from India, and, according to Max Müller, the imperialistic Aryans still had a mission to link all parts of the world with their cultural practices. Grammatical structures destined the Aryans to be the "prominent actors in the great drama of history." The "Aryan nations," Max Müller concluded, were assured victory in the "struggle . . . with the Semitic and Turanian races."[112] His linguistic determinism closely resembled a racialist view of world history, even if it celebrated words and conjugation patterns rather than the Aryan body.

By the late 1860s German anthropologists had all but rendered comparative philology irrelevant in discussions of the Aryan race. As Andrew Zimmerman has argued, nearly all the practices of anthropology, centered as they were on the collecting, measuring, and display of objects, originated in a distrust of language and narrative.[113] The head of the Berlin Anthropological Society, Rudolf Virchow, specifically rejected linguistic genealogies as an indication of whether Europeans were of Aryan descent in "The Overpopulation of Europe" (1874). Virchow credited Friedrich Max Müller with having divided the continent's inhabitants into Aryans, Semites, and Turanians. But he feared only archaeology and the study of pigment and craniums could prevent "the decision about the ethnological standing of a people" from being "surrendered to the hands of language scholars." Virchow confined philologists to making judgments about the political alliances of human communities and their historical fate. In his view, language revealed nothing about "blood relations"; it merely "nationalizes and de-nationalizes." To evaluate whether Europeans were of Aryan descent, anthropologists had to consider the physiological ideal of the race. In the mid-1870s Virchow thus solicited the help of schoolteachers in gathering the physical data necessary to classify the inhabitants of imperial Germany but neglected considerations of language.[114]

As the definition of the Aryan physical type fell to anthropologists, Indians were excluded from the family, limiting the term's applicability to a small, original white population.[115] The Aryan homeland likewise moved further westward to northern Germany itself. The prospect that Europeans had racial ties to Indian Aryans forced a reversal of the biblical migration narratives that once traced the German ancestry back to an Asian Garden of Eden. The British ethnologist Robert Latham was the first to argue that Sanskrit speakers originated on the southeastern border of Lithuania in the Baltic regions. His *Elements of Comparative Philology* (1862) denied any substantial ties between Sanskrit and the modern languages of India. It was far more likely, in his view, that one language had traveled east, than that a larger assembly had departed India.[116] This perspective seemed to be confirmed by the discovery of ancient skeletal remains, such as the bones of Neanderthal man found in a limestone cave in Rhenish Prussia in 1857 and those discovered in Brixham Cave in 1858.

A debate then ensued over whether the Aryans had originated in Asia or Europe. Several linguists supported the idea of an Asian homeland based on the supposed affinities between the Semitic and Indo-European language families.[117] In 1873 the Orientalist Friedrich Delitzsch reported that only he himself, Pott, and August Schleicher denied the possibility of an *Urverwandtschaft.* Others, including Lassen, Renan, Burnouf, and Pictet, accepted the possibility of an early connection.[118] The Europeanist camp mustered linguistic, anthropological, and archaeological evidence to elevate Proto-Germans into the exalted position once held by ancient Indians. In 1868 Theodor Benfey placed the Aryan *Urheimat* just north of the Black Sea, between the Caspian Sea and the mouth of the Danube. This was justified, in his view, by the fact that there were no Proto-Indo-European words for lions, tigers, or camels.[119] Lazar Geiger claimed in 1869 that only middle and western Germany had the tree vegetation necessary to explain lexical similarities in Indo-European languages. The beech tree, whose name supposedly remained constant throughout the family, had not yet reached Holland at the start of the Christian period, but could be found in the Baltic provinces of Prussia.[120] Similarly, J. G. Cuno assumed the Indo-Europeans had originated where most of their current members now lived. Only northern Germany and eastern Europe could have provided a continuous space large enough to host what he assumed to have been an original population numbering in the millions.[121] Scholars in favor of Asian origins countered these arguments with the fact that salt was known to Europeans but not found in tongues directly descended from Sanskrit.[122]

The allure of Europe representing the primordial Aryan homeland derived from racialist arguments concerning the body. In 1878 Theodor Pösche dubbed Indo-Europeans "the blonds," describing the family as a "special, very distinguished human tribe" whose homeland was in eastern Europe, not Asia. Rudolf Virchow himself claimed in 1884 that based on skin pigmentation, hair color, and skull formation "a kind of autochthonism was to be established for the peoples built according to Germanic type in the north." The Scandinavian Karl Penka concurred that Europeans were a blond race with dolichocephalic skulls who had conquered Europe from the north. In the early 1900s prehistoric archaeologists such as Gustaf Kossinna likewise rallied the material evidence of weapons and tools to locate the Indo-European homeland along the western coast of the Baltic and bordering areas of the North Sea.[123] The new priority that bodies and material artifacts held over words in the classification of human communities reversed the Aryan myth as it had been invented by comparative philologists. As the Italian Enrico de Michelis stated, by 1903 Asia was no longer "the cradle but the grave the Aryans."[124]

Ernest Renan and the "Languages of Steel"

If Friedrich Max Müller fabricated images of an "Aryan race," comparative philology's most vocal advocate in France created its foil in a "Semitic race." Race and religion were the cornerstones of the Hebraicist Ernest Renan's language studies. Like Max Müller he brought linguistic evidence to bear on the history of religion, extrapolating from characteristic grammatical forms maxims that purportedly illuminated the inner life of "Semites." Renan's fame derives largely from his immensely popular *Life of Jesus* (1863), a controversial text for which he was expelled from his chair in Hebrew, Chaldean, and Sryiac at the Collège de France. In 1835 D. F. Strauss had distressed the German theological establishment by arguing that scriptural accounts of Jesus's life were mere myths grounded in Jewish messianic expectations.[125] Renan shocked Catholic ecclesiastics by denying the divinity of Jesus and stressing the aesthetic and emotional appeal of Christianity over supernatural aspects of the faith. Philology was the demon that took Renan on the path to sacrilege. His research into the origin of religious thought began with the study of language in the 1840s. The force with which language influenced the cultural practices of speakers sufficed for Renan as an explanation for why the ancient Hebrews had experienced monotheism but failed at other forms of historical progress.

When Renan applied the techniques of comparative philology to the Semitic tongues in the 1840s he reaped the fruits of a discipline that had cultivated an early French connection. Paris had once been the coveted haven of Europe's aspiring Orientalists; many German comparativists trained in the French capital. Some, such as Julius Klaproth or Julius Mohl, chose to stay where the manuscripts were more plentiful and the opportunities for learning Sanskrit, Farsi, Turkish, Arabic, or Assyrian more abundant.[126] Centers for studying non-European languages, such as the École des langues orientales vivantes (est. 1795) and the Société asiatique de Paris (est. 1822), were available at an early date in France.[127] Abraham Hyacinthe Anquetil-Duperron (1731–1805) had supplied the royal library with a stock of manuscripts useful for learning languages other than Hebrew, Arabic, Turkish, and Chinese.[128] Based on Persian sources, he published in 1771 the first Latin translation of the *Zend-Avesta.* This attracted the eye of the Farsi and Arabic scholar Silvestre de Sacy (1758–1838), who in 1793 deciphered the Pahlavi inscriptions of the Sassanid kings. When Napoleon declared all Englishmen on French soil to be prisoners of war in 1802, Alexander Hamilton, a member of the Asiatick Society of Calcutta was trapped in Paris and catalogued Sanskrit manuscripts. A French translation of Jones's *Asiatick Researches* had appeared in 1803, and Hamilton became a magnet for continental Europeans interested in the language. His students included Friedrich Schlegel and Franz Bopp, but also the first French Sanskritist, Antoine-Léonard de Chézy (1774–1832), who received the first European chair in that language at the Collège de France in 1814.

This generation of French Orientalists was disinclined toward approaching language comparatively and historically given the persistence of a national tradition of universal or philosophical grammar.[129] In the sixteenth century Port-Royal grammarians had evoked language comparison while searching for the rational structures of the mind, and early French Orientalists continued to approach language in this vein. Silvestre de Sacy, for example, published an essay called *Principles of General Grammar* in 1803, issuing reprints in 1810 and 1815. There was no French equivalent to the massive comparative charts published in J. C. Adelung's *Mithridates* (1806). Schlegel's *Essay on the Language and Wisdom of the Indians* was not translated into French until 1837. When France lost three of its founding Orientalists, François Champollion, Chézy, and J. P. Abel-Réumsat in 1832, the avant-garde of language studies had long since passed to German grammarians.

The young Christian Lassen helped transplant the techniques of comparative-historical philology across the Rhine when he received a Prussian state grant to study Sanskrit manuscripts in 1824. Under his guidance, a fellow student of Chézy, Eugène Burnouf (1801–52), applied German scholarship to Pali, the sacred language of Buddhists in Sri Lanka and Indochina. Cowritten with Lassen, Burnouf's *Essay on Pâli* (1826) argued that the liturgical language had evolved from Sanskrit. The work marked the first application of historical grammar to the Indian dialects and was an important moment in connecting the idiom of the Vedas to modern India.[130] It also suggested to Burnouf that language comparison could illuminate the history of religious ideas, in this case Buddhism. Burnouf extended his case study of Pali to a broader comparative analysis of Sanskrit and Farsi, which enabled him to reconstruct the ancient language of the Zoroastrian books. His *Commentary on the Yançа* (1835) asserted that Avestan was contemporary to Vedic Sanskrit. Burnouf later deciphered the cuneiform inscriptions of Persepolis based on knowledge of Avestan, an endeavor that enabled the first readings of Assyrian since the inscriptions had been translated into the language of Babylon.[131] Since 1829 Eugène Burnouf had been offering a course in comparative grammar to students of the École normale. In 1832 he ascended to the joint chairs vacated by Chézy at the Collège de France and by Champollion at the École. The inaugural address Burnouf held at the Collège, "On the Language and Literature of Sanskrit" (1832) proposed that "comparative analysis" could connect the *Rig Veda* to the *Zend-Avesta*.[132] His famous course on the *Rig Veda* acquainted students, such as Friedrich Max Müller and, briefly in 1849, Ernest Renan, with a linguistic approach to comparative mythology.

At the time of his death, Burnouf had few followers in France itself, his legacy passing largely to German scholars and to the Geneva Orientalist Adolphe Pictet. As he had been the sole representative of comparative philology in France, the sense of discovery relayed by Ernest Renan in the early 1840s is not surprising. Abbé Arthur-Marie Le Hir had taught Renan Hebrew grammar at the Saint-Suplice seminary, while he attended Étienne Quatremère's lectures at the Collège de France. Le Hir was an accomplished Orientalist and introduced Renan to the comparative study of Hebrew, Greek, and Latin, a perspective he later extended to the entire Semitic family.[133] In 1845 a disillusioned Renan descended the steps of Saint-Suplice, never to return, and dedicated his life to the "science of the future."[134]

Renan later claimed to have been "a philologist by instinct."[135] But his success in the field was more the product of diligent research than inspiration. By the time Renan won the Volney prize in linguistics in 1847 for an essay on the Semitic language family, he had acquired a thorough knowledge of German scholarship on Hebrew, reading the likes of Gesenius, Ewald, Fürst, and Klaproth. His essay *On the Origin of Language* (1848) reviewed, for a French audience, developments that had defined comparative philology from Herder and Humboldt to Grimm and Bopp. Far more successfully than Burnouf, Renan publicly celebrated the field as a "science of the human spirit." He styled himself as the spokesmen for German scholarship in France, earning his reputation by applying Bopp's techniques to Hebrew and related tongues. His *General History and Comparative System of the Semitic Languages* (1845) charted the unique grammatical evolution of Aramaic, Hebrew, and Arabic from their origin to the conquest of the East African coast. Whereas Bopp restricted himself to a sober survey of Indo-European languages, however, Renan extrapolated from an "internal history" of the Semitic tongues to an analysis of "the Semitic spirit"[136] and its religious and cultural proclivities.

Race was as malleable and ambiguous a term for Renan as it was for Friedrich Max Müller. Like his British colleague, he believed race "held the secret to all events in the history of humanity." Unlike Max Müller, however, Renan never assumed that race could be defined biologically except at the start of history. The "enormous cross-breeding of blood and ideas" made this impossible.[137] "Languages," he concluded, "virtually supplanted race in distinguishing between human groups, or, to put it another way, the meaning of the word 'race' changed. Race became a matter of language, religion, laws, and customs more than of blood."[138]

For this reason, Renan was more skeptical than Max Müller about philology's claiming ethnological privileges. There are "linguistic races," he argued, but these "have nothing to do with anthropological race." Language, in his view, was a "very insufficient criterion for race."[139] The few moments when Renan did persist in attributing racial qualities to linguistic groups, it was not in the context of distinguishing Aryans from Semites. Both belonged to the "great perfectible race." Biological race was only a factor separating this "civilized" pair from Africans, Chinese, and Native Americans. When envisioned in physical terms, in fact, Aryans and Semites were "two twins" who had become "strangers." They had "no other sign of their parentage" than "imperceptible analogies in language, some common ideas that recall certain localities, and above all an air of family in the essential aptitudes and external traits."[140] Renan concluded that the Semitic birthplace lay just to the west of the Aryan homeland identified by Burnouf. Both tribes had come down from the heights of the Imaus mountain range to live in the region stretching from Kashmir to the fertile crescent.[141]

Language, however, revealed for Renan differences in the "intellectual aptitudes and moral instincts" of Aryans and Semites.[142] He argued that comparative philology made possible "an embryology of the human spirit," allowing scholars to return to the first formative moment in the emergence of a cultural group.[143] For Renan, language and religion were both the unreflective, intuitive creations of national spirit. Consistency in the evolution of language ensured that the initial idea behind its formation remained binding through history. Nothing could ever "be created or added" to a language that did not conform to its essence.[144] Language emerged "fully formed" at the start of a nation's history "like Minerva from the head of Jupiter."[145] Moreover, once created, language constituted an "indestructible individuality," an "organic whole, endowed with its own life . . . and laws."[146] This explained why there was no evidence of "languages being able to correct themselves." The Semitic languages in particular, Renan insisted, exemplified the principle of internal organic consistency. Jacob Grimm considered a language healthy when it resisted the imposition of foreign elements. Renan used the notion that language constituted "an indestructible individuality" to essentialize Aryan and Semitic races.[147]

Much of the *Origin* was dedicated to refuting the large contingent of German Orientalists who derived the most common Hebrew roots from Proto-Indo-European forms.[148] Scholars such as Gesenius, Ewald, and Julius Fürst tried to prove that Hebrew roots, which were disyllabic and composed of three radicals, had evolved from simpler roots still found in Indo-European tongues. Although admitting the ultimate possibility of shared descent, Renan insisted that the grammatical systems of the families were "profoundly distinct."[149] Nothing authorized the "hypothesis of the Semitic languages' primitive monosyllabism";[150] they could never have "attain[ed] through any series of developments the essential processes" characteristic of Aryan tongues.[151]

Desiring to isolate Semitic languages from Indo-European forms, Renan dubbed them "languages of steel."[152] Comparative-historical philology had taken so long to complete a Semitic grammar because the tongues involved had "an interior life so inactive that they were incapable of revealing the organism . . . and laws" of the family. These tongues were "metallic," according to Renan, lacking the "fluidity" and "aptitude for transformations" characteristic of the Indo-European family.[153] Hebrew had ceased all historical development. This was apparent in the materialist metaphors Hebrew evoked to describe the nonphysical world, a relic, Renan argued, of the earliest stage of linguistic signification. Writing had likewise preserved the roots of the language as if each radical were a "perfectly pure diamond." The convention of omitting vowels and only "representing the skeleton of words" was "excellent for the preservation of roots." From its origins to the present "not one letter was lost." The "equal and unified" pronunciation of Hebrew had also prevented accented syllables from swallowing or absorbing weaker ones.[154]

Most decisive for the rigid structure of the Hebrew language was, however, its grammar. The roots of words, Renan argued, were "unassailable . . . safe, more intact"; they were "a bedrock that no infiltration can penetrate."[155] He explained that Hebrew "displayed a marked tendency to amass expressions of relation outside the essential root." In his view, agglutination was the dominant grammatical structure of Hebrew, "a steadfast procedure." As agglutination had been characteristic of the most primitive first languages, he argued, its persistence testified to the antiquity of Hebrew. Inflective languages, among which he included Sanskrit, were, by contrast, "laden with inflections for expressing infinitely delicate references in thought."[156] Semitic sentences failed to develop the "art of establishing reciprocity" among component grammatical elements, never forming an organic unit. Inflecting languages enjoyed the advantage of building sentences that were "like a body whose parts are connected."[157]

The *General History* translated this account of linguistic difference into an exploration of the respective cultural contributions Aryans and Semites had made to world history. Renan held language to be "the requisite mold of a people's intellectual performance."[158] Speakers were "imprisoned once and for all in the grammar"[159] of their particular idiom. In his interpretation, the principle features of Semitic grammar rendered speakers within the family incapable of science and philosophy. Languages such as Hebrew had a "physical and sensual character" in which "abstraction is unknown and metaphysics impossible."[160] Semitic roots had evolved in "imitation of nature" so that the ideas they embodied always tended toward realism, materiality, and the sensual.[161] Verb conjugation patterns likewise resulted in "inferior faculties of reasoning," while preserving "a vital taste for realism and a great delicacy of sensations." Semitic languages supposedly lacked the type of interior sentence construction that facilitated reason and science; the art of subordinating lesser parts of a sentence, as well as an organic combination of parts, was the privilege of Indo-European tongues. In his view, philosophy had its only roots in India and Greece among "a curious and vital race."[162]

Similarly, Renan held Semitic roots to be "absolutely incapable of giving birth to mythology." In his view, the divination of nature's primitive forces had been the source of all mythology. Flexible Indo-European verbs had embellished stories for a series of divine beings. Almost all Aryan roots, Renan concluded, "contain . . . a hidden god." By contrast, the "physical image" that dominated metaphors in Semitic languages held a power over religious thought, just as "the sun over the flower"; their realism "always obscured abstract deductions." Semitic speakers were only capable of thinking in terms that were "profoundly monotheistic." Foreign mythologies, for example, had always been reduced into "dull historical accounts" by the literal bent of their languages.[163] Despite an abhorrence of metaphysics, Semitic peoples thus had "a superior instinct" for monotheism, according to Renan. They were possessed of "sure and steady intuitions" that had unveiled the true divinity. Without "effort," "reflection[,] or reason" the Hebrew people had mysteriously attained "the most purified form of religion that antiquity knew."[164] The "desert is monotheistic," Renan concluded, "sublime in its immense uniformity."[165] Hebrew grammar endowed its speakers with the ability to "simplify the human spirit" and establish a "most reasonable religion."[166]

Renan deduced all further aspects of the Semitic character from the primordial desire for monotheism.[167] In contrast to the ancient Aryans, Semitic speakers had consistently sacrificed complexity, nuance, and multiplicity for unity. This resulted in their becoming a "race incomplete in its own simplicity." Following Christian Lassen's model in the *Indian Antiquities,* Renan depicted Semitic speakers almost exclusively with negative qualities.[168] He concluded that intolerance and immobility had been a necessary condition of monotheism. Believing God's power to explain everything, Semitic peoples had shown no curiosity and no "freedom of thought, spirit of examination[,] or individual research." After introducing the world to monotheism they had exited history. The Semites lacked poetry and a creative imagination, a sense for laughter, and all the fine arts except music, as well as an advanced civil life. The "great superiority of the Aryan race" rested in the advantages of inflection. Indo-European languages displayed "a marvelous suppleness in how they express the most intimate relations among things" in the inflection of nouns, in the varied tenses and moods of their verbs, in composite words, and finally in the "delicacy of their particles."[169]

These arguments served Renan's purposes as a chronicler of Christianity by diminishing the importance of Hebraic monotheism. As Maurice Olender has argued, Renan wished to "Aryanize" the birthplace of both civilization and religion by reconciling what he saw as the dual ancestry of western Christianity.[170] If Europe was Aryan in its linguistic system, how could it be Semitic in faith? According to Renan the Semitic spirit had produced monotheism by no fault of its own. The truth of one God descended on the Hebrews without thought, reflection, or imagination. The rigid structures of language reinforced their religious instincts, while preventing Semitic speakers from perfecting or developing religion. According to Renan there had been "fundamentally . . . nothing Jewish about Jesus."[171] "Christianity over time rid itself of nearly everything it took from the race," he argued, "so that those who consider Christianity to be the Aryan religion par excellence are in many respects correct."[172]

Renan and Max Müller may have eliminated biological race from their considerations of linguistic difference. The sharp distinction they drew between the language-based cultural proclivities of Aryans and Semites reinforced, however, an equally pernicious attempt to write the ancient Hebrews out of the religious and cultural history of Europe. Inverting biblical narratives of God's chosen people had been a feature of Orientalist rhetoric since Friedrich Schlegel equated the Germanic homeland with an Eastern terrestrial paradise. Renan and Max Müller contributed to this by essentializing the linguistic abilities of Aryans and Semites. Comparative philology offered a paradigm for relating grammar, thought, and cultural practices that was similar to racial theory in its determinism. National tongues were an instinctive product of an inner spirit or soul. They remained forever true to the principle guiding their development through history and offered an all-encompassing explanation for the actions and beliefs of speakers.

The Linguistic Anti-Humanism of August Schleicher

Materialist concerns for how the body affected linguistic diversity did eventually enter the German language sciences. The Jena comparativist

August Schleicher revived his field's traditional ties to the natural sciences, transforming comparative philology into a discipline he called *Linguistik*. Linguistics distinguished itself, in Schleicher's view, as the field that "took language as an object." Traditional philology, by contrast, approached language as a "means" to "penetrate the spiritual essence and life of one or more nations." In his conception, language lay beyond the "free will . . . and determination of the individual." Thus the laws governing its development fell to the natural, not the historical, sciences. For Schleicher, language was an internally sufficient system that developed in complete independence of the needs or intentions of its users. The goal of linguists was to document "the reign of unchanging, natural laws" that the "will and caprice" of human beings could not alter.[173] The only external explanation for linguistic change could be found, he believed, in the physiology of linguistic organs.

Like many nineteenth-century linguists, Schleicher began his studies as a theologian and a liberal. His father, a doctor, had taken part in the founding of the first *Burschenschaft* in Jena before moving his family to Meinigen, Thuringia. Schleicher himself was an active participant in the gymnastics movement of the *Turner*, a vain effort to stave off the tuberculosis which killed him at age forty-seven. As a theology student, Schleicher resided in Tübingen with the local Hegelians. Switching there to philology, he studied Hebrew, Sanskrit, Arabic, and Farsi with Heinrich Ewald, who had recently been exiled for his defense of Hannover's constitution. In 1843 Schleicher took up classical languages with Friedrich Ritschl and Friedrich Welcker in Bonn. There he caught the attention of Prince Georg von Sachsen-Meiningen, who funded two years of travel to Paris, London, and Vienna during the revolutionary years 1848–50. During this time, Schleicher also served as a foreign correspondent for the *Augsburger Allgemeine Zeitung* and the *Kölnische Zeitung*. His open support of the 1848 Revolutions concerned the Hapsburg police enough to spy on him in Vienna and Prague.[174] Schleicher's first academic post was as a classicist at the Charles University of Prague. Here he stayed until 1858 when he was appointed to the University of Jena.

Schleicher started his career collecting fairy tales and folklore in Lithuania, emerging as the first expert on Slavic languages and situating them within the larger Indo-European family. As such, he exemplifies a new generation of comparative linguists whose specialty lay not in Sanskrit or Indology. A concern for linguistic genealogies, partly inspired by Ritschl's comparative reconstruction of manuscripts, drew Schleicher deeper into the internal structures of languages themselves. As Sebastiano Timpanaro has noted, there is a strong affinity between the way nineteenth-century linguists classified languages and reconstructed a lost mother tongue, and the method by which classicists classified manuscripts genealogically.[175] Schleicher's massive *Compendium of the Comparative Grammar of the Indogermanic Languages* (1861) synthesized and extended half a century of research into the family related to Sanskrit. Its principle ambition was to reconstruct the original Proto-Indo-European language with the same certainty as Karl Lachmann reconstructed the archetype of Lucretius. In Schleicher's view, phonetic changes represented a decline from an original state of perfection and were thus analogous to textual corruptions.[176]

Schleicher's understanding of linguistic history merged Hegelian philosophy with Humboldt's typologies. In Tübingen Schleicher confronted Hegel's legacy and adopted the division he proposed between prehistory and a later period in which humans became self-consciously reflective. According to Hegel's *Lectures on the Philosophy of History* (1837), neither the creation of language nor its perfection had been "acts of a will becoming conscious of itself."[177] The elaborate, first national tongues appeared long before their speakers "attained historical existence."[178] Language, moreover, became "poorer and less subtle" with the advent of reason, will, freedom, and action.[179] Schleicher translated this perspective into a strict division between a "prehistoric period," in which language developed to its fullest perfection, and a "historical period" characterized by the "decline" of language. His monograph *On the Comparative History of Language* (1848) explained that "history and language formation" were "mutually exclusive activities within the human spirit."[180] "The more freely the spirit unfolds," Schleicher noted, "the more it extracts itself from language. That is why sounds are worn away and the richness of forms is lost."[181]

The prehistoric development of all languages followed Humboldt's linguistic typology, according to Schleicher, with isolating, agglutinating, and inflecting languages representing progressive stages of intellectual maturity. Schleicher followed Hegel in assuming all languages embarked on the same historical trajectory toward structural perfection.[182] Not all completed the transition from isolation to inflection, however. Monosyllabic tongues, such as Chinese, had remained mired in the first evolutionary stage of the prehistoric period. Agglutinating languages, including Finnish and Turkish, had only achieved the second level before entering a historical period of degeneration.[183]

Schleicher's distinction between the prehistoric and historical periods of language development did not discourage research into the undocumented past. On the contrary, Schleicher was the first to reconstruct a hypothetical ancestor for the Indo-European family. Earlier philologists had assumed the existence of a mother tongue no longer extant; Schleicher derived its likely forms from evidence surviving in its descendents.[184] Comparative charts in his *Compendium* listed cognate forms of various words and grammatical patterns as they appeared in different languages. At the top of each column, he then added the most likely reconstructed *Urform*. So confident was Schleicher in his reconstructions that in 1868 he published a controversial fable ("The Sheep and the Steed") in the supposed Indo-European *Ursprache*.[185] His student Johannes Schmidt (1843–1901) exposed this primitive language as a scientific fiction, suggesting that its components had actually originated at widely different periods. But later linguists applied the methodology of reversing patterns of historical development to arrive at a language's hypothetical origin more successfully.[186]

The division of the Indo-European *Ursprache* into its known descendents preoccupied Schleicher in the early 1850s, and he devised the influential model of a "family tree" to document their separation. This idea of a genealogical tree likely came from Ritschl, who was one of the first to study the genealogy of a manuscript tradition in depth.[187] "The First Divisions of the Indo-Germanic *Urvolk*" (1853) visually represented the descent of the language family in the form of a *Stammbaum*. This model was updated twice, once in 1860 and then in 1863 following Schleicher's encounter with the genealogical chart Charles Darwin presented in *The Origin of Species* (1859). The antiquity of a given linguistic group's departure from the homeland could be measured based on how far to the east or west it had progressed.[188]

Linguistic images, such as Schleicher's family tree, preceded and influenced the pattern of branching genealogical descent that Darwin and other natural scientists adopted in the 1860s.[189] Philologists welcomed the model as well, but with greater reservation. The family tree most effectively depicts the diffusion of languages over distances that completely sever speakers from each other geographically, as in the evolution of South African Afrikaans from Dutch. In most cases the division of languages is a gradual process. Yet Schleicher's diagram sug-

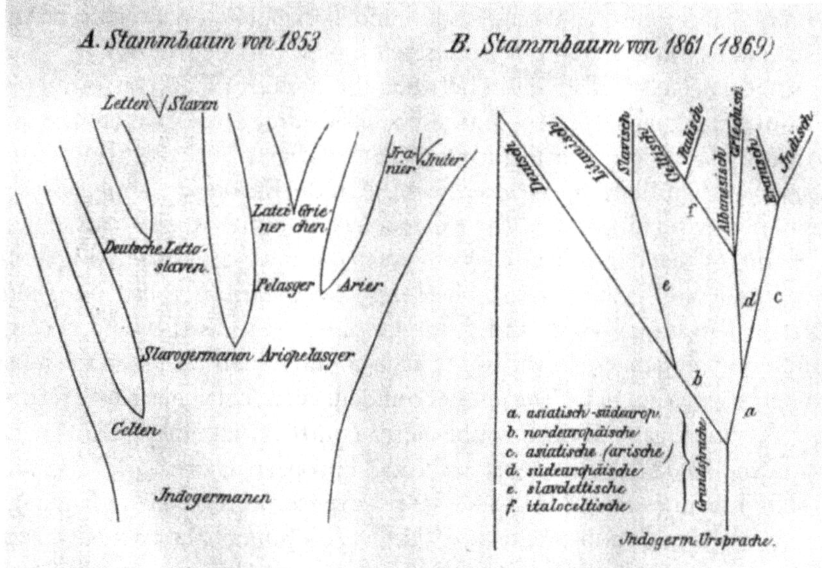

Two of the genealogical trees by which August Schleicher depicted the branching descent of Indo-European languages from a single source.

gested that the branching of tongues transpired within a short time span and that once separate, no further influences were possible.[190] Johannes Schmidt, added a corrective to the family tree in the form of a "wave theory" of linguistic diffusion, proposing in 1872 that sound changes in the Indo-European languages had spread over geographic areas. This eased the abrupt splits in Schleicher's model and indicated how certain languages or dialects might have borrowed neighboring attributes without being direct descendents.[191] Schmidt's own student Paul Kretschmer increasingly emphasized the horizontal transmission of linguistic facts so that linguistic kinship appeared to be acquired by means of contact not by inheritance.[192]

Schleicher's exclusion of human influence from the first period of language development reinforced its perceived autonomy. *Europe's Languages in Systematic Overview* (1850) set language apart from speakers as an autonomous natural organism. National tongues went through periods of growth, maturity, and decline independently of the will and consciousness of speakers. "Languages are organisms of nature," Schleicher stated, "They have never been directed by the will of man; they rose, and developed themselves according to definite laws; they grew old and died out."[193] Even within the historical period, Schleicher concluded, the process of language degeneration "lies . . . equally beyond the free determination of will." The regularity of "erosion" across the spectrum of national tongues could only be explained by the "uniform constitution" of human "speech organs." The sole influence speakers had on language was in the area of syntax and stylistics.[194]

Many German linguists accepted Schleicher's aligning their field with the natural sciences while qualifying his treatment of language as an autonomous organism. Friedrich Max Müller, for example, maintained that linguistics was a physical science comparable to geology. His first lecture in the *Science of Language* (1861) supported Schleicher's detaching the field from the historical sciences based on the claim that it was "not in the power of man" to produce or prevent language change.[195] At the same time, Max Müller considered it "sheer mythology" to speak of language "as a thing by itself, as living a life of its own, as growing to maturity, producing offspring, and dying away." The human soul was the "soil" without which a language did not grow. What he termed the "natural growth of language" was determined by two forces: phonetic decay and dialectic regeneration. Neither of these was "under the control of man," nor "produced by an inward principle of growth."[196]

In the 1860s Schleicher tied language change more consistently to the physiology of speakers' bodies. An encounter with Darwinian theory reinforced his turn to materialism. Schleicher received a German translation of *The Origins of Species* in 1863 from the young Ernst Haeckel (1834–62), then an associate professor of zoology at the Friedrich Schiller University of Jena. He responded with a letter dedicated to Haeckel that evaluated "Darwinism Tested by the Science of Language" (1863). Schleicher found evidence in Darwin's work that biology and linguistics were converging. This implied, on the one hand, that Darwinian notions of descent and the struggle for existence applied to languages and language groups. According to Schleicher, "Arian" tongues were "the conquerors in the struggle for existence." Competition in the "field of human speech" allowed for "comparatively few favored races"; they had "already supplanted or dethroned numerous other idioms," causing the "extinction of a vast multitude."[197] On the other hand, Schleicher believed evolutionary biology needed the support of linguistics. Only the "glossologist" could confirm the evolutionary patterns of the natural world, possessing in writing more positive proofs for branching descent and transmutation.[198]

Schleicher's acceptance of Darwinism was more threatening to linguists than the call to natural science. Max Müller feared Schleicher erased the distinction language drew between human and animal. The popularity of the Indologist's public lectures derived from his ability to muster philology in the fight against Darwinism.[199] He blamed Britons' uncritical acceptance of Darwin on their ignorance of Kantian philosophy. Kant had proclaimed the categories of thought to be prior to experience; reason therefore could not have evolved from man's animal faculties.[200] The connection between language and conceptual thought disproved for Max Müller any evolutionary continuity between people and animals. "The one great barrier between the brute and man," he asserted, "is Language. Man speaks, and no brute has ever uttered a word. Language is our Rubicon, and no brute will dare to cross it."[201]

Schleicher himself, however, cited the physiology of speakers as grounds for retaining language as the "prime criterion" in the scientific classification of human communities. Language, he insisted, was "something with a material existence"; speech had "a material, bodily basis." Schleicher concluded in 1865 that "language is the audible symptom of the brain and speech organs, with nerves, bones, muscles, etc." Different types of lungs, noses, larynxes, throats, and oral cavities produced particular sounds. He admitted that a "comparative investigation of the speech organs of linguistically diverse peoples" had not yet begun. It was likely, however, that language diversity resulted from "minimal differences in the character of the brain and the speech organs."[202] Comparative linguistics was therefore far more effective than physical anthropology in ordering the world's peoples. "How inconstant are such matters as cranial shape and other racial traits!" Schleicher exclaimed. Far more important were the "no less material, though infinitely finer, bodily characteristic, of which the symptom is language."[203] Language study could make more precise physical distinctions within the same race, while showing the ties between racial groups who shared similar tongues.

For Schleicher race alone was not an adequate concept for classifying human beings. Yet the attempt to explain language diversity with direct reference to racial categories found adherents among Africanists in the late nineteenth century. As Sara Pugach has illustrated, the African linguist Carl Meinhof (1857–1944) derived the unfamiliar sounds of African tongues from the racialized bodies of their speakers. The first professor of African Languages at the Colonial Institute of Hamburg, Meinhof applied the principles of Indo-European linguistics to a comparative grammar of Bantu tongues in 1906, having earlier made an effort to reconstruct the likely vocabulary of *Ur*-Bantu.[204] At his pioneering phonetics laboratory in Hamburg, Meinhof insisted that students first observe African subjects speaking and absorb their pronunciation visually before learning languages aurally. African bodies were a chief preoccupation of linguistic research.[205] Racial assumptions likewise underlay Meinhof's division of African languages into Bantu, Hamitic, and Sudanic families, as they did his affirmation of the notorious Hamitic hypothesis. By this view, the cursed descendents of Ham entered northern Africa as a relatively light-skinned conquering tribe closely related to speakers of Semitic languages and eventually intermixed with local black natives assumed to be of lesser cultural and racial value.[206] Meinhof's classification of African languages had a direct impact on the state ethnologists who devised the apartheid-era homelands policy for the Republic of South Africa.[207]

Schleicher's model of language evolving independently of speakers' willful control ultimately proved inadequate in explaining linguistic change over time. Scholars outside of Germany criticized Schleicher's historicism and his insistence that the moment of a language's creation predetermined its subsequent evolution. The American William Dwight Whitney (1827–94) and the French linguist Michel Bréal (1832–1915) also rejected his radical separation of languages and speakers. Schleicher's model of the natural organism verged on a caricature, Whitney suggested. In his view, language was the cultural and historical product of people's action, a voluntary institution, rather than an autonomous natural being subject to set laws. For Whitney and Bréal, the problem of language change could only be solved by ceasing to regard language as an autonomous entity that lived independently of its users. As will be seen in chapter 6, they insisted on the importance of a speaker's free will, redefining language as a social institution and an instrument of communication and interaction. The will, needs, and intention of the speaker were the true forces behind language change, not the inner principle governing the linguistic organism.

Neogrammarians and the Problem of Historical Agency

Linguists in Germany recognized this crisis of historical agency but instead attributed language change to ***unconscious*** psychological mechanisms. The school of Neogrammarians that coalesced in Leipzig in the 1870s assumed language evolved independently of the conscious will and intention of human communities. Its members eliminated the *Volksgeist* as an agent of historical change and restricted themselves to a positivistic "study of forms." The circle's chief theorists included two comparativists, the Heidelberg professor Hermann Osthoff (1847–1909) and his Leipzig colleague Karl Brugman (1849–1919), as well as the Germanist Hermann Paul (1846–1921). These linguists documented how national tongues evolved, conducting detailed, even atomistic, investigations of grammatical change over time. Their explanations for this change eventually drew attention to structuralist aspects of language production, but with specific attention to the physical mechanisms of the body.

In the 1878 text known as the Neogrammarian manifesto, Osthoff and Brugman urged linguists to cease regarding language as "something that exists outside and above the individual and lives a life of its own." Language had "its true existence only in the individual," and "all changes in the life of language can only ensue from individual speakers."[208] Linguists thus had to conduct research on "the speaking person" in order to understand how "human language lives and progresses." Nevertheless, Osthoff and Brugman had a restricted notion of the impact speakers had on language. The pair did not consider the communicative or pragmatic aspects of the speech act. In their view, the physics of the "human mechanism for speech" propelled language evolution. This mechanism had "a dual front"; it was driven by both the "psychic" and "corporal" functions of the body.[209]

This focus did not obviate the traditionally historical focus of German linguistics. The strength of the Neogrammarian reputation rests on the precision with which the school identified exceptionless laws governing sound change through time. "All sound change," Osthoff and Brugman argued, "occurs according to exceptionless laws . . . the direction of sound change is . . . always the same among all members of a linguistic community."[210] Karl Verner (1846–96) inspired this claim when he eliminated one year earlier the exceptions plaguing Grimm's

Law on the Germanic sound shifts. Verner demonstrated that the position of the accent in Indo-European words was responsible for the seemingly irregular behavior of the spirants resulting from the first Germanic sound shift; whether the spirant remained voiceless or became voiced was predictable.[211]

However, Osthoff and Brugman did urge linguists not to endow the origins of a language with the formative powers. Neogrammarians preferred to research the "most recent phases" of the Indo-European languages, as well as the "living vernaculars." Only this would clear the methodological "fog" that a focus on archaic origins had produced. To understand historical change, the pair insisted, linguists must "step out of the murky hypothetical atmosphere of the workshop on which the base Indo-Germanic forms are forged and into the clear air of tangible reality and the present."[212] They criticized previous comparativists, including Schleicher, for concentrating on the "purely hypothetical" reconstruction of the Indo-European "base forms." The focus on origins and linguistic prehistory was an inadequate basis for achieving "a correct notion of the way language develops."[213] Texts, such as Wilhelm Scherer's *On the History of the German Language* (1868) likewise shifted scholars' attention from the written letter to the spoken word. Phonetics and dialectology were gateways to what the Neogrammarians termed the physiology of sound.

For Neogrammarians, the regularity of sound change derived from the consistency of speakers' physical and psychological responses to language. How speakers "appropriated the language inherited from their ancestors," as well as how consciousness "reproduced and modified sound images" were "essentially the same at all times."[214] This made it possible, according to Osthoff and Brugman, to investigate barely documented periods of linguistic history. The "principle of analogy" could be used to project patterns of linguistic change backward in time. There was no reason to assume that the "physical activities" people engaged in when "adopting, reproducing, and gradually changing" inherited forms was "in past centuries substantially different" than in the present.[215] In 1880 the Neogrammarian Hermann Paul conceded that the expectation of sound laws being exceptionless could only be a "working hypothesis." Osthoff and Brugman's claim had to be relativized. Nevertheless, the school retained the focus on sound laws as the only "pillars" that could provide the field of linguistics with "solid ground under foot."[216]

Despite the theoretical emphasis on reintroducing the speaker to considerations of sound change, Neogrammarians still treated language as if it were an autonomous entity with a historical existence. "The sound laws of language," Hermann Osthoff asserted, "operate nearly blind, with the blind necessity of nature."[217] In practice, the focus Neogrammarians placed on external forms tended to isolate individuals from the process of language change.[218] Osthoff's essay "The Physiological and Psychological Moment in the Building of Linguistic Forms" (1879) argued that sound change "occurs unbeknownst to the speaker, thus purely mechanically" without "human desire or disinterest."[219] Physiologically, speakers were propelled by "the unconscious desire to spare energy" to substitute sounds that were "less energetic" and demanded "less effort" from linguistic organs.[220] Physical affinities among the speakers of a given language ensured that bodily organs reacted in a similar fashion; one individual substitution could also spark a collective transformation through "imitation." Osthoff likewise attributed linguistic diversity and the progressive diffusion of language families to "changes in the linguistic organs." The "differing climate of the mountains," he explained "creates different lungs, chests, larynxes in mountain dwellers, that of the plains creates the same organs differently among inhabitants of the valleys."[221]

The psychological factors shaping the laws of sound change were also "unconscious" and transpired at the level of the collective, rather than the individual. Osthoff borrowed from the work of the psychologist Johann Friedrich Herbart (1776–1841) to explain a process of "association creation" in language. Any sound changes that appeared random or irregular were actually the product of the "psychological drives" that transformed the spoken word. Concepts were "brought into unconscious connection . . . their forms influenced and their sounds transformed" by means of psychologically associated ideas.[222] Here, too, human will and desire had little control over the way speakers contributed to the historical evolution of language. Language change occurred by means of automatic physical and mental responses.

The emphasis the Neogrammarians placed on psychology and the role of the speaker eventually caused a crisis of historicism within German linguistics. Osthoff, Brugman, and their Leipzig colleagues sought to identify sources of sound change over time. But the explanatory mechanisms they chose to replace mystical forces such as the *Volksgeist* had a universalizing dimension to them. As Hermann Paul detailed in his *Principles of the History of Language* (1880), the laws of psychology remained constant over time. The linguist therefore had to research the "general conditions for the life of a historically developing object."[223] Paul, as will be seen, contributed to the new discipline of general linguistics that emerged in the late nineteenth century, discussing the conditions that made language possible. The always present concern he and other Neogrammarians showed for the synchronic dimensions of language study makes it less surprising that Ferdinand de Saussure, the founder of modern structuralism, emerged from within their ranks. The next chapter traces a growing reaction against the strict historicism of German language studies, both abroad and among those who applied psychology to comparative linguistics. It likewise shows how the turn to psychology reanimated old debates concerning the relationship between language and mental structures. The late eighteenth-century affinity between philosophy and language study was reborn, as a psychological approach to language again raised the problem of linguistic signification.

6

Speakers and Subjectivity

Toward a Crisis of Linguistic Historicism, 1850–1900

The University of Leipzig holds a remarkable, yet often unrecognized place in the history of twentieth-century French philosophy. Two of the theorists most responsible for launching a "linguistic turn" in the human sciences trained in the philosophical faculty of the Saxon capital. Seven years after Friedrich Nietzsche left the city for Basel in 1869, Ferdinand de Saussure began his university studies there. The pair never crossed paths in Leipzig and in any event frequented different departments, classical philology and comparative linguistics respectively. Yet they shared an important mentor in Georg Curtius, the adventurous classicist who acquainted Greek scholars with comparative philological techniques. Nietzsche followed Curtius's pleas to enhance classical studies by adopting the philosophical perspective and scientific rigor of linguistics. Himself a disciple of Friedrich Ritschl, Curtius introduced Nietzsche to an extensive literature in comparative philology and language theory. Saussure, in turn, entered the University of Leipzig after reading Curtius's *Principles of Greek Etymology* (1858). Once there, he "followed regularly the course of Curtius,"[1] joining his Grammatical Society along with members of the local school of Neogrammarians.

The near of meeting of the prominent fin-de-siècle scholars rivals any number of missed historical encounters. One can only imagine the list of eager flies on the wall. Claude Lévi-Strauss, Michel Foucault, and other structuralists and poststructuralists built upon the way Nietzsche and Saussure used language to critique knowledge, subjectivity, and forms of social interaction. Could the talented students have entertained these authors so early in their careers? A rising star in classical philology, Nietzsche had yet to repudiate a tradition that many scholars have seen as a mere obstacle on the path to philosophy. A prodigy among the Neogrammarians, Saussure had recently published a highly regarded, radically historical study that reconstructed the vowel system of Proto-Indo-European. Neither scholar had yet assumed the guise most familiar to the twentieth century. Is the Leipzig connection purely coincidental? To what extent did the encounter with comparative German philology propel Nietzsche and Saussure on their respective intellectual trajectories?

This chapter situates the work of Friedrich Nietzsche (1844–1900) and Ferdinand de Saussure (1857–1913) at the culmination of a century of reflecting on the autonomous powers of language. Their vision of words constructing the very subjects that spoke them represents an extension of earlier concerns for how national tongues shaped culture and community. Comparativists once attributed an authoritative role to origins and an inner principle of growth when considering how language shaped thought and identity. Both Nietzsche and Saussure challenged the origin paradigm, while subjecting speakers to a new set of linguistic demands. Their respective theories of language responded to a crisis of historicism that a predominance of organic metaphors had spawned among German-trained scholars. Late nineteenth-century linguists had difficulty explaining sound change over time, especially after August Schleicher detached language from human communities and discounted the illusive *Volksgeist* as a motor of linguistic change. Seeking other causes behind the evolution of national tongues, his successors reintroduced speakers and drew on the principles of psychology to explain the regularity of linguistic development. This shift encouraged analysis of the unconscious desires and drives that influenced language production. It also favored general theories of language use and the systematic description of how an idiom operates at a given time regardless of its origins and past history.

The chapter opens with the broader political context in which speculative psychology entered the field of linguistics, suggesting that a reconsideration of speakers did not resurrect faith in their agency and cognitive authority. The linguists Moritz Lazarus (1824–1903) and Heymann Steinthal (1823–99) applied the principles of collective psychology to clarify the relationship between language and national spirit in the years surrounding the *Reichsgründung*. Loyal Prussians and German Jews, this team minimized the importance of origins in nationality, refuting a view increasingly popular in the German Empire that a shared language implied joint ethnic descent. Within the context of *Völkerpsychologie*, or comparative research on the "psychology of peoples," Steinthal and Lazarus defined the nation as a discursive community united by a self-conscious process of identification. Steinthal, in particular, insisted that national tongues had their inception in instinctual life and the unconscious. This dehistoricized the origin of language question and drew attention to general laws of language operation. He likewise applied psychology to Wilhelm von Humboldt's consideration of the impact language had on thought, rekindling the linguistic critique of metaphysics that J. G. Hamann and J. G. Herder had initiated in the late eighteenth century.

Nietzsche and Saussure developed the implications German linguists drew from the encounter with psychology and the effort to reintegrate the speaker into considerations of language. The role of instincts and aesthetic drives in the formation of words undermined for Nietzsche the pretensions conceptual thought made to objective truth. He critically reappropriated the genealogical method to unveil what he perceived as the unstable linguistic foundations of rational science and theology. By the mid-1880s Nietzsche came to regard the cognitive subject itself as a linguistic fiction—a grammatical convention that had through history assumed untoward philosophical significance. Saussure's transition from historical to synchronic linguistics likewise built upon late nineteenth-century precedents. The Neogrammarian Hermann Paul and other critics within the German philological tradition asserted the need to investigate language states as if frozen in time. Saussure drew on their perspective, but without heeding their plea to reinvest speakers with semiotic agency. Both Saussure and Nietzsche questioned on the basis of language whether human subjects possessed a sovereign consciousness and could claim privileged knowledge of the worlds they inhabited. Their respective conceptions of language redefined human subjectivity and the epistemological capabilities of speakers. Yet Nietzsche's critical appropriation of genealogy and the origin motif found little immediate resonance in Germany. The turn toward structuralism was also of limited scope and of relatively short duration. Nietzsche and Saussure were language scholars untypical of their age and only found a substantial following outside of Germany in the twentieth century.

VÖLKERPSYCHOLOGIE AND THE NATION: MORITZ LAZARUS

A speculative form of collective psychology entered the language sciences within the broader nationalist project of *Völkerpsychologie* that two Jewish intellectuals, Moritz Lazarus and Heymann Steinthal, organized following the failed Revolutions of 1848–49. As linguists, this pair believed themselves well equipped to unravel the cultural significance of language as the chief constituent and objective manifestation of the *Volksgeist.* The application of psychology, in their view, aided in explaining the elusive ebb and flow of the German national consciousness. The ambition to unite the study of language, nationality, and collective psychology inspired Lazarus and Steinthal's *Zeitschrift für Völkerpsychologie und Sprachwissenschaft* (Journal of Comparative Psychology and Linguistics), which began in 1860. The publication branched beyond the field of linguistics proper to include essays on mythology, religion, art, literature, law, statistics, trade practices, and domestic life. Steinthal, in particular, devoted attention to mythology as an authentic expression of the national spirit, engaging in a bitter dispute on the respective merits of Hebrew monotheism and "Aryan" polytheism in the 1860s.[2] The journal touched a range of thinkers from Wilhelm Dilthey to Sigmund Freud, Thomas Mann, and Franz Boas.[3] The experimental psychologist Wilhelm Wundt most directly carried on the tradition of *Völkerpsychologie,* tracing in a ten-part work of that name the correspondence between language and human mental processes at different stages in history.[4] Many language scholars, such as Hermann Paul, shunned the journal's focus on collective psychology, however. Lazarus and Steinthal's idealism and their speculative methods ran counter to the model of natural science that more mainstream linguists, such as August Schleicher, advocated.

Lazarus and Steinthal were moderate liberals who supported a Prussian solution to German unification and never questioned the ultimate authority of the state.[5] However, their discursive model of the linguistic community departed from the standard of the time in rejecting the allure of formative origins. Lazarus and Steinthal generally assumed nationality emerged in a process of subjective identification; through language the individual developed a self-conscious awareness of participating in a larger community. This notion detached nationhood from ethnicity, but soon represented a last gasp of moderation in a new era of *Realpolitik* and radical nationalism. Especially after German unification, many conservative nationalists favored an increasingly radical *völkisch* vision of a quasi-racial linguistic community. This indicates how substantially the strand of linguistic thought that culminated in a repudiation of origins departed from the more mainstream essentialist and racialist notion of authentic German national culture that infused the various national philologies and public opinion.

Prussia had initially separated citizenship rights from language and cultural heritage following its reconstitution as a state after the Napoleonic occupation. As Friedrich Wilhelm III declared to his Polish provinces in 1815, "You shall be integrated into my kingdom without having to disavow your nationality. . . . Your language shall be used alongside German in all public proceedings."[6] A law from 1817 protected the use of both German and Polish in the courts; in 1842 the state likewise guaranteed that children of linguistic minorities would receive instruction in their mother tongue. All schools were to teach German, but this expectation arose from pragmatic considerations of how best to facilitate communication and the business of administration. A similar policy of linguistic toleration applied to Danish-speaking areas of the kingdom following Prussia's incorporation of the Duchy of Schleswig. Even nationalists assembling at the Frankfurt Parliament in 1848–49 voiced almost universal opposition to the idea of forced Germanization or even discrimination against other language groups or nationalities; the nation-state they imagined was not limited to an exclusive community of German speakers. The goals of political integration and inspiring loyalty to the state trumped more idealistic visions of German cultural unity.[7]

As a child, Lazarus experienced the delicate balance of language, culture, and national loyalty that characterized the small towns of Posen in East Prussia. He was born into a family of rabbis, his hometown of Filehne inhabited by a third each of Polish Catholics, German Protestants, and Jews. The young Lazarus noticed that the confessional groups "were of different descent and spoke different languages" and found himself observing "national developments in the cultural diversity of all forms of life." This marked for him the "personal beginnings of *Völkerpsychologie*," while suggesting that German statehood must incorporate a diversity of ethnic backgrounds.[8] Lazarus received a local Talmudic education before entering the gymnasium at Braunschweig where his advisor, a student of the psychologist Johann Friedrich Herbart (1776–1841), encouraged him to study languages in Berlin. After completing his doctorate, Lazarus obtained a professorship in comparative psychology in the Swiss city of Bern. He quickly rose to the post of dean and then rector of the university, supporting Steinthal on the proceeds. He returned to Berlin later in his career, helping to found the Hochschule für Wissenschaft des Judentums. After 1880 he was increasingly active in Judaic studies, eventually leaving the journal he founded with Steinthal to write *The Ethics of Judaism* (1898–99).

While a doctoral student, Lazarus published a defense titled *Prussia's Moral Privileges in Germany* (1850) that made manifest the political ambitions behind *Völkerpsychologie*. Prussia was the "true pillar and guardian" of the German national spirit, Lazarus argued.[9] Following Hegel, he honored the state as an ethical forum; in his view, individuals became moral through their identification with and assimilation into the state. The state's ethical responsibilities included, in turn, "executing the national idea."[10] German unification depended on the strength of "the spiritual and moral power that permeates a *Volk*," and only Prussia, in his view, possessed the "intelligence" and cultural fortitude necessary to assert its "inner spiritual power."[11] In a letter to T. A. Krüger, Lazarus stated his intention "to pursue . . . these thoughts further . . . academically and carry them out in a more scholarly venue."[12] The *Zeitschrift für Völkerpsychologie und Sprachwissenschaft* provided "politics with a scientific foundation,". developing a theory of the national spirit that the state could theoretically harness and direct.[13]

Psychology, a field Lazarus dubbed the "science of Spirit," was, in his view, best suited to clarify the laws by which "the inner spirituality or ideal activity of a people" developed.[14] He and Steinthal initially imagined the *Volksgeist* as pure idea or a transcendent subject with its own creative powers. Gradually, however, the journal came to regard spirit as substance, looking at its concrete manifestations. The dual nature of the *Volksgeist* justified Lazarus's dividing the project of *Völkerpsychologie* into two spheres of investigation. The "psychology of national history" devised a general theory that explained how the *Volksgeist* operated. This project had structuralist ambitions, seeking the universal "psychological laws" that governed sociability and intersubjective experience across history. "Psychological ethnology," by contrast, investigated actually existing national spirits with the descriptive, particularistic tools of anthropology and history.[15] Despite this intention, Wilhelm Dilthey (1833–1911), who met Lazarus and Steinthal in Berlin, rightly chastised the project's inhospitality to empirical research. Comparative psychology proceeded largely as a philosophy of history, rather than as an investigation of concrete acts.[16]

Lazarus and Steinthal attributed to language scholars "the most important role" in *Völkerpsychologie.* Language was, on the one hand, the objective manifestation of the national spirit and thus an important topic for empirical research. One could, for example, scrutinize vocabulary to determine the "size of the conceptual circle" belonging to a nation or to discover whether a people valued material objects, religion, emotion, or abstract thought.[17] On the other hand, national tongues supposedly produced "an instinctive worldview and logic" that unified communities.[18] They acted as an "adhesive" solidifying the intersubjective life of a nation.[19] In Steinthal's view, language enabled "the apperception of one person through another." When engaging in a conversation, for example, language enabled speakers of the same tongue to bare their souls and become "united in spirit." Members of a linguistic community "reciprocally take each other into themselves so that they together form a nation."[20] Using language as an instrument of communication and sociability helped create the sense of self-consciousness involved in being part of a nation.

The nation that emerged from this understanding of language was a voluntary discursive community whose members inhabited a shared spiritual realm. The mere inheritance of a shared mother tongue was not sufficient to form a nation. Lazarus realized the difficulty of distinguishing national languages from dialects or accounting for the persistence of vernacular speech and slang in a standardized idiom.[21] Therefore only "a mass of people who regard themselves as a *Volk*" constituted a nation;[22] the nation existed "merely in the subjective view of [its] members."[23] "The individual himself determines his nationality in a subjective manner"; Lazarus explained, "he reckons himself part of a nation."[24] Lazarus and Steinthal virtually eliminated the importance of common descent and biological relation in the linguistic definition of nationality. "The branches of a nation do not all grow from one trunk," Lazarus asserted."[25] Physical characteristics only conditioned a nation to the extent that they shaped subjective feelings of identification. The potato, for example, was now a symbol of Irish nationality, but there was no causal relationship between nutrition it provided and the Irish national spirit.[26]

This perspective enabled Lazarus and Steinthal to express their loyalty as German nationals while still preserving a self-consciously Jewish identity. In a lecture titled "What Is National?" held before the Hochschule für die Wissenschaft des Judentums in December 1880, Lazarus specifically rejected "all blood and racial theory" as "the overflow of a grossly sensual materialism."[27] His reflections were provoked by the anti-Semitic speeches the Prussian court preacher Alfred Stöcker held the same year to draw workers away from social democracy. Lazarus countered that nationality consisted solely in the subjective identification an individual felt for a community; it was facilitated by language, but also through education, art, law, and statecraft.

Emphasizing the discursive function of the national tongue resonated with the conception of language once favored by the dynastic states of central Europe. In the eighteenth and early nineteenth centuries, language had been of concern to officials only to the extent that vernaculars presented a potential barrier to effective administration. However, statisticians like Richard Böckh (1824–1907), who argued in Lazarus and Steinthal's journal for the necessity of the state's surveying linguistic practices, were instrumental in creating a new official correlation between language and nationality in Prussia. Starting in 1817 and 1828 Prussia began gathering statistics in its eastern provinces to determine how many people could not use German in public venues and religious services.[28] The grandson of the classicist August Boeckh assisted in evaluating the findings of Prussia's first comprehensive linguistic survey in 1861, serving as the director of Berlin's statistical office from 1875 to 1902.

Böckh's essay "The Statistical Importance of the *Volkssprache* as a Mark of Nationality" (1866) argued that the mother tongue was "the true criterion of nationality."[29] In his view, a shared mother tongue fostered the common consciousness which united members of the nation; it also provided a necessary instrument of communication. Böckh rejected a wide array of factors as inconclusive evidence of national affiliation. These included political loyalties, geographical location, and traditions of law, dress, customs, food, domestic life, as well as intellectual and cultural achievements. "Physique" and "signs of descent" were also irrelevant, in his view. Language alone was the "true pillar of nationality."[30] From Böckh's perspective, Jews were thus full members of the German nation, Yiddish being a German dialect comparable to Saxon or Frisian.[31]

Censuses of the type Böckh recommended encouraged a linguistic definition of nationhood among a wide swath of Prussian citizens. The modern administrative state was, as Eric Hobsbawn suggests, complicit in fostering popular nationalism and suggesting the viability of language as a political instrument.[32] By 1866, the year of the decisive Prussian victory over Austria, increased exposure to standardized German in schools and an expansion of the literary market had familiarized the educated middle class and the petit bourgeoisie with the notion of a national language. As Claus Ahlzweig writes, a series of lectures, brochures, and popular publications indicate that broad segments of the population had embraced a nationalist ideology of the mother tongue by the time of German unification in 1871.[33] As this occurred, the linguistic definition of German nationhood ceased to be the purview of a progressive and liberal opposition and was drawn into a broader-based conservative nationalism.

Under Otto von Bismarck, the German Empire initially refrained from defining nationhood in ethnocultural terms, fearing that this might jeopardize the integrity of Germany's fragile borders. The individual states retained purview over linguistic matters.[34] Nevertheless, Prussia itself did steer the politics of language in its eastern provinces. As part of the *Kulturkampf,* Bismarck imposed the first restrictions on the use of Polish. In 1872–73 German became the compulsory language of instruction for all subjects in elementary schools in Upper Silesia and West Prussia, and for all subjects except religion in Posnan. He declared German the sole language of public life in 1876. These measures did not aim at Germanizing Poles but at winning over the loyalty of peasants and the emerging Polish middle class by weakening the influence of the nobility and clergy.[35] In 1908 a new imperial law concerning societies (*Reichsvereinsgesetz*) made German the required language of all assemblies and associations, as an attempt to regulate and censor nationalists in the east. Alsace-Lorraine received special exemption to permit French as an official second language of assemblies in its districts.[36]

By the Wilhelmine period, language had emerged as a driving force in the type of radical (*völkisch*) nationalism that brought the state closer to an expansionist and ethnocultural definition of nationhood. As

Roger Chickering has shown, the German Language Association, founded in 1885 by Hermann Riegel, resembled other patriotic societies of the period, including the Pan-German League and the German Colonial Society.[37] Attracting a membership of 34,280 by 1914, the organization dedicated itself to "strengthening the general national consciousness of the German people,"[38] using its journal and popular *Verdeutschungsbücher* (Germanizing books) to help "purify" the mother tongue. The association won the support of powerful agencies, successfully convincing ministries, local government offices, and professional associations to rid their vocabulary of Anglicisms. At stake, Chickering suggests, was the question of whose language would symbolize, express, mediate, and constitute the German national experience. The association drew from the ranks of the educated Protestant middle class, public employees and university graduates wishing to assert their cultural leadership.[39]

In the 1890s a radical faction of the association made language central to an overtly racialist definition of a Pan-Germanic *Urvolk*. Founded by the purist Adolf Reinecke in 1896, *Heimdall: Journal for Pure Germandom and Pan-Germandom* embraced language as the most important criterion for membership in the German race. The publication was named for the third son of Wotan and cited J. G. Fichte when declaring German to be an especially pure *Ursprache*. Radical Germanizers, such as Reinecke and Hermann von Pfister-Schwaighusen, tried to "correct" their native tongue and the conventions with which it was written by appealing to archaic forms. Runes, for example, were to be used in all ceremonial occasions.[40] Reinecke likewise drew on linguistic research to legitimate territorial expansion, seeking to include all German speakers within a larger Reich. Like other radical nationalists of the period, adherents to this movement were decidedly anti-Semitic. And they appealed to the supposed precedent of early nineteenth-century philologists to justify their perverted policies.

This radical form of linguistic nationalism, which forced the acquisition of colonies and fueled German militarism, claimed continuity with a Romantic conception of the *Volk*. However, it represents a nostalgic and artificial revival of ideas once mustered to challenge the legitimacy of the dynastic state. Individuals within the comparatively liberal and Enlightened field of linguistics had long since questioned whether a binding relationship existed between language, nationhood, and ethnic or racial descent. Within the *völkisch* ideology of Wilhelmine radicals, language symbolized a shared ethnicity and racial allegiance. As will be seen, outside the field of comparative linguistics, other German philologists also continued to search for formative points of origin and subscribed to racialist histories of German national descent. Even a republican, such as the Prussian historian Friedrich Meinecke, claimed in 1907 that Germans defined themselves a *Kulturnation,* based on a shared inheritance of language, religion, and customs.[41]

The Psychology of Language: Heymann Steinthal

Within the relatively liberal field of linguistics, comparative philologists such as Heymann Steinthal began moving away from the origin paradigm and examining the general laws that governed the life of language. Born the son of a linen salesman in Gröbzig, Anhalt, Steinthal attended Hebrew school before entering the University of Berlin to study linguistics. His main contribution to the field was to revive interest in the linguistic writings of Wilhelm von Humboldt, which he edited in 1884. As a Jew Steinthal never obtained a full professorship in Germany or a position in the Prussian Academy of Sciences, although he taught at his alma mater starting in 1856. Yet his influential critique of Humboldt reanimated discussion of the epistemological significance of language and relayed to the late nineteenth century an earlier tradition in the philosophy of language. Steinthal's reflections directly influenced Friedrich Nietzsche's appreciation of language's origin in unconscious instincts, as well as his linguistic critique of conceptual thought. Steinthal's contemporaries, the Neogrammarians, however, remained suspicious of the way he applied psychology to the field, as it deviated markedly from the positivist leaning of much late nineteenth-century linguistics.

The principles of psychology offered Steinthal a tool for curbing what he perceived as Humboldt's lingering faith in universal rational structures. Agreeing with Humboldt's dictum that language was a "creative organ of thought," Steinthal denied that national tongues harbored philosophical truth. In his view, all linguistic forms arose from the unconscious and reflected the nationally specific structures that shaped instinctual life. Language lacked stable reference points in the external world, as well as any foundation in logic or rationality. For this reason the addition of psychology to linguistics confirmed the autonomy with which language intervened in the thought process. For

The comparative linguist Heymann Steinthal in the year he published the edited works of Wilhelm von Humboldt (1884). From Ingrid Belke, ed. *Moritz Lazarus und Heymann Steinthal: Die Begründer der Völkerpsychologie in ihren Briefen* (Tübingen: Mohr, 1983). (Courtesy Leo Baeck Institute, New York)

Steinthal cognition depended on the symbolic forms of language as they were forged by instinct and the unconscious.

Humboldt's chief weakness, according to Steinthal, was to have promoted a "dualistic" view of language.[42] He wrongly resorted to "mysticism"[43] when reconciling theoretical, a priori assumptions about language as a system with historical case studies.[44] Intrigued, nonetheless, Steinthal pursued a question central to Humboldt's project, taking up "the fight against the enemy within and emerging victorious."[45] Specifically, he sought to clarify "the relationship of language to thought and of grammatical forms to the logical forms of thought."[46] Steinthal adopted Humboldt's notion that the inner form of language was a mechanism for explaining the supposed consistency with which national tongues shaped the mind. Unlike his predecessor, however, Steinthal asserted that the inner form of language provided the only applicable standards of rationality. There was no preexisting metaphysical world to which language referred; its effectiveness could not be measured by external markers.[47]

The new perspective Steinthal brought to Humboldt emerged in a fusion of Hegelian philosophy and the psychology of Johann Friedrich Herbart. As a student of comparative philology in Berlin, Steinthal had worked closely with Carl Wilhelm Ludwig Heyse (1797–1855), the main representative of Hegelianism in linguistics. Heyse suggested to Steinthal and Lazarus how Hegel's understanding of Spirit (*Geist*) and historical development could be applied to linguistics. The pair first met in Heyse's classroom and quickly solidified a close intellectual and personal friendship; Steinthal later married his friend's sister, Jeanette. In Steinthal's view Humboldt had wrongly regarded Spirit as "power without substrate," "an impetus to activity," without connection to its actual manifestations in the empirical world. He applied Hegel's notion of objective spirit to Humboldt's view of language, in order to explain how Idea became immanent.[48]

The solution to resolving Humboldt's contradictions was for Steinthal to eliminate metaphysics. His predecessor should never have approached language as "a being . . . to be understood in ontological categories."[49] Steinthal, like Ernest Renan, assumed the soul created language without reasoned reflection. The question of its origin therefore fell to psychology, not metaphysics. The linguist, Steinthal insisted, "leaves behind the metaphysical ground upon which the antinomies of Humboldt's dialectic rest and transfers the question over to the field of psychology. . . . He called language . . . '*energeia*,' a 'work of the spirit': from this we learn that its contemplation belongs to psychology."[50] Steinthal aimed to isolate the psychological mechanism that enabled language to emerge from the lower functions of the soul. This perspective emphasized universal, rather than historical, dimensions in the production of language.

Steinthal's treatise *Grammar, Logic, and Psychology: Their Principles and Relations to Another* (1855) embedded language and rationality within the psychological processes that governed instinctual life. The text was written while the author resided in Paris, funded by the Volney prize in linguistics, which he received for an essay on African languages in 1851. For three years Steinthal studied Chinese, Tibetan, southeast and central Asian languages, as well as West African languages at Collège de France and the École des langues orientales vivantes. During this time, he became well acquainted with Ernest Renan. Although rejecting Renan's interpretation of the Semitic instinct for monotheism,[51] Steinthal agreed that language was "an organ of the soul"[52] that spontaneously appeared with the development of other psychological functions. The text specifically brought psychology to bear against the "logical formalism" of Karl Ferdinand Becker.[53] Becker claimed to have discovered universal metaphysical categories lurking in the grammatical forms of the world's tongues. Steinthal countered that the forms of language were not vestiges of transcendental rationality, but rather psychological phenomena that emerged from the soul.

Similar to Fichte and the German idealists, Steinthal derived the origin of language from ahistorical laws governing the human mind. For him, though, language emerged in a pre-rational soul subject only to universal psychological principles. "Language always originates from the soul of a person in the same fashion," he explained, "and this source is eternally the same. Language is an emanation, an unfolding of the soul. It always occurs with natural, organic necessity when the development of the soul reaches a certain point. . . . Thus the soul creates language today, as it did in primitive times."[54] He assumed the soul had a life before the onset of speech; its earliest "agitations" included "feeling, sensation, intuition" that produced a primitive form of consciousness. Language only emerged after people became conscious of their consciousness. And the transition to self-awareness occurred without the subject's will or intention. An initial "passage from soul to spirit" produced a type of "instinctive self-consciousness" that was the prerequisite for language.[55] The actual "breaking through of language" transpired through speech. According to Steinthal, "perception of intuition" was nothing more than "setting intuition to sound."[56] The first sounds fixed "the inner linguistic form of intuition," a principle that subsequently guided development of conceptual thought.[57] For Steinthal, the soul thus created language and thought at the same moment.

The third stage in the evolution of human consciousness required the maturation of language out of its original embryonic state. As the inner form of language crystallized, regulating the relationship between sound and mental presentations, speakers gained the capacity for conceptual thought. Reasoned reflection demanded that the mind analyze and manipulate representations (*Vorstellungen*). These were presentations (*Anschaungen*) that entered the consciousness after being shaped by a combination of sound and the inner form of language. Mental representations always took symbolic form in language as they entered the consciousness. Grammar and syntax then submitted representations to logical evaluation, creating concepts. In this way language allowed the mind to evolve from a purely receptive organ to an active force capable of self-consciously manipulating ideas.[58]

Several psychological principles that Steinthal adopted from Herbart explained how language allowed an individual to be conscious of the presentations that entered the mind. A disaffected Kantian, Herbart believed there were no innate ideas or concepts; the soul was formed through contact with the sensible world. Feelings and desires produced presentations in the mind, which variously sank and rose across the threshold of consciousness. The psychological process of apperception determined which representations entered the consciousness. Steinthal concluded that this mechanism controlled the "content of thought"[59] by determining the "images, comparisons, and metaphors" through which the individual experienced his or her sense impressions.[60] For this reason, Steinthal considered representations "a purely psychological form, the manner by which intuitions, thought, and their content are present in consciousness."[61] Apperception likewise determined how new ideas mingled with existing concepts. Masses of strong and weak representations were always already present in the consciousness. Apperception stepped in "to make connections in what once seemed disjointed, contradictory, and incomprehensible."[62]

Language was the dominant "medium of apperception," according to Steinthal. He considered it to be a "sixth sense,"[63] which filtered into consciousness the content of the soul, as well as sensations from the empirical world. "Speaking," he explained, "means essentially and primarily to understand oneself."[64] Out of the dark chambers of the soul where sensations and ideals lurked, "tower up sounds into full consciousness."[65] Words also governed the "negotiations between one soul and another."[66] Language was a condition of communication and understanding for Steinthal. "Sound," he wrote, "builds a bridge between both, extending the consciousness of one into that of the other."[67] This justified applying the mechanisms of individual psychology to the linguistic community as a whole. Members of a nation shared in a collective consciousness because the same sounds and grammatical structures molded their subjective awareness of the soul and external world, as well as their perceptions of each other.

The second psychological process Steinthal tied to language regulated conceptual thought. The consciousness, Herbart had suggested, was too narrow to simultaneously embrace all impressions and ideas. The mind had to rely on language to compress presentations into symbolic form. Steinthal and Lazarus concluded that language was central to a process termed "condensation [*Verdichtung*] of thought." The word was the "furnace of intuition, the workshop of concepts"[68] which resulted in giving "an eternally discursive character to thought."[69] The compression of thought was a psychological phenomenon common to the individual. But, as Lazarus argued, it also allowed for collective progress in human history. Language was the receptacle for the "endless sum of prior thoughts, an unspeakably rich treasure of the spirit."[70] It transmitted concepts developed by earlier generations and allowed for continuity in the national spirit of a people.

The causes of national diversity within this complex were twofold, emanating from the "inner linguistic form" and phonetic considerations.[71] Steinthal concluded that the production of sound depended on "language organs" and on the "individual constitution of the body."[72] At the same time, the inner form of language varied according to "the way instinctive self-consciousness appropriates intuitions and transforms them into representations."[73] Present in the deep recess of the soul, "instinctive freedom" or "subjectivity" gave form to a language's grammatical structures.[74] Steinthal's *Classification of Languages* (1850) ranked national tongues based on the degree to which they had perfected an inner form. One could test "the power of language to condense, as well as its efficacy in fostering nimble, versatile and . . . clear thought," he believed, by studying the "imperfect languages of wild people" in which the process of abstraction "remained unfinished."[75] Most peoples, Steinthal proposed, had a "compulsion to express the content of thought ever more precisely." This impulse created the formal elements of language. Inflection, isolation, and agglutination were for him the "different effects of psychological drives, various externalizations of the diverse means to imagine the self."[76] But such distinctions only emerged at a relatively advanced stage in a nation's history. Some peoples still presided over prehistoric languages that had never perfected an inner form. Steinthal divided the world's tongues into two main groupings: "languages with forms" which include the Indo-European and Semitic families, as well as Egyptian and Basque, and "formless languages" such as Chinese, Turkish, Finnish, and Mongolian, and also Native American, Polynesian, and African languages. The fully matured languages of the Indo-European family "adapted most readily to the forms of self-conscious thought-activity";[77] their grammar structures separated categories of being and doing and distinguished content from form. By contrast, Steinthal's case study *The Mende-Negro Languages, Presented Psychologically and Phonetically* (1867) offered a profile of the "primitive" mind, as it grouped the Mende, Vai, Susu, and Bambara languages of northwestern Sudan into one family.[78]

The powers Steinthal attributed to language reinforced its autonomy as a constructive force that molded the inner life of subjects and their experience of the world. National tongues, in his view, created "their forms independently of logic in absolute autonomy."[79] There were no external standards of rationality for evaluating the adequacy of linguistic representations. "Autonomy reigns in language," he argued in 1871, "it can create and transform . . . spontaneously . . . : thus it is everywhere and above all in control; and no logic claims the right to made demands of it."[80] Nor was language responsible for accurately mirroring an empirical world. National tongues depicted objects "entirely and exclusively based on their own laws . . . which arise from the nature of their own goals and means, and are not dictated by the objects being represented."[81] One could only measure the strength of a language's life force. "If language is autonomous," Steinthal reckoned, "its excellence only lies in letting this autonomy govern with proper force; the force of a language's autonomy is the objective measure of its excellence."[82]

Cognition thus depended for Steinthal on an autonomous medium which unconscious instincts had endowed with independent drives and desires. In his view national tongues had their origin in the pre-rational soul and only mistakenly had been linked to logic or a prelinguistic form of rationality. Language was neither bound to abstract metaphysical structures nor to the objects and ideas it represented. As a result, the unconscious held sway over conceptual thought, and human subjects never achieved complete sovereignty over discursive practices. Steinthal's fusion of psychology and linguistics likewise highlighted the general conditions governing the life of language. He contributed to the dehistoricization of language study by depicting national tongues as the products of universal laws regulating consciousness.[83] Rather than document specific historical transformations in the grammar or lexicon of languages, he speculated on the general conditions of language production. Language, in Steinthal's definition, was the verbal expression of the soul's inner life. He further divided the speech act into three elements (the "capacity for language," the "physiological ability to produce articulated sounds," and "linguistic material"),[84] from which Waltraud Bumann has suggested Ferdinand de Saussure derived his tripartite distinction of language, *langue,* and *parole.*[85]

Language and Genealogy: Friedrich Nietzsche

The young Friedrich Nietzsche found intriguing Steinthal's synthesis of words and desires, as well as his displacing the origin of language onto the unconscious. The central role language assumed in Nietzsche's increasingly ambitious cultural criticism extended the implications of Steinthal's drawing attention to the instinctual, unconscious drives lurking beneath conceptual language. Through Steinthal's transmission, Nietzsche likewise became familiar with the linguistic critique of Kantian metaphysics that Hamann and Herder initiated in the late eighteenth century. These two perspectives fueled Nietzsche's epistemological skepticism and his radical critique of human subjectivity as it developed after the *Reichsgründung.* A number of scholars have tied Nietzsche's background in the classics to his mature philosophical oeuvre.[86] Comparative philology, not the classics, however, provided the precedent for discussing how words and grammar molded the mind. Nietzsche embraced the discipline's constructivist view of language while making a radical critique of genealogy, and the origin paradigm, occasion for unmasking the creative powers of language.

Born in the small village of Röcken twenty miles from Leipzig, the young Friedrich Nietzsche followed a well-trod nineteenth-century path of defection from theology to philology. After attending the prestigious Schulpforta boarding school on a scholarship, Nietzsche initially pursued the career of his late father. When philology brought on in Nietzsche a crisis of faith, he transferred to Leipzig to begin classical studies with Friedrich Ritschl, quickly rising as a star student. Nietzsche came to regard language as a philosophical problem during the initial moments of his disaffection with classical philology. As Federico Gerratana has shown, the restless doctoral student took increasing notice of the natural scientific dimensions of linguistics and its model of language during his last years in Leipzig.[87] Nietzsche's notes from the brief period of his military service in 1867–68 list Steinthal's *Philology, History, and Psychology in their Mutual Relations* (1864) and Curtius's lectures as important counterparts to August Boeckh's encyclopedia of philology. According to Gerratana, the pretensions linguistics had to being a natural science offered Nietzsche an escape from what he regarded as the pitfalls of historical knowledge. The methodology of linguistics stood in sharp contrast to the intuitive, individual character of philological interpretation. "Amazing is the progress of comparative philology," Nietzsche noted in his journal.[88] An "all too strong subjectivity" had spread like an "epidemic" through classical studies. A "natural sci. understanding of the essence of language," would, in Nietzsche's view, allow for a "natural sci. manner of contemplating antiquity."[89]

By the late 1860s language appeared to Nietzsche as a key to investigating the human condition. The "most beautiful triumph" of comparative philology, in his view, was its "philosophical perspective."[90] The field encouraged observers to "step back toward the beginnings of all culture . . . and seek a path to the problems of thought."[91] "It must be a philosopher," he suggested in a notebook entry, "who concerns himself with it [language]."[92] Specifically, Nietzsche believed that a scientific approach to language would enable a "description of instinctive life, its laws, etc."[93] His inaugural lecture at the University of Basel, therefore, described the field of language studies as "one portion history, a portion natural science, and a portion aesthetics." The scientific basis of linguistics enabled one to "probe the deepest instinct of man, the language instinct [*Sprachinstinkt*]."[94]

Nietzsche's own fragment "On the Origin of Language" (1869–70) explored the philosophical and psychological issues of concern to Steinthal and other linguists. The piece documents Nietzsche's emerging interest in the relationship between language and thought, as well as the two tacks that guided his future reflections on the topic. He rejected "all earlier naïve standpoints" that language could be the conscious creation of individuals or a community. Rather, it had to be treated as "the product of an instinct." A reading of Eduard von Hartmann's *Philosophy of the Unconscious* (1869), especially a chapter titled "The Unconscious in the Emergence of Language," guided Nietzsche's interpretation of the origin of language.[95] And notably, Hartmann's synopsis credited Heymann Steinthal when declaring language to be the product of "unconscious mental activity."[96] The chapter cited his claim that language could not be the product of "conscious thinking spirit."[97] Rather, as Hartmann explained, the evolution of each national tongue "can only be explained based on one instinct common to humanity—to create language."[98] He followed Steinthal in suggesting that language mediated which sense impressions entered the consciousness and which converged to form abstract concepts. "Every conscious human thought [is] first possible with language," Hartmann asserted. "Progress in the development of language" was the "condition," rather than the "consequence," of advances in thought.[99]

Hartmann's transmission likewise acquainted Nietzsche with the legacy of the linguistic metacritique of Kant. Nietzsche noted in 1869 that "the deepest philosophical insights are already contained in language"; he ventured further that the conceptual categories *subject* and *object* in Kantian philosophy were merely "abstracted from the grammatical sentence." In Kant's hands, "the subject and predicate developed into the substance and accidence."[100] These insights informed Nietzsche's later critique of metaphysics and bestowed a second life on the tradition of Hamann and Herder. Hartmann had commented on how the pair interpreted the "philosophical worth of grammatical forms." Linguistic distinctions between subject and predicate, subject and object had, Hartmann recounted, shaped the history of philosophy, especially Kant's notion of judgment.

Until 1873 when Nietzsche began preparing lectures on rhetoric, however, he idealized primordial language as representing an uncorrupted moment of human origin. Specifically, he posited the existence of two different types or levels of language. Earliest language had been an unconscious product of the instincts and thus maintained an essential connection to the innermost being and will of its creator. From this had grown an impoverished language of conscious representation; the images of the early period had been symbolized ever more strictly in words and concepts. For Nietzsche, contemporary languages sustained an illusionary Apollonian world where logic, grammar, and abstractions agreed upon by convention were understood as real.[101] In the years surrounding *The Birth of Tragedy from the Spirit of Music* (1872), Nietzsche probed the artistic realm of unconscious language production in the hopes of peeling back what he saw as the artifices of representation. Only the self-consciously aesthetic language of the genius, in his view, was capable of giving adequate expression to real existence.

Nietzsche considered music, in particular, to be the paradigm against which to measure the limitations and possibilities of language. The fragment "On Music and Words" (1871) proclaimed music to be the privileged first language of humanity (*Ursprache*). In his view, the art form had originated in a primordial, Dionysian sphere of existence and maintained an exclusive bond to what Nietzsche termed the "original Oneness, the ground of Being."[102] Following Arthur Schopenhauer, Nietzsche interpreted music "as the immediate language of the will."[103] The spoken word, by contrast, emerged as an "imitation of the language of music," preserving a weaker, yet ever-present resonance with the world of primitive desire.[104] Nietzsche contradicted Schopenhauer in insisting that the "whole realm of drives, the interplay of feelings, sensations, emotions, and acts of will" could only be known through representations, not directly in their essence. There was no direct "bridge" leading to the "kernel" of being; one encountered only its "expression in images." Words were therefore valid "symbols" of these images. The "*duality* . . . built into *the essence of language*" ensured that each national tongue preserved a musical core. Each language had a "tonal background" that was universal and intelligible in that it "echoed" the shared primeval past of human beings. The "will" found symbolic expression in "the tone of the speaker."[105]

The *Birth of Tragedy* distinguished "two main currents" in the history of Greek poetry according to whether language was "used to imitate the world of appearance or that of music."[106] Lyric poetry and folk tales, Nietzsche argued, showed a remarkable affinity with music.

In contrast to epics and the opera, the content of words and concepts did not threaten the musicality of these verbal art forms.[107] Nietzsche especially believed that the dramatic dithyrambs of Greek antiquity, choric poems or chants sung by revelers in honor of Dionysus, were musical mirrors of the cosmos. Like the chorus in Attic tragedy, lyric poetry allowed for a "mysterious marriage"[108] of the worlds of will and appearance. Its Apollonian language made music visible. Words recalled in the tone of the speaker the primordial "oneness of nature" without collapsing into empty concepts and content.

In his Romantic desire to tap into a lost world of will and desire, the early Nietzsche revealed a veneration for intact origins that resembled the nostalgic genealogies of earlier philologists. The *Birth of Tragedy* mythologized the *Ursprache* as both a formative and redemptive force in the development of German national culture. Ancient Greece and its linguistic practices offered Nietzsche an idealized model for strengthening the new nation-state. He feared that modern Germany was "caught in the net of Alexandrian culture"[109] to the extent that the prestige assigned to knowledge and conscious intelligence was having a corrosive influence on instinctual life. The "imminent rebirth of Greek antiquity" would allow the "German genius" to free itself from "the leading strings of Romance culture."[110] The tradition of German philosophy and, especially, of German music from Bach to Beethoven and Wagner, promised a "gradual reawakening of the Dionysiac spirit."[111] This retrospective on Greek culture was framed within a larger Indo-European context. Greek mythology, Nietzsche noted, especially the tale of Prometheus, was "indigenous to the entire community of Aryan races." Tragic vision and the heroic striving toward universality was an Aryan ambition, diametrically opposed to the passive, feminine, Semitic myth of the fall.[112]

The relative optimism of the *Birth of Tragedy* evaporated with Nietzsche's denial in the winter of 1872–73 that one could resurrect an absolute language of representation. Music, he concluded, was not the language of nature that directly expressed the *Ur-eine*. Nor could the artist convincingly construct such a world artificially. This change reflects Nietzsche's break with Richard Wagner, but also a new sensitivity to the rhetorical dimension of human expression.[113] While preparing a lecture course called "The History of Greek Eloquence" he lost faith in the representational function of language. Words had no preexisting referents in an authentic realm of existence; their artistic qualities existed alone for their own pleasure and purposes. This perspective altered the expectations Nietzsche held out for origins. No longer a formative moment of truth which endured despite the vagaries of time, the origin of language highlighted the total caprice of concepts.

One of the main sources for Nietzsche's depiction of ancient rhetoric was Gustav Gerber's *Language as Art* (1871). The text presented a history of German language philosophy from Hamann, Herder, Humboldt, Bernhardi, and Grimm through Max Müller, Steinthal, and Lazarus. Nietzsche's linguistic critique of epistemology clearly built upon the inspiration of the *Metakritiker.* Gerber had wished to mesh the observations of comparative philology with August Boeckh's concern for the "'artistic use' of language"—rhetoric, aesthetics, and poetics.[114] He developed "what Kant began to examine as the 'critique of pure reason' . . . as a critique of impure reason, what has become objective, thus as a critique of language."[115] This project necessitated, in Gerber's view, first and foremost an analysis of the "artistic character of language."[116] Agreeing with Heymann Steinthal, he suggested that any discussion must derive the origin of language from "the nature of man."[117] Only for Gerber living language was an unconscious creation of the *Kunsttrieb,* specifically, or the instinct for art. For Nietzsche this perspective undermined the claim that knowledge and ethical systems, built as they were on conceptual language, actually referenced stable, preexisting universal principles.

"On Truth and Lying in an Extra-Moral Sense" (1873) developed the intellectual implications of language originating in an artistic impulse. Nietzsche opened the essay by questioning why human beings had such an intense "desire for truth" given that their perspective on the world was as provincial as the gnat's. He argued that the "legislation of language" had established the "first laws of truth" in a fit of deception.[118] People had trusted the unstable foundations of language because the very idea of truth enabled them to escape a bellicose state of nature. Only by regarding language as an "adequate expression of all realities"[119] was reliable communication possible. Accepting the illusion that words referred to things allowed early humans to live in mutual trust and security. The invention of truth thus had "pleasant, life-preserving consequences."[120] Society, however, thereby exchanged a set of lies for the truth. Deception and false representation acquired a normative moral value, which Nietzsche exposed as self-destructive.

Faith in truth depended for Nietzsche on a process of forgetting.

People had to deny and repress the actual origins of language in order to believe in the accuracy of representations, for acknowledging the rhetorical foundation of words would have destabilized the shaky edifice of truth. Nietzsche's critique of representational language assumed that "language itself is the result of purely rhetorical arts." The artistic impulses that transformed nerve stimuli into images and these into sounds and words were dominated by metaphors and arbitrary transferences. The origin of language was therefore not "a logical process."[121] The relationship of a word to its referent was always partial, transferable, and reversible, subject to three tropes: synecdoche, metaphor, and metonymy.[122] Signs, for this reason, were arbitrary, not "correspond[ing] at all to the original entities." The sounds that stood for the image of an object or idea were "based as little as rhetoric is upon that which is true, upon the essence of things." Language "designate[d] only the relations of things to men."[123] Things in themselves did not pass into consciousness, but "the manner in which we stand toward them."[124]

Language, consequently, could never instruct speakers about the true nature of objects. It could only convey a subjective impulse. The lectures on rhetoric offer an early formulation of Nietzsche's perspectivism, or the notion that full and essential knowledge of the world cannot be had.[125] One could only ever encounter the partial images that nerve impulses made of objects. On this basis Nietzsche concluded that truth was nothing but "a mobile army of metaphors, metonyms, anthropomorphisms," "in short, a sum of human relations which were poetically and rhetorically heightened, transferred, and adorned, and after long use seem solid, canonical, and binding to a nation. Truths are illusions about which it has been forgotten that they *are* illusions."[126] Abstract language was most guilty of perpetuating the illusion of truth. Concepts, Nietzsche asserted, claimed the greatest scientific authority while repressing most violently their origins in rhetoric.[127]

Nietzsche took greatest issue with the continued social sanction of these illusions and the life-denying implications this had for the individual. In his view, society imposed a moral obligation to be "truthful" and uphold established metaphors. To lie collectively became mandatory for everyone. And people soon did so unconsciously. An edifice of false concepts acquired the "rigid regularity of a Roman columbarium," according to Nietzsche, and this increasingly detached human beings from "the concrete world of primary impressions."[128] Constantly repressing his desires, man forgot himself as "an artistically creative subject."[129]

The power of illusions was not absolute for Nietzsche, however. Truth may have been "the sepulcher of intuition," but humanity's repressed instincts repeatedly returned, forcing people to reckon with the "terrible powers which constantly press[ed] upon" them.[130] The second section of his essay proposed a revaluation of the individual's relationship to language that tapped into the life-affirming potential of artistic drives. Recognizing the rhetorical foundations of knowledge would, in his view, liberate "intuitive man." Nietzsche envisioned a new, life-affirming relationship to language and truth. The "liberated intellect" would approach the existing edifice of concepts like a "scaffolding and plaything for his boldest artifices."[131] Future individuals would "speak in sheer forbidden metaphors and unheard of conceptual compounds . . . smashing and scorning old conceptual barriers."[132]

"On Truth and Lying" signaled a new relationship to origins and the rewards Nietzsche hoped to reap by practicing linguistic genealogy. As Michel Foucault has argued, Nietzsche inverted the traditional German attempt to capture the exact essence and identity of things by uncovering their origins. Origins were a site of truth in the older view; they signified the existence of immobile forms that preceded the historical world.[133] After 1873 Nietzsche no longer dreamed of resurrecting an ideal cultural starting point for Germany, one that reached back to a primordial period of authentic being. Rather, he began to write the "history of an error we call truth."[134] Genealogy, for the later Nietzsche, offered a powerful form of cultural criticism. Reconstructing the history of language could identify the accidents, errors, and false appraisals that gave birth to conventional standards of truth and morality. Nietzsche's form of genealogy suggested that stable ontological categories did not lie at the root of metaphysics but arose in the exteriority of accidents. It likewise dispelled the chimera of historical continuity and the prospect that a formative moment of origin secretly animated the present.[135] Etymology and the history of language had value for Nietzsche as philosophical critique; philology did not sustain substantial identities and the illusion of authenticity but unraveled them.

The *Genealogy of Morals: An Attack* (1887) offered a case study of how etymology could destabilize the Christian "ethics of pity" by exposing its profane origins. It marks a new concern for the effects language change had on cultural development, but also inaugurates Nietzsche's linguistic critique of metaphysics. The *Genealogy of Morals* approached words as shapers of events that had through history transformed and molded culture and human communities. Specifically, he expected "the science of linguistics" to shed new light on "the evolution of moral ideas."[136] In Nietzsche's view, compassion and self-denial posed "the greatest danger for humanity." For similar to "a narcotic drug," these values turned the will against life.[137] He hoped to cure Europe of Christianity by investigating how human beings had constructed the value judgments good and evil.[138] Nietzsche concluded that the Christian world had attributed transcendental significance to arbitrary linguistic conventions. Language, he suggested, had mysteriously acquired ontological status as speakers mistook linguistic distinctions for absolute metaphysical categories.

Tracing the history of terms for "good" allowed Nietzsche to present Christian values as an aberration from the vital morality of a master race. Etymology proved that the spiritual designation "good" derived from concepts of "nobility" in the sense of a social elite. By contrast, the term "bad" had once referred to the common, plebian, or base folk. These value judgments had affirmed the strength of a ruling elite and given free rein to their instincts and desire. Dominant individuals expressed their natural passions and creativity, unhampered by transcendental notions of right and wrong. This morality had a racial content for Nietzsche, having been introduced by an "Aryan race of conquerors." The "good, noble, pure, originally the fair-haired" stood in contrast to a "dark, black-haired native population"[139] who represented "human retrogression." Their influence had domesticated the original instincts of the invaders and transformed a noble people into "the mass of sickly and effete creatures whom Europe is beginning to stink of today."[140]

The "snare of language" explained for Nietzsche how a weak class of slaves could have usurped moral authority from this ruling elite.[141] He argued that the Christian notion of the soul was a strategic invention of the oppressed. But the peculiarities of Indo-European grammar had conditioned all people to honor their ideas. The strength of the nobility, in his view, had taken the form of un-self-conscious activity. Like birds of prey, the masters obeyed natural urges. Devious in their revenge, however, priests suggested that all activity was "conditioned by an agent—the 'subject.'" They separated the pure expression of strength from "a neutral agent" that could freely choose to rein in or unleash its power. Once guided by a soul, human subjects felt an unnatural moral responsibility to curtail their natural aggression. Nietzsche insisted that "no such agent exists"; there was no being behind the doing. Instead, the "dupe of linguistic habits" had naturalized the illusion that an autonomous subject lurked behind every action. This sleight of hand gave the "appearance of free choice."[142]

The *Genealogy of Morals* specifically exposed as a linguistic fiction the desire to submit to self-imposed responsibility or "guilt" (*Schuld*). The moral category of bad conscience or duty had emerged, in Nietzsche's view, from the economic sphere of contracts and legal obligations.[143] All feelings of obligation had their inception in material debts (*Schulden*). When a person became unable to meet his obligations, he had once been expected to offer compensation in the form of bestowing pleasure. Powerful creditors had enjoyed watching the weak suffer pain; the economic contract served as a legal warrant to exercise cruelty.[144] Denied the opportunity to impose pain on others, the weak directed their instincts inward, denying and mortifying themselves to gain a modicum of pleasure. Like a "wild beast hurling itself against the bars of its cage," the slave class fetishized God as a form of self-punishment.[145] This signified a redemptive moment in the ascetic, self-denying ideals of Christian morality for Nietzsche. The faithful wrongly assumed that there was inherent meaning in the universe, a set of universal ethical ideals that justified self-denial. Yet their attempt to create meaning out of a void testified to another type of desire. Even a "will to nothingness, a revulsion from life" preserved for Nietzsche a kernel of the same will to power needed to rejuvenate the decadent culture of modern Europe.[146]

Notebook entries from 1885 to 1886 show Nietzsche expanding the linguistic critique of metaphysics at which he hinted in the essay "On the Origin of Language." In a fragment on the predicate and in later passages from *Beyond Good and Evil* (1886) and the *Twilight of the Idols* (1888), Nietzsche dismantled what he considered to be an untenable metaphysical edifice built upon chance grammatical structures. Analysis of language led him, on the one hand, to question the authority of the coherent, knowing subject. The confidence philosophers invested in the transcendental subject, as a stable center of knowledge, was, in Nietzsche's view, merely a projection of misplaced faith in the grammatical subject. Nietzsche likewise asserted that familiar ontological categories, such as Being, substance, and causation, were illusions evoked by nothing more than grammatical habits. These linguistic conventions, he hoped to show, hid a more brutal reality governed by an ever-present will to power.

At the center of Nietzsche's epistemological skepticism lay a critique of the subject-predicate sentence structure. The predicate found in Indo-European languages, he feared, raised the "erroneous idea that the subject was cause." Everything that happens, he noted, "relates predicatively to some kind of subject." For this reason, "man believes himself to be cause, perpetrator."[147] It was a "falsification of facts," in his view, to conclude that "the subject 'I' is the condition of the predicate 'think.'" Philosophers were merely "following grammatical habits" when they assumed that "behind every activity something is active."[148] For Nietzsche the transcendental subject, like the soul, had "a merely apparent existence."[149] The "I," in his view, was "a fable a fiction, a play on words." It was a "surface phenomenon of consciousness, an accessory to the act."[150] The "grammatical custom that adds a doer to every deed"[151] obfuscated a deeper reality in which all appearances and actions stemmed from "one basic form of will . . . the will to power."[152]

Philosophy had become implicated in a "crude fetishism" of the grammatical subject due to an error in evaluating free will. According to Nietzsche, people wanted to believe "in the will as the cause in general."[153] The practice of attributing actions to a grammatical subject enabled them to imagine a sovereign intention behind every cause.[154] Priests, for example, wanted individuals to bear responsibility for their actions so they could judge and punish others; they had invented the soul in order to impose punishments in the name of God. This "disaster of an error"[155] had implications for the faith philosophers placed in God and the existence of fixed essences. Language wrongly became the measure of reality for Nietzsche, so that "every word, every sentence" became proof of a divinely inspired rational order. "'Reason' in language," Nietzsche elaborated, "oh what a deceitful old woman! I am afraid we are not getting rid of God because we still believe in grammar."[156] Language, in his view, gave birth to a false theology and prevented philosophers from questioning inherited metaphysical structures.

Nietzsche notably associated these pitfalls with the Indo-European language family, recalling earlier forms of linguistic determinism. The "strange family resemblance" he perceived in Indian, Greek, and German thought stemmed, in his view, from a "common philosophy of grammar." Bound by the "spell of particular grammatical functions," Indo-European speakers had succumbed to the "unconscious domination and direction" of language.[157] Furthermore, Nietzsche compared the tyranny of language to "the spell of *physiological* value judgments and racial conditioning."[158] He assumed that a language's "tempo of style" was "grounded in the character of the race." Germans, for example, were incapable of "presto" in their language, developing instead a style that was "ponderous, lumbering, solemnly awkward, . . . long-winded and boring."[159]

Nietzsche's radical critique of reason and subjectivity did not end in despair. The practice of genealogy gave philosophers the unique opportunity to "rise above the belief in grammar" and renounce their seductive "governess."[160] Starting with *Beyond Good and Evil,* his own writing increasingly turned to fragments, aphorisms, metaphors, and parodies as a more legitimate means of creating meaning than the conceptual language of logic. The language of transgression, madness, impropriety, and excess was preferable to scientific discourse for Nietzsche because it openly avowed its deception and admitted to being an artistic construct.[161] Nietzsche likewise explored how a new relationship to language could enhance the creativity of dynamic individuals and further their will to power. For people who self-consciously wielded the power of language, each moment of linguistic production imposed values that molded human society. By manipulating the spoken and written word, the strong gained an ability to change existing values within language itself and within broader cultural or moral systems. For the late Nietzsche, human beings had the capacity to exploit the unconscious foundations of language as creative possibilities and to translate them into a conscious will, force, and action.[162] This emancipatory practice depended on a critical view of origins and a new relationship to genealogy.

Structuralist Linguistics: Ferdinand de Saussure

Ferdinand de Saussure likewise responded critically to the idealization of origins within fin-de-siècle German linguistics, himself probing the limits of the speaking subject's agency. Whereas Nietzsche critically reappropriated the genealogical method, Saussure met the crisis of historicism facing linguistics by emphasizing the synchronic dimensions of language. The recognized father of structuralist linguistics all but eliminated the allure origins and diachronic change held for his followers. At any given moment in history, language appeared to Saussure as an autonomous system of signification whose laws operated without the knowing participation of speakers. Signs, in his view, were arbitrary so that speakers lacked a stable foundation for intervening in the language state that confronted them. Like Nietzsche, Saussure denied the existence of stable external referents in either the material or metaphysical world. In his view signs represented nothing more than a series of relational values determined by structures internal to the language system itself. For this reason the idea of a self-determining speaking subject was merely an illusion conjured by a false sense of language having external referents.

Saussure's synchronic approach to linguistics is frequently seen as a radical departure from the past. His *Course on General Linguistics* (1916) often assumes iconic status as a "zero hour" in intellectual history, a new point of departure for twentieth-century structuralists.[163] And it certainly inspired a new style of humanistic inquiry. In his inaugural lecture to the Collège de France in 1961, the anthropologist Claude Levi-Strauss recognized Saussure as the founder of a new science of signs or semiotics that had applications across the human sciences.[164] Historians of linguistics, however, rightly maintain the necessity of situating Saussure within the German tradition of comparative philology.[165] He trained under the Neogrammarians in Leipzig, exhibiting an extraordinary talent for historical linguistics before transferring his energies to the general study of language.

Saussure's interest in synchronic linguistics evolved gradually out of his comparative-historical studies. There was no abrupt moment of conversion nor any dramatic defection from the German field. In fact, other linguists trained in the same milieu questioned the origin paradigm at the same time. In the last quarter of the nineteenth century, the inability to explain language change over time drew the attention of some Neogrammarians, for example, to the role of the speaker. Saussure adapted aspects of the methodology Hermann Paul presented in his *Principles of the History of Language*, building on a critique of historical-mindedness internal to the Neogrammarian movement itself. Philologists outside of Germany, such as the American William Dwight Whitney (1827–94), also explored problems of language use, rather than continuing to regard language as an independent organism with its own internal mechanisms of growth. This attention to the role of language in communication and social interaction raised synchronic concerns. Saussure borrowed terminology and the impetus to create a general theory of language from figures trained within the German philological tradition, as well as from informed critics abroad. Unlike Whitney, Michel Bréal (1832–1915), and other French critics of German science, however, Saussure never endowed the speaking subject with full semiotic agency, preferring to uphold the autonomy of the linguistic system. His theory of representation limited the ability of the subject to transcend the arbitrary structures that governed thought.

The young Genevan's initiation to the German tradition occurred via a local star in Indo-European philology. A family friend introduced Saussure to Adolphe Pictet, a compatriot and author of the *Origins of the Indo-Europeans or the Primitive Aryans* (1859). By age twelve, Saussure had read several chapters of the book and presented Pictet with the outline of a "general system of language."[166] The older son of a distinguished academic family, he entered the University of Geneva in 1875 intending to study chemistry but found himself drawn to courses in Indo-European languages, especially the classical European tongues. Having read Georg Curtius's *Principles of Greek Etymology* (1858), Saussure decided to register at the University of Leipzig in the fall of 1876, just as the structuralist psychologist Wilhelm Wundt was establishing his psychology laboratory there. The founder of structuralist linguistics trained at the same university where Wundt explored the structures of conscious experience, and Saussure later classified linguistics as a field within social psychology. He attended Curtius's classes in comparative grammar and spent two years working closely with Karl Brugmann, Hermann Osthoff, Karl Verner, and August Leskien. With the exception of a year in Berlin, where he studied Sanskrit, Saussure remained in Leipzig until obtaining his doctorate in 1880.

The precocious student earned his credentials as a historical linguist by the age of twenty-one, publishing a rigorous *Memoir on the Primitive System of Vowels in the Indo-European Languages* in 1878. The text proposed recognizing the existence of another phoneme in Proto-Indo-European in order to explain patterns of vowel alteration in the languages known to derive from it. Saussure tackled the problem of the sounds associated with the vowel "a," exemplifying the type of historical reconstruction that was the hallmark of the Neogrammarians. After it was deciphered, cuneiform Hittite was found to contain a phoneme that behaved as Saussure had predicted; the student had discovered what in theory were later termed Indo-European laryngeals. More importantly, as Jonathan Culler has suggested, the *Memoir* may have helped Saussure conceive of language as a system of purely relational items. The author did not define the substance of the missing phoneme but presented a formal missing "sonant coefficient."[167]

The historically minded *Memoir* was Saussure's only major lifetime publication. Two Geneva colleagues, Charles Bally and Albert Sechehaye, compiled the *Course in General Linguistics* posthumously from students' lecture notes. Already during his Leipzig years, however, Saussure engaged debates on the general state of language that transpired both within and in opposition to the German tradition. In the early phases of his career Saussure formed an interest in synchronic linguistics, fueled by intellectual encounters with William Dwight Whitney and Hermann Paul. American and French scholars reacted first to the extreme historicism of the German tradition, challenging the predominance of organicist metaphors that treated language as an autonomous force independent of human affairs.[168] Whitney, Paul, and Bréal encouraged researchers to consider the intentions, behavior, and mindset of speakers when analyzing language, as well as the situation in which language was used. Only by ceasing to regard national tongues as living beings beyond the control of speakers could the general conditions that shaped language be investigated. John Joseph has established that Saussure met Whitney during a shared stay in Berlin in the spring of 1879. In his view Whitney's critique of the German philological tradition influenced Saussure's conception of the institutional nature of language and the need to develop synchronic linguistic inquiry.[169]

A professor of Sanskrit and Comparative Philology at Yale, Whitney trained in Berlin and Tübingen during the early 1850s, returning to Germany periodically to conduct research on his *Sanskrit Grammar* (1879). He was the person most responsible for transplanting German philological techniques to the United States, often competing with Friedrich Max Müller for the ear of English-speaking audiences. Whitney, however, rejected the perceived historical excesses of German linguistic theory. Especially after 1870 he berated Schleicher and Max Müller for their organicism and for a naturalistic model of language change that downplayed the agency of human speakers. Steinthal he faulted as well for a metaphysical mysticism that threatened the inductive, empirical methods of true science. "Language is not an emanation of the soul, nor a physical organism," Whitney explained, "but an institution, or part of human culture."[170] Words did not have a life of their own, in his view; rather, language was a conventional tool of communication that speakers tailored toward their own purposes.

The great faux pas of German linguistics, according to Whitney, was a propensity to eliminate the speaker from discussions of language change. As he wrote in the *Life and Growth of Language* (1875), his colleagues wrongly "den[ied] the agency of the human will in the changes of speech."[171] Instead they relied on a "mysterious natural process, in which men have no part," assuming that there were "organic forces in speech itself which—by fermentation, or digestion, or crystallization . . . produce new material and alter old."[172] Whitney countered that "individual minds, capable of choice, under wide-reaching motives and inducements" produced language change.[173] The intervention of conscious human will altered the linguistic framework inherited by a given community. This change in perspective followed from Whitney's declaring language to be the "most ancient and valuable of man's social institutions."[174] No longer an autonomous organism with its own internal laws of development, language was a tool subject to human needs and desires. An elaborate system of arbitrary signs allowed speakers to communicate preexisting ideas and coordinate their actions; language was a pragmatic instrument. Any little "bit of linguistic growth," Whitney concluded, was "the act of a human being, working toward definable ends under the government of recognizable motives."[175]

Whitney challenged the very foundations of German linguistics, and the Neogrammarians heard his call. August Leskien translated the *Life and Growth of Language* in 1876, and the text had a significant impact on the Leipzig circle.[176] The commemoration Brugmann wrote upon Whitney's death, for example, credited the American with helping German Indo-Europeanists to "turn against a number of widely spread methodological flaws in the[ir] research."[177] Saussure noted Whitney's influence on his own development in several manuscript pages. And Konrad Koerner has concluded that Whitney was a major source for Saussure's conceiving of language as a social system. Whitney suggested that understanding language change required exploring the relationship between the individual and the speech community. He likewise affirmed that language could be conceived as a totality and introduced Saussure to the term "value" and to the distinction between substance and form.[178]

Next to Whitney, Hermann Paul exerted the greatest influence on Saussure. His explanation for the regularity of language change likewise directed Saussure's attention to synchronic linguistics.[179] Paul's *Principles of the History of Language* insisted that "clear views as to the conditions of the life of language" were necessary for establishing "a thoroughly trustworthy basis for historical investigation."[180] Paul distinguished between historical grammar and a "descriptive" branch of linguistics concerned with the general conditions of language use. The scholar, in his view, could not "avoid describing states of language" nor the way individual speech acts contributed to the life of a tongue. Those aspects of language study that "claim exemption from historical observation" included "general reflections upon the individual employment of language, and about the relation of the individual speaker to the general use of language."[181] Paul's conception of linguistics as a double science was an important foundation for Saussure's distinction between diachronic and synchronic language study.[182]

The proper object of linguistic study was for Paul a sequence of "linguistic states" (*Zustände*), each of which was governed by the use of language "at a given date within a certain community."[183] He reconstructed an underlying system of speech, comparable to Saussure's *langue,* that evolved historically but could not be understood with reference to origins or genealogy alone. Descriptive linguistics, as Paul understood it, explored the "general usage of language" (*allgemeinen Sprachusus*).[184] The linguist analyzed the "entire sum of the products of the linguistic activity of the entire sum of individuals in their reciprocal relations." Ideally this field considered "all the groups of sound ever spoken, heard, or represented, with the associated ideas, whose symbols they were; all the numerous relations entered into by the elements of speech in the minds of individuals." But Paul conceded that a "gulf" existed between one's powers and the possibilities.[185] Linguists could at most "obtain a certain average, by which the strictly normal part of language—namely, its usage is defined."[186]

The dichotomy between language usage and the individual's linguistic expression (*parole*) emerged as one of Saussure's main concerns. He took an opposing view to Paul, insisting that *langue* was independent of individual speech. For Saussure language as a system was not complete in the individual; it existed only in the multitude. *Langue* and *parole* were separate objects of research.[187] Paul's focus on the individual reflects his own grounding in psychology, as well as his dispute with the comparative psychologists Steinthal and Lazarus. Paul insisted that "every linguistic creation is always the work of one single individual only."[188] The representatives of *Völkerpsychologie* had mistakenly applied the laws governing the psychical process of the single mind to nations. According to Konrad Koerner, Saussure's insistence that language was independent of the individual and external to her was an overreaction to Paul's contention that language could only be observed in the individual speaker. He recognized difficulties in Paul's position and favored a sociological approach over the psychology of the individual.[189]

Significantly, Paul asserted that individual speakers always had an unconscious impact on language. He allowed little consideration of the will and intention behind linguistic activity. All linguistic formulations had an "involuntary character" in Paul's analysis. They were "created without preconceived intention, at all events without an intention of establishing anything lasting, and without consciousness on the part on an individual of his creative activity."[190] Individual linguistic activity affected language use. But the "forces at work" that ultimately shaped the general conditions for the life of language "flow[ed] from this dark chamber of the unconscious in the mind."[191] The physical organs of speakers, as well as psychical processes of association and analogy, determined how language was produced and evolved historically.

The French philologists with whom Saussure resided for ten years after leaving Leipzig reserved a more assertive role for the speaking subject. Saussure had joined the Société de linguistique de Paris before leaving Geneva; soon after arriving in the French capital in 1880 he became its assistant secretary charged with writing summaries of biweekly meetings. Michel Bréal arranged for Saussure to be appointed lecturer in Germanic languages, Sanskrit, Latin, Farsi, and Lithuanian at the École pratique des hautes études. Since the 1860s and especially following the Franco-Prussian war of 1870, French linguists had been distancing themselves from the German masters under whom many had trained. The extent to which figures such as Bréal, Gaston Paris (1839–1903), and Antoine Meillet (1866–1936) shaped Saussure's disaffection with historicism is debated. Hans Aarsleff insists that Bréal gave Saussure's "new linguistics its fresh French cast" and resurrected an eighteenth-century concern for representation and signification.[192] Koerner counters that French influence on Saussure's general theory of language was "slight, if not negligible."[193] Saussure did not present any portion of the later *Course* in Paris, and his students did not pursue the precepts of his synchronic linguistics.[194] Regardless of Bréal's direct impact on Saussure, his concerns reveal the disfavor into which German linguistics was falling internationally by the late nineteenth century.

The son of French Jewish émigrés, Michel Bréal was born in Rhenish Bavaria but returned to Alsace when his father died in 1837. His early career was dedicated to establishing a German school of comparative philology in France. Bréal had studied Sanskrit with Bopp and Albrecht Weber in Berlin and made his reputation by translating the former's *Comparative Grammar* into French in 1866. Bopp, according to Bréal, had rightly dispelled the "mysticism" of the Romantic fascination with India and first developed the principle of uniformitarianism, assuming language was always subject to the same laws and basic conditions. Bopp had also refused to succumb to the excessive naturalism of Schleicher, whose *Compendium* Bréal opted not to translate.[195] In the 1870s the French scholar increasingly turned against comparative German philology, however, raising concerns shared by Whitney about the conditions of language change. His inaugural lecture at the Collège de France faulted German comparativists for a "purely external study of words."[196] A focus on origins and evolution had detached form from meaning, as if language scholars merely documented "a fourth natural realm" devoid of human intention.[197] Bréal imagined language to be a semiotic system and proposed like Whitney that signs were both arbitrary and conventional.

For Bréal conscious, rational agents were the source of linguistic change. Observers should recall that "language is a human act; it has no reality outside of human activity. . . . Everything in language comes from man and is addressed to man."[198] He coined the term "semantics" in 1883 to describe the discipline that explored how speakers created linguistic meaning and engaged in processes of signification. For Bréal, speech was "foremost a means of communication"; "our speech organs" were "at the service of our thinking and only convey what is going on in the mind."[199] The evolution of language thus depended on the activities of speakers and hearers as they gave meaning to the world and sought to be understood.

In the closing decades of the nineteenth century, linguists attempted to restore to speakers a portion of the agency that comparative-historical philology denied them. The difficulty of explaining linguistic change over time compromised the autonomy of language as an entity presumably driven by its own internal laws. Scholars trained in the German tradition raised problems of meaning and signification in the 1870s, questioning the Neogrammarian focus on original forms and their evolution through time. Saussure's resurrection of the sign and his concern for processes of signification followed, in this sense, a broader trend. His work evolved as part of an internal reaction to the historicization of language within Germany that considered language to be a social institution and means of communication. Neogrammarians and their critics alike were on the cusp of creating a quasi-structuralist science of language states when Saussure took on the project.

Saussure assumed a professorship in the history and comparison of Indo-European languages at the University of Geneva in 1891. Not until 1906, however, did he offer the lectures on "general linguistics" for which he is famed. Saussure delivered three courses on the topic before 1911. Unlike other scholars responding to the German historical tradition, Saussure did not emphasize the free will and autonomy of speaking subjects. Rather, the "militant anti-humanism"[200] of which structuralism has been accused, can be tied to his subsuming individual speakers to the vagrancies of a linguistic system. Structuralism and its disregard for the subject ironically emerged out of the quintessential humanist discipline, philology. Saussure returned questions of representation to the heart of linguistics, while radically curtailing the semiotic agency of individuals. Signs were arbitrary and their value depended on a temporally fixed set of linguistic relations. Language, in his model, preserved its autonomy and destabilized the human subject.

Starting in 1870, Saussure recalled in the *Course*, Whitney and the Neogrammarians began to investigate "the principles that govern the life of languages."[201] He credited his predecessors with dismantling organicist metaphors and depicting language instead as "a product of the collective mind of linguistic groups." Yet Saussure feared that the fundamental problems of general linguistics still awaited solution.[202] The *Course* sought to rectify the methodological flaws plaguing comparative-historical philology by defining the object of linguistic inquiry. This, according to Saussure, included "all manifestations of human speech" (*langage*)[203] and could be broken down into two distinct entities: language proper (*langue*) and speaking (*parole*). The separation of these key terms followed from Saussure's conception of the basic speaking-circuit. The execution of a particular speech act was, in his view, always individual, willful, and intellectual. Speaking or *parole* allowed a person to combine linguistic units uniquely so that she might express her thoughts. It was a psychophysical process that could never be studied in its totality given its inevitable heterogeneity.

The "social crystallization of language" presented Saussure with the true object of linguistic study. Like Whitney and Paul, he assumed language was foremost a "social product."[204] *Langue* resembled a general "storehouse" filled by the members of a linguistic community; it contained the "grammatical system" and the "sum of word-images" present in their minds. Saussure assumed for this reason that language was never "complete in any speaker; it exists perfectly only within the collectivity."[205] He defined *langue* more specifically as a "self-contained whole," a homogeneous "system of distinct signs corresponding to distinct ideas."[206] This system could be studied independently of all other aspects of natural language. It had its own internal arrangement and rules that remained untouched by individual acts of speaking.

Autonomy was a defining characteristic of language in Saussure's conception. The system he envisioned was, for one, not "affected by the will of the depositaries,"[207] either as individual speakers or a community. Participants could never "create or modify" *langue* on their own; speakers merely assimilated a system of signs passively and made use of it without premeditation.[208] The arbitrary nature of the linguistic sign likewise contributed to this autonomy, as Saussure imagined it. He followed Whitney in assuming that "language is a convention and the nature of the sign that is agreed upon does not matter."[209] But Saussure did not share the American's confidence that ready-made ideas existed before words. In his view, signs did not unite a thing and a name, but a concept and a sound-image. And the bond uniting the pair was entirely unmotivated. The arbitrary nature of the sign was, on the one hand, the result of Saussure's recognizing the historicity of language.[210] Sound and meaning were in constant flux; the particular combination of signified and signifier shifted according to contingent historical processes.[211]

On the other hand, Saussure denied that the signified possessed an essential internal core that might stand outside of time and resist change. The meaning of any given word was not predicated on its etymology, but rather on its location within the system of language currently available to speakers. Language states were "determined by nothing except the momentary arrangement of terms."[212] The signified existed only in relation to a signifier whose meaning depended on its relative position within the larger system of language. For this reason the sign had to be studied at the moment of its articulation and as a point of intersection within a particular synchronic state. Laws of sound change and other historical realities never affected a given system as a whole; the evolution of specific linguistic elements had to be studied outside the totality. Saussure therefore strictly separated synchronic and diachronic approaches to linguistics. For him, the science of language states could succeed "only by completely suppressing the past."[213] To interpret language as a product of its own genealogical development wrongly denied the self-sufficiency of the system.

The arbitrariness of the sign did not convey creative choice upon the speaker, however. Unlike Locke, Saussure did not regard language as "a contract pure and simple," a "rule to which all freely consent."[214] Neither individuals nor the community could "modify" or "control the linguistic sign."[215] Despite appearances, it was effectively fixed and immutable with respect to the users of language. Signs resisted arbitrary substitution because a given language state was "always the product of historical forces."[216] The power of tradition prohibited willful change and replacement. The arbitrary nature of the sign likewise protected it from any attempts at modification. Speakers had no "reasonable basis" for evaluating the appropriateness of a sign because the signified existed solely in conjunction with an arbitrary sound-image.[217] An individual could not present arguments for substituting a freely chosen sign as the more natural or correct designation.

The purely relational identity of the sign rendered the structure of language self-sufficient. For Saussure, language was "a system of pure values."[218] The meaning of signs was relational, a factor of their ties to other elements in the linguistic system. Scholars of language should therefore approach language as they would a game of chess. The value of a linguistic unit, like that of a game piece, was made up "solely of relations and differences with respect to . . . other terms."[219] Only the simultaneous presence of other elements bestowed value on a given signifier. Saussure concluded that "language is a form not a substance."[220] Its component parts were based entirely on relations of identity and difference, calculated formally without regard for what might be considered the substantial or material content of the signifier. He identified two specific types of relationships that existed in a language-state: associative and syntagmatic. Both gave value to linguistic units based on an internal framework of binary opposites.

Saussure's rejection of nomenclaturism bestowed autonomy on

language as a system for creating meaning. "There are no pre-existing ideas," Saussure explained, "and nothing is distinct before the appearance of language."[221] Specifically, Saussure imagined language and thought as two parallel domains, both originally "shapeless and confused." The "floating realm of thought" existed alongside "phonic substance." The "indefinite plane of jumbled ideas" was "equally vague" as the "plane of sounds" until language provided demarcation. Language, for Saussure, was not a "mold"; it did not create "a material phonic means for expressing ideas." Rather, language "serve[d] as a link between thought and sound" delimiting units of both. The choice of a given "slice of sound" to name a given idea was completely arbitrary; neither had a foundation outside the relative framework provided by language. But Saussure insisted that thought and sound were as inseparable as the recto and verso of a sheet of paper. The structures of language gave form to thought in a similar manner: the observer could "neither divide sound from thought nor thought from sound."[222] Knowledge, by implication, was always particular to the system of identity and difference that governed the interaction of linguistic units. The relative value of linguistic signs set the parameters for thought, and there was no escaping the structures of the system.

Saussure's perspective on the autonomy of language differed substantially from the view of earlier comparativists, yet its implications for the speaking subject were equally severe. August Schleicher imagined the life and growth of national tongues transpiring in complete isolation from human beings. Languages, in his view, followed an internal principle of development that remained unchanged from the first moment of its inception. Renan and Friedrich Max Müller likewise assumed that linguistic conventions determined the thought patterns and cultural practices of human communities. Language actively shaped the human experience by presenting a grammar that united members of a nation. Even Steinthal and the Neogrammarians, who attempted to recognize the contributions of speakers, concluded that language change occurred in an unconscious realm. Hidden psychological and physiological mechanisms influenced the origin and evolution of national tongues. In these cases, the authority of a language derived from its historical continuity. Origins remained a formative moment in these narratives, creating habits of thought and behavior that nations and human subjects could not escape.

The structuralist model of Ferdinand de Saussure dissolved the agency of speakers in a synchronic field. Human beings ceased to be transcendental subjects with the potential to operate outside of a linguistic system. There was no privileged center from which the knowing subject could survey a metaphysical or empirical reality. From a structuralist perspective, the subject is neither sovereign nor self-sufficient; she is defined by a system of relations whose very existence escapes her gaze. The play of difference and the multiplicity of linguistic relations create subject positions that individuals subsequently inhabit.[223] This perspective undermined traditional Western notions of the subject. As Jonathan Culler has argued, a whole tradition of discourse about humanity had taken the self as a conscious subject that endowed the world with meaning. Saussure displaced the sovereign subject from its function as center or source. Speakers were dissolved into a set of interpersonal systems that worked unconsciously through them. The self was no longer identified with a unified, homogeneous consciousness, but with the unintended result of conventional systems of relation. There is thus no attempt within structuralism to achieve empathetic understanding or to reconstruct a situation as it might have been consciously grasped by an individual subject.[224]

Saussure's perspective detached language from perceived human essences, whether national, racial, moral, or ontological. Structuralism overturned the remnants of an expressive theory of language, in which national tongues were guided by the spirit and proclivities of speakers. According to Saussure, correlating language with an essential being succumbed to the very type of organicism he sought to avoid by "assuming that the 'genius' of a race or ethnic group tends constantly to lead language along certain fixed routes."[225] Saussure dismissed as "largely an illusion" the prospect of reconstructing the cultural life of human communities based on archaic linguistic states.[226] Language, in his view, did contribute to a sense of "ethnic unity" (*éthnisme*), but only to the extent that this entailed a "social bond."[227] Words did not point to shared cultural origins and common genealogical descent. Rather, the discursive function of language encouraged communities to engage in the same religious, governmental, and cultural practices.

Both Saussure and Nietzsche helped reinstitute the study of language as a central concern of the human sciences. Saussure proposed a new science of semiology designed to examine "the life of signs within society."[228] Linguistics provided the "master-pattern for all branches of semiology" because, in Saussure's view, language was "the most complex and universal of all systems of expression."[229] This perspective opened a new avenue for understanding human subjects and the laws of social interaction. During the 1950s and 1960s Saussurian-inspired structuralism became a prominent intellectual movement in France, though not in Germany, after Lévi-Strauss suggested that all social practices could be interpreted as circuits of signification and exchange. Language and culture were analogous, in his view. Both were complex systems for creating meaning that relied on signs, relations of exchange, and the negotiation of identity and difference.

Nietzsche likewise reinstated rhetoric as a principle concern of the modern human sciences. He is responsible for displacing philosophy with discourse analysis as the architectonic discipline of the twentieth century.[230] Language, in his view, functioned as a "prison-house,"[231] proscribing historically contingent yet temporally fixed systems of relating ideas, signs, and the material world. For Nietzsche the aesthetics of the metaphor detached words and concepts from their referents so that language remained autonomous of all it represented. He likewise suspected that the transcendental subject was a grammatical fiction, a mirage emanating from a subject-predicate sentence structure. Yet, unlike Saussure, Nietzsche held open the possibility of salvaging a playful, postmodern subject who, once rid of her illusions, embraced the creative potential of language. Transforming the practice of genealogy into a tool of liberation, he demonstrated to Foucault and other poststructuralists how one might break the spell of discursive conventions.

A concern for the constructive powers of language was the logical conclusion of the comparative philological tradition. Nietzsche and Saussure were both heirs to a century-long tradition of language study in Germany that had in the course of extensive empirical research developed a strikingly modern appreciation for the way words and grammatical structures shape knowledge, human communities, and cultural identity. Their radical critique of subjectivity is rooted in a linguistic tradition that is neither as French nor as *post*modern as often assumed. The rise of autonomous language in nineteenth-century Germany helped set the stage for the linguistic turn of twentieth-century France.

Conclusion

The French comparativist Antoine Meillet (1866–1936) echoed the sentiments of Ernest Renan when he affirmed in 1923 that German scholars had erected "a solid edifice in comparative grammar." Up to this point, he argued, Germans had dominated the field of linguistics "in very large part." Yet Meillet believed this tradition showed "signs of decline" in the early twentieth century. Comparative philology resembled a "machine fatigued by extended use," one that had "lost its profitability."[1] Himself trained in comparative Indo-European studies, Meillet insisted that any explanation of linguistic change must approach language as a social phenomenon. German scholars had erred in assuming language was "a being that existed for itself, independently of the people who employed it." Outsiders to the tradition had recently reintroduced the speaker into considerations of language, and Meillet expected "new voices" soon to "emancipate" linguistics from its German heritage. Among other things, he admonished, students should consider a new field of "general linguistics" that was emerging from the work of W. D. Whitney and Ferdinand de Saussure.[2]

By the end of World War I, German linguistics had lost its international preeminence to various forms of European structuralism and to the United States as an emerging center for research on language.[3] The field ultimately failed to integrate and respond to the two most innovative critics it had itself produced. German scholars did not fail to recognize the significance of Saussure as a linguistic theorist. The *Course on General Linguistics* was immediately reviewed and often cited in German literature; it was even assimilated into interwar neo-Kantian "organicist" linguistics.[4] Yet the sober, methodological form of structuralism that took root in Germany was often dismissed as a continuation of positivism and thus lacking in social significance.[5] German critics treated Saussure with "indifference" and displayed little sensitivity toward the methodological implications of structuralist principles, preferring a historical approach to language.[6] Not until 1931 was the *Course* actually translated into German. Discussion of Saussure as a foundational thinker was far more prevalent in Geneva, Copenhagen, and Prague than in German cities and universities. German linguists generally assumed that structuralism broke away from a native tradition of linguistic investigation that grew out of Herder, Humboldt, and Grimm. In their view, the characteristically French focus on language as a tool of communication was more amenable to structuralism than the German appreciation of language as a living force uniting members of the *Volk*.[7] In truth, a German tradition of linguistic thought had at least in part produced Saussure after itself challenging the primacy of the *Volksgeist* as a mechanism for explaining change over time.

Nietzsche's evocation of language in the dismantling of illusory systems of truth and totality likewise found little reception among his German devotees. The fin-de-siècle German avant-garde enlisted Nietzsche in salvationist projects of cultural and political redemption very distinct from the deconstructive visions of later followers. In the early twentieth century Nietzsche inspired transvaluative programs of regeneration designed to overcome an impending sense of nihilism. This focus on creative, positive reconstruction precluded serious engagement with Nietzsche's canonical texts on language.[8] The philosophical implications of his linguistic work did not gain a more serious audience for another fifty years. Under the custodianship of Elisabeth Förster-Nietzsche, Nietzsche's early legacy was also annexed by the most extreme, anti-Semitic members of the *völkisch,* eugenicist, and Alldeutsch nationalist movements. These circles ironically transformed Nietzsche into a prophet of Aryan racism and a purified and de-Judaized German Christianity.[9] The alternative concepts of language offered by Saussure and Nietzsche found far greater resonance among social scientists, literary scholars, and philosophers in France and the United States, especially after the second world war.

German language scholars resisted the challenge Saussure and Nietzsche posed to the origin paradigm that had dominated comparative philology through most of the nineteenth century. Instead, the various fields of philology and linguistics gravitated, as Suzanne Marchand has shown, toward a deepening historicism and toward an illiberal, neo-Romantic fascination with cultural particularism.[10] The German universities were a center of conservatism and reaction after World War I, hostile to the Weimar Republic and the encroaching forces of modernism and democratization; classical philologists, especially, feared irrelevance as political commentators and national cultural mentors.[11] Political commitments alone, however, cannot explain the relative German neglect of Saussure and structuralism. The notion of language existing as a synchronic system was compatible after World War I with allegiance to a fascist state, racism, and ideological nationalism, just as it could support an egalitarian notion of a social order without internal hierarchies.[12] However, resuming the search for origins and appealing to the vital force of the *Volksgeist* enabled German language scholars to reassert more effectively the cultural relevance of a field increasingly drawn into conservative and National Socialist circles under the Weimar Republic and Third Reich.

The academic fields presiding over the points of origin from which nineteenth-century philologists traced German descent continued their search for a national cultural essence. In the 1890s Germanists integrated various neo-idealist methodologies that arose in reaction to positivism into their exploration of national literature. This entailed, on the one hand, distinguishing a supposedly inward, vital, metaphysically oriented German soul from the technical, rational, and urban society ascribed to western civilization.[13] On the other hand the new field of *Volkskunde* encouraged German philologists to consider how landscape, blood, soil, and the legacy of the ancient Germanic tribes had shaped cultural production. This perspective bound the problem of origins directly to considerations of racial and ethnic descent. August Sauer, for example, professor of German philology in Prague, sought "new evidence" for evaluating German literature in "the previously unfathomed depths of the most authentic tribalism" and in the physical reality that gave it form.[14]

Under the dual pressure of postwar pessimism and cultural historical specialization, German classicists abandoned the ideal of aristocratic, universalist humanism in exchange for a similar historicism. A universal definition of *Kultur* as the sum of human achievement was gradually replaced by the model of *Kulturen,* organically conceived cultures each driven by an instinctive will to form.[15] During the Wilhelmine period, the progressive and cosmopolitan aspects of J. G. Herder's thoughts were similarly distorted into a national chauvinism bordering on racism, retroactively transforming Herder into a prophet of militant nationalism.[16] A neo-Romantic appreciation of Greek culture and religion emphasized ritual and subrational aspects of Greek life, increasingly distancing German classicists from more social-scientific scholars in Britain and France.[17] The field of Indology also gravitated toward a neo-Romantic concern for mysticism, art, spiritualism, and aestheticism after World War I, while criticizing the stringent methods of text-critical analysis that had dominated classical philology.[18]

Comparativists once again entered the debate on the likely location of the Indo-European *Urheimat* after research on the topic had dwindled in the climate of sober positivism that characterized the Neogrammarians. Archaeologists, prehistorians, and scholars of race reopened the problem; linguists joined the fray riding the coattails of these popular disciplines and challenging their authority to interpret origin myths.[19] Advocates of locating the *Urheimat* in northern Europe drew National Socialist racial theory into linguistic scholarship, while prominent representatives of the central Asian thesis tended to be persecuted under the Third Reich.[20] Both sides of the debate, however, tapped into what Clemens Knobloch terms the "purity imperative of origin myths" and upheld the fundamental intersection of language, race, and *Volk*.[21] By contrast, in 1939, the structuralist Nikolai Trubetzkoy (1890–1938), a Russian linguist and friend of Roman Jakobson in the Prague school, declared the problem of locating the Indo-European homeland invalid; it was ridiculous, in his view, to seek the primal seat of an entity that never existed and for which solid evidence could never be found.[22]

Even the notorious Houston Stuart Chamberlain (1855–1927) laid claim to comparative philology in his immensely popular *Foundations of the Nineteenth Century* (1899), declaring his age to have been the "century of philology." Published in German, the racist tract sought legitimacy and a gloss of erudition in the "safety anchor" provided by philology. According to Chamberlain, Indologists had "unearthed buried possessions of mankind" testifying to the "genuine individuality" of the Aryan race and its Germanic vanguard. Their knowledge of the deep Indo-European past exploded the "myth of the peculiar aptitude of the Jew for religion," while intensifying the "belief in our strength" and "our independent capacity for much that is of the highest."[23] Chamberlain claimed philological support for his obscene vision of a Germanic religion in which Jesus was "morally" a Jew, but Aryan by race.[24] Chamberlain mobilized the field of philology within a radical cult of Germanism that gave credence to Nazi racism and may have predisposed readers to join the NSDAP.[25]

Linguistic research itself was dominated in Germany by the various national philologies and their *völkisch*-organicist rhetoric through the first half of the twentieth century.[26] General linguistics did not earn its independence as a fully professionalized field with its own institutional structures until the 1950s. Thus, language scholars needed training in a specific area of cultural history or literary analysis, usually Indology, in order to receive a full professorship; even in the 1920s it was impossible to habilitate exclusively as a linguist. Most people with an interest in linguistics styled themselves as philologists and regarded their research as an aid or instrument in historical analysis.[27] German language scholars did follow the broader turn-of-the-century European and American trend to interpret language within a social framework and as part of communicative practice. Only in Germany this most often resulted in language appearing as an expression of national or ethnic identity and in scholars researching culturally articulated linguistic practice with the aid of other disciplines, such as *Volkskunde*.[28] German linguistics focused not on the totality of language as a synchronic system, but on the importance of language within a totality composed of *Geist, Volk,* and *Kultur*.[29]

A new vitalist and organicist school of linguistics dominated German universities from 1918 to 1945, and the type of historicism it advocated stood in direct opposition to both Nietzsche and Saussure. These linguists rejected the apparent atomism, materialism, and methodological individualism of the late nineteenth century, focusing instead on collectivity and proclaiming language to be energy, force, and the foundation of a dynamic world order. At the start of the century Karl Vossler, a student of Romance languages, led a generational revolt against the perceived positivism of the Neogrammarians, fearing that in their specialization and expertise they had sacrificed national cultural leadership for the minutiae of science. An approach to language that was synthetic, spiritual, organic, and German was to provide new relevance to a discipline threatened by the onslaught of realism, the natural sciences, and technical advance.[30] Scholars such as the Germanist Hennig Brinkmann held language to be an autonomous life force that renewed and regenerated the nation by reanimating traditional forms.[31] Each linguistic fact could be placed in relation to a latent order that defined the totality of a language and in turn the spirit, worldview, and culture of the national collective.[32] This perspective drew on a Humboldtian tradition of regarding language as *energeia*, but for vitalist scholars the nation had expanded beyond the notion of linguistic community designated by the Romantic concept *Volk* to include a pronounced racial dimension.[33]

The German linguists who came of age after World War I rejected the biological materialism of the Neogrammarians and stood opposed to physical or materialist theories of race. The Jew who spoke and wrote perfect German symbolized for Nazi theorists how insecure the relationship between language and race was; individuals could pass all too easily from one native tongue to another. As Christopher Hutton argues, language scholarship under National Socialism was not characterized by a conflation of linguistic and racial categories but by a particular attitude toward the gap between language and ties of blood and kinship. Linguists under the Third Reich assumed a collective act of will was required to maintain the appropriate links between language, race, ethnicity, and heritage. A *völkisch* "cult of the mother tongue" was to prevent language and race from drifting further apart.[34] The impossibility of mapping linguistic genealogies onto parallel conceptions of biological descent had been apparent by the mid-nineteenth century. Nazi scholars of Yiddish did not speculate on the likely origin and descent of eastern European Jews. Instead they mapped the spread of Yiddish as a dialect and criticized its speakers for an "unhealthy" attitude toward preserving the mother tongue.[35] Recognizing disparate origins for language and race could equally have resulted in linguists assuming that the conscious adoption of German nationality was a choice open to any individual regardless of perceived racial heritage.

The National Socialist mobilization of origin motifs more closely resembles a suspect form of historical citation than the natural outgrowth of a nineteenth-century linguistic tradition. Historicism in linguistics and reference to the *Volksgeist* as a driving force of linguistic change had often served to unsettle existing political structures and challenge religious orthodoxies, just as Aryan racial theory could have liberal or progressive applications. In the nineteenth century the study of language as a field tended to attract more liberal and cosmopolitan thinkers away from the traditional national philologies and theology due to the often destabilizing implications of comparative-historical analysis. The linguists who came of age in the Wilhelmine and post–World War I eras differed from their predecessors in an often reactionary use of tropes and concepts introduced in the Romantic period. In 1932 the Celticist Leo Weisgerber thus claimed his generation was "renewing piece by piece" Humboldt's project and finally defining the nation based on language as Herder and Grimm had wished. For Weisberger, this continuity gave German linguistics its "vitality" (*Lebenskraft*).[36] Evoking memories of the early nineteenth century bestowed legitimacy on an increasingly radical *völkisch* perspective while self-consciously linking an increasingly aggressive militaristic state with an earlier, more benign form of cultural nationalism.

Defining the nation as a homogeneous linguistic community united by virtue of its members' "pure" descent from a single point of origin was, nevertheless, a problematic proposition from the start. When taken as a marker of national genealogy and as evidence of untarnished ethnic descent, language could be mobilized to exclude perceived minorities from the German nation. A historical appreciation of linguistic meanings and structures could more easily be used to reinforce a quasi-biological understanding of cultural identity being transmitted through the mother tongue. Assigning a formative role to origins and relative autonomy to inner principles of linguistic growth likewise tended to privilege the *Volksgeist* or other national essence as determining patterns of thought and interaction. By contrast, the notion of a discursive community composed of speakers who freely wield linguistic signs in the service of mutual exchange would seem to emphasize the autonomy and agency of individual participants. When placed in the constellations as such ideas assumed in the first half of the twentieth century, the German tradition of linguistic thought could be mustered in support of a criminal regime. This, however, was not a necessary outcome and not the only legacy of comparative philology.

Following World War II, the theories of language developed by Ferdinand de Saussure and Friedrich Nietzsche reemerged to inspire social scientists and philosophers west of the Rhine River. As a project for rejuvenating the social sciences in the 1950s, structuralism built upon the theory of signs developed in the *Course;* for a diverse group of anthropologists, psychologists, historians, and literary critics, language became an analogy for other aspects of human life. Structuralists were united by their common adoption of concepts from Saussurian linguistics and a concurrent methodological privileging of underlying rules over events. By contrast, greater reception of Nietzsche's thought distinguished a younger generation of poststructuralists in the later half of the 1960s who, following Michel Foucault, sought to reopen questions of history and subjectivity, while retaining their predecessors' concern for the workings of linguistic and systemic forces.[37] The alternative French legacy of comparative philology stressed the autonomy of language and pursued the implications this had for the process of subject formation and for individual agency. In every respect, structuralists and poststructuralists extended the criticisms Saussure and Nietzsche had launched against the paradigm of formative origins in linguistic thought.

That linguistics became the paradigmatic human science in postwar France ironically hinges on a delayed reception of Saussure. After World War I Russian and Swiss scholars dominated the field of structuralist linguistics. Not until the mid-1950s did modern linguistics enter the French university, where the comparative Indo-Europeanist Antoine Meillet dominated the scene; even then structuralist linguistics remained very marginal and only lay siege to Paris and the Sorbonne gradually from the provinces.[38] The anthropologist Claude Lévi-Strauss first learned of Saussure from Roman Jakobson, a leading figure in Russian formalism, during his wartime exile at the New School for Social Research in New York City. The feverish activity that surrounded the reception of structuralist linguistics in early-1960s France, as well as the ingenuity with which it was applied to the human sciences, relates to this tardiness. France had likewise been cut off from the linguistic turn in analytic philosophy, unaware of the Vienna school that had nurtured Ludwig Wittgenstein and been bypassed as its representatives sought refuge from National Socialism in Anglo-Saxon countries.[39]

Structuralist linguistics offered the possibility of achieving a new form of objectivity and rationality in a series of sciences perceived as lacking formalism.[40] Instead of trusting how individual subjects created meaning, structuralism as a method aimed to uncover the subconscious, buried, yet universal mental structures that made thought possible and upon which lived experience, culture, and society were built. These hidden structures were believed to constitute an independently existing order of reality, and their laws could be known with scientific precision. To this end, Saussure's understanding of the language system provided a model. Lévi-Strauss thus believed the structures of kinship systems, totems, and myths mimicked language; Roland Barthes asserted in 1964 that all sign systems were already language systems; and Jacques Lacan conceived of the unconscious as being structured like a language. Following Saussure, structuralists envisioned these complex systems existing as a network of relationships that united and linked their various elements. Nothing in the system had an intrinsic meaning or identity; the significance of any given item was determined relationally among other elements, and the meaning of signs could be determined objectively. What a given sign designated was thus less important than how it fit into a larger symbolic order.

This perspective resulted in a self-conscious departure from a traditional "humanist" appreciation of subjectivity and historicity, especially as most recently represented in French existential phenomenology. In the context of postfascist and postcollaborationist Europe, the notion of an autonomous, unified subject capable of choice and self-determination had been a powerful mechanism for grappling with questions of responsibility. Structuralism undermined the idea of a transcendental subject capable of perpetual self-fashioning and privileged knowledge, countering that deep linguistic processes actually constructed the self at a level beneath consciousness. For this reason, the advent of structuralism has often been linked to a conservative turn in French intellectual life and in French politics under Charles de Gaulle's Fifth Republic. Disenchanted with political activism, the reality of Russian communism, and any new ideological commitments, intellectuals gravitated to what Lévi-Strauss called a cooler temporality of rules, codes, and structures.[41] Structuralism offered disengagement from existential Marxism's model of the committed intellectual. For this reason, it was perhaps less appealing in postwar Germany, where confronting history and preserving the autonomy of subjects as ethical agents was more imperative.

In the last chapter of *The Savage Mind* (1962), Lévi-Strauss thus questioned the assumptions Jean-Paul Sartre made about the absolute freedom of transcendent consciousness and the privileged status of human beings as historical agents. For Lévi-Strauss the "ultimate goal of the human sciences" was "not to constitute, but to dissolve man." Human beings had to be integrated back into the objective structures of nature so they could be studied "as if they were ants."[42] In his view, historical subjects were merely surface phenomena, a mirage of sorts hovering above a deeper reality. Sartre's belief that human beings forged their own existence as masters of history was, from an anthropological perspective, a local and contingent form of self-perception; it was equivalent to the myths of "savages" in that it revealed more about imperial power relations in the present than fundamental truths about reality. Language, for Lévi-Strauss, was likewise not an instrument for the self-creation of free subjects, but a realm independent of human agency. Speakers did not freely endow linguistic signs with meaning. Rather, language was "human reason which has its reasons and of which man knows nothing."[43] Saussure's linguistics had prepared this perspective by divesting signs of stable, external reference points in subjective intention or material reality.

In his most structuralist phase Michel Foucault also rejected the humanist assumption that man was an active, conscious subject of history. The *Order of Things* (1966) proposed that the recent centrality of man conceived as an autonomous subject was merely an illusion and historicized the manner in which the illusion took shape, especially in the nineteenth century.[44] Man, in Foucault's view, was "a recent invention" and "one perhaps nearing its end."[45] His work detailed how human subjects had been produced and constituted by a succession of linguistic regimes that had determined at various points in history what entailed valid knowledge. The patterns or codes that had governed empirical analyses of labor, life, and language set the parameters of the historical worlds that humans inhabited. For Foucault, human agency was subsumed within larger patterns of defining or categorizing reality. Language set these grids in a discursive realm that paid little heed to external referents or realities. Thus, once the modern episteme began to crumble, Foucault wagered, "man would be erased, like a face drawn in the sand at the edge of the sea."[46]

Friedrich Nietzsche's approach to language provided a useful foundation for what Foucault described as his life work: creating a genealogy of the modern subject.[47] In the *Order of Things,* he credited Nietzsche with returning "language . . . into the field of thought directly"; he had been "the first to connect the philosophical task with a radical reflection upon language." At the start of the nineteenth century, Foucault surmised, language had become "detached from representation"; this revealed language as an "enigmatic multiplicity that must be mastered." Nietzsche, in turn, opened up a "philosophical-philological" space from which to reassemble the "fragmented being of language" into a new synthesis.[48] His questioning the representational accuracy of language allowed Foucault to shift the focus of his own analysis away from what was said toward considerations of power, for example, who spoke and the reasons that gave rise to what was said. It was supposedly in the "possessor of the word" that language would be gathered together in its entirety.[49] Foucault's own philological examination of discourse likewise borrowed from Nietzsche,[50] as did the assumption that language as a semi-autonomous agent shaped thought patterns and the formation of subjects.

A renewal of philosophy, especially as was inspired by Nietzsche, helped define the shift toward poststructuralism within French circles after 1966.[51] Increasingly, Foucault saw in Nietzsche's view of subject formation a model for addressing the problem of individual agency without succumbing to Sartrean subjectivism. His notion of genealogy also allowed Foucault and other poststructuralists to raise the question of history, which had been dismissed by the emphasis on synchronic analysis within structuralism.[52] Language had been central to Nietzsche's contributions in both these areas and remained so for poststructuralists. These scholars rejected the presumption of totality and closure that characterized the structuralist approach to language. In their view, the underlying structures that made meaning possible were not fixed; the relationships among elements in a society, culture, or text were constantly being reworked and negotiated. By undermining the formative quality of origins, Nietzsche drew attention to the contingencies and power struggles that shaped the formation of subjects and discourses in history. He suggested that the meaning of a sign was not stable, but instead constantly being produced, proliferated, undermined, and contested. The political implications of this position were potentially ambiguous, with possibilities for both emancipatory cultural engagement and a reactionary dismissal of ethics in the name of relativism.

In his inaugural lecture at the Collège de France (1970), Foucault presented three concepts of language that he believed underlay recent approaches to philosophy. Each of these he rejected for its apparent complicity in eliding the "reality of discourse" as an "event" central to the articulation and contestation of power and to the constitution of human subjects. Three misleading assumptions about language had helped disguise the will-to-power as a will-to-truth. First, belief that a speaker "directly animat[ed] the empty forms of language with his aims" supported the "philosophy of the founding subject." In this view, man "grasps by intuition the meaning lying deposited within [empty things]" and freely disposes of signs, marks, and traces. Secondly, the opposing theme of "originating experience" proclaimed that "things are already murmuring meaning which our language has only to pick up." The conditions of possibility for speaking of and in the world were thus "a primordial complicity with the world." The third attempt to discover rationality within the workings of language appeared to place discourse at the center of the philosophical enterprise, but at heart attributed an essentializing "consciousness of self" to all things. The idea of "universal mediation" allowed language to "elevate[] particularities to the status of concepts"; but it assumed that things and events "unfold[ed] the secret of their own essence" as they took form in language.[53]

The constructivist understanding of language that itself underlies Foucault's philosophy has deep roots in nineteenth-century Germany. Language scholars had by the fin-de-siècle unraveled the three presumptions Foucault dismissed in his inaugural lecture for wrongly retaining faith in the stability of prelinguistic points of reference. The *Order of Things* identified only a few, and not necessarily the most important, of the comparative philologists and language scholars that bestowed autonomy on words and grammatical structures starting in the late eighteenth century. Foucault's self-declared genealogy should not be dismissed as entirely fictitious, however, despite its near teleological neglect of historical contingency and contemporary concerns. Starting in the late eighteenth century, theologically inspired Protestant theorists, including J. G. Hamann and J. G. Herder, translated the notion of God's living word into an appreciation of language as an independent organism; national tongues were imagined to build communities of people united by the force of common origins and shared thought patterns. This perspective could potentially undermine the agency of speaking subjects, depicting individuals themselves as being formed by the structures and historical whims of language.

The supposed "death of man" within nineteenth-century German reflections on language was, however, never absolute. For Nietzsche and Foucault, as for Hamann, Herder, Grimm, and their followers, recognizing the contingency of linguistic forms was also a precondition for effective action, offering a strategic advantage in the reconstruction of alternative communities, new knowledge, and more potent forms of subjectivity. The philologist who broke through the deceptions of languages that claimed transparency simultaneously wielded the power to direct them in his own image. In this respect, the shadow of Babel extended only so far over nineteenth-century language scholarship. The ambition to master language in the diversity of its historical and cultural forms ultimately withstood the cautions of a God troubled by human conceit.

Notes

Introduction

1. Ernest Renan, "Souvenirs d'Enfance et de Jeunesse," in *Oeuvres Complètes de Ernest Renan,* ed. Henriette Psichari (Paris: Calmann-Lévy, 1947–58), 2:865–66.
2. Ernest Renan, *L'Avenir de la Science, Pensées de 1848* in *Oeuvres Complètes,* 3:841, 845.
3. Renan, *L'Avenir de la Science,* 3:830.
4. Renan, *L'Avenir de la Science,* 3:832–33.
5. Renan, *L'Avenir de la Science,* 3:821.
6. Renan, *L'Avenir de la Science,* 3:839, 847.
7. Renan, *L'Avenir de la Science,* 3:832.
8. Anthony Grafton, *Defenders of the Text: The Traditions of Scholarship in an Age of Science, 1450–1800* (Cambridge, Mass.: Harvard University Press, 1991), 4.
9. In the early 1860s, for example, the German émigré scholar Friedrich Max Müller delivered his lively Lectures on the Science of Language to substantial crowds in London.
10. Ernest Renan, "Les Études Savantes en Allemagne," in *Oeuvres Complètes,* 1:186, 182.
11. See Olga Amsterdamska, *Schools of Thought: The Development of Linguistics from Bopp to Saussure* (Boston: D. Reidel, 1987); and Hans Arens, *Sprachwissenschaft: Der Gang ihrer Entwicklung von der Antike bis zur Gegenwart* (Munich: Karl Alber, 1955).
12. For a discussion of this relationship see Indra Sengupta, *From Salon to Discipline: State, University and Indology in Germany, 1821–1914* (Hei-

delberg: Ergon, 2005).

13. The term *Ursprache* referred to an original, first language from which other languages were derived. It could be the lost "mother" tongue of a specific family, comparable to Proto-Indo-European, or the divine first language of revelation spoken before Babel.
14. Maurice Olender, *The Languages of Paradise: Race, Religion, and Philology in the Nineteenth Century,* trans. Arthur Goldhammer (Cambridge, Mass.: Harvard University Press, 1992).
15. See E. J. Hobsbawm, *Nations and Nationalism since 1780: Programme, Myth, Reality* (Cambridge: Cambridge University Press, 1990), 51–63.
16. George Williamson, *The Longing for Myth in Germany: Religion and Aesthetic Culture from Romanticism to Nietzsche* (Chicago: University of Chicago Press, 2004), 16.
17. A recent exception to this includes David Hoyt and Karen Oslund, eds., *Language Study and the Politics of Community in Global Context* (New York: Rowland & Littlefield, 2006). Most histories of linguistics are concerned with the provenance of scientific "discoveries," the formation of schools, and questions of influence. Comparative-historical philology is often regarded as a founding moment in the emergence of the modern, scientific discipline. Classic histories of the field include Theodor Benfey, *Geschichte der Sprachwissenschaft und orientalischen Philologie in Deutschland* (Munich: J. G. Cotta Buchhandlung, 1869); Berthold Delbrück, *Einleitung in das Sprachstudium: Ein Beitrag zur Geschichte und Methodik der vergleichenden Sprachforschung* (Leipzig: Breitkopf und Hartel, 1880); and Holger Pedersen, *Sprogvidenskaben i det nittende Aarhundrede* (1924), translated into English by John Webster Spargo as *Linguistic Science in the Nineteenth Century: Methods and Results* (Cambridge, Mass.: Harvard University Press, 1931). Other early histories written by distinguished linguists include Rudolf von Raumer, *Geschichte der germanischen Philologie vorzugsweise in Deutschland* (Munich: R. Oldenbourg, 1870) and Vilhelm Thomsen, *Geschichte der Sprachwissenschaft bis zum Ausgang des 19. Jahrhunderts: Kurzgefasste Darstellung der Hauptpunkte,* trans. Hans Pollak (Halle: M. Niemeyer, 1927). More recent surveys include Amsterdamska, *Schools of Thought;* Arens, *Sprachwissenschaft;* Arno Borst, *Der Turmbau von Babel: Geschichte der Meinungen über Ursprung und Vielfalt der Sprachen und Völker* (Stuttgart: Anton Hiersemann, 1958–63; David Cram, Andrew Linn, and Elke Nowak, eds., *History of Linguistics,* vol. 2, *From Classical to Contemporary Linguistics* (Philadelphia: John Benjamins, 1999); Andreas Gardt, *Geschichte der Sprachwissenschaft in Deutschland* (New York: Walter de Gruyter, 1999); R. H. Robins, *A Short History of Linguistics* (New York: Longman, 1990); and James Stam, *On the Origin of Language: The Fate*

of a Question (New York: Harper & Row, 1976). More concerned with the history of ideas are Hans Aarsleff, *From Locke to Saussure: Essays on the Study of Language and Intellectual History* (Minneapolis: University of Minnesota Press, 1982); and Roy Harris and Talbot J. Taylor, *Landmarks in Linguistic Thought: The Western Tradition from Socrates to Saussure* (New York: Routledge, 1989). Historians of science have also written on the "parasite tendency" of linguistics to borrow scientific models from (and lend them to) botany, anatomy, geology, and evolutionary theory. See, for example, Henry M. Hoenigswald and Linda F. Wiener, *Biological Metaphor and Cladistic Classification: An Interdisciplinary Perspective* (Philadelphia: University of Pennsylvania Press, 1987); and Konrad Koerner, ed., *Linguistics and Evolutionary Theory: Three Essays by August Schleicher, Ernst Haeckel, and Wilhelm Bleek,* vol. 6 of *Amsterdam Classics in Linguistics, 1800–1925* (Philadelphia: John Benjamins, 1983).

18. Historians distinguish broadly between a state-centered model of citizenship typical of France and Britain and an ethnocultural vision of nationhood, which was based on an ideal of linguistic unity and took root east of the Rhine River. Hobsbawm, *Nations and Nationalism,* 51–63; Rogers Brubaker, *Citizenship and Nationhood in France and Germany* (Cambridge, Mass.: Harvard University Press, 1992).
19. See Hobsbawm, *Nations and Nationalism;* Brubaker, *Citizenship and Nationhood in France and Germany.*
20. Bernhard Giesen, *Intellectuals and the Nation: Collective Identity in a German Axial Age,* trans. Nicholas Levis and Amos Weisz (Cambridge: Cambridge University Press, 1993).
21. Benedict Anderson, *Imagined Communities: Reflections on the Origin and Spread of Nationalism* (London: Verso, 1983), 71–72, 83–84.
22. Hobsbawm, *Nations and Nationalism,* 51–58.
23. See, for example, Werner Besch, "Dialekt, Schreibdialekt, Schriftsprache, Standardsprache: Exemplarische Skizze ihrer historischen Ausprägung im Deutschen," in *Dialektologie: Ein Handbuch zur deutschen und allgemeinen Dialketforschung,* ed. Werner Besch et al., 2:961–90 (New York: Walter de Gruyter, 1983).
24. Andreas Gardt, ed., *Nation und Sprache: Die Diskussion ihres Verhältnisses in Geschichte und Gegenwart* (New York: Walter de Gruyter, 2000); and Claus Ahlzweig, *Muttersprache—Vaterland: Die deutsche Nation und ihre Sprache* (Opladen: Westdeutscher Verlag, 1994).
25. Michael Townson, *Mother-Tongue and Fatherland: Language and Politics in Germany* (New York: Manchester University Press, 1992).
26. Martin Jay, "Should Intellectual History Take a Linguistic Turn? Reflections on the Habermas-Gademer Debate," in *Modern European Intellectual History: Reappraisals and New Perspectives,* ed. Dominick LaCapra

and Steven L. Kaplan (Ithaca: Cornell University Press, 1982), 87–90.

27. Jay, "Should Intellectual History Take a Linguistic Turn?" 89.

28. Martin Jay acknowledges precedents to the "linguistic turn" in the German theologians Johann Gottfried Hamann and Friedrich Schleiermacher, who did associate language and thought. But he characterizes them as "relatively isolated figures"; the powerful idealist movement had little use for the irrational hermeneutics of Hamann and his followers. See Jay, "Should Intellectual History Take a Linguistic Turn?" 87, 90.

29. Anthony Grafton and Lisa Jardine, *From Humanism to the Humanities: Education and the Liberal Arts in Fifteenth- and Sixteenth-Century Europe* (London: Duckworth, 1986).

30. Anthony J. La Vopa, "Specialists against Specialization: Hellenism as Professional Ideology in German Classical Studies," in *German Professions, 1800–1950,* ed. Geoffrey Cocks and Konrad Jarausch, 27–45 (New York: Oxford University Press, 1990); and R. Steven Turner, "The Growth of Professional Research in Prussia, 1818 to 1848—Causes and Context," *Historical Studies in the Physical Sciences* 3 (1971): 137–82.

31. Robert S. Leventhal, "The Emergence of Philological Discourse in the German States, 1770–1810," *Isis* 77 (1986): 243–60; and R. Steven Turner, "Historicism, *Kritik,* and the Prussian Professoriate, 1790–1840," in *Philologie und Hermeneutik im neunzehnten Jahrhundert: Zur Geschichte und Methodologie der Geisteswissenschaften,* ed. Helmut Flashar, Karfried Gründer, and Axel Horstmann, 2:450–89 (Göttingen: Vandenhoeck and Ruprecht, 1979).

32. See Andreas Kilcher, *Die Sprachtheorie des Kabbala als ästhetisches Paradigma: Die Konstruktion einer ästhetischen Kabbala seit der Frühen Neuzeit* (Stuttgart: Metzler, 1998).

33. Quentin Skinner, "Moral Ambiguity and the Art of Persuasion in the Renaissance," in *Proof and Persuasion: Essays on Authority, Objectivity, and Evidence,* ed. Suzanne Marchand and Elizabeth Lunbeck (Brepols, 1996), 26.

34. John Locke, *An Essay Concerning Human Understanding,* ed. Peter H. Nidditch (Oxford: Clarendon Press, 1975).

35. Skinner, "Moral Ambiguity and the Art of Persuasion," 41.

36. Robert Markley, *Fallen Languages: Crises of Representation in Newtonian England, 1600–1740* (Ithaca: Cornell University Press, 1993).

37. Debora Kuller Shuger, *The Renaissance Bible: Scholarship, Sacrifice, and Subjectivity* (Berkeley: University of California Press, 1994), 21.

38. Shugar, *Renaissance Bible,* 45. See also Wolf Peter Klein, "Christliche Kabbala und Linguistik orientalischer Sprachen im 16. Jahrhundert: Das Beispiel von Guillaume Postel (1510–1581)," *Beiträge zur Geschichte der Sprachwissenschaft* 11 (2001): 1–26.

39. Jonathan Sheehan, *The Enlightenment Bible: Translation, Scholarship, Culture* (Princeton: Princeton University Press, 2005), 90ff.
40. Jonathan Sheehan, *Enlightenment Bible,* 234.
41. John Edward Toews, *Becoming Historical: Cultural Reformation and Public Memory in Early Nineteenth-Century Berlin* (Cambridge: Cambridge University Press, 2004), xxi.
42. See Douglas Kibbee, "Théorie linguistique et droits humains linguistiques: perspectives tirées de l'histoire des communautés linguistiques en France," in *DiversCité,* electronic journal of the Université du Québec à Montréal (1998); and "The 'People' and Their Language in 19th-century French Linguistic Thought," in *The Emergence of the Modern Language Sciences: Studies on the Transition from Historical-Comparative to Structural Linguistics in Honour of E. F. K. Koerner,* ed. Sheila Embleton, Hans-Josef Niederehe, and John E. Joseph, 111–28 (Philadelphia: John Benjamins, 1999).
43. This provided the inspiration for Darwin's theory of species differentiation. See Stephen Alter, *Darwinism and the Linguistic Image: Language, Race, and Natural Theology in the Nineteenth Century* (Baltimore: Johns Hopkins University Press, 1999).
44. Thomas Trautmann, *Aryans and British India* (Berkeley: University of California Press, 1997), 8; and Bruce Lincoln, *Theorizing Myth: Narrative, Ideology, and Scholarship* (Chicago: University of Chicago Press, 1999), 70.
45. See, for example, Umberto Eco, *The Search for the Perfect Language,* trans. James Fentress (Cambridge, Mass.: Blackwell, 1995), 7ff.
46. On the Romantic "spiral" of historical development see M. H. Abrams, *Natural Supernaturalism: Tradition and Revolution in Romantic Literature* (New York: W. W. Norton, 1971).
47. Michel Foucault, "Nietzsche, Genealogy, History," in *The Foucault Reader,* ed. Paul Rabinow, 76–100 (New York: Pantheon Books, 1984).
48. Toews, *Becoming Historical,* xxi.
49. Anthony Grafton, "Invention of Traditions and Traditions of Invention in Renaissance Europe: The Strange Case of Annius of Viterbo," in *The Transmission of Culture in Early Modern Europe,* ed. Anthony Grafton and Ann Blair (Philadelphia: University of Pennsylvania Press, 1990), 31.
50. Jonathan Sheehan, *Enlightenment Bible,* 233.
51. Antoine Berman, *The Experience of the Foreign: Culture and Translation in Romantic Germany,* trans. S. Heyvaert (Albany: State University of New York Press, 1992), 106–8.
52. Markus Hundt, *"Spracharbeit" im 17. Jahrhundert: Studien zu Georg Philipp Harsdörffer, Justus Georg Schottelius und Christian Gueintz* (New York: Walter de Gruyter, 2000), 4.

53. See Sara Smart, "Justus Georg Schottelius and the Patriotic Movement," *Modern Language Review* 84 (1989): 95.
54. See Rolf Schneider, *Der Einfluß von Justus Georg Schottelius auf die deutschsprachige Lexikographie des 17./18. Jahrhunderts* (New York: Peter Lang, 1995); and Stefan Sonderegger, "Zu Grimmelshausens Bedeutung für die detusche Sprachgeschichte," in *Wahrheit und Wort: Festschrift für Rolf Tarot zum 65. Geburtstag,* ed. Gabriela Scherer and Beatrice Wehrli, 427–35 (Berlin: Peter Lang, 1996).
55. See Wolfgang Huber, *Kulturpatriotismus und Sprachbewußtsein: Studien zur deutschen Philologie des 17. Jahrhunderts* (New York: Peter Lang, 1984).
56. Smart, "Justus Georg Schottelius," 97.
57. Huber, *Kulturpatriotismus und Sprachbewußtsein,* 237.
58. Hundt, *"Spracharbeit" im 17. Jahrhundert,* 4.
59. On print culture and the public sphere see Isabel Hull, *Sexuality, State, and Civil Society in Germany, 1700–1815* (Ithaca: Cornell University Press, 1996); and Ian McNeely, *The Emancipation of Writing: German Civil Society in the Making, 1790s–1820s* (Berkeley: University of California Press, 2003).
60. E. M. Butler, *The Tyranny of Greece over Germany* (New York: Macmillan Company, 1935); Robert Holub, *Heinrich Heine's Reception of German Grecophilia: The Function and Application of the Hellenic Tradition in the First Half of the Nineteenth Century* (Heidelberg: Carl Winter, 1981); and Suzanne Marchand, *Down from Olympus: Archaeology and Philhellenism in Germany, 1750–1970* (Princeton: Princeton University Press, 1996).
61. See Uwe Puschner, *Die völkische Bewegung im wilhelminischen Kaiserreich: Sprache, Rasse, Religion* (Darmstadt: Wissenschaftliche Buchgesellschaft, 2001).
62. Léon Poliakov, *The Aryan Myth: A History of Racist and Nationalist Ideas in Europe,* trans. E. Howard (London: Chatto & Heinemann for Sussex University Press, 1974) and George Mosse, *Toward the Final Solution: A History of European Racism* (New York: Howard Fertig, 1978).
63. See Olender, *Languages of Paradise.*
64. Abigail Green, *Fatherlands: State-Building and Nationhood in Nineteenth-Century Germany* (Cambridge: Cambridge University Press, 2001), 7.
65. James J. Sheehan, "What Is German History? Reflections on the role of the Nation," *Journal of Modern History* 53 (1981): 1–23.
66. Roger Chickering, "Language and the Social Foundations of Radical Nationalism in the Wilhelmine Era," in *1870/71–1989/90: German*

Unifications and the Change of Literary Discourse, ed. Walter Pape, 61–78 (New York: Walter de Gruyter, 1993).

67. Rainer Kipper, *Der Germanenmythos im Deutschen Kaiserreich* (Göttingen: Vandenhoeck & Ruprecht, 2002).
68. Michel Foucault, *The Order of Things: An Archaeology of the Human Sciences,* trans. R. D. Lang (New York: Pantheon Books, 1970), 282, 233.
69. Historians of linguistics have taken Foucault's account of comparative historical philology quite seriously. Brigitte Schlieben-Lange, for example, supports his notion of a radical epistemic break in linguistic thought around the year 1800. See *Idéologie: Zur Rolle der Kategorisierungen im Wissenschaftsprozess* (Heidelberg: Carl Winter, 2000); and "Überlegungen zur Sprachwissenschaftsgeschichtsschreibung," in *Europäische Sprachwissenschaft um 1800: Methodologische und historiographische Beiträge zum Umkreis der "idéologie,"* ed. Brigitte Schlieben-Lange, Hans-Dieter Dräxler, Franz-Josef Knapstein, Elisabeth Bolck-Duffy, and Isabel Zollna, 11–24 (Münster: Nodus, 1989).
70. Foucault, *Order of Things,* 297.
71. Foucault, *Order of Things,* 386.
72. Foucault, *Order of Things,* 384.
73. Linda Dowling, *Language and Decadence in the Victorian Fin-de-Siècle* (Princeton: Princeton University Press), xii.
74. See, for example, the discussion in David West, *An Introduction to Continental Philosophy* (Cambridge: Polity Press, 1996), 154ff.
75. Charles Taylor, *Hegel* (London: Cambridge University Press, 1978), 18–21.
76. Lia Formigari, *Signs, Science and Politics: Philosophies of Language in Europe, 1700–1830,* trans. William Dodd (Philadelphia: John Benjamins, 1993), 187.
77. Aarsleff, *From Locke to Saussure;* Ulrich Ricken, *Linguistics, Anthropology, and Philosophy in the French Enlightenment,* trans. Robert E. Norton (New York: Routledge, 1994); Brigitte Nerlich, *Change in Language: Whitney, Bréal, and Wegener* (New York: Routledge, 1990).
78. Konrad Koerner, *Practicing Linguistic Historiography,* (Amsterdam: John Benjamins, 1989); Sheila Embleton, John E. Josepf, and Hans-Josef Niederehe, eds., *The Emergence of the Modern Language Sciences: Studies on the Transition from Historical-Comparative to Structural Linguistics in Honour of E. F. K. Koerner,* vol. 1 *Historiographical Perspectives* (Philadelphia: John Benjamins, 1999).

Chapter 1

1. Wilhelm von Humboldt, "Fragmente der Monographie über die

Basken" (1801/2), in *Wilhelm von Humboldts Werke,* ed. Albert Leitzmann et al. (Berlin: B. Behr, 1903–36), 7:599–602.

2. See Wilhelm von Humboldt, "Über Denken und Sprechen" (1795/96), in *Wilhelm von Humboldts Werke,* 7:582–83.
3. Humboldt, "Fragmente der Monographie über die Basken," 7:601.
4. Wilhelm von Humboldt, "Grundzüge des allgemeinen Srpachtypus," n.d., in *Wilhelm von Humboldts Werke,* 5:214.
5. Wilhelm von Humboldt, "Ankündigung einer Schrift über die vaskische Sprache und Nation, nebst Angabe des Gesichtspunctes und Inhalts derselben" (1812), in *Wilhelm von Humboldts Werke,* 3:291.
6. See Humboldt's discussion of American languages in "Grundzüge des allgemeinen Srpachtypus," 5:164ff.
7. This has been noted by Jere Paul Surber in *Metacritique: The Linguistic Assault on German Idealism,* ed. Jere Paul Surber (Amherst, N.Y.: Humanity Books, 2001), 41.
8. Ricken, *Linguistics, Anthropology, and Philosophy,* 71–73, 177.
9. Locke, *Essay Concerning Human Understanding,* 104ff.
10. Gottfried Wilhelm Leibniz, "Unvorgreiffliche Gedancken, betreffend die Ausübung und Verbesserung der Teutschen Sprache," in *History of Linguistics: Eighteenth- and Nineteenth-Century German Linguistics,* ed. Christopher M. Hutton (London: Routledge, 1995), 1:255, 257–58.
11. Gottfried Wilhlem Leibniz, *New Essays on Human Understanding,* trans. and ed. Peter Remnant and Jonathan Bennett (Cambridge: Cambridge University Press, 1996), 49, 50.
12. Talbot J. Taylor, *Mutual Misunderstanding: Skepticism and the Theorizing of Language and Interpretation* (Durham: Duke University Press, 1992), 32.
13. Locke, *Essay Concerning Human Understanding,* 408.
14. Leibniz suggested that humankind's original vocabulary might have been based on an aesthetic harmony between words and things or on a sound symbolism that was lost through time. Christopher M. Hutton has argued that Leibniz shared a Kabalistic belief about the hidden truths found in combinations of letters and was willing to consider that sounds could be independent bearers of meaning (introduction to *History of Linguistics,* 1:xvi). See also Lia Formigari, *Signs, Science and Politics,* 187.
15. Locke, *Essay Concerning Human Understanding,* 720–21.
16. Ricken, *Linguistics, Anthropology, and Philosophy,* 76–77.
17. It is a stretch to suggest that Locke sowed the seeds of Romanticism by claiming that national languages reflect or even determine the way the members of that linguistic group think. In Locke's view, word choice was an individual act; it was not communities of speakers who chose to

attribute a particular sign to an idea. But he did awaken the eighteenth century's interest in the origin of language and in the interdependent historical evolution of language and cognition. See Harris and Taylor, *Landmarks in Linguistic Thought,* 113, 118–19.

18. See Aarsleff, *From Locke to Saussure,* 335, 345–46.
19. On rationalist tendencies in Locke's thought see Ricken, *Linguistics, Anthropology, and Philosophy,* 78, 140.
20. Étienne Bonnot de Condillac, *An Essay on the Origin of Human Knowledge, Being a Supplement to Mr. Locke's Essay on the Human Understanding,* ed. Robert G. Weyant (Gainesville, Fla.: Scholars' Facsimiles & Reprints, 1971), 11.
21. Ricken, *Linguistics, Anthropology, and Philosophy,* 174ff; Formigari, *Signs, Science and Politics,* 187.
22. Condillac, *Essay on the Origin of Human Knowledge,* 51ff, 173.
23. Condillac, *Essay on the Origin of Human Knowledge,* 61.
24. Condillac, *Essay on the Origin of Human Knowledge,* 298.
25. Ricken, *Linguistics, Anthropology, and Philosophy,* 179–80.
26. Condillac, *Essay on the Origin of Human Knowledge,* 283ff.
27. Condillac, *Essay on the Origin of Human Knowledge,* 325–41.
28. Ricken, *Linguistics, Anthropology, and Philosophy,* 104; Harris and Taylor, *Landmarks in Linguistic Thought,* 131.
29. Condillac, *Essay on the Origin of Human Knowledge,* 253.
30. Harris and Taylor, *Landmarks in Linguistic Thought,* 131–34.
31. Hans Aarsleff, "The Berlin Academy under Frederick the Great," *History of the Human Sciences* 2 (1989): 195.
32. Mary Terrall, *The Man Who Flattened the Earth: Maupertuis and the Sciences in the Enlightenment* (Chicago: University of Chicago Press, 2002), 234.
33. Terrall, *Man Who Flattened the Earth,* 250, 233.
34. Aarsleff, *From Locke to Saussure,* 178–86.
35. Condillac himself responded to this question in book 3 of his *Cours d'études pour l'instruction du Prince de Parme.* See Aarsleff, *From Locke to Saussure,* 189.
36. Ricken, *Linguistics, Anthropology, and Philosophy,* 185–87.
37. *Nouveaux Mémoires de l'Académie Royale des Sciences et Belle-Lettres* (1770) (Berlin: Chrétien Fréderic Voss, 1772), 25.
38. Aarsleff, *From Locke to Saussure,* 189.
39. Étienne Bonnot de Condillac, *Essay on the Origin of Human Knowledge,* ed. Hans Aarsleff (Cambridge: Cambridge University Press, 2001), 5, 3, 6.
40. Johann David Michaelis, *A Dissertation on the Influence of Opinions on Language, and of Language on Opinions* (New York: AMS Press, 1973),

35.

41. Michaelis, *Dissertation on the Influence,* 2–3.
42. Michaelis, *Dissertation on the Influence,* 10.
43. Michaelis, *Dissertation on the Influence,* 33.
44. Jonathan Hess, *Germans, Jews, and the Claims of Modernity* (New Haven: Yale University Press, 2002), 29ff.
45. For example, Michaelis argued that stories surrounding the term "celestial manna" indicated that the linguistic conventions of Middle Eastern tongues had distorted religious truth. Both the Arabs and the Hebrews claimed that the substance miraculously supplied as food to the children of Israel during their progress through the wilderness came from heaven or "fell." Scripture associates manna with dew. And, Michaelis feared, Moses had obscured that the substance was "no more than a gum exuding from plants" when he made use of Israelite expressions that wrongly held that dew "came from above" not from the earth. According to Michaelis, "the Jews in Jesus' time went still farther, making this error a handle to disparage the miracle of the multiplication of the loaves." Recognizing errors in the metaphors associated with dew in Arabic and Hebrew and subsequently transferred to manna would confirm Christ's claim that the bread Moses gave his children did not come from heaven. Michaelis, *Dissertation on the Influence,* 55–56.
46. Jonathan Sheehan argues that Michaelis's translations of scripture intended to evoke "vertigo" in readers. See *The Enlightenment Bible,* 206ff.
47. Michaelis, *Dissertation on the Influence,* 12.
48. Johann Gottfried Herder, *On the Origin of Language: Two Essays,* trans. Alexander Gode (Chicago: University of Chicago Press, 1966), 151.
49. James C. O'Flaherty, *Johann Georg Hamann* (Boston: Twayne Publishers, 1979), 136.
50. James C. O'Flaherty, *The Quarrel of Reason with Itself: Essays on Hamann, Michaelis, Lessing, Nietzsche* (Columbia, S.C.: Camden House, 1988), 135.
51. O'Flaherty, *Quarrel of Reason with Itself,* 171.
52. Johann Georg Hamann, "Aesthetica in Nuce: Eine Rhapsodie in kabbalistischer Prose," in Hamann, *Sämtliche Werke,* ed. Josef Nadler (Wuppertal: R. Brockhaus, 1999), 2:211; O'Flaherty, *Quarrel of Reason with Itself,* 63–64.
53. O'Flaherty, *Quarrel of Reason with Itself,* 115.
54. Hamann, "Aesthetica in Nuce," 2:197.
55. Robert E. Norton, *Herder's Aesthetics and the European Enlightenment* (Cornell University Press, 1991), 65.
56. Johann Georg Hamann, "Des Ritters von Rosencreuz letzte Willenserk-

lärung über den göttlichen und menschlichen Ursprung der Sprache," in *Sämtliche Werke,* 3:32.

57. Hamann, "Aesthetica in Nuce," 2:206.
58. Frederick Beiser, *The Fate of Reason: German Philosophy from Kant to Fichte* (Cambridge, Mass.: Harvard University Press, 1987), 17.
59. F. Ernest Stoeffler, *German Pietism during the Eighteenth Century* (Leiden: Brill, 1973), 240.
60. James C. O'Flaherty, *Unity and Language: A Study in the Philosophy of Johann Georg Hamann* (Chapel Hill: University of North Carolina Press, 1952), 19.
61. O'Flaherty, *Unity and Language,* 19.
62. Johann Georg Hamann, *Briefwechsel,* ed. Walther Ziesemer and Arthur Henkel (Wiesbaden: Insel, 1955), 1:393.
63. Johann Georg Hamann, *Johann Georg Hamann's, des Magus in Norden, Leben und Schriften,* ed. Karl Hermann Gildemeister (Gotha, F. A. Perthes, 1863–75), 5:122.
64. Hamann, *Johann Georg Hamann's,* 5:7.
65. Hamann, *Briefwechsel,* 7:173.
66. Johann Georg Hamann, "Tagebuch eines Christens," in *Sämtliche Werke,* 1:52.
67. Johann Georg Hamann, "Versuch über eine akademische Frage," in *Sämtliche Werke,* 2:121–26.
68. Hamann, "Versuch über eine akademische Frage," 2:122.
69. Johann Gottfried Herder, "Ueber die neuere Deutsche Literatur: Erste Sammlung von Fragmenten," in Herder, *Herders Sämtliche Werke,* ed. Bernhard Suphan (Berlin: G. Olms, 1967), 1:148–49.
70. Norton, *Herder's Aesthetics,* 94.
71. Johann Gottfried Herder, "Ueber die neue Deutsche Literatur: Erste Sammlung von Fragmenten, 2. Ausgabe," in *Herders Sämtliche Werke,* 2:12–17.
72. Aarsleff, *From Locke to Saussure,* 187.
73. Aarsleff, *From Locke to Saussure,* 195.
74. Herder, *On the Origin of Language,* 87.
75. Herder, *On the Origin of Language,* 103, 108–10.
76. Herder, *On the Origin of Language,* 101.
77. Jean-Jacques Rousseau, "Discourse on the Origin of Inequality among Men," in *The Essential Rousseau,* trans. Lowell Bair (New York: New American Library, 1975), 157–62.
78. Kurt Müller-Vollmer, "Von der Poetik zur Linguistik—Wilhelm von Humboldt und der romantische Sprachbegriff," in *Universalismus und Wissenschaft im Werk und Wirken der Brüder Humboldt,* ed. Klaus Hammacher and John Pickering (Frankfurt: Vittorio Klostermann, 1976), 12.

79. Herder, *On the Origin of Language,* 109.
80. Herder, *On the Origin of Language,* 138.
81. Herder, *On the Origin of Language,* 117.
82. Herder, "Über den Ursprung der Sprache," in *Herders Sämtliche Werke,* 5:146.
83. Johann Gottfried Herder, "Abschiedspredigt, Bückeburg, 1769," in *Herders Sämtliche Werke,* 31:125.
84. Arnd Bohm, "Herder and the Politics of Adamic Language," In *Herder Jahrbuch,* ed. Karl Menges, Regine Otto, and Wulf Koepke (Stuttgart: J. B. Metzler, 2000), 21–32.
85. In the essay *Origin of Language* (1781), a text written as an unpublished addendum to the *Discourse,* which Herder could not have known, Rousseau argued that humans did not invent language as a tool to meet specific needs. Primitive language was expressive, not utilitarian; it was "due not to need but passion." Like Herder and Hamann, Rousseau believed the earliest Middle Eastern and Asian languages must have been highly figurative, sensuous, and poetic, designed to express feelings not rational ideals. The first tongues were those of poets; only with increasing grammatical sophistication had their musical, rhythmic, and melodic qualities later been silenced. See Rousseau, "Discourse on the Origin," 11–13.
86. Dae Kweon Kim, *Sprachtheorie im 18. Jahrhundert* (Saint Ingbert: Röhrig, 2002), 147ff.
87. Herder, "Über den Ursprung der Sprache," 5:37–38.
88. Herder, "Über den Ursprung der Sprache," 5:155.
89. Taylor, *Hegel,* 13ff.
90. Herder, "Ueber die neuere Deutsche Literatur," 1:151.
91. Herder, "Ueber die neue Deutsche Literatur," 2:13.
92. Herder, "Ueber die neuere Deutsche Literatur," 1:152–55.
93. Johann Gottfried Herder, "Ideen zur Philosophie der Geschichte der Menschheit," *Herders Sämtliche Werke,* 9:348.
94. Herder, "Ueber die neue Deutsche Literatur," 2:12–13.
95. Herder, "Ideen," 9:358, 363.
96. Herder, "Ideen," 9:343, 346.
97. Herder, "Ideen," 9:141.
98. Herder, "Ideen," 9:363.
99. Herder, "Ideen," 9:348.
100. Johann Gottfried Herder, "Briefe zu Beförderung der Humanität," in *Herders Sämtliche Werke,* 17:287.
101. Herder, "Ueber die neue Deutsche Literatur," 2:13.
102. Herder, "Ueber die neue Deutsche Literatur," 2:14.
103. Herder, "Ideen," 9:364–65.

104. Herder, "Ideen," 9:365.
105. French, for example, was often mistaken as a derivative of Celtic, not Latin, because of the two languages' mutual reliance on word order, not morphology, to construct meaningful sentences. See Robins, *Short History of Linguistics,* 185–87.
106. Robert L. Miller, *The Linguistic Relativity Principle and Humboldtian Ethnolinguistics* (The Hague: Mouton, 1968), 95.
107. Pietro Perconti, *Kantian Linguistics: Theories of Mental Representation and the Linguistic Transformation of Kantism* (Münster: Nodus, 1999), 13f. See also Jürgen Villers, *Kant und das Problem der Sprache: Die historischen und systematischen Gründe für die Sprachlosigkeit der Transzendentalphilosophie* (Constance: Verlag am Hockgraben, 1997).
108. Surber, *Metacritique,* 53.
109. Johann Georg Hamann, "Metakritik über den Purismum der Vernunft," in *Sämtliche Werke,* 3:286.
110. Hamann, "Metakritik," 3:286.
111. Surber, *Metacritique,* 14–19.
112. See Beiser, *Fate of Reason,* 40.
113. Hamann, "Metakritik," 3:286.
114. Beiser, *Fate of Reason,* 43.
115. Surber, *Metacritique,* 86.
116. Johann Gottfried Herder, "Metakritik zur Kritik der reinen Vernunft," in *Herders Sämtliche Werke,* 21:31.
117. Herder, "Metakritik," 21:25.
118. Surber, *Metacritique,* 13.
119. Perconti, *Kantian Linguistics,* 24f.
120. Perconti, *Kantian Linguistics,* 24ff.
121. Perconti, *Kantian Linguistics,* 61ff.
122. Anthony J. La Vopa, *Fichte: The Self and the Calling of Philosophy, 1762–1799* (Cambridge: Cambridge University Press, 2001), 192–93.
123. Formigari, *Signs, Science and Politics,* 172–73.
124. Johann Gottlieb Fichte, "Von der Sprachfähigkeit und dem Ursprunge der Sprache," *Sämtliche Werke,* ed. I. H. Fichte (Berlin: Veit, 1846), 8:301.
125. Fichte, "Von der Sprachfähigkeit," 8:304–5.
126. Stam, *On the Origin of Language,* 182; Lia Formigari, "Idealism and Idealistic Trends in Linguistics and in the Philosophy of Language," in *Sprachtheorien der Neuzeit I: Der epistemologische Kontext neuzeitlicher Sprach-und Grammatiktheorien,* ed. Peter Schmitter (Tübingen: Gunter Narr, 1999), 242.
127. Formigari, "Idealism and Idealistic Trends,"242.
128. Stam, *On the Origin of Language,* 185.

129. Cited in Stam, *On the Origin of Language,* 185–86.
130. Isobel Armstrong, *Language as Living Form in Nineteenth-Century Poetry* (Sussex: Harvester Press, 1982), 4.
131. Fichte, "Von der Sprachfähigkeit," 8:309.
132. Fichte, "Von der Sprachfähigkeit," 8:309.
133. Surber, *Metacritique,* 30.
134. Helmut Gipper, "Sprachphilosophie in der Romantik," in *Sprachphilosophie—Philosophy of Language—la philosophie du langue. Ein internationales Handbuch—An International Handbook of Contemporary Research—Manuel international des recherches contemporaines,* ed. Marcelo Dascal, Dietfried Gerhardus, Kuno Lorenz, and Georg Meggle (Berlin: Walter de Gruyter, 1992), 1:216.
135. Karl Heinrich Ludwig Pölitz (1772–1838), Georg von Reinbeck (1766–1849), and Vater pursued a theory of language as the external presentation of internal representations. But their focus on universal grammar generally excluded them from the university institutionalization of linguistics which favored an empirical, comparative-historical approach. See Perconti, *Kantian Linguistics,* 61.
136. August F. Bernhardi, *Sprachlehre* (New York: Georg Olms, 1973), 1:8.
137. Bernhardi, *Sprachlehre,* 2:129.
138. Gipper, "Sprachphilosophie in der Romantik," 216.
139. August Wilhlem Schlegel, "Miscellen," in *Europa: Eine Zeitschrift,* ed. Friedrich Schlegel (Stuttgart: J. Cotta, 1963), 2:193–95.
140. Jürgen Trabant, "How Relativistic are Humboldt's 'Weltansichten?" in *Explorations in Linguistic Relativity,* ed. Martin Pütz and Marjolijn Verspoor, 25–44 (Philadelphia: John Benjamins, 2000).
141. Michael Heath, introduction to Wilhelm von Humboldt, *On Language: The Diversity of the Human Language-Structure and its Influence on the Mental Development of Mankind,* trans. Peter Heath (New York: Cambridge University Press, 1988), xxv.
142. Paul R. Sweet, "Wilhelm von Humboldt, Fichte, and the Idéologues (1794–1805): A Re-Examination," *Historiographia Linguistica* 15, no. 3 (1988): 361.
143. Miller, *Linguistic Relativity Principle,* 90.
144. Wilhelm von Humboldt, "Über Denken und Sprechen," in *Wilhelm von Humboldts Werke,* 7:582.
145. Formigari, "Idealism and Idealistic Trends," 177.
146. Wilhelm von Humboldt, "Über das vergleichende Sprachstudium in Beziehung auf die verschiedenen Epochen der Sprachentwicklung," in *Wilhelm von Humboldts Werke,* 4:25.
147. Wilhelm von Humboldt, "Grundzüge des allgemeinen Sprachtypus," *Wilhelm von Humboldts Werke,* 5:252.

148. Cited in Sweet, "Humboldt, Fichte and the Idéologues," 354.
149. These divisions were replicated in all languages and "flowed . . . necessarily and on their own out of the categories of relation." See Humboldt, "Grundzüge," 5:452.
150. Christian Stetter, "'Über Denken und Sprechen': Wilhelm von Humboldt zwischen Fichte und Herder," in *Wilhelm von Humboldts Sprachdenken: Symposium zum 150. Todestag,* ed. Hans-Werner Scharf (Essen: Reimar Hobbig, 1989), 36.
151. The extent of Humboldt's debt to J. G. Herder is rightly disputed. Nowhere does he directly acknowledge the influence of his predecessor, and textual evidence that might indicate a direct exchange of ideas is ambiguous. The two families met several times, but without forming any significant attachment. See Sweet, "Humboldt, Fichte, and the Idéologues," 360.
152. Wilhelm von Humboldt, "Ueber den Nationalcharakter der Sprachen" *Wilhelm von Humboldts Werke,* 4:424, 430, 433.
153. Martin L. Manchester, *The Philosophical Foundations of Humboldt's Linguistic Doctrines* (Philadelphia: University of Pennsylvania Press, 1985), 104f.
154. Sweet, "Humboldt, Fichte and the Idéologues," 184–87; Manchester, *Philosophical Foundations,* 105.
155. Humboldt, *On Language,* 46.
156. Jeffrey Grossman, "Wilhelm von Humboldt's Linguistic Ideology: The Problem of Pluralism and the Absolute Difference of National Character—Or, Where Do the Jews Fit In?" *German Studies Review* 20, no. 1 (1997): 12; Ruth Römer, *Sprachwissenschaft und Rassenideologie in Deutschland* (Munich: Wilhelm Fink, 1985), 153ff.
157. Humboldt, "Grundzüge," 5:428.
158. Heath, introduction, xvii.
159. Humboldt, "Grundzüge," 5:374.
160. Formigari, *Signs, Science and Politics,* 178.
161. Humboldt, "Grundzüge," 5:374–75.
162. Humboldt, "Grundzüge," 5:377.
163. Formigari, *Signs, Science and Politics,* 188.
164. Humboldt, "Einleitung in das gesammte Sprachstudium," in *Wilhelm von Humboldts Werke,* 7:622.
165. See Müller-Vollmer, "Von der Poetik zur Linguistik."
166. Humboldt, *On Language,* 49.
167. Humboldt, "Grundzüge," 5:433.
168. Humboldt, "Grundzüge," 5:387–88.
169. Humboldt, *On Language,* 21.
170. Heath, introduction, x.

171. Humboldt, *On Language,* 112–13.
172. Humboldt, *On Language,* 216.
173. Manchester, *Philosophical Foundations,* 129, 133.
174. Manchester, *Philosophical Foundations,* 131–33.
175. Humboldt, *On Language,* 216–18.
176. Humboldt, *On Language,* 216, 230.
177. Manchester, *Philosophical Foundations,* 136–41.
178. August F. Bernhardi, *Anfangsgründe der Sprachwissenschaft* (1805), 4–7.
179. Formigari, "Idealism and Idealistic Trends," 241.
180. Siegfried J. Schmidt, *Sprache und Denken als sprachphilosophischs Problem von Locke bis Wittgeinstein* (The Hague: Martinus Nijhoff, 1968).
181. Leventhal, "Emergence of Philological Discourse," 248f.
182. Anthony Grafton, "Polyhistor into *Philolog:* Notes on the Transformation of German Classical Scholarship, 1780–1850," *History of Universities* 3 (1983): 162–71, 182–83; Vopa, "Specialists against Specialization."
183. Turner, "Historicism, *Kritik,* and the Prussian Professoriate."
184. Stam, *On the Origin of Language,* 187.

Chapter 2

1. Heinrich Julius Klaproth, *Geographisch-historische Beschreibung des östlichen Kaukasus, zwischen den Flüssen Terek, Aragwi, Kur und dem Kaspischen Meere* (Weimar: Landes-Industrie-Comptoir, 1814), 24.
2. In Julius Klaproth, *Asia Polyglotta* (Paris: J. M. Eberhart, 1823). Franz Bopp introduced the term "Indo-European" in his 1857 *Vergleichende Grammatik,* and it was adopted by non-German-speaking linguists; he himself preferred "Indo-Classical" because it recognized the importance of ancient Greek to the family.
3. The term was used by Friedrich August Pott in "Indogermanischer Sprachstamm," in *Allgemeine Encyklopädie der Wissenschaften und Künste,* ed. J. S. Ersch and J. G. Gruber, 2nd ser., sect. 18 (Leipzig: J. F. Gleditsch, 1840), 20.
4. Susanne Zantop, for example, has shown South America to have been the subject of German "colonial fantasies" (*Colonial Fantasies: Conquest, Family, and Nation in Precolonial Germany, 1770–1870* [Durham: Duke University Press, 1997]); Sheldon Pollack and Jonathan Hess have argued that Germans colonized Jews as an "other" internal to Europe (Pollack, "Deep Orientalism? Notes on Sanskrit and Power beyond the Raj," in *Orientalism and the Postcolonial Predicament,* ed. Carol A. Breckenridge and Peter van der Veer, 76–133 [Philadelphia: University of Pennsylvania Press, 1993]; Hess, "Johann David Michaelis and the

Colonial Imaginary: Orientalism and the Emergence of Radical Antisemitism in Eighteenth-Century Germany," *Jewish Social Studies* 6, no. 2 [2000]: 56–101); central European involvement in the failing Ottoman Empire has likewise been depicted as a case of German Orientalism sustaining imperial expansion (K. E. Flemming, "*Orientalism,* the Balkans, and Balkan Historiography," *American Historical Review* 105, no. 4 [2000]: 1218–33).

5. Trautmann, *Aryans and British India,* 55.
6. Trautmann, *Aryans and British India,* 9.
7. Han F. Vermeulen, "Frühe Geschichte der Völkerkunde oder Ethnographie in Deutschland, 1771–1791," in *Völkerkunde Tagung 1991,* ed. Mattias S. Laubscher and Bertram Turner (Munich: Akademischer Verlag München, 1994), 1:332–33.
8. Leibniz, "Unvorgreiffliche Gedancken," 1:278.
9. Leibniz, *New Essays on Human Understanding,* 286.
10. Leibniz, *New Essays on Human Understanding,* 285.
11. August Ludwig Schlözer, *Allgemeine Nordische Geschichte* (Halle: Johann Justinus Gebauer, 1771), 291.
12. August Ludwig Schlözer, *Vorstellung seiner Universal-Histoirie* (Göttingen, 1772), 103.
13. Schlözer, *Vorstellung seiner Universal-Histoirie,* 103.
14. Schlözer, *Allgemeine Nordische Geschichte,* 266–85.
15. Jürgen Osterhammel, *Die Entzauberung Asiens: Europa und die asiatischen Reiche im 18. Jahrhundert* (Munich: C. H. Beck, 1998), 250.
16. On Adelung see Ulrich Wyss, *Die wilde Philologie: Jacob Grimm und der Historismus* (Munich: C. H. Beck, 1979) 96ff.
17. Johann Christoph Adelung, *Mithridates oder allgemeine Sprachkunde mit dem Vater Unser als Sprachprobe in bey nahe fünfhundert Sprachen und Mundarten,* vol. 1 (New York: Georg Olms Verlag, 1970), xi.
18. Osterhammel, *Entzauberung Asiens,* 132.
19. For an early nineteenth-century account of the history of the comparative scholarship on German and Farsi see Bernhard Dorn, *Ueber die Verwandtschaft des persischen, germanischen und griechisch-lateinischen Sprachstammes* (Hamburg: J. A. Meissner, 1827), 91–135.
20. Johann Christoph Adelung, *Aelteste Geschichte der Deutschen, ihrer Sprache und Litteratur, bis zur Völkerwanderung* (Leipzig, 1806), 349.
21. Adelung, *Aelteste Geschichte der Deutschen,* 351.
22. See Otto Schrader, *Sprachvergleichung und Urgeschichte: Linguistish-historische Beiträge zur Erforschung des indogermanischen Altertums* (Jena: Hermann Costenoble, 1906), 5.
23. Adelung, *Mithridates,* 11.
24. William Jones, "The Third Anniversary Discourse on the Hindus," in *A*

Reader in Nineteenth-Century Historical Indo-European Linguistics, ed. Winfred Lehmann (Bloomington: Indiana University Press, 1967), 15.

25. Trautmann, *Aryans and British India,* 39ff.
26. Jürgen Lütt, "Einleitung," in "Utopie-Projektion-Gegenbild: Indien in Deutschland," special issue, *Zeitschrift für Kulturaustasuch* 37, no. 3 (1987): 391–93.
27. Hans Aarsleff, *The Study of Language in England, 1780–1860* (Princeton: Princeton University Press, 1967), 3–5, 139.
28. Amos Leslie Willson, *A Mythical Image: The Ideal of India in German Romanticism* (Durham: Duke University Press, 1964), 71.
29. Willson, *Mythical Image,* 50.
30. Othmar Frank, *Das Licht vom Orient* (Leipzig: Besson, 1808), 21, 31.
31. Heinrich Friedrich Link, *Die Urwelt und das Altertum erläutert durch die Naturkunde* (Berlin: Ferdinand Dümmler, 1821–22). In the second edition of this work (1834), Link retracts his claim that Avestan was the mother of Sanskrit in favor of the thesis that Sanskrit was the language most closely related to their common mother.
32. Dorn, *Ueber die Verwandtschaft des persischen,* 12.
33. Sengupta, *From Salon to Discipline,* 1.
34. Edgar Lohner, ed. *Ludwig Tieck und die Brüder Schlegel: Briefe* (Munich: Winkler Verlag, 1972), 135–36.
35. Chen Tzoref-Ashkenazi, "The Nationalist Aspect of Friedrich Schlegel's On the Language and Wisdom of the Indians," in *Sanskrit and 'Orientalism': Indology and Comparative Linguistics in Germany, 1750–1958,* ed. Douglas T. McGetchin, Peter K. J. Park, and Damodar SarDesai (New Delhi: Manohar, 2004), 110.
36. Peter K. J. Park, "A Catholic Apologist in a Pantheistic World: New Approaches to Friedrich Schlegel," in *Sanskrit and 'Orientalism,'* 91.
37. Tzoref-Ashkenazi, "Nationalist Aspect of Friedrich Schlegel," 110.
38. Tzoref-Ashkenazi, "Nationalist Aspect of Friedrich Schlegel," 119.
39. Friedrich Schlegel, *Über die Sprache und Weisheit der Indier: Ein Beitrag zur Begründung der Alterthumskunde* (Heidelberg: Mohr und Zimmer, 1808), 66.
40. Schlegel, *Über die Sprache und Weisheit der Indier,* 105, 175.
41. Tzoref-Ashkenazi, "Nationalist Aspect of Friedrich Schlegel," 109.
42. Schlegel, *Über die Sprache und Weisheit der Indier,* 3–4, 16,3 28.
43. Schlegel, *Über die Sprache und Weisheit der Indier,* 38, 35, 44.
44. Schlegel. *Über die Sprache und Weisheit der Indier,* 44, 41, 50–51, 45.
45. Friedrich Schlegel, "Vorlesungen über Universalgeschichte," in *Kritische Ausgabe seiner Werke,* ed. Ernest Behler (Munich: Verlag Ferdinand Schöningh, 1960), 9:17–18, 3.
46. Schlegel, "Vorlesungen über Universalgeschichte," 9:12, 17, 19.

47. Schlegel, *Sprache und Weisheit der Indier,* 180f. and 197f. See also Manfred Petri, *Die Urvolkhypothese: Ein Beitrag zum Geschichtsdenken der Spätaufklärung und des deutschen Idealismus* (Berlin: Duncker & Humblot, 1990), 194–95.
48. Friedrich Schlegel, "Philosophie der Geschichte," in *Kritische Ausgabe seiner Werke,* 9:31–49.
49. Schlegel, *Über die Sprache und Weisheit der Indier,* 194.
50. Schlegel, *Über die Sprache und Weisheit der Indier,* 195.
51. Konrad Koerner, "Friedrich Schlegel and the Emergence of Historical-Comparative Grammar," in *Practicing Linguistic Historiography,* 285.
52. Sengupta, *From Salon to Discipline,* 19–24.
53. Sengupta, *From Salon to Discipline,* 103.
54. Peter P. J. Park, "Return to Enlightenment: Franz Bopp's Reformation of Comparative Grammar," in *Language Study and the Politics of Community in Global Context,* ed. David Hoyt and Karen Oslund (New York: Rowland & Littlefield, 2006), 62.
55. Salomon Lefmann, *Franz Bopp: Sein Leben und seine Wissenschaft,* vol. 1 (Berlin: Georg Reimer, 1891), 10–14.
56. Cited in Lefmann, *Franz Bopp,* 31.
57. Lefmann, *Franz Bopp,* 33.
58. Koerner, "Friedrich Schlegel," 285.
59. Franz Bopp, *Vocalismus oder sprachvergleichende Kritiken über Jacob Grimm's deutsche Grammatik und Graff's althochdeutschen Sprachschatz mit Begründung einer neuen Theorie des Ablauts* (Berlin: Nicolaische Buchhandlung, 1836), 1.
60. Bopp, *Über das Conjugationssystem der Sanskritsprache in Vergleichung mit jenem der griechischen, lateinischen, persischen und germanischen Sprache,* ed. K. J. Windischmann (Frankfurt: Andreäische Buchhandlung, 1816), 11.
61. Berthold Delbrück, *Introduction to the Study of Language: A Critical Survey for the History and Methods of Comparative Grammar of the Indo-European Languages,* trans. Eva Channing (London: Trübner, 1882), 19.
62. Franz Bopp, *Über das Conjugationssystem,* 8–9. Emphasis added.
63. Bopp, *Über das Conjugationssystem,* 7.
64. *International Encyclopedia of Linguistics,* ed. William Bright, vol. 2 (New York: Oxford University Press, 1992), 213–15.
65. Bopp, *Über das Conjugationssystem,* 8.
66. R. E. Asher and J. M. Y. Simpson, eds., *Encyclopedia of Language and Linguistics* (New York: Pergamon, 1994), 5:2576ff.
67. See Vivien Law, "Processes of Assimilation: European Grammars of Sanskrit in the Early Decades of the Nineteenth Century," in *La linguistique*

entre mythe et histoire, ed. Daniel Droixhe (Münster: Nodus-Publikation, 1993), 254–57.

68. Ernst Windisch, *Geschichte der Sanskrit Philologie und indischen Altertumskunde* (Strassburg: K. J. Trübner, 1917), 72, 74–76.
69. Park, "Return to Enlightenment," 74–75.
70. For a good analysis of how Bopp's understanding of inflection and Indo-European roots evolved see Delbrück, *Introduction to the Study of Language,* 3–16.
71. A. W. Schlegel's final appointment to the philosophical faculty in Bonn was not official until 1822, although he assumed his duties in 1818. See Sengupta, *From Salon to Discipline,* 25.
72. A. W. Schlegel, "Ueber den gegenwärtigen Zustand der Indischen Philologie. Geschrieben im Sommer 1819," *Indische Bibliothek* 1 (1820), 22.
73. Windisch, *Geschichte der Sanskrit Philologie,* 76.
74. Sengupta, *From Salon to Discipline,* 56.
75. Lefmann, *Franz Bopp,* 73.
76. Law, "Processes of Assimilation," 257.
77. Delbrück, *Introduction to the Study of Language,* 17.
78. Franz Bopp, *Vergleichende Grammatik,* iii. The citation is taken from the preface to the first edition. For a discussion of what Bopp meant by "physical" and "mechanical," see Delbrück, *Introduction to the Study of Language,* 3–16.
79. Delbrück, *Introduction to the Study of Language,* 18.
80. Bopp, *Vergleichende Grammatik,* 201.
81. Bopp, *Vergleichende Grammatik,* 203.
82. Bopp, *Vergleichende Grammatik,* 196–97.
83. Bopp, *Vergleichende Grammatik,* 198.
84. Bopp, *Vergleichende Grammatik,* 203.
85. Bopp, *Vergleichende Zergliederung des Sanskrit,* (Berlin: Druckerei der Königlichen Akademie der Wissenschaften, 1824), 14.
86. Delbrück, *Introduction to the Study of Language,* 31.
87. See Pott's review article "Researches into the Origin and Affinity of the Principal Languages of Asia and Europe. By Lieut. Colon. Vans Kennedy," *Jahrbücher für wissenschaftliche Kritik,* no. 8 (July 1832): 61.
88. See the article on Klaproth in *Encyclopaedia Britannica,* 8th edition, vol. 8 (1857), 105.
89. In Klaproth, *Asia Polyglotta.*
90. Klaproth, *Asia Polyglotta,* 35, 40.
91. Klaproth, *Asia Polyglotta,* 42–44.
92. Klaproth, *Asia Polyglotta,* 43.
93. Julius Klaproth, "Obersvations sur la critique faite par M. Sam. Lee . . . ,

par M. le baron Silvestre de Sacy," *Nouveau Journal Asiatique* 5 (1830): 112–13.

94. Pott, "Indogermanischer Sprachstamm," 19. Contemporary scholars point to the area just north and between the Caspian and Black seas and trace Indo-European migration based on the diffusion of the domesticated horse. On the intersection of linguistics and archaeology in theories of the Indo-European homeland see Colin Renfrew, *Archaeology and Language: The Puzzle of Indo-European Origins* (London: Pimlico, 1998); J. Mallory, *In Search of the Indo-Europeans: Language, Archaeology, and Myth* (London: Thames and Hudson, 1989); and Katherine Kress, *Indo-European Homeland Hypotheses: A Critical Examination of Linguistic Arguments* (Ottawa, 1995).
95. Pott, "Indogermanischer Sprachstamm," 20.
96. Georg Heinrich August Ewald, "Plan dieser Zeitschrift," *Zeitschrift für die Kunde des Morgenlandes* 1 (1837): 7.
97. An account of this trip is published as *Reise in den Kaukasus und nach Georgien unternommen in den Jahren 1807 und 1808, auf Veranstaltung der kaiserlichen Akademie der Wissenschaften zu St. Petersburg,* 2 vols. (Berlin, 1812–14). See also *Geographisch-historische Beschreibung.*
98. Sergei Ouvaroff, "Projet d'une Académie Asiatique," *Études de philologie et de critique.* 2nd ed. (Paris: Didot Frères, 1845), 1–48.
99. Klaproth published accounts of these travels in *Die russische Gesandtschaft nach China im Jahre 1805* (Leipzig, 1809), and "Bemerkungen über die chinesisch-russische Grenze, gesammelt auf einer Reise an derselben, im Jahre 1806," *Archiv für asiatische Litteratur* (1810).
100. Susan Layton, *Russian Literature and Empire: Conquest of the Caucasus from Pushkin to Tolstoy* (Cambridge: Cambridge University Press, 1994), 75–77.
101. Christian Martin Frähn, *Indications bibliographiques relatives pour la plupart à la littérature historico-géographique des Arabes, des Persans et des Turcs, spécialement destinées à nos employés et voyageurs en Asie* (Saint Petersburg: Académie impériale des sciences, 1845), xii.
102. After Frähn's appointment, Czar Alexander I asked Sylvestre de Sacy to recommend scholars to fill two new positions in Arabic and Farsi at the Central Pedagogical Institute in Saint Petersburg. The two Frenchmen engaged were later instrumental in establishing the Oriental Institute for Translation, which opened in 1823 by the Asian Department of the Foreign Ministry.
103. Dorn, *Ueber die Verwandtschaft des persischen,* 12.
104. Dorn, *Ueber die Verwandtschaft des persischen,* 51.
105. See the works by Bernhard Dorn, *Beiträge zur Geschichte der kaukasis-*

chen Länder (Saint Petersburg: Royal Academy of Sciences, 1841–47), and *Beiträge zur Kenntnis der iranischen Sprache* (Saint Petersburg: Royal Academy of Sciences, 1860).

106. Klaproth, *Asia Polyglotta,* 35.
107. Klaproth, *Asia Polyglotta,* 40.
108. Klaproth, *Reise in den Kaukasus,* 2:585.
109. Julius Klaproth, *Tableau historique, géographique, et politique du Caucase et des provinces limitrophes entre la Russie et la Persie* (Paris: Ponthieu et C., 1827), 70.
110. Klaproth, *Reise in den Kaukasus,* 2:287.
111. Schmidt described Mongolian as a field "in which not only no one is active, but also in which no one has ever broken ground" and noted the lack of reference materials available in Mongolian and Tibetan, either as published by Europeans or complied by native speakers. He had to rely on odd sources such as a Mandschu-Mongolian comparative grammar composed under Chinese Emperor Kanghi who had done battle with the Mongolians, or a grammar and dictionary published in Calcutta 1834 by a Hungarian traveler who had learned Tibetan from a lama. See Isaac Jacob Schmidt, *Grammatik der tibetischen Sprache* (Leipzig: Leopold Voss, 1839), ix–x, and *Grammatik der mongolischen Sprache* (Saint Petersburg: Kaiserliche Akademie der Wissenschaften, 1831), vii.
112. Isaac Jacob Schmidt, *Forschungen im Gebiete der älteren religiösen, politischen und literärischen Bildungsgeschichte der Völker Mittel-Asiens, vorzüglich der Mongolen und Tibeter* (Leipzig: Zentralantiquariat der DDR, 1972), 1–2.
113. Isaac Jacob Schmidt, *Grammatik der mongolischen Sprache,* vi.
114. Isaac Jacob Schmidt, *Forschungen,* 28.
115. Wilhlem Schott, *Über die sogenannten Indo-Chinesischen Sprachen insonderheit das Siamische* (Berlin: Druckerei der königlichen Akademie der Wissenschaften, 1856), 161.
116. Wilhelm Schott, ed., *Werke des tschinesischen Weisen Kung-fu-dsu und seiner Schüler: Zum erstenmal aus der Ursprache ins Deutsche übersetzt und mit Anmerkungen begleitet* (Halle, Rengersche Verlags-Buchhandlung, 1826–32), 1:v–vi.
117. Wilhelm Schott, *Chinesische Sprachlehre: Zum Gebrauche bei Vorlesungen und zur Selbstunterweisung* (Berlin: Ferdinand Dümmler, 1857), 1–2. Julius von Klaproth likewise studied Japanese with the help of a Chinese-Japanese dictionary after meeting a Japanese language teacher in Russia in 1805–6 at a school created by Catherine II.
118. Heinrich Julius Klaproth, writing as Wilhelm Lauterbach, *Dr. William Schott's vergebliche Übersetzung des Confucius aus der Ursprache, eine litterarische Betrügerei* (Leipzig: Ponthieu, Michelson and Comp., 1828),

11.

119. Koerner, "Friedrich Schlegel," 280.

120. Gordon Hewes, "Disputes on the Origin of Language," in *Sprachphilosophie—Philosophy of Language—La philosophie du langage. Ein internationales Handbuch—An International Handbook of Contemporary Research—Manuel international des recherches contemporaines,* ed. Marcelo Dascal, Dietfried Gerhardus, Kuno Lorenz, and Georg Megle (Berlin: Walter de Gruyter, 1992), 2:936.

121. Wilhelm von Humboldt, *Über die Verschiedenheit des menschlichen Sprachbaues und ihren Einfluß auf die geistige Entwicklung des Menschengeschlechts,* ed. Donatella Di Cesare (Munich: Ferdinand Schöningh, 1998), 378ff.

122. Carl Friedrich Neumann, "Sprache und Schrift der Chinesen," in *Asiatische Studien* (Leipzig: Johann Ambrosius Barth, 1837), 4.

123. That the Societé Asiatique in Paris wanted copies of the Sanskrit type that Bopp had made for the Berlin Academy of Sciences in 1824 suggests the relative strength of German Indology. See Windisch, *Geschichte der Sanskrit Philologie,* 65, 78.

124. Klaproth, *Reise in den Kaukasus,* 1:v.

125. Thus, when the Indologist Friedrich Max Müller took an Oxford chair in Sanskrit in 1851, he was struck by the paltry state of Oriental studies in England. See Patricia Casey Sutcliffe, "F. M. Müller and Dwight Whitney as Exporters of Nineteenth-Century German Philology: A Sociological Analysis of the Development of Linguistic Theory" (PhD diss., University of Texas, Austin, 2000), 93.

126. For August Ludwig Schlözer's coining the term "Semitic languages," see Justin Stagl, "August Ludwig Schlözers Entwurf einer 'Völkerkunde' oder 'Ethnographie seit 1772,'" *Ethnologische Zeitschrift Zurich* 2 (1974), 75.

127. Jon D. Levenson, *The Hebrew Bible, the Old Testament, and Historical Criticism* (Louisville, Ky.: Westminster/John Knox Press, 1993), 4ff.

128. See Arno Beyer's summary in *Deutsche Einflüsse auf die englische Sprachwissenschaft im neunzehnten Jahrhundert* (Göppingen: Kümmerle Verlag, 1981), 184–86.

129. Wilhelm Gesenius, *Ausführliches grammatisch-kritisches Lehrgebäude der hebräischen Sprache mit Vergleichung der verwandten Dialekte* (Leipzig: Friedrich Christian Wilhelm Vogel, 1817), x.

130. Wilhelm Gesenius, *Geschichte der hebräischen Sprache und Schrift. Eine philologische Einleitung in die Sprachlehren und Wörterbücher der hebräischen Sprache* (Leipzig: Friedrich Christian Wilhelm Vogel, 1815), 13.

131. Gesenius, *Geschichte,* 25.

132. Gesenius, *Geschichte,* 19.

133. Gesenius, *Geschichte,* 20.
134. Gesenius, *Geschichte,* 30.
135. See John William Rogerson, *Old Testament Criticism in the Nineteenth Century: England and Germany* (London: Society for Promoting Christian Knowledge, 1984), 52ff.
136. Williamson, *Longing for Myth,* 153.
137. Williamson, *Longing for Myth,* 154; and Rogerson, *Old Testament Criticism,* 29.
138. Williamson, *Longing for Myth,* 155.
139. The article is reprinted in Johannes Bachmann, *Ernst Wilhelm Henstenberg: Sein Leben und Wirken* (Gütersloh: Bertelsmann, 1880), 2:187.
140. Bachmann, *Ernst Wilhelm Henstenberg,* 2:177–283.
141. Rogerson, *Old Testament Criticism,* 51.
142. Sengupta, *From Salon to Discipline,* 54–56.
143. Rogerson, *Old Testament Criticism,* 92–93.
144. Heinrich Ewald, *The History of Israel,* trans. Russell Martineau (London: Longmans, Green, and Co., 1869), 1:50–51.
145. Ewald, *History of Israel,* 1:65.
146. Rogerson, *Old Testament Criticism,* 97.
147. Rogerson, *Old Testament Criticism,* 91.
148. Williamson, *Longing for Myth,* 167ff.
149. Levenson, *Hebrew Bible,* 11–12.
150. Levenson, *Hebrew Bible,* 14.
151. Benfey, *Geschichte der Sprachwissenschaft,* 691ff.
152. Reinhard G. Lehmann, *Friedrich Delitzsche und der Babel-Bibel-Streit* (Göttingen: Vandenhoeck & Ruprecht, 1994), 31–33.
153. Friedrich Delitzsch, *The Hebrew Language Viewed in Light of Assyrian Research* (London: Williams and Norgate, 1883), vi.
154. Suzanne Marchand, "German Orientalism and the Decline of the West," *Proceedings of the American Philosophical Society* 145, no. 4 (2001): 473.
155. David Sorkin, *The Transformation of German Jewry, 1780–1840* (New York: Oxford University Press, 1987), 99ff.
156. Peter Freimark, "Language Behavior and Assimilation: The Situation of the Jews in Northern Germany in the First Half of the Nineteenth Century," *Yearbook of the Leo Baeck Institute* 24 (1979): 173–74.
157. Jacob Toury, "Die Sprache als Problem der jüdischen Einordnung in den deutschen Kulturraum," in *Gegenseitige Einflüsse deutscher und jüdischer Kultur: Internationales Symposium,* ed. Walter Grab (Tel Aviv, 1982), 82–86.
158. Cited in Toury, "Sprache als Problem," 91.
159. Freimark, "Language Behavior and Assimilation," 162–63.
160. George Mosse, "Jewish Emancipation: Between *Bildung* and

Respectability," in *The Jewish Response to German Culture: From the Enlightenment to the Second World War,* ed. Juduha Reinharz (Hanover: University Press of New England, 1985), 6–7.

161. Hannah Franziska Augstein, "Linguistics and Politics in the Early Nineteenth Century: James Cowles Prichard's Moral Philology," *History of European Ideas* 23, no. 1 (1997): 5.
162. Cited in Beyer, *Deutsche Einflüsse,* 184–85n.
163. Julius Fürst, *Lehrgebäude der aramäischen Idiome mit Bezug auf die Indo-Germanischen Sprachen* (Leipzig: Karl Tauchmitz, 1835), ix–x.
164. Heinrich Ewald, "Abhandlung über den Zusammenhang des Nordischen (Türkischen), Mittelländischen, Semitischen und Koptischen Sprachstammes," in *Abhandlungen der königlichen Gesellschaft der Wissenschaften in Göttingen* (Berlin, 1862), 10:4, 71, 74.
165. See the biographical sketch in Theodor Benfey, *Kleinere Schriften,* ed. Adalbert Bezzenberger (Berlin: H. Reuther's Verlagsbuchhandlung, 1890), 1:xiii.
166. Benfey, *Kleinere Schriften,* 1:xv.
167. See Theodor Benfey, *Die persischen Keilinschriften mit Uebersetzung und Glossar* (Leipzig: Brockhaus & Avenarius, 1847), and his review of Hermann Brockhaus's *Vendidad* and Friedrich Spiegel's *Avesta* in the *Göttingische Gelehrte Anzeigen* (1850): 1193–1236, (1852): 1953–76, and (1853): 57–93.
168. Henry Hoenigswald, "Historiography as Source: The Afterlife of Theodor Benfey," in *Lingua et traditio: Geschichte der Sprachwissenschaft und der neueren Philologien,* ed. Hans Helmut Christmann and Richard Baum (Tübingen: Gunter Narr Verlag, 1994), 424.
169. Theodor Benfey and Moriz A. Stern, *Ueber die Monatsnamen einiger alter Völker insbesondere der Perser, Cappodocier, Juden und Syrer* (Berlin: G. Reimer, 1836), 121.
170. Theodor Benfey, *Pantschatantra: Fünf Bücher indischer Fabeln, Märchen und Erzählungen aus dem Sanskrit übersetzt* (Leipzig: Brockhaus, 1859), 1:xxiii.
171. Christian Charles Josias Bunsen, *Outlines of the Philosophy of Universal History Applied to Language and Religion* (London: Longman, Brown, Green, and Longmans, 1854), 1:172ff.
172. Theodor Benfey, *Ueber das Verhältniss der ägyptischen Sprache zum semitischen Sprachstamm.* Leipzig: F. A. Brockhaus, 1844), vi–vii.
173. See the discussion in Delbrück, *Introduction to the Study of Language,* 78.
174. On Benfey's repudiation of the term root see Theodor Benfey, "Pott: Etymologische Forschungen auf dem Gebiete der Indo-Germanischen Sprachen" (1837), in *Kleinere Schriften,* 4:30ff.

175. On this theory see Theodor Benfey, "Ein abschnitt aus meiner vorlesung über 'vergleichende Grammatik der indo-germanischen sprachen,'" *Zeitschrift für vergleichende Sprachforschung auf dem Gebiete des deutschen, grieschischen, und lateinischen* 9 (1860): 81–132.
176. See the discussion in Delbrück, *Introduction to the Study of Language,* 86.
177. Theodor Benfey, "Müller: Lectures on the Science of Language" (1862), in *Kleinere Schriften,* 4:129.
178. Benfey, "Müller," 4:128–29.
179. Beyer, *Deutsche Einflüsse,* 184.
180. Pott, "Indogermanischer Sprachstamm," 14.
181. August Wilhelm Schlegel, "De l'origine des hindous," in *Essais littéraires et historiques* (Bonn: E. Weber, 1842), 489.
182. Pott, "Indogermanischer Sprachstamm," 12.
183. Koerner, "Friedrich Schlegel," 281.
184. See Koerner, "Friedrich Schlegel," 282.
185. Augstein, "Linguistics and Politics," 4–5.
186. Humboldt, *Über die Verschiedenheit des menschlichen Sprachbaues,* 368.
187. Humboldt, *Über die Verschiedenheit des menschlichen Sprachbaues,* 371–73. See also Augstein, "Linguistics and Politics," 7.
188. Humboldt, *Über die Verschiedenheit des menschlichen Sprachbaues,* 368.
189. Grossmann, "Wilhelm von Humboldt's Linguistic Ideology," 25.
190. Grossmann, "Wilhelm von Humboldt's Linguistic Ideology," 37–38.
191. Ismar Schorsch, *From Text to Context: The Turn to History in Modern Judaism* (Hanover: University Press of New England, 1994), 59.
192. Jacob Katz, *From Prejudice to Destruction: Anti-Semitism, 1700–1933* (Cambridge, Mass.: Harvard University Press, 1980) 76–83.
193. Sorkin, *Transformation of German Jewry,* 22.
194. Olender, *Languages of Paradise,* 9ff,
195. Olender, *Languages of Paradise,* 139ff.
196. Sheldon Pollack has argued that German Orientalism was from its inception directed inward toward Europe and the internal colonization of Jews in the National Socialist period. See his "Deep Orientalism?" See also Ritchie Robertson, "'*Urheimat Asien*': The Re-Orientation of German and Austrian Jews, 1900–1925," *German Life and Letters* 49, no. 2 (1996): 182–92; and Nadia Malinovich, "Orientalism and the Construction of Jewish Identity in France, 1900–1932," *Jewish Culture and History* 2, no. 1 (1999): 1–25.
197. Johann Heinrich Kalthoff, *Handbuch der hebräischen Altertümer* (Münster: Theissingsche Buchhandlung, 1840), 3, 5, 6.
198. Kalthoff, *Handbuch,* 409–10.

Chapter 3

1. Johann Gottlieb Fichte, *Reden an die deutsche Nation* (Berlin: Realschulbuchhandlung, 1808), 114–17, 139–44.
2. Lincoln, *Theorizing Myth,* 48.
3. Cited in Klaus von See, *Deutsche Germanen-Ideologie vom Humanismus bis zur Gegenwart* (Frankfurt: Athenäum, 1970), 68ff.
4. See Uwe Meves, "Zur Namesgebung 'Germanist,'" in *Wissenschaftsgeschichte der Germanistik im 19. Jahrhundert,* ed. Jürgen Fohrmann and Wilhelm Voßkamp (Stuttgart: J. B. Metzler, 1994), 25–47.
5. See Susan A. Crane, *Collecting and the Historical Consciousness in Early Nineteenth-Century Germany* (Ithaca: Cornell University Press, 2000).
6. Peter Hans Reill, *The German Enlightenment and the Rise of Historicism* (Berkeley: University of California Press, 1975), 208.
7. Williamson, *Longing for Myth,* 84ff.
8. Friedrich Heinrich von der Hagen, "Ueber die Grundsätze der neuen Bearbeitung vom Liede der Nibelungen," *Eunomia: Eine Zeitschrift des 19. Jahrhunderts* 1 (1805): 254.
9. Joachim Burkhard Richter, *Hans Ferdinand Maßmann: Altdeutscher Patriotismus im neunzehnten Jahrhundert* (Berlin: Walter de Gruyter, 1992), 43ff.
10. Cited in Eckhard Grunewald, *Friedrich Heinrich von der Hagen: Ein Beitrag zur Frühgeschichte der Germanistik* (Berlin: de Gruyter, 1988), 2.
11. Grunewald, *Friedrich Heinrich von der Hagen,* 338.
12. Grunewald, *Friedrich Heinrich von der Hagen,* 41–42.
13. Hagen, "Grundsätze der neueren Bearbeitung," 255–56.
14. "Old, vigorous works" were reduced, in their hands, to "linguistic curiosities and rarities" slated to be "buried . . . in libraries" (Hagen, "Grundsätze der neueren Bearbeitung," 256).
15. Werner Bahner and Werner Neumann, eds., *Sprachwissenschaftliche Germanistik: Ihre Herausbildung und Begründung* (Berlin: Akademie-Verlag, 1985), 160–65.
16. Jacob Grimm, "Über Etymologie und Sprachvergleichung" (1854), in *Kleinere Schriften* (Berlin: Ferdinand Dümmler, 1879), 1:309.
17. Jacob Grimm, *Deutsche Grammatik,* ed. Wilhelm Scherer (Göttingen: Dieterichsche Buchhandlung, 1819), 1:xviii.
18. Toews, *Becoming Historical,* 322.
19. See Sigmar Hellerich, *Religionizing, Romanizing Romantics: The Catholico-Christian Camouflage of the Early German Romantics: Wackenroder, Tieck, Novalis, Friedrich and August Wilhelm Schlegel* (New York: Peter Lang, 1995), xix ff.
20. Williamson, *Longing for Myth,* 72ff.

21. Williamson, *Longing for Myth,* 73.
22. Murray B. Peppard, *Paths through the Forest: A Biography of the Brothers Grimm* (New York: Holt, Rinehart and Winston, 1971), 49–50, 67.
23. Toews, *Becoming Historical,* 340.
24. Toews, *Becoming Historical,* 342.
25. "Wissenschaftshistorische Stufen sprachgeschichtlicher Forschung I: Geschichte der Sprachgeschichtsforschung entlang der Zeitlinie," in *Sprachgeschichte: Ein Handbuch zur Geschichte der deutschen Sprache und ihrer Erforschung,* ed. Werner Besch, Oskar Reichmann, and Stefan Sonderegger (Berlin: Walter de Gruyter, 1984), 1:309–15.
26. Gunhild Ginschel, *Der junge Jacob Grimm, 1805–1819* (Berlin: Akademie-Verlag, 1967), 331.
27. Cited in Konrad Koerner, "Jacob Grimm's Place in the Foundation of Linguistics as a Science," in *Practicing Linguistic Historiography,* Studies in the History of the Language Sciences 50 (Amsterdam: John Benjamins, 1989), 305–6.
28. Bahner and Neumann, *Sprachwissenschaftliche Germanistik,* 130.
29. Ginschel, *Der junge Jacob Grimm,* 362.
30. Schlegel, *Über die Sprache und Weisheit der Indier,* 33–34.
31. Grimm, *Deutsche Grammatik,* 1:xxiv, xiv.
32. Grimm, *Deutsche Grammatik,* 1:xxiv.
33. Twentieth-century linguists divide the Germanic languages into northern, western, and eastern subgroups. The North Germanic languages include Icelandic, Faroese, Danish, Swedish, and Norwegian; English, German, Dutch, and Frisian compose the West Germanic languages. The members of the eastern group, Gothic, Burgundian, and Vandalic are all extinct and little is known of them except for Gothic, for which a fourth-century Bible translation is extant.
34. Hans Frede Nielsen, "Jacob Grimm and the 'German' Dialects," in *The Grimm Brothers and the Germanic Past,* ed. Elmer H. Antonsen (Philadelphia: John Benjamins, 1990), 25–26.
35. Grimm, *Deutsche Grammatik,* 1:546.
36. Grimm, *Deutsche Grammatik,* 1:xxi–xxii.
37. These are the examples Grimm presented in the *Geschichte der deutschen Sprache* (Leipzig: Weidmannische Buchhandlung, 1848), 1:842.
38. Grimm, *Deutsche Grammatik,* 1:547.
39. The term *Umlaut* refers to changes in the vowel that can express a variety of grammatical functions such as noun plurals ("*Bruder*" [brother] becomes "*Brüder*"), the subjunctive case ("*wir waren*" [we were] becomes "*wir wären*" [we would be]), and adjective comparison, as in the word for "big" ("*groß*" becomes "*größer*"). See Grimm, *Deutsche Grammatik,* 2:73.

40. Grimm, *Deutsche Grammatik,* 1:546.
41. The earliest Germanic tongues revealed only "pure changes to the root vowel"; later versions could be identified by the extent to which they "give up their roots and relinquish their vowel changes," compensating for this loss through "compound constructions." The newer Germanic languages were, according to Grimm, distinguished by "the appending of an auxiliary root." See Grimm, *Deutsche Grammatik,* 2:74.
42. Grimm was inspired to recast the first volume of the work after reviewing Rask's *Undersögelse om det gamle Nordiske eller Islandske Sprogs Oprindelse* (1818), which argued that sounds are a central body of linguistic evidence. Rask, not Grimm, was the first to note that cognate languages display systematic sound-correspondences that can be stated as rules. The nineteenth-century linguist Holger Pedersen suggested for this reason that the Germanic sound shifts identified by Grimm should actually be known as "Rask's Law," although most historians now agree that this overstates the credit due to Rask. It was the 1822 edition of Grimm's grammar that established the importance of phonology in historical linguistics, an area of study ignored by Bopp and only applied to the Indo-European languages by August Friedrich Pott in 1833. See Koerner, *Practicing Linguistic Historiography,* 304.
43. Jacob Grimm, *Deutsche Grammatik,* 2nd edition (Göttingen: Dieterichsche Buchhandlung, 1822), 1:584.
44. Proto-Germanic is the language believed to have been spoken around the North Sea and the Baltic before 1000 BC. One third of its vocabulary lacks Indo-European cognates, most notably words having to do with the ocean such as, in English, sea, ship, and boat. See Asher and Simpson, *Encyclopedia of Language and Linguistics,* 3:1426.
45. Grimm, *Deutsche Grammatik,* 2nd ed., 1:584–85.
46. R. L. Trask, *Historical Linguistics* (New York: St. Martin's Press, 1996), 224–26.
47. Grimm, *Deutsche Grammatik,* 2nd ed., 1:590, 588.
48. Benfey, *Geschichte der Sprachwissenschaft,* 38.
49. Toews, *Becoming Historical,* 347.
50. Grimm, *Deutsche Grammatik,* 1:xxvi.
51. Toews, *Becoming Historical,* 345.
52. Toews, *Becoming Historical,* 342.
53. Asher and Simpson, *Encyclopedia of Language and Linguistics,* 3:1419–20.
54. Jacob Grimm, *Kleinere Schriften,* 3:320. See also Klaus von See, *Barbar, Germane, Arier: Die Suche nach der Identität der Deutschen* (Heidelberg: Carl Winter, 1994), 138.
55. James J. Sheehan, "What Is German History?" 1–23.

56. Besch, "Dialekt, Schreibdialekt, Schriftsprache, Standardsprache," 978.
57. Toews, *Becoming Historical,* 344.
58. Grimm, *Deutsche Grammatik,* 2nd ed., 1:xiii.
59. Grimm, *Deutsche Grammatik,* 2nd ed., 1:xiii.
60. Chauncy Jeffries Mellor, *Scholarly Purpose and National Purpose in Jacob Grimm's Work on the 'Deutsches Wörterbuch'* (Chicago: University of Chicago Press, 1972), 361.
61. Grimm, *Deutsche Grammatik,* 1:10.
62. Walter Haas, *Jacob Grimm und die deutschen Mundarten* (Stuttgart: Steiner, 1990), 6ff.
63. Johann Andreas Schmeller, *Über Schrift und Schriftunterricht: Ein ABC-Büchlein in die Hände Lehrender,* ed. Hermann Barkey (Munich: Bayerische Akademie der Wissenschaften, 1965), 41.
64. Schmeller, *Über Schrift und Schriftunterricht,* 41.
65. Schmeller, *Über Schrift und Schriftunterricht,* 11.
66. Schmeller, *Über Schrift und Schriftunterricht,* 42. He later devised the first historically based phonetic transcription adequate to the phonology of the German dialects.
67. Peter Wiesinger, "Johann Andreas Schmeller als Sprachsoziologe," in *Linguistic Method: Essays in Honor of Herbert Pernzl,* ed. Irmengard Rauch and Gerald F. Carr (New York: Mouton, 1979), 591.
68. Johann Andreas Schmeller, *Die Mundarten Bayerns grammatisch dargestellt von Johann Andreas Schmeller* (Munich: Karl Thienemann, 1821), x.
69. Franz Josef Stalder, *Probe eines schweizerischen Idiotikons; hie und da mit etymologischen Bemerkungen untermischt* (1805).
70. Johann Andreas Schmeller, "Sprache der Baiern," in Ludwig Rockinger, *An der Wiege der bayerischen Mundart-Grammatik und des bayerischen Wörterbuchs* (Aalen: Scienta, 1985), 70.
71. Celia Appelgate, *A Nation of Provincials: The German Idea of Heimat* (Berkeley: University of California Press, 1990), 13.
72. Johann Andreas Schmeller, "*Lauter gemähte Wiesen für die Reaktion*": *Die erste Hälfte des 19. Jahrhunderts in den Tagebüchern Johann Andreas Schmellers,* ed. Reinhard Bauer and Ursula Münchhoff (Munich: Serie Piper, 1990), 67.
73. Schmeller, *Die Mundarten Bayerns,* ix.
74. Schmeller, *Die Mundarten Bayerns,* x.
75. Schmeller, *Die Mundarten Bayerns,* 21f.
76. Schmeller, *Die Mundarten Bayerns,* 30.
77. Bernd Naumann, "Heymann Steinthals Position in der Geschichte der Sprachwissenschaft," in *Germanistik und Deutschunterricht im Zeitalter der Technologie,* ed. N. Oellers (Tübingen: Niemeyer, 1988), 1:90; and

Richard J. Brunner, *Johann Andreas Schmeller: Sprachwissenschaftler und Philologe* (Innsbruck: Institut für vergleichende Sprachwissenschaft, 1971), 66.

78. Ludwig M. Eichinger and Bernd Naumann, eds., *Johann Andreas Schmeller und der Beginn der Germanistik* (Munich: R. Oldenbourg, 1988), 41.
79. Schmeller, *Die Mundarten Bayerns,* 30.
80. Schmeller, *Die Mundarten Bayerns,* 163.
81. Johann Christoph Adelung, *Über die Geschichte der deutschen Sprache, über Deutsche Mundarten und Deutsche Sprachlehre* (Leipzig: Johnann Gottlieb Immanuel Breitkopf, 1781), 37.
82. Jacob Grimm, *Deutsche Grammatik,* 1:x.
83. Jacob Grimm, *Deutsche Grammatik,* 1:xxxiii.
84. Jacob Grimm, *Deutsche Grammatik,* 1:xxxiii.
85. Cited in Ronald Feldmann, *Jacob Grimm und die Politik* (Kassel: Bärenreiter, 1971), 110.
86. See Feldmann, *Jacob Grimm,* 111–12.
87. Jacob Grimm, *Deutsche Grammatik,* 2nd ed. 1:xiii.
88. Jacob Grimm, *Geschichte der deutschen Sprache,* 1:828.
89. See Feldmann, *Jacob Grimm,* 54ff.
90. Schmeller, *Die Mundarten Bayerns,* vi–vii.
91. Schmeller, "*Lauter gemähte Wiesen für die Reaktion,*" 195.
92. Uwe Meves, "Zum Institutionalisierungsprozeß der deutschen Philologie: Die Periode der Lehrstuhlerrichtung," in *Wissenschaftsgeschichte der Germanistik,* 186.
93. Jörg Jochen Müller, "Germanistik—Eine Form bürgerlicher Opposition," in *Germanistik und deutsche Nation, 1806–1848: Zur Konstitution bürgerlichen Bewußtseins,* ed. Jörg Jochen Müller (Stuttgart: J. B. Metzler, 2000), 39ff.
94. The recollections of students who took German in the *Vormärz* are remarkably devoid of nationalist pathos. See Rüdiger Gans, "Erfahrungen mit dem Deutschunterricht: Eine Analyse autobiographischer Zeugnisse im Zusammenhang mit der Geschichte des Bildungsbürgertums im 19. Jahrhundert," in *Muttersprachlicher Unterricht im neunzehnten Jahrhundert: Untersuchungen zu seiner Genese und Institutionalisierung,* ed. Hans-Dieter Erlinger and Clemens Knoblauch (Tübingen: Niemeyer, 1991), 29.
95. Reinhart Koselleck, "Einleitung—Zur anthropologischen und semantischen Strukture der Bildung," in *Bildungsbürgertum im 19. Jahrhundert,* ed. Reinhart Koselleck (Stuttgart: Klett-Cotta, 1985), 2:11–46.
96. Wolfgang Kaschuba, "Deutsche Bürgerlichkeit nach 1800. Kultur als symbolische Praxis," in *Bürgertum im 19. Jahrhundert,* ed. Jürgen Kocka

(Göttingen: Vandenhoeck & Ruprecht, 1995), 2:92–127.

97. Jürgen Kocka, "Das europäische Muster und der deutsche Fall," in *Bürgertum im 19. Jahrhundert,* 1:19.

98. Karen Hagemann, "Of 'Manly Valor' and 'German Honor': Nation, War, and Masculinity in the Age of the Prussian Uprising against Napoleon," *Central European History* 30, no. 2 (1997): 206–7.

99. Hagemann, "Of 'Manly Valor' and 'German Honor,'" 203–8.

100. Brigit Benes, *Wilhelm von Humboldt, Jacob Grimm, August Schleicher: Ein Vergleich ihrer Sprachauffassungen* (Winterthur: P. G. Keller, 1958), 65.

101. See Toews, *Becoming Historical,* 348. This bias partially explains Grimm's exclusive focus on the importance of consonants in the Germanic sound shifts.

102. Jacob Grimm, "Über den Ursprung der Sprache," in *Kleinere Schriften,* 1:281.

103. Jacob Grimm, *Deutsche Grammatik,* 3:343.

104. Jacob Grimm, *Deutsche Grammatik,* 3:343.

105. See Jacob Grimm, "Über Frauennamen aus Blumen" (1852), in *Kleinere Schriften,* 2:366–401.

106. Jacob Grimm, *Deutsche Grammatik,* 1:46.

107. Jacob Grimm, *Deutsche Grammatik,* 1:46.

108. Jacob Grimm, *Deutsche Grammatik,* 1:35.

109. Jacob Grimm, *Deutsche Grammatik,* 1:28.

110. Jacob Grimm, *Deutsche Grammatik,* 1:xi.

111. Jacob Grimm, *Deutsche Grammatik,* 1:30.

112. John M. Ellis, *One Fairy Story Too Many: The Brothers Grimm and their Tales* (Chicago: University of Chicago Press, 1983), 32.

113. Jacob Grimm and Wilhelm Grimm, *Deutsches Wörterbuch von Jacob und Wilhelm Grimm* (Munich: Deutscher Taschenbuch Verlag, 1984), 1:xiii.

114. Wolfgang Mommsen, *Bürgerliche Kultur und politische Ordnung, 1831–1933: Künstler, Schriftsteller und Intellektuelle in der deutschen Geschichte, 1831–1933* (Frankfurt: Fischer Taschenbuch Verlag, 2000), 59.

115. Claudia Bartels, "Deutschunterricht ohne Deutschlehrer," in *Satzlehre-Denkschulung-Nationalsprache: Deutsche Schulgrammatik zwischen 1800 und 1850,* ed. Hans Dietrich Erlinger and Clemens Knobloch (Münster: Nodus Publikationen, 1989), 21. See also Raumer, *Geschichte der germanischen Philologie,* 685.

116. Gans, "Erfahrungen mit dem Deutschunterricht," 22.

117. Hans Dieter Erlinger and Clemens Knobloch, "Einleitung," in Erlinger and Knobloch, *Muttersprachlicher Unterricht im neunzehnten Jahrhundert,* 1–2.

118. Gans, "Erfahrungen mit dem Deutschunterricht," 13.

119. Dieter Langewiesche, *Nation, Nationalismus, Nationalstaat in Deutschland und Europa* (Munich: C. H. Beck, 2000), 181–89.

120. Christopher Clark, "Germany: 1815–1848: Restoration or Pre-March," in *Nineteenth-Century Germany: Politics, Culture and Society 1780–1918,* ed. John Breuilly (New York: Oxford University Press, 2000), 61.

121. Werner Besch, "Die Entstehung und Ausbreitung der neuhochdeutschen Schriftsprache/Standardsprache," in Besch, Reichmann, and Sonderegger, *Sprachgeschichte,* 2:1783ff.

122. Schmeller, "Sprache der Baiern," 73.

123. In Rockinger, *An der Wiege,* 198–99.

124. Schmeller, *Die Mundarten Bayerns,* 4.

125. Bayerische Staatsbibliothek, *Johann Andreas Schmeller, 1785–1852: Gedächtnisausstellung zum 200. Geburtsjahr* (Munich: R. Oldenbourg, 1985), 155ff.

126. Johann Andreas Schmeller, "Über die sogenannten Cimbern der VII und VIII Communen auf den Venedischen Alpen und ihre Sprache," in *Abhandlungen der philosophisch-philologischen Classe der königlichen bayerischen Akademie der Wissenschaften* (Munich: Mich. Lindauerschen Hofbuchdruckerey, 1838), 2:3; and Schmeller, *Sogenanntes Cimbrisches Wörterbuch, das ist Deutsches Idiotikon der VII und VIII Communi in den Venetianischen Alpen,* ed. Joseph Bergmann (Vienna: Kaiserl.-Königl. Hof-und Staatsdruckerei, 1855).

127. Schmeller, *Die Mundarten Bayerns,* vi.

128. Johann Andreas Schmeller, *Bayerisches Wörterbuch. Sammlung von Wörtern und Ausdrücken . . . mit unkundlichen Belegen* (Stuttgart: J. G. Cotta, 1827–37), 1:ix.

129. Richter, *Hans Ferdinand Maßmann,* 268.

130. Schmeller, *Bayerisches Wörterbuch,* 1:dedication.

131. Schmeller, *Bayerisches Wörterbuch,* 1:vii.

132. Asher and Simpson, *Encyclopedia of Language and Linguistics,* 7:3681.

133. Schmeller, *Bayerisches Wörterbuch,* 1:vii.

134. Schmeller, *Bayerisches Wörterbuch,* 1:xv.

135. Schmeller, *Bayerisches Wörterbuch,* 1:ix.

136. See Eberhard Dünninger, "Heimat und Geschichte bei Johann Andreas Schmeller," in Eichinger and Naumann, *Johann Andreas Schmeller und der Beginn der Germanisitik,* 205.

137. Grimm, *Deutsche Grammatik,* 2nd ed., 1:xi.

138. See Eric W. Gritsch, "Luther and the State: Post-Reformation Ramifications," in *Luther and the Modern State in Germany: Sixteenth-Century Essays and Studies,* ed. James D. Tracy, 45–60 (Kirksville, Mo.: Sixteenth

Century Journal Publishers, 1986).

139. Jacob Grimm, *Deutsche Mythologie* (Göttingen: Dieterichsche Buchhandlung, 1835; reprint, Granz: Akademische Druck-und Verlagsanstalt, 1953), 1:3.

140. Jacob Grimm, *Deutsche Mythologie,* 1:4.

141. Jacob Grimm, *Deutsche Mythologie,* 1:5.

142. Jacob Grimm, *Deutsche Mythologie,* 1:xxxvii–xxxviii.

143. Jacob Grimm, *Deutsche Mythologie,* 1:v.

144. Jacob Grimm, *Deutsche Rechtsalterthümer* (Darmstadt: Wissenschaftliche Buchgesellschaft, 1955), 1:xviii.

145. Jacob Grimm, *Deutsche Mythologie,* 1:10.

146. Carola L. Gottzmann, "Die altnordischen Studien und Publikationen von Wilhelm und Jacob Grimm zur Literatur, Sprache, Ur-und Frühgeschichte, Rechtsgeschichte, Geschichte und Runologie" *Brüder Grimm Gedenken* 7 (1987), 64.

147. Wilhelm Grimm, "Die altnordische Literatur in der gegenwärtigen Periode" (1820), in *Kleinere Schriften,* ed. Gustav Hinriches (Berlin: Ferdinand Dümmler, 1882–87), 2:83–84.

148. See Wilhelm Grimm, *Über deutsche Runen* (Göttingen: Dieterichsche Buchhandlung, 1821).

149. Toews, *Becoming Historical,* 318.

150. Toews, *Becoming Historical,* 363.

151. R. Hinton Thomas, *Liberalism, Nationalism, and the German Intellectuals (1822–1847): An Analysis of the Academic and Scientific Conferences of the Period* (Cambridge: W. Heffler & Sons, 1951), 81ff.

152. Jacob Grimm, "Über die wechselseitigen beziehungen und die verbindung der drei in der versammlung vertretenen wissenschaften," in *Kleinere Schriften,* 7:557.

153. Grimm and Grimm, *Deutsches Wörterbuch,* 1:lxviii.

154. Jacob Grimm, *Geschichte der deutschen Sprache,* 1:iv.

155. Jacob Grimm, *Geschichte der deutschen Sprache,* 1:v.

156. Benfey, *Geschichte der Sprachwissenschaft,* 457.

157. Jacob Grimm, *Geschichte der deutschen Sprache,* 2:800.

158. Raumer, *Geschichte der germanischen Philologie,* 640.

159. Jacob Grimm, *Geschichte der deutschen Sprache,* 1:xiii.

160. Koerner, "Jacob Grimm's Place," 312–13.

161. Jacob Grimm, *Geschichte der deutschen Sprache,* 1:5.

162. Jacob Grimm, *Geschichte der deutschen Sprache,* 1:7.

163. Raumer, *Geschichte der germanischen Philologie,* 640.

164. Toews, *Becoming Historical,* 367–68.

165. Toews, *Becoming Historical,* 368.

166. Jacob Grimm, *Geschichte der deutschen Sprache,* 1:482.

167. Jacob Grimm, *Geschichte der deutschen Sprache,* 1:438.
168. Jacob Grimm, *Geschichte der deutschen Sprache,* 2:1035.
169. Jacob Grimm, *Geschichte der deutschen Sprache,* 2:837.
170. Jacob Grimm, *Geschichte der deutschen Sprache,* 1:vi.
171. Cited in Heinz Gollwitzer, "Zum politischen Germanismus des neunzehnten Jahrhunderts," in *Festschrift für Hermann Heimpel zum 70. Geburtstag,* ed. Hermann Heimpel and Theodor Schieder, vol. 1 (Göttingen: Vandenhoeck & Ruprecht, 1971), 289.
172. Cited in Roland Pozorny, *Hoffmann von Fallersleben: Ein Lebens-und Zeitbild* (Berg: Türmer, 1982), 121.
173. Langewiesche, *Nation, Nationalismus, Nationalstaat,* 181–89.
174. Brian Vick, *Defining Germany: The 1848 Frankfurt Parliamentarians and National Identity* (Cambridge, Mass.: Harvard University Press, 2002), 110, 203.
175. Schmeller, "*Lauter gemähte Wiesen für die Reaktion,*" 271.
176. See also Eberhard Dünninger, "Heimat und Geschichte," 207.
177. Feldmann, *Jacob Grimm und die Politik,* 250.
178. Jacob Grimm, "Über den Ursprung der Sprache," 1:277.
179. Jacob Grimm, *On the Origin of Language,* trans. Raymond A. Wiley (Leiden: Brill, 1984), 6.
180. Jacob Grimm, *On the Origin of Language,* 7.
181. Jacob Grimm, *On the Origin of Language,* 8.
182. Toews, *Becoming Historical,* 371.
183. Raumer, *Geschichte der germanischen Philologie,* 611, 687–88.
184. Cited in Meves, "Zum Institutionalisierungsprozeß der deutschen Philologie," 180–81.
185. Cited in Meves, "Zum Institutionalisierungsprozeß der deutschen Philologie," 182.
186. Meves, "Zum Institutionalisierungsprozeß der deutschen Philologie," 186ff.
187. Meves, "Zum Institutionalisierungsprozeß der deutschen Philologie," 45.
188. Cited in Wolfgang Höppner, *Das "Ererbte, Erlebte und Erlernte" im Werk Wilhelm Scherers: Ein Beitrag zur Geschichte der Germanistik* (Cologne: Böhlau, 1993), 211.
189. Jürgen Sternsdorff, *Wissenschaftskonstitution und Reichsgründung: Die Entwicklung der Germanistik bei Wilhelm Scherer: Eine Biographie nach unveröffentlichen Quellen* (Frankfurt: Peter Lang, 1979), 70–73.
190. Sternsdorff, *Wissenschaftskonstitution und Reichsgründung,* 147ff.
191. See Wilhelm Scherer, *Geschichte der deutschen Literatur* (Berlin: Thomas Knaur, 1883).
192. Cited in Höppner, *"Ererbte, Erlebte und Erlernte"* 213.

193. Scherer, *Geschichte der deutschen Sprache,* ix.
194. Kurt R. Jankowsky, introduction to Jankowsky, ed., *Wilhelm Scherer: Zur Geschichte der deutschen Sprache* (Philadelphia: John Benjamins, 1995), xvii.
195. Scherer, *Geschichte der deutschen Sprache,* x.
196. Jankowsky, xvi.
197. Scherer, *Geschichte der deutschen Sprache,* x–xi.
198. Scherer, *Geschichte der deutschen Sprache,* vii.
199. Scherer, *Geschichte der deutschen Sprache,* 21.
200. Scherer, *Geschichte der deutschen Sprache,* 85–88.
201. Scherer, *Geschichte der deutschen Sprache,* 165.
202. Scherer, *Geschichte der deutschen Sprache,* 156–58.
203. Scherer, *Geschichte der deutschen Sprache,* 162–63.
204. See Franz Greß, *Germanistik und Politik: Kritische Beiträge zur Geschichte einer nationalen Wissenschaft* (Stuttgart: Frommann-Holzboog, 1971), 35–36.
205. See, for example, Scherer, *Geschichte der deutschen Sprache,* 154.
206. Jankowsky, xxiv.
207. Sternsdorff, *Wissenschaftskonstitution und Reichsgründung,* 175.
208. Jost Hermand, *Geschichte der Germanistik* (Reinbeck bei Hamburg: Rowohlt Taschenbuchverlag, 1994), 54–55.
209. Sengupta, *From Salon to Discipline,* 89, 101.
210. Meves, "Zum Institutionalisierungsprozeß der deutschen Philologie," 196.
211. Wolf von Schierbrand, ed., *The Kaiser's Speeches Forming a Character Portrait of Emperor Wilhelm II* (New York: Harper & Brothers, 1902), 214.

Chapter 4

1. Friedrich August Wolf, "Darstellung der Alterthums-Wissenschaft," in *Kleine Schriften in lateinischer und deutscher Sprache* (Halle: Verlag der Buchhandlung des Waisenhauses, 1807), 2:817–21.
2. Friedrich Schlegel, *Über die Sprache und Weisheit der Indier,* ix–x.
3. Schlegel, *Über die Sprache und Weisheit der Indier,* 218–19.
4. August Friedrich Pott, *Etymologische Forschungen auf dem Gebiete der Indo-Germanischen Sprachen, mit besonderem Bezug auf die Lautumwandlung im Sanskrit, Griechischen, Lateinischen, Littauischen und Gothischen* (Lemgo: Meyersche Hof-Buchhandlung, 1833), 1:xiv.
5. La Vopa, "Specialists against Specialization," 31f.
6. Grafton, "Polyhistor into *Philolog,*" 162–71, 182–83; Marchand, *Down from Olympus,* 24–35.

7. La Vopa, "Specialists against Specialization," 34.
8. La Vopa, "Specialists against Specialization," 40.
9. Friedrich August Wolf, "Darstellung der Alterthumswissenschaft," in *F. A. Wolf's Vorlesung über die Encyclopädie der Alterthumswissenschaft,* ed. J. D. Gürtler (Leipzig: August Lehnhold, 1831), 63, 47.
10. Wolf, "Darstellung der Alterthumswissenschaft," 48.
11. Wolf, "Darstellung der Alterthumswissenschaft," 49.
12. Friedrich August Wolf, "Einleitung in die Alterthumswissenschaft," in *F. A. Wolf's Vorlesung über die Encyclopädie der Alterthumswissenschaft,* 43–44.
13. Wolf, "Darstellung der Alterthumswissenschaft," 52.
14. Wolf, "Einleitung in die Alterthumswissenschaft," 24.
15. See Friedrich August Wolf, *Allgemeine Grammatik als Grundlage des Unterrichts in jeder besonderen Sprache* (Görlitz: C. G. Anton, 1810), 12.
16. Wolf, "Darstellung der Alterthumswissenschaft," 1:75.
17. Wolf, *Allgemeine Grammatik,* 13ff.
18. Wolf, "Darstellung der Alterthumswissenschaft," 1:56.
19. Ernest Vogt, "Der Methodenstreit zwischen Hermann und Böckh," in *Philologie und Hermeneutik im neunzehnten Jahrhundert: Zur Geschichte und Methodologie der Geisteswissenschaften,* ed. Mayotte Bollack and Heinz Wismann (Göttingen: Vandenhoeck and Ruprecht, 1983), 1:107.
20. See Otto Jahn, *Gottfried Hermann: Eine Gedächtnissrede* (Leipzig: Weidmannsche Buchhandlung, 1849), 12ff.
21. John Edwin Sandys, *A History of Classical Scholarship* (New York: Hafner, 1958), 3:92.
22. Marchand, *Down from Olympus,* 7–16.
23. Manfred Fuhrmann, *Brechungen: Wirkungsgeschichtliche Studien zur antik-europäischen Bildungstradition* (Stuttgart: Klett-Cota, 1982), 135–36.
24. See in particular Walter Rüegg, "Die Antike als Begründung des deutschen Nationalbewußtseins," in *Antike in der Moderne,* ed. Wolfgang Schuller, 261–87 (Constance: Universitätsverlag Konstanz, 1985); and Manfred Fuhrmann, "Die Querelle des Anciens et des Modernes, der Nationalismus und die deutsche Klassik," in *Brechungen: Wirkungsgeschichtliche Studien zur antik-europäischen Bildungstradition,* 129–49 (Stuttgart: Klett-Cotta, 1982).
25. See August Boeckh's reflections on the founding of the university in Berlin: "Ueber den Sinn und Geist der Gründung der Berliner Universität," in *Gesammelte kleine Schriften* (Leipzig: B. G. Teubner, 1858), 2:131–47.
26. See Marchand, *Down from Olympus,* 24–28.
27. La Vopa, "Specialists against Specialization," 34.

28. Wilhelm von Humboldt, "Latium und Hellas oder Betrachtungen über das classische Alterthum," in *Wilhelm von Humboldts Werke,* 3:137–38.
29. Klemens Menze, *Wilhelm von Humboldt und Christian Gottlob Heyne* (Ratingen bei Düsseldorf: Henn, 1966), 36.
30. Marchand, *Down from Olympus,* 28.
31. Humboldt, "Latium und Hellas," 3:166.
32. Humboldt, "Latium und Hellas," 3:163.
33. Wilhelm von Humboldt, "Geschichte des Verfalls und Untergangs der griechischen Freistaaten," in *Werke in fünf Bänden,* ed. Andreas Flitner and Klaus Giel (Berlin: Rütten & Loening, 1961), 2:87–89.
34. Friedrich Ast, "Über den Geist des Altertums und dessen Bedeutung für unser Zeitalter," in *Kleine Pädagogische Texte,* vol. 17, *Dokumente des Neuhumanismus* (Berlin: Julius Beltz, 1931), 1:16.
35. See Johann Arnold Kanne, *Ueber die Verwandtschaft der griechischen und teutschen Sprache* (Leipzig: Wilhelm Rein, 1804).
36. Cited in Hans Loewe, *Friedrich Thiersch, Ein Humanisten Leben* (Munich: Oldenbourg, 1913), 132.
37. Each of the modern European languages embodied one quality of Greek. Portuguese, for example, resembled the Ionian dialect; Spanish was akin to Doric and Aeolian in that it was "magnificent, solemn, and proud." See Ast, "Über den Geist des Altertums," 1:28–29.
38. Ast, "Über den Geist des Altertums," 1:28.
39. Ast, "Über den Geist des Altertums," 1:21.
40. Ast, "Über den Geist des Altertums," 1:15–16.
41. Franz Passow, "Die griechische Sprache, nach ihrer Bedeutung in der Bildung deutscher Jugend," in *Archiv deutscher Nationalbildung,* ed. Reinhold Bernhard Jackmann and Franz Passow (Berlin: Friedrich Maurer, 1812), 1:126.
42. Franz Passow, "Der griechischen Sprache pädagogischer Vorrang vor der lateinischen, von der Schattenseite betrachtet," in *Vermischte Schriften,* ed. W. A. Passow (Leipzig: F. A. Brockhaus, 1843), 23.
43. Passow, "Der griechischen Sprache," 115.
44. Passow, "Der griechischen Sprache," 107–8.
45. Humboldt, "Latium und Hellas," 3:169.
46. Humboldt, "Latium und Hellas," 3:167.
47. See, for example, Krüger's attack on Georg Curtius and the comparative method in the epilogue of his *Griechische Sprachlehre für Schulen* (Leipzig: R. W. Krüger, 1875), 202–14.
48. Gottfried Hermann, *Acta Societatis Graecae* (Leipzig: C. H. Funkhänel, 1836–40), xii–xiii.
49. Bahner and Neumann, *Sprachwissenschaftliche Germanistik,* 342.
50. Conrad Bursian, *Geschichte der classischen Philologie in Deutschland von*

den Anfängen bis zur Gegenwart (Leipzig: R. Oldenbourg, 1883), 2:972.

51. Wilhelm Kroll, *Geschichte der klassischen Philologie* (Berlin: Walter de Gruyter, 1919), 124.
52. Sandys, *History of Classical Scholarship,* 3:205ff.
53. Benfey, *Geschichte der Sprachwissenschaft,* 640. See his account of the application of comparative-historical techniques to the classical languages, 972ff.
54. The dialect of Athens and its surroundings, Attic became the received standard form of Greek due partially to the literary prestige of the city. The northern kingdom of Macedon adopted the literary form of Attic as the language of the royal court toward the end of the fifth century BC, so it was the form of Greek that was spread over the whole of the eastern Mediterranean and beyond by the Macedonian conquests. The three principal earlier Greek dialects were Doric, Aeolic, and Ionic. See Asher and Simpson, *Encyclopedia of Language and Linguistics,* 3:1494.
55. Benfey, *Geschichte der Sprachwissenschaft,* 642.
56. Bahner and Neumann, *Sprachwissenschaftliche Germanistik,* 342.
57. Helmut Flashar, "Die methodisch-hermeneutischen Ansätze von Friedrich August Wolf und Friedrich Ast," in *Philologie und Hermeneutik im neunzehnten Jahrhundert,* 1:30–31.
58. Marchand, *Down from Olympus,* xx.
59. Karl Christ, "Aspekte der Antike-Rezeption in der deutschen Altertumswissenschaft des 19. Jahrhunderts," in *Die Antike im 19. Jahrhundert in Italien und Deutschland,* ed. Karl Christ and Arnaldo Momigliano (Berlin: Duncker & Humblot, 1988), 26.
60. August Boeckh, *Encyklopädie und Methodologie der philologischen Wissenschaften,* ed. Ernst Bratuscheck (Leipzig: B. G. Teubner, 1886), 21.
61. Boeckh, *Encyklopädie und Methodologie,* 300.
62. Boeckh, *Encyklopädie und Methodologie,* 28.
63. Axel Horstmann, "August Boeckh und die Antike-Rezeption im 19. Jahrhundert," in *Die Antike im 19. Jahrhundert,* 72.
64. Grafton, "Polyhistor into *Philolog,*" 181.
65. These lectures were compiled and published in 1886 after Boeckh's death largely from his personal notes and those of his students by Ernst Bratuscheck. See Boeckh, *Encyklopädie und Methodologie,* 56.
66. See Horstmann, "August Boeckh," 45.
67. Boeckh, *Encyklopädie und Methodologie,* 10.
68. Boeckh, *Encyklopädie und Methodologie,* 10–11.
69. According to Axel Horstmann, this broad definition of philology, which could include the study of medieval German texts and newer European literature presented classicists with an unrecognized problem of legitima-

tion. See Horstmann, "August Boeckh," 69.

70. Ulrich Muhlack, "Zum Verhältnis von Klassischer Philologie und Geschichtswissenschaft im 19. Jahrhundert," in *Philologie und Hermeneutik im neunzehnten Jahrhundert,* 1:230.
71. Boeckh, *Encyklopädie und Methodologie,* 17.
72. Boeckh, *Encyklopädie und Methodologie,* 57.
73. Horstmann, "August Boeckh," 55–60.
74. See Horstmann, "August Boeckh," 45.
75. Gottfried Hermann, *Ueber Herrn Professor Böckhs Behandlung der griechischen Inschriften* (Leipzig: Gerhard Fleischer, 1826), 3.
76. Hermann, *Ueber Herrn Professor Böckhs Behandlung,* 4.
77. Hermann, *Ueber Herrn Professor Böckhs Behandlung,* 9.
78. Cited in Vogt, "Der Methodenstreit zwischen Hermann und Böckh," 116.
79. Boeckh, *Encyklopädie und Methodologie,* 6. See also Brigitte Hauger's remarks in *Johan Nicolai Madvig: The Language Theory of a Classical Philologist* (Munster: Nodus, 1994), 46.
80. Boeckh, *Encyklopädie und Methodologie,* 12.
81. Boeckh, *Encyklopädie und Methodologie,* 763.
82. Boeckh, *Encyklopädie und Methodologie,* 276.
83. Boeckh, *Encyklopädie und Methodologie,* 763.
84. Hauger, *Johan Nicolai Madvig,* 195.
85. Williamson, *Longing for Myth in Germany,* 237.
86. Williamson, *Longing for Myth in Germany,* 121–50.
87. Williamson, *Longing for Myth in Germany,* 149.
88. See Heinrich Thiersch, *Friedrich Thiersch's Leben,* vol. 1 (Leipzig: Winter'sche Verlagshandlung, 1866).
89. Heinrich Thiersch, *Friedrich Thiersch's Leben,* 1:72ff.
90. Friedrich Thiersch, *Ueber die Epochen der bildenden Kunst unter den Griechen,* 2nd edition (Munich: Literarisch-artistische Anstalt, 1829), 110.
91. Friedrich Thiersch, *Ueber die Epochen der bildenden Kunst,* 6.
92. Friedrich Thiersch, *Ueber die Epochen der bildenden Kunst,* 110.
93. Friedrich Thiersch, *Ueber die Epochen der bildenden Kunst,* 6.
94. Friedrich Thiersch, *Ueber die Epochen der bildenden Kunst,* 18–19.
95. Friedrich Thiersch, *Ueber die Epochen der bildenden Kunst,* 110–11.
96. Friedrich Thiersch, *Ueber die Epochen der bildenden Kunst,* 24–25.
97. See Traian Stoianovich, *Balkan Worlds: The First and Last Europe* (Armonk, N.Y.: M. E. Sharpe, 1994).
98. Flemming, "*Orientalism,* the Balkans," 1221.
99. Andrea Fuchs-Sumiyoshi. *Orientalismus in der deutschen Literatur* (New York: Georg Olms, 1984), 12.

100. Johannes Irmscher, *Der Philhellenismus in Preußen als Forschungsanliegen* (Berlin: Akademie Verlag, 1966), 2:11.
101. For a detailed, early twentieth-century examination of Thiersch's newspaper articles on the state of Greece during the revolution and the course of the German regency and Otto's reign, see Hans Loewe, *Friedrich Thiersch und die griechische Frage* (Munich: Oldenbourg, 1913).
102. Christopher Hauser, *Anfänge bürgerlicher Organisation: Philhellenismus und Frühliberalismus in Sudwestdeutschland* (Göttingen: Vandenhoeck & Ruprecht, 1990).
103. See Hans Eideneier, "Hellenen und Philhellenen," in *Griechen und Deutsche: Bilder vom Andern,* ed. Kirsten Fast and Jan Peter Thorbecke, 63–75 (Darmstadt: H. Austhes, 1982).
104. Wolf Seidl, *Bayern in Griechenland: Die Geburt des griechischen Nationalstaates und die Regierung König Ottos* (Munich: Prestel, 1981), 106ff.
105. Seidel, *Bayern in Griechenland,* 149ff.
106. Friedrich Thiersch, *L'État actuel de la Grèce et des moyens d'arriver à sa restauration* (F. A. Brockhaus, 1833), 1:194.
107. While on the Peloponnesus, Thiersch discovered in the archaic dialect of the Zakonians in Brastos what he considered to be irrefutable linguistic evidence for the continuity thesis. Other travelers to Greece and Turkey, including the Bavarian historian and Orientalist Jakob Philipp Fallmerayer (1790–1861) returned as antiphilhellenes. See Friedrich Thiersch, "Über die Sprache der Zakonen," in *Abhandlungen der Akademie der Wissenschaften* (Munich, 1835), 511ff.
108. Thiersch, *L'État actuel de la Grèce,* vol. 1, 198.
109. Thiersch, *L'État actuel de la Grèce,* vol. 1, 194.
110. Thiersch, *L'État actuel de la Grèce,* vol. 1, 325.
111. Williamson, *Longing for Myth in Germany,* 145–48.
112. See Friedrich Schlegel, *Über die Sprache und die Weisheit der Indier,* and Peter von Bohlen, *Das alte Indien, mit besonderer Rücksicht auf Aegypten,* 2 vols. (Königsberg: Gebrüder Bornträger, 1830).
113. Karl Otfried Müller, "Ueber den angeblich ägyptischen Ursprung der griechischen Kunst," in *Kleine deutsche Schriften über Religion, Kunst, Sprache und Literatur, Leben und Geschichte des Alterthums,* ed. Eduard Müller (New York: Georg Olms, 1979), 2:524.
114. Karl Otfried Müller, "Ueber den angeblich ägyptischen Ursprung," 534.
115. Karl Otfried Müller, "Ueber den angeblich ägyptischen Ursprung." 526.
116. Karl Otfried Müller, "Ueber den angeblich ägyptischen Ursprung," 536.
117. Josine H. Blok, "Proof and Persuasion in *Black Athena I:* The Case of K. O. Müller," in "Black Athena: Ten Years After," ed. Wim M. J. van Binsbergen, *Talanta: Proceedings of the Dutch Archaeological and Historical Society,* vol. xxviii–xxix (1996–97): 189.

118. Karl Otfried Müller, "Ueber den angeblich ägyptischen Ursprung," 533.
119. Karl Otfried Müller, "Ueber den angeblich ägyptischen Ursprung," 536.
120. Karl Otfried Müller, *Orchomenos und die Minyer: Geschichte Hellenischer Stämme und Städte* (Graz: Akademische Druck-und Verlagsanstalt, 1969), 1:2.
121. Karl Otfried Müller, *Orchomenos und die Minyer,* 1:2.
122. Karl Otfried Müller, *Die Dorier: Geschichte Hellenischer Stämme und Städte* (Graz: Akademische Druck-und Verlagsanstalt, 1969), 2:1.
123. Karl Otfried Müller, *Die Dorier,* 2:1.
124. Karl Otfried Müller, *Die Dorier,* 2:16.
125. Martin Bernal's assertion that Müller took no notice of new developments in fields related to the classics is incorrect; Müller's turn away from Egypt should not be seen as the result of purely "externalist reasons," such as racism or a belief in progress (Martin Bernal, *Black Athena: The Afroasiatic Roots of Classical Civilization* [New Brunswick, N.J.: Rutgers University Press, 1987], 1:315–16).
126. Karl Otfried Müller, "Friedrich Thiersch: Über die Epochen der bildenden Kunst unter den Griechen," in *Kleine deutsche Schriften,* 2:318.
127. In 1836, for example, Müller praised Raphael Kühner's attempt to apply the techniques of historical grammar developed by Jacob Grimm to school grammars of the Greek language, demonstrating a thorough knowledge of the significance of sound shifts for etymology, as well as of the value of comparing the inflection patterns of Greek and other Indo-European verbs. See Karl Otfried Müller, "Ausführliche Grammatik der Griechischen Sprache wissenschaftlich und mit Rücksicht auf den Schulgebrauch ausgearbeitet von Raphael Kühner," in *Kleine deutsche Schriften,* 1:336ff. See also Karl Otfried Müller, "Lehre von den Partikeln der griechischen Sprache von J. A. Hartung," in *Kleine deutsche Schriften,* 1:327ff.
128. Karl Otfried Müller, "Acta Societatis Graecae," *Kleine deutsche Schriften,* 1:12.
129. Karl Otfried Müller, "Acta Societatis Graecae," 1:12.
130. Bernal, *Black Athena,* 1:310 and 314f.
131. Karl Otfried Müller, "Acta Societatis Graecae," 1:13.
132. Karl Otfried Müller, "Acta Societatis Graecae," 1:8–9.
133. Karl Otfried Müller, *Die Etrusker* (Graz: Akademische Druck-und Verlagsanstalt, 1965), 1:9–10.
134. Karl Otfried Müller, *Geschichte der griechischen Literatur bis auf das Zeitalter Alexanders,* ed. Eduard Müller (Breslau: Josef Max und Komp., 1841), 1:8.
135. Karl Otfried Müller, *Geschichte der griechischen Literatur,* 1:5.
136. Karl Otfried Müller, *Handbuch der Archäologie der Kunst* (Breslau: Josef

Max und Komp., 1848), 257.

137. Karl Otfried Müller, *Prolegomena zu einer wissenschaftlichen Mythologie* (Göttingen: Vandenhoeck und Ruprecht, 1825), 336.

138. Karl Otfried Müller, "Friedrich Thiersch. Über die Epochen der bildenden Kunst unter den Griechen," in *Kleine deutsche Schriften,* 2:319.

139. Edgar Quinet, *Oeuvres complète de Edgard Quinet,* vol. 1, *Le Génie des Religions* (Paris: Librairie Germer-Baillière, 1877), 56.

140. Friedrich Gottlieb Welcker, "Ueber die Bedeutung der Philologie," in *Kleine Schriften zur griechischen Literaturgeschichte* (Osnabrück: Otto Zeller, 1973), 4:2–3.

141. Welcker, "Ueber die Bedeutung der Philologie," 4:4–5.

142. Friedrich Gottlieb Welcker, *Griechische Götterlehre* (Göttingen: Dietersche Buchhandlung, 1857–63), 1:10.

143. August Boeckh, "Von der Philologie, besonders der klassischen in Beziehung zur morgenländischen: Rede zur Eröffnung der elften Versammlung Deutscher Philologen, Schulmänner und Orientalisten, gehalten zu Berlin am 30. September 1850," in *Kleine Schriften,* 2:188–89.

144. Georg Curtius, "Philologie und Sprachwissenschaft," in Georg Curtius, *Kleine Schriften,* ed. Ernst Windisch, vol. 1, *Ausgewählte Reden und Vorträge* (Leipzig: S. Hirzel, 1886), 149.

145. See Ernst Windisch, *Georg Curtius: Eine Charakteristik* (Berlin: Calvary & Co., 1887), as well as Georg Curtius, *Zur Kritik der neuesten Sprachforschung* (Leipzig: S. Hirzel, 1885).

146. Georg Curtius, *The Results of Comparative Philology in Reference to Classical Scholarship,* trans. F. H. Trithen (Oxford: Francis Macpherson, 1851), 4.

147. Curtius, *Results of Comparative Philology,* 31.

148. Sebastiano Timpanaro, *The Genesis of Lachmann's Method,* ed. and trans. Glenn W. Most (Chicago: University of Chicago Press, 2005), 122.

149. Curtius, *Results of Comparative Philology,* 10.

150. Curtius, *Results of Comparative Philology,* 59.

151. Curtius, *Results of Comparative Philology,* 8.

152. Curtius, "Philologie und Sprachwissenschaft," 137.

153. Curtius, "Philologie und Sprachwissenschaft," 147.

154. Curtius, "Philologie und Sprachwissenschaft," 143.

155. Benfey, *Geschichte der Sprachwissenschaft,* 637.

156. Adolf Deissmann, *Bible Studies: Contributions Chiefly from Papyri and Inscriptions to the History of the Language, the Literature, and the Religion of Hellenistic Judaism and Primitive Christianity,* trans. Alexander Grieve (Edinburgh: T&T Clark, 1901), 173.

157. Deissmann, *Bible Studies,* 63.

158. Karl Barth, *Protestant Theology in the Nineteenth Century: Its Background*

and History (Valley Forge, Pa.: Judson Press, 1973), 597–606.

159. Richard Rothe, *Zur Dogmatik* (Gotha: Perthes, 1863), 238. The English translation is from Stanley E. Porter, *The Language of the New Testament: Classic Essays* (Sheffield: Sheffield Academic Press, 1991), 51.
160. Hermann Cremer, *Biblisch-theologisches Wörterbuch der neutestamentischen Gräcität* (Gotha: F. A. Perthes), xv.
161. Georg Benedikt Winer, *A Treatise on the Grammar of New Testament Greek: Regarded as a Sure Basis for New Testament Exegesis,* trans. W. F. Moulton (Edinburgh: T&T Clark, 1882), 2–3.
162. Deissmann, *Bible Studies,* 70–77.
163. See J. M. Rife, "The Greek Language of the New Testament," in *The International Standard Bible Encyclopedia,* ed. Geoffrey W. Bromiley (Grand Rapids, Mich.: W. B. Eerdmans, 1982), 2:571.

Chapter 5

1. Ludwig Schemann, *Gobineaus Rassenwerk: Aktenstücke und Betrachtungen zur Geschichte und Kritik des Essai sur l'inégalité des races humaines* (Stuttgart: Fr. Fromann, 1910), 117–18.
2. See the chapter titled "The Different Languages are Unequal, and Correspond perfectly in relative merit to the races that use them," in Arthur Comte de Gobineau, *Essay on the Inequality of the Human Races,* trans. Adrian Collins (New York: Howard Fertig, 1967), esp. 188, 193, 196, 203–4. See also Ulrich Ricken, "Sprachtheoretische und weltanschauliche Rezeption der Aufklärung bei August Friedrich Pott (1802–1887)," in *History and Historiography of Linguistics,* ed. Hans-Josef Niederehe and Konrad Koerner, 2:619–32 (Philadelphia: John Benjamins, 1990).
3. Cited in Schemann, *Gobineaus Rassenwerk,* 117.
4. Friedrich August Pott, *Die Ungleichheit menschlicher Rassen hauptsächlich vom sprachwissenschaftlichen Standpunkte, unter besonderer Berücksichtigung von des Grafen von Gobineau gleichnamigem Werke* (Lemgo: Meyer'sche Hofbuchhandlung, 1956).
5. Schemann, *Gobineaus Rassenwerk,* 117ff.
6. Many histories of Aryan racial theory draw direct lines of continuity linking Germany's Oriental Renaissance to the violent anti-Semitism of the Third Reich. According to Leon Poliakov, Raymond Schwab, and René Gérard, German Orientalists wrongly translated observations of linguistic affinity into a fatal theory of racial descent. Raymond Schwab, for example, readily drew on the metaphor of "language as a weapon of war," generalizing that the "confusion of linguistic facts and ethnic theories perpetuated . . . more ravages than . . . the wars of faith" (Raymond

Schwab, *The Oriental Renaissance: Europe's Rediscovery of India and the East 1680–1880,* trans. Gene Patterson-Black and Victor Reinking [New York: Columbia University Press, 1984], 184–87). Both he and René Gérard believed they were able to identify a particular German affinity for the "irrational," the "unconscious," and the "mystic," virtues supposedly extolled in Indian texts (Schwab, *Oriental Renaissance,* 482–84; René Gérard, *L'Orient et la pensée romantique allemande* [Paris: M. Didier, 1963], 1–2, 257). Léon Poliakov put an "emphasis on biology," a basic element of Aryan theory as it was formulated by Friedrich Schlegel, and assumed that a conflation of the concepts of language and race had already taken place in the first German empire (Poliakov, *Aryan Myth,* 197 and 74f). He likewise justified "short-circuiting fifteen centuries of history" with the claim that the roots of Nazi racism could be found in pre-Christian Germanic myths of origin (Poliakov, *Aryan Myth,* 4–5).

7. Pott, "Indogermanischer Sprachstamm," 79.
8. Pott, "Indogermanischer Sprachstamm," 26.
9. Hans Siegert, "Zur Geschichte der Begriffe 'Arier' und 'arisch,'" *Wörter und Sachen: Zeitschrift für Indogermanische Sprachwissenscahft, Volksforschung und Kulturgeschichte* n.s. 4 (1941–42), 84.
10. Friedrich Schlegel, "Über den Anfang unserer Geschichte und die letzte Revolution der Erde, als wahrscheinliche Wirkung eines Kometen. Von J. G. Rhode," *Jahrbücher der Literatur* 8 (1819), 459.
11. Friedrich Schlegel, "Über den Anfang unserer Geschichte," 454, 452.
12. Friedrich Schlegel, "Über den Anfang unserer Geschichte," 458–59.
13. Friedrich Schlegel, "Über den Anfang unserer Geschichte," 459–60.
14. Christian Lassen, "Über Herrn Professor Bopps grammatisches System der Sanskrit-Sprache," *Indische Bibliothek* 3 (1830), 70.
15. Lassen, "Über Bopps grammatisches System," 70–71.
16. August Wilhelm Schlegel, "De l'origine des Hindous," 474–75.
17. August Wilhelm Schlegel, "De l'origine des Hindous," 469.
18. August Wilhelm Schlegel, "De l'origine des Hindous," 473.
19. August Wilhelm Schlegel, "De l'origine des Hindous," 515–16.
20. Christian Lassen, *Indische Alterthumskunde* (Bonn: H. B. König, 1847), 1:388.
21. Lassen, *Indische Alterthumskunde,* 1:390–91.
22. Lassen, *Indische Alterthumskunde,* 1:388.
23. Lassen, *Indische Alterthumskunde,* 1:385.
24. Lassen, *Indische Alterthumskunde,* 1:390–91.
25. Lassen, *Indische Alterthumskunde,* 1:390, 514.
26. Lassen, *Indische Alterthumskunde,* 1:387, 389, 401.
27. Lassen, *Indische Alterthumskunde,* 1:400, 408.

28. Lassen, *Indische Alterthumskunde,* 1:513.
29. Lassen, *Indische Alterthumskunde,* 1:411.
30. Lassen, *Indische Alterthumskunde,* 1:414.
31. Lassen, *Indische Alterthumskunde,* 1:417.
32. Lassen, *Indische Alterthumskunde,* 1:414–16.
33. John E. Joseph, "Language, Body, Race: From Aristotle and Epicurus to Descartes and Locke" (paper prepared for the Young Scholars' Summer Institute on the Concept of Language, Research Triangle Park, N.C., August 2003).
34. See Jeffrey Wollock, *The Noblest Animate Motion: Speech, Physiology and Medicine in Pre-Cartesian Linguistic Thought* (Philadelphia: John Benjamins, 1997).
35. Joseph, "Language, Body, Race," 18.
36. Charles Bouton, *Neurolinguisitcs: Historical and Theoretical Perspectives,* trans. Terence MacNamee (New York: Plenum, 1991), 68–75.
37. Römer, *Sprachwissenschaft und Rassenideologie,* 132.
38. Pott, *Die Ungleichheit menschlicher Rassen,* 41.
39. August Friedrich Pott, *Anti-Kaulen oder Mythische Vorstellungen vom Ursprunge der Völker und Sprachen* (Lemgo: Meyer'sche Hofbuchhandlung, 1863), 298.
40. August Friedrich Pott, *Einleitung in die allgemeine Sprachwissenschaft: Zur Literatur der Sprachkunde Europas,* ed. E. F. K. Koerner (Amsterdam: John Benjamins, 1974), 202.
41. Pott, *Anti-Kaulen,* 291.
42. Pott, *Anti-Kaulen,* 171.
43. Ricken, "Sprachtheoretische und weltanschauliche Rezeption der Aufklärung," 620.
44. Delbrück, *Introduction to the Study of Language,* 35.
45. Pott, *Etymologische Forschungen,* 1:xxiv.
46. Pott, *Eymologische Forschungen,* 1:xxv.
47. Pott, *Eymologische Forschungen,* 1:xxv.
48. Pott, *Eymologische Forschungen,* 1:xxvii.
49. Pott, *Eymologische Forschungen,* 1:xxvi–xxvii.
50. Pott, *Eymologische Forschungen,* 1:xxv.
51. Pott, *Etymologische Forschungen,* 1:xiii.
52. Pott, *Eymologische Forschungen,* 1:xxi.
53. Pott, "Indogermanischer Sprachstamm," 1.
54. August Friedrich Pott, *Die Zigeuner in Europa und Asien. Ethnographisch-linguistische Untersuchung vornehmlich ihrer Herkunft und Sprache* (Halle: Ed. Heynemann, 1844), 1:58.
55. Pott, *Die Zigeuner in Europa und Asien,* xv. Twentieth-century linguists actually see the relationship to be much closer, classifying the sixty or

more dialects of Romany as Indo-Aryan languages spoken by peoples of non-Aryan descent. See the article "Romani," in Asher and Simpson, *Encyclopedia of Language and Linguistics*, 7:3603–4.

56. Siegert, "Zur Geschichte der Begriffe 'Arier' und 'arisch,'" 90ff.
57. Siegert, "Zur Geschichte der Begriffe 'Arier' und 'arisch,'" 97.
58. Bouton, *Neurolinguisitcs*, 138–43, 147.
59. Römer, *Sprachwissenschaft und Rassenideologie*, 132–33.
60. Römer, *Sprachwissenschaft und Rassenideologie*, 134.
61. Römer, *Sprachwissenschaft und Rassenideologie*, 126–29.
62. Pott, *Etymologische Forschungen*, 1:xxv.
63. Pott, *Etymologische Forschungen*, 2:ix.
64. Pott, *Ungleichheit menschlicher Rassen*, vii, x, viii.
65. Pott, *Ungleichheit menschlicher Rassen*, 8, 178.
66. Pott, *Ungleichheit menschlicher Rassen*, xxxiii.
67. Pott, *Ungleichheit menschlicher Rassen*, 81.
68. Pott, *Ungleichheit menschlicher Rassen*, 84.
69. Pott, *Ungleichheit menschlicher Rassen*, 183.
70. Pott, *Ungleichheit menschlicher Rassen*, 85–86.
71. See Pott's essays in the *Zeitschrift der deutschen morgenländischen Gesellschaft*, vols. 2, 6, 5, 8: "Ueber das verwandtschaftliche Verhältniß zwischen den Kasser-und Kongo-Sprachen"; "Ueber die Kihiau-Sprache"; "Die Sprachen Südafrikas"; and "Sprachen aus Afrikas Innern und Westen."
72. Pott, *Ungleichheit menschlicher Rassen*, 88. His article "Sprachen aus Afrika's Inneren und Westen" (1854) had attracted Gobineau's attention because it cited him.
73. Hutton, introduction to *History of Linguistics*, 4:xxi.
74. See Williamson, *Longing for Myth in Germany*, 74, 217–19.
75. Hannah Franziska Augstein, "Linguistics and Politics in the Early Nineteenth Century: James Cowles Prichard's Moral Philology," *History of European Ideas* 23, no. 1 (1997): 1–18.
76. Hannah Franziska Augstein, "Aspects of Philology and Racial Theory in Nineteenth-Century Celticism—the Case of James Cowles Prichard," *Journal of European Studies* 28, no. 4 (1998): 366.
77. James Cowles Prichard, "On the various methods of Research which contribute to the Advancement of Ethnology, and of the relations of that Science to other branches of Knowledge," in *Report of the British Association for the Advancement of Science* (London: John Murray, 1848), 230–53.
78. Trautmann, *Aryans and British India*, 132.
79. Trautmann, *Aryans and British India*, 171.
80. Aarsleff, *Study of Language in England*, 166ff.

81. J. W. Burrow, "The Uses of Philology in Victorian England," in *Ideas and Institutions of Victorian Britain,* ed. Robert Robson (London: G. Bell & Sons, 1967), 194–97.
82. Friedrich Max Müller, "Comparative Mythology" (1856), in *Chips from a German Workshop,* vol. 2, *Essays on the Science of Religion* (London: Longmans, Green, and Co., 1867), 19.
83. Friedrich Max Müller, "On the Relation of the Bengali to the Arian and Aboriginal Languages of India," in *Report of the Seventeenth Meeting of the British Association for the Advancement of Science, 1847* (London: John Murray, 1848), 325.
84. Max Müller, "On the Relation," 327.
85. This is Thomas Trautmann's term, *Aryans and British India,* 173.
86. Max Müller, "On the Relation," 347.
87. Max Müller, "On the Relation," 321.
88. Max Müller, "On the Relation," 328.
89. Max Müller, "On the Relation," 330, 348.
90. Max Müller, "On the Relation," 349.
91. Friedrich Max Müller, *Suggestions for the Assistance of Officers in Learning the Languages of the Seat of War in the East* (London: Longman, Brown, Green, & Longmans, 1854), 29–30.
92. Nirad C. Chaudhuri, *Scholar Extraordinary: The Life of Professor the Rt. Hon. Friedrich Max Müller, P.C.* (London: Chatto & Windus, 1974), 316ff.
93. Bunsen, *Outlines of the Philosophy of Universal History,* 1:349–52.
94. Trautmann, *Aryans and British India,* 197, 212.
95. Friedrich Max Müller, "Inaugural Lecture. On the Results of the Science of Language," delivered to the Imperial University of Strassburg, 23 May 1873, in *Chips from a German Workshop,* vol. 3, *Essays on Literature, Biography, and Antiquities* (London: Longmans, Green, and Co., 1870), 187.
96. George Stocking, *Victorian Anthropology* (New York: Free Press, 1987), 67.
97. Adalbert Kuhn, "Die sprachvergleichung und die urgeschichte der indogermanischen völker," *Zeitschrift für vergleichende Sprachforschung auf dem Gebiete des Deutschen, Griechischen und Lateinischen* 4 (1855), 81.
98. Schrader, *Sprachvergleichung und Urgeschichte,* 32.
99. Friedrich Max Müller, *Biographies of Words and the Home of the Aryas* (London: Longmans, Green, and Co., 1887), 89–90.
100. Immanuel Kant, *The Critique of Pure Reason,* trans. Friedrich Max Müller (New York: MacMillan, 1907), lxxvii.
101. See the genealogy Max Müller himself gave for his understanding of lan-

guage and thought in *The Science of Thought* (London: Longsmans, Green, and Co., 1887), 43–45.

102. Max Müller, *Science of Thought*, 26–29, 30, 548–49.
103. Max Müller, *Science of Thought*, 83.
104. Max Müller, *Science of Thought*, 419.
105. Friedrich Max Müller, *Lectures on the Science of Language* (London: Longmans, Green, and Co, 1866), 396.
106. Ronald W. Neufeldt, *Friedrich Max Müller and the Rg-Veda: A Study of Its Role in His Work and Thought* (Calcutta: Minerva Associates, 1980), 109–12.
107. Max Müller, *Lectures on the Science of Language*, 394.
108. Joseph M. Kitagawa and John S. Strong, "Friedrich Max Müller," in *Nineteenth-Century Religious Thought in the West*, ed. Ninian Smart (New York: Cambridge University Press, 1985), 3:199–202.
109. Friedrich Max Müller, "Semitic Monotheism" (1860), in *Chips from a German Workshop*, 1:352.
110. Max Müller, "Semitic Monotheism," 1:357.
111. Friedrich Max Müller, *A History of Ancient Sanskrit Literature* (London: Williams and Norgate, 1859), 3.
112. Max Müller, *History of Ancient Sanskrit Literature*, 14–15.
113. Andrew Zimmerman, *Anthropology and Antihumanism in Imperial Germany* (Chicago: University of Chicago Press, 2001), 48.
114. Zimmerman, *Anthropology and Antihumanism*, 135ff.
115. Trautmann, *Aryans and British India*, 184–87.
116. Trautmann, *Aryans and British India*, 178–81; and Schrader, *Sprachvergleichung und Urgeschichte*, 90–91.
117. Schrader, *Sprachvergleichung und Urgeschichte*, 102–3.
118. Friedrich Delitzsch, *Studien über indogermanisch-semitische Wurzelverwandtschaft* (Leipzig: J. C. Hinrichs'sche Buchhandlung, 1873), 3–21.
119. In the foreword to August Fick, *Wörterbuch der indogermanischen Grundsprache in ihrem Bestande vor der Völkertrennung: Ein sprachgeschichtlicher Versuch* (Göttingen: Vandenhoeck & Ruprecht, 1868), ix. See also Schrader, *Sprachvergleichung und Urgeschichte*, 92.
120. Lazarus Geiger, "Über die Ursitze der Indogermanen," in *Zur Entwicklungsgeschichte der Menschheit*, 113–50 (Stuttgart: I. G. Cotta, 1878); see also Schrader, *Sprachvergleichung und Urgeschichte*, 93–94.
121. J. C. Cuno, *Forschungen im Gebiete der Völkerkunde* (Berlin: Gebrüder Bornträger, 1871); see also Schrader, *Sprachvergleichung und Urgeschichte*, 97–98.
122. Schrader, *Sprachvergleichung und Urgeschichte*, 101.
123. Schrader, *Sprachvergleichung und Urgeschichte*, 110–12, 116–17.
124. Cited in Rolf Peter Sieferle, "Indien und die Arier in der Rassentheorie,"

Zeitschrift für Kulturaustausch 37 (1987): 453.

125. Williamson, *Longing for Myth in Germany,* 224.

126. James Darmesteter, *Essais Orientaux* (Paris: Librairie Centrale des Beaux-Arts, 1883), 3–4, 29–31.

127. Prussia offered its Orientalists comparable university support, but the first seminar for Oriental languages was not founded until after unification and the onset of German imperialism in 1887.

128. In 1754 he had joined the East India Company as a mercenary solider, hoping to discover Veda manuscripts, but war confined him to studying Farsi in Surate. Yet in 1761 Anquetil-Duperron returned to France with 180 manuscripts in Avestan, Farsi, Sanskrit, and Pahlavi.

129. Lionel Gossman notes an exception to this in *La Curne de Sainte-Palaye*'s work on Old French and Provençal literature. See Lionel Gossman, *Medievalism and the Ideologies of the Enlightenment: The World and Work of La Curne de Sainte-Palaye* (Baltimore: Johns Hopkins, 1968).

130. Darmsteter, *Essais Orientaux,* 33–34.

131. Darmsteter, *Essais Orientaux,* 23.

132. Eugène Burnouf, "De la langue et de la littérature sanscrite," *Revue des deux mondes* 1 (1833): 275.

133. Jean Pommier, *La Jeunesse cléricale d'Ernest Renan* (Paris: Les Belles Lettres, 1933), 118.

134. Ernest Renan, "Souveniers d'Enfance et de Jeunesse," in *Oeuvres Complètes,* 2:869.

135. Renan, "Souveniers d'Enfance et de Jeunesse," 2:864.

136. Ernest Renan, "Histoire générale et systèmes comparés des langues sémitiques," in *Oeuvres Complètes,* 8:140.

137. Ernest Renan, "Nouvelles Considérations sur le caractère general des peoples sémitique, et en particulier sur leur tendance au monotheism," *Journal Asiatique* (1859), 446, 448–49.

138. Ernest Renan, "Histoire du peuple d'Israël," in *Oeuvres Complètes,* 6:32.

139. Ernest Renan, "Des services rendus par la philologie," *Oeuvres Complètes,* 8:1224, 1230.

140. Renan, "Histoire générale," 8:577–78.

141. Renan, "Histoire générale," 8:586–87.

142. Renan, "Histoire générale," 8:577.

143. Ernest Renan, "De l'origine du langue," in *Oeuvres Complètes,* 8:37.

144. Renan, "De l'origine du langue," 8:59–61.

145. Renan, "De l'origine du langue," 8:53.

146. Renan, "De l'origine du langue," 8:46–47.

147. Renan, "De l'origine du langue," 8:55–56.

148. See especially the following passages: Renan, "De l'origine du langue," 8:57–59; and Renan, "Histoire générale," 8:538–44.

149. Renan, "Histoire générale," 8:544–45.
150. Renan, "De l'origine du langue," 8:58–59.
151. Renan, "De l'origine du langue," 8:61.
152. Renan, "De l'origine du langue," 8:63.
153. Renan, "Histoire générale," 8:137.
154. Renan, "Histoire générale," 8:529–30.
155. Renan, "Histoire générale," 8:541.
156. Renan, "Histoire générale," 8:517.
157. Renan, "Histoire générale," 8:522.
158. Renan, "Histoire générale," 8:157.
159. Renan, "De l'origine du langue," 8:55.
160. Renan, "De l'origine du langue," 8:97.
161. Renan, "Histoire générale," 8:157.
162. Renan, "Histoire générale," 8:145.
163. Renan, "Nouvelles Considérations," 430–32.
164. Renan, "Histoire générale," 8:144–45.
165. Renan, "De l'origine du langue," 8:147.
166. Renan, "De l'origine du langue," 8:97.
167. Renan, "Histoire générale," 8:146.
168. Renan, "Histoire générale," 8:155–56. Renan believed Lassen had confirmed his thesis independently. But whether Renan had truly written his analysis before discovering the German author as claimed is questionable. Many defining passages in the *Histoire* were lifted word for word from the earlier *Origin,* but the latter text showed no hint of the sharp foils Renan drew between Aryans and Semites in 1855.
169. Renan, "De l'origine du langue," 8:98.
170. Olender, *Languages of Paradise,* 69–70.
171. Cited in Olender, *Languages of Paradise,* 69.
172. Ernest Renan, "Marc-Aurèle et la Fin du Monde Antique," in *Oeuvres Complètes,* 5:1142.
173. August Schleicher, *Die Sprachen Europas in systematischer Uebersicht* (1850), in *Sprachvergleichende Untersuchungen* (Frankfurt: Minerva, 1983), 1–3.
174. Salomon Lefmann, *August Schleicher: Skizze* (Leipzig: B. G. Teubner, 1870), 7, 15.
175. Robins, *Short History of Linguistics,* 197.
176. Sebastiano Timpanaro, *Genesis of Lachmann's Method,* 119.
177. G. W. F. Hegel, *Reason in History: A General Introduction to the Philosophy of History,* trans. Robert S. Hartman (Englewood Cliffs, N.J.: Prentice, 1997), 78.
178. Hegel, *Reason in History,* 74.
179. Hegel, *Reason in History,* 77.

180. August Schleicher, "Zur vergleichenden Sprachengeschichte," in *Sprachvergleichende Untersuchungen,* 20–21.
181. Schleicher, "Zur vergleichenden Sprachengeschichte," 17–18.
182. Gardt, *Geschichte der Sprachwissenschaft in Deutschland,* 281.
183. Schleicher, "Zur vergleichenden Sprachengeschichte," 22.
184. Robins, *Short History of Linguistics,* 197.
185. Schleicher, "Eine Fabel in indogermanischer Ursprache," *Beiträge zur vergleichenden Sprachforschung auf dem Gebiete der arischen, celtischen und slawischen Sprachen* 5 (1868), 206.
186. The twentieth-century decipherment of the Hittite script, for example, used in Anatolia during the second millennium BC, uncovered the first known Indo-European language to have separated from the common mother and substantially revised its forms. See Robins, *Short History of Linguistics,* 199.
187. Timpanaro, *Genesis of Lachmann's Method,* 121–22.
188. August Schleicher, "Die ersten Spaltungen des indogermanischen Urvolks," *Kieler Allgemeine Monatsschrift für Wissenschaft und Literatur* (1853): 786–87; see also Schrader, *Sprachvergleichung und Urgeschichte,* 54.
189. See Alter, *Darwinism and the Linguistic Image.*
190. Robins, *Short History of Linguistics,* 198.
191. Dialects were always depicted as having evolved latest in Schleicher's linguistic tree; Schmidt accounted for their presence early in a language's history by considering geographic encounters among groups of speakers. See Schrader, *Sprachvergleichung und Urgeschichte,* 64–65.
192. Timpanaro, *Genesis of Lachmann's Method,* 126.
193. August Schleicher, *Darwinism Tested by the Science of Language,* trans. Alex Bikkers (London: J. C. Hotten, 1869), 21.
194. Schleicher, *Die Sprachen Europas,* 2.
195. Max Müller, *Lectures on the Science of Language,* 138.
196. Max Müller, *The Science of Language,* 42.
197. Schleicher, "Darwinism Tested by the Science of Language," 62, 64.
198. Alter, *Darwinism and the Linguistic Image,* 74–76.
199. Elizabeth Knoll, "The Science of Language and the Evolution of the Mind: Max Müller's Quarrel with Darwinism," *Journal of the History of the Behavioral Sciences* 22, no. 1 (1986): 6.
200. Knoll, "Science of Language," 10–12.
201. Max Müller, *Science of Language,* 392.
202. August Schleicher, "On the Significance of Language for the Natural History of Man" (1865), trans. J. Peter Maher, in *Linguistics and Evolutionary Theory,* 76.

203. Schleicher, "On the Significance of Language," 78–79.
204. See Carl Meinhof, *Grundriß einer Lautlehre der Bantusprachen* (Berlin: D. Reimer, 1899); and *Grundzüge einer vergleichenden Grammatik der Bantusprachen* (Berlin: D. Reimer, 1906).
205. Sara Pugach, "Afrikanistik and Colonial Knowledge: Carl Meinhof, the Missionary Impulse, and African Language and Culture Studies in Germany, 1887–1919" (Ph.D. Diss., University of Chicago, 2001), 258.
206. See Pugach, "Afrikanistik and Colonial Knowledge," especially chapter two.
207. Sara Pugach, "Carl Meinhof and the German Influence on Nicholas van Warmelo's Ethnograophic and Linguistic Writing, 1927–35," *Journal of Southern African Studies* 30, no. 4 (2004): 825–45.
208. Hermann Osthoff and Karl Brugman, *Morphologische Untersuchungen auf dem Gebiete der indogermanischen Sprachen* (Leipzig: S. Hirzel, 1878), 1:xii.
209. Osthoff and Brugman, 1:iii.
210. Osthoff and Brugman, 1:xiii.
211. Kurt R. Jankowsky, "Development of Historical Linguistics from Rask and Grimm to the Neogrammarians," in *Sprachtheorien der Neuzeit II: Von der Grammaire de Port-Royal (1660) zur Konstitution moderner linguistischer Disziplinen,* ed. Peter Schmitter (Tübingen: Gunter Narr, 1996), 20.
212. Osthoff and Brugman, 1:viii–ix.
213. Osthoff and Brugman, 1:vi–vii.
214. Osthoff and Brugman, 1:xiii.
215. Hermann Osthoff, "Das physiologische und psychologische Moment in der sprachlichen Formenbildung," *Sammlung gemeinverständlicher wissenschaftlicher Vorträge von Virchow und Hotzendorff* 327 (1879): 8.
216. Osthoff and Brugman, 1:xiv.
217. Hermann Osthoff, *Das Verbum in der Nominalkomposition im Deutschen, Griechischen, Slavishen und Romanischen* (Jena: H. Costenoble, 1878), 326.
218. Gerhard Helbig, *Geschichte der neueren Sprachwissenschaft: Unter dem besondern Aspekt der Grammatik-Theorie* (Leipzig: VEB Bibliographisches Institut, 1973), 19.
219. Osthoff, "Das physiologische und psychologische Moment," 13–14.
220. Osthoff, "Das physiologische und psychologische Moment," 15–16.
221. Osthoff, "Das physiologische und psychologische Moment," 19–20.
222. Osthoff, "Das physiologische und psychologische Moment," 5.
223. Herman Paul, *Prinzipien der Sprachgeschichte,* 2nd edition (Halle: M. Niemeyer, 1886), 1.

Chapter 6

1. Ferdinand de Saussure, "Souvenirs de F. de Saussure concernant sa jeunesse et ses études," *Cahiers Ferdinand de Saussure* 17 (1960): 22.
2. See Williamson, *Longing for Myth in Germany,* 219–29.
3. Laura Otis, *Organic Memory: History and the Body in the Late Nineteenth and Early Twentieth Centuries* (Lincoln: University of Nebraska Press, 1994), 98.
4. Wilhelm Max Wundt, *Völkerpsychologie: Eine Untersuchung der Entwicklungsgesetze von Sprache, Mythus und Sitte,* 2 vols. (Leipzig: Wilhelm Engelmann, 1900–1909).
5. Williamson, *Longing for Myth in Germany,* 220.
6. Cited in Johann Karl Kretzschmer, *Friedrich Wilhelm III: Sein Leben, sein Wirken und seine Zeit: Ein Erinnerungsbuch für das preussische Volk* (Danzig: Friedrich Samuel Gerhard, 1842), 2:289.
7. Vick, *Defining Germany,* 110.
8. Ingrid Belke, ed., *Moritz Lazarus und Heymann Steinthal: Die Begründer der Völkerpsychologie in ihren Briefen* (Tübingen: J. C. B. Mohr, 1983), 1:xv.
9. Moritz Lazarus, *Die sittliche Berechtigung Preußens in Deutschland* (Berlin: Carl Schultze, 1850), ix.
10. Lazarus, *Die sittliche Berechtigung Preußens,* 104.
11. Lazarus, *Die sittliche Berechtigung Preußens,* 5.
12. Belke, *Moritz Lazarus und Heymann Steinthal,* 1:58.
13. Moritz Lazarus and Heymann Steinthal, "Einleitende Gedanken über Völkerpsychologie, als Einladung zu einer Zeitschrift für Völkerpsychologie und Sprachwissenschaft," *Zeitschrift für Völkerpsychologie und Sprachwissenschaft* 1 (1860/61): 9–10.
14. Moritz Lazarus, "Ueber den Begriff und die Möglichkeit einer Völkerpyschologie," in *Deutsches Museum: Zeitschrift für Literatur, Kunst und öffentliches Leben,* ed. Robert Prutz (Leipzig: J. C. Hinrichs'sche Buchhandlung, 1851), 112–13.
15. Moritz Lazarus, "Einige synthetische Gedanken zur Völkerpsychologie," *Zeitschrift für Völkerpsychologie und Sprachwissenschaft* 3 (1865): 26–27.
16. Georg Eckardt, ed., *Völkerpsychologie—Versuch einer Neuentdeckung: Texte von Lazarus, Steinthal, und Wundt* (Weinheim: Psychologie Verlags Union, 1997), 25, 74.
17. Lazarus, "Einige synthetische Gedanken zur Völkerpsychologie," 52.
18. Heymann Steinthal, *Grammatik, Logik, und Psychologie: Ihre Principien und ihr Verhältniss zu Einander* (Berlin: Ferdinand Dümmler, 1855), 391–92.
19. Lazarus, "Einige synthetische Gedanken zur Völkerpsychologie," 41.

20. Lazarus, "Einige synthetische Gedanken zur Völkerpsychologie," 40.
21. Lazarus, "Einige synthetische Gedanken zur Völkerpsychologie," 36.
22. Lazarus, "Einige synthetische Gedanken zur Völkerpsychologie," 35.
23. Lazarus, "Einige synthetische Gedanken zur Völkerpsychologie," 35.
24. Lazarus, "Einige synthetische Gedanken zur Völkerpsychologie," 35.
25. Lazarus, "Einige synthetische Gedanken zur Völkerpsychologie," 32.
26. Lazarus, "Einige synthetische Gedanken zur Völkerpsychologie," 39.
27. Moritz Lazarus, *Was heißt national?* (Berlin: Ferdinand Dümmler, 1880), 21.
28. Leszek Belzyt, *Sprachliche Minderheiten im preußischen Staat, 1815–1914: Die preußische Sprachenstatistik in Bearbeitung und Kommentar* (Marburg: Verlag Herder-Institut, 1998), 9.
29. Richard Böckh, "Die statistische Bedeutung der Volkssprache als Kennzeichen der Nationalität," *Zeitschrift für Völkerpsychologie* 4 (1866): 265.
30. Böckh, "Die statistische Bedeutung der Volkssprache," 264.
31. Hobsbawm, *Nations and Nationalism,* 99.
32. Hobsbawm, *Nations and Nationalism,* 99.
33. Ahlzweig, *Muttersprache-Vaterland,* 165, 170.
34. Eva Rimmele, *Sprachenpolitik im Deutschen Kaiserreich vor 1914: Regierungspolitik und veröffentlichte Meinung in Elsaß-Lothringen und den östlichen Provinzen Preußens* (Frankfurt: Peter Lang, 1996), 166.
35. Brubaker, *Citizenship and Nationhood in France and Germany,* 129.
36. Rimmele, *Sprachenpolitik im Deutschen Kaiserreich,* 166.
37. Chickering, "Language and the Social Foundations of Radical Nationalism," 76.
38. Cited in Puschner, *Die völkische Bewegung,* 29.
39. Chickering, "Language and the Social Foundations," 74.
40. Puschner, *Die völkische Bewegung,* 30ff.
41. Friedrich Meinecke, *Weltbürgertum und Nationalstaat: Studien zur Genesis des deutschen Nationalstaates* (Munich: R. Oldenbourg, 1911), 1–20.
42. Heymann Steinthal, *Die Classification der Sprachen, dargestellt als die Entwickelung der Sprachidee* (Berlin: Ferdinand Dümmler, 1850), 16. See also Waltraud Bumann, *Die Sprachtheorie Heymann Steinthals, dargestellt im Zusammenhang mit seiner Theorie der Geisteswissenschaften* (Meisenheim am Glan: Anton Hain, 1966), 18.
43. Steinthal, *Die Classification der Sprachen,* 17.
44. Heymann Steinthal, *Der Ursprung der Sprache im Zusammenhange mit den letzten Fragen alles Wissens, Eine Darstellung, Kritik und Fortentwickelung der vorzüglichsten Ansichten* (Berlin: Ferdinand Dümmler, 1888), 106.
45. Heymann Steinthal, "Offenes Sendschreiben an Herrn Professor Pott"

(1852), in *Kleine Sprachtheoretische Schriften,* ed. Waltraud Bumann (New York: Georg Olms, 1970), 5.
46. Steinthal, *Die Classification der Sprachen,* 24.
47. See Heymann Steinthal, "Philologie, Geschichte und Psychologie in ihren gegenseitigen Beziehungen," in *Kleine sprachtheoretische Schriften,* 436–511.
48. Steinthal, *Der Ursprung der Sprache,* 109.
49. Steinthal, *Der Ursprung der Sprache,* 109.
50. Steinthal, *Der Ursprung der Sprache,* 109.
51. Heymann Steinthal, "Zur Charakteristik der semitischen Völker," *Zeitschrift für Völkerpsychologie und Sprachwissenschaft* 1 (1860): 328–45.
52. Steinthal, *Grammatik, Logik, und Psychologie,* 234.
53. Steinthal, *Grammatik, Logik, und Psychologie,* 47.
54. Steinthal, *Grammatik, Logik, und Psychologie,* 232.
55. Steinthal, *Grammatik, Logik, und Psychologie,* 295, 298.
56. Steinthal, *Grammatik, Logik, und Psychologie,* 235.
57. Steinthal, *Grammatik, Logik, und Psychologie,* 306.
58. Steinthal, *Grammatik, Logik, und Psychologie,* 319–23.
59. Steinthal, "Zur Sprachphilosophie," 270.
60. Steinthal, "Zur Sprachphilosophie," 270.
61. Steinthal, "Zur Sprachphilosophie," 279.
62. Steinthal, "Zur Sprachphilosophie," 270.
63. Steinthal, "Zur Sprachphilosophie," 296.
64. Heymann Steinthal, *Abriss der Sprachwissenschaft,* vol. 1 of *Einleitung in die Psychologie und Sprachwissenschaft* (Berlin: Ferdinand Dümmler, 1871), 370.
65. Steinthal, "Zur Sprachphilosophie," 295.
66. Steinthal, "Zur Sprachphilosophie," 296.
67. Steinthal, *Abriss der Sprachwissenschaft,* 285.
68. Steinthal, "Zur Sprachphilosophie," 303.
69. Steinthal, "Zur Sprachphilosophie," 297.
70. Moritz Lazarus, "Verdichtung des Denkens in der Geschichte: Ein Fragment," *Zeitschrift für Völkerpsychologie und Sprachwissenschaft* 2 (1863): 67.
71. Steinthal, *Grammatik, Logik, und Psychologie,* 374.
72. Steinthal, *Grammatik, Logik, und Psychologie,* 375.
73. Steinthal, *Grammatik, Logik, und Psychologie,* 375.
74. Steinthal, *Grammatik, Logik, und Psychologie,* 380.
75. Steinthal, "Zur Sprachphilosophie," 303.
76. Steinthal, *Die Classification der Sprachen,* 74.
77. Steinthal, *Die Classification der Sprachen,* 91.

78. See Heymann Steinthal, *Die Mande-Neger-Sprachen: Psychologisch und Phonetisch Betrachtet* (Berlin: Ferdinand Dümmler, 1867).
79. Steinthal, *Abriss der Sprachwissenschaft,* 62.
80. Steinthal, *Abriss der Sprachwissenschaft,* 67.
81. Steinthal, *Abriss der Sprachwissenschaft,* 62.
82. Steinthal, *Abriss der Sprachwissenschaft,* 68.
83. Clemens Knobloch, *Geschichte der psychologischen Sprachauffassung in Deutschland von 1850 bis 1920* (Tübingen: Max Niemeyer, 1988), 60; and Eckardt, *Völkerpsychologie,* 21.
84. Steinthal, *Grammatik, Logik, und Psychologie,* 137–38.
85. Bumann, *Die Sprachtheorie Heymann Steinthals,* 43.
86. See James I. Porter, *Nietzsche and the Philology of the Future* (Stanford: Stanford University Press, 2000); and Manfred Riedel, ed., "*Jedes Wort ist ein Vorurteil": Philologie und Philosophie in Nietzsches Denken* (Cologne: Böhlau, 1999).
87. Federico Gerratana, "'Jetzt zieht mich das Allgemein-Menschliche an': Ein Streifzug durch Nietzsches Aufzeichnungen zu einer 'Geschichte der litterarischen Studien,'" in "*Centauren-Geburten" Wissenschaft, Kunst und Philosophie beim jungen Nietzsche,* ed. Tilman Borsche, Federico Gerratana, and Aldo Venturelli (New York: Walter de Gruyter, 1994), 343.
88. Friedrich Nietzsche, *Friedrich Nietzsche's Frühe Schriften,* ed. Hans Joachim Mette, Karl Schlechta, and Carl Koch (Munich: C. H. Beck, 1994), 3:338.
89. Nietzsche, *Frühe Schriften,* 5:268.
90. Nietzsche, *Frühe Schriften,* 1:369.
91. Nietzsche, *Frühe Schriften,* 3:338.
92. Nietzsche, *Frühe Schriften,* 5:268.
93. Nietzsche, *Frühe Schriften,* 5:195.
94. Nietzsche, *Frühe Schriften,* 5:285.
95. Compare Nietzsche's obscure reference to "the bees—the anthill" in "On the Origin of Language" (in *Friedrich Nietzsche on Rhetoric and Language,* ed. Sander Gilman, C. Blair, and D. Parent [New York: Oxford University Press, 1989], 209), to Hartmann's passage: "Nur der Masseninstinct kann sie (die Sprache) geschaffen haben, wie er im Leben des Bienenstockes, des Thermited-und Armeisenhaufens waltet" (Eduard von Hartmann, *Philosophie des Unbewussten* [Berlin: Carl Duncker, 1873], 258). See Claudia Crawford, *The Beginnings of Nietzsche's Theory of Language* (New York: Walter de Gruyter, 1988), 18.
96. Hartmann, *Philosophie des Unbewussten,* 260. See also the reference to Steinthal in the index, as well as the numerous references to his essay on the origin of language and to *Völkerpsychologie* generally.

97. Hartmann, *Philosophie des Unbewussten,* 260.
98. Hartmann, *Philosophie des Unbewussten,* 258.
99. Hartmann, *Philosophie des Unbewussten,* 258–59.
100. Nietzsche, "On the Origin of Language," 209.
101. Crawford, *Beginnings of Nietzsche's Theory,* 178.
102. Friedrich Nietzsche, *The Birth of Tragedy from the Spirit of Music,* trans. Francis Golffing (New York: Anchor Books, 1956), 32.
103. Nietzsche, *Birth of Tragedy,* 101.
104. Nietzsche, *Birth of Tragedy,* 45.
105. Friedrich Nietzsche, "On Music and Words" (1871), trans. Walter Kaufmann, in *Between Romanticism and Modernism: Four Studies in the Music of the Later Nineteenth Century,* ed. Carl Dahlhaus (Berkeley: University of California Press, 1980), 107–8.
106. Nietzsche, *Birth of Tragedy,* 44.
107. Nietzsche, "On Music and Words," 109.
108. Nietzsche, *Birth of Tragedy,* 36.
109. Nietzsche, *Birth of Tragedy,* 109.
110. Nietzsche, *Birth of Tragedy,* 96, 121, 123.
111. Nietzsche, *Birth of Tragedy,* 119.
112. Nietzsche, *Birth of Tragedy,* 63–64.
113. See Ernst Behler, "Die Sprachtheorie des frühen Nietzsche," in Borsche, Gerratana, and Venturelli, *"Centauren-Geburten,"* 102ff.
114. Gustav Gerber, *Die Sprache als Kunst* (Hildesheim: Gerog Olms, 1961), iii.
115. Gerber, *Die Sprache als Kunst,* 244.
116. Gerber, *Die Sprache als Kunst,* 260.
117. Gerber, *Die Sprache als Kunst,* 118ff.
118. Friedrich Nietzsche, "On Truth and Lying in an Extra-Moral Sense" (1873), in Nietzsche, *Friedrich Nietzsche on Rhetoric and Language,* 247.
119. Nietzsche, "On Truth and Lying," 248.
120. Nietzsche, "On Truth and Lying," 248.
121. Nietzsche, "On Truth and Lying," 249.
122. See Nietzsche, *Friedrich Nietzsche on Rhetoric and Language,* xiii.
123. Nietzsche, "On Truth and Lying," 248.
124. Friedrich Nietzsche, "Description of Ancient Rhetoric" (1872–73), in Nietzsche, *Friedrich Nietzsche on Rhetoric and Language,* 21, 23.
125. Nietzsche, *Friedrich Nietzsche on Rhetoric and Language,* xiv f.
126. Nietzsche, "On Truth and Lying," 250.
127. Michel Haar, "Nietzsche und die Sprache," in *"Jedes Wort ist ein Vorteuil": Philologie und Philosophie in Nietzsches Denken,* ed. Manfred Riedel (Cologne: Böhlau Verlag, 1999), 68.

128. Nietzsche, "On Truth and Lying," 250–51.
129. Nietzsche, "On Truth and Lying," 252.
130. Nietzsche, "On Truth and Lying," 254.
131. Nietzsche, "On Truth and Lying," 255.
132. Nietzsche, "On Truth and Lying," 256.
133. Foucault, "Nietzsche, Genealogy, History," 79.
134. Foucault, "Nietzsche, Genealogy, History," 80.
135. Foucault, "Nietzsche, Genealogy, History," 81.
136. Friedrich Nietzsche, *The Genealogy of Morals,* trans. Francis Golffing (New York: Anchor Books, 1956), 188.
137. Nietzsche, *The Genealogy of Morals,* 154–55.
138. Nietzsche, *The Genealogy of Morals,* 151.
139. Nietzsche, *The Genealogy of Morals,* 163–64.
140. Nietzsche, *The Genealogy of Morals,* 176.
141. Nietzsche, *The Genealogy of Morals,* 178.
142. Nietzsche, *The Genealogy of Morals,* 178–79.
143. Nietzsche, *The Genealogy of Morals,* 197.
144. Nietzsche, *The Genealogy of Morals,* 197.
145. Nietzsche, *The Genealogy of Morals,* 218.
146. Nietzsche, *The Genealogy of Morals,* 299.
147. Friedrich Nietzsche, *Friedrich Nietzsche: Nachgelassene Fragmente, 1885–1887,* in *Friedrich Nietzsche: Sämtliche Werke. Kritische Studienausgabe,* ed. Giorgio Colli and Mazzino Montinari (Munich: Deutscher Taschenbuch Verlag, 1988), 12:98, 101.
148. Friedrich Nietzsche, *Beyond Good and Evil: Prelude to a Philosophy of the Future,* trans. Judith Norman (Cambridge: Cambridge University Press, 2002), 17–18.
149. Nietzsche, *Beyond Good and Evil,* 49.
150. Friedrich Nietzsche, *Twilight of the Idols,* trans. Duncan Large (Oxford: Oxford University Press, 1998), 28.
151. Nietzsche, *Twilight of the Idols,* 18.
152. Nietzsche, *Beyond Good and Evil,* 36.
153. Nietzsche, *Twilight of the Idols,* 18.
154. Nietzsche, *Nachgelassene Fragmente,* 102.
155. Nietzsche, *Twilight of the Idols,* 18.
156. Nietzsche, *Twilight of the Idols,* 18–19.
157. Nietzsche, *Beyond Good and Evil,* 20.
158. Nietzsche, *Twilight of the Idols,* 19.
159. Nietzsche, *Beyond Good and Evil,* 29.
160. Nietzsche, *Beyond Good and Evil,* 35.
161. Daniel Müller, *Wider die "Vernunft in der Sprache": Zum Verhältniss von Sprachkritik und Sprachpraxis im Schreiben Nietzsches* (Tübingen: Gunter

Narr, 1995), 62ff.

162. Crawford, *Beginnings of Nietzsche's Theory,* xiv ff.

163. See for example, Edith Kurzweil, *The Age of Structuralism: Lévi-Strauss to Foucault* (New York: Columbia University Press, 1980).

164. Jonathan Culler, *Saussure* (Hassocks, Sussex: Harvester Press, 1976), 96.

165. See Sheila Embleton, John E. Joseph, and Hans-Josef Niederehe, eds., *The Emergence of the Modern Language Sciences: Studies on the Transition from Historical-Comparative to Structural Linguistics in Honour of E. F. K. Koerner,* vol. 1, *Historiographical Perspectives* (Philadelphia: John Benjamins, 1999); Konrad Koerner, *Ferdinand de Saussure: Origin and Development of His Linguistic Thought in Western Studies of Language* (Braunschweig: Vieweg & Sohn, 1973); and Amserdamska, *Schools of Thought.*

166. Saussure, "Souvenirs de F. de Saussure," 17.

167. Culler, *Saussure,* 66.

168. See Nerlich, *Change in Language.*

169. John E. Joseph, "Saussure's Meeting with Whitney, Berlin 1879," *Cahiers Ferdinand de Saussure* 42 (1988): 205ff.

170. Stephen George Alter, "William Dwight Whitney and the Science of Language" (Ph.D. diss., University of Michigan, 1993), 346.

171. William Dwight Whitney, *The Life and Growth of Language: An Outline of Linguistic Science* (New York: Dover, 1979), 146.

172. Whitney, *Life and Growth of Language,* 145.

173. Whitney, *Life and Growth of Language,* 146.

174. Whitney, *Life and Growth of Language,* 319.

175. Whitney, *Life and Growth of Language,* 145–46.

176. Konrad Koerner, "L'importance de William Dwight Whitney pour les jeunes linguistes de Leipzig et pour Ferdinand de Saussure," in Konrad Koerner, *Saussurean Studies/Etudes Saussuriennes* (Geneva: Editions Slatkine, 1988), 3f.

177. Karl Brugmann, "Zum Gedächtniss W. D. Whitney's," *Journal of the American Oriental Society* 19 (1897): 80.

178. Koerner, *Ferdinand de Saussure,* 79–92.

179. Koerner, "Hermann Paul and Synchronic Linguistics," in *Saussurian Studies,* 23.

180. Hermann Paul, *Principles of the History of Language,* trans. H. A. Strong (College Park, Md.: McGrath Publishing, 1970), 9.

181. Paul, *Principles of the History of Language,* xlviii.

182. Koerner, "Hermann Paul and Synchronic Linguistics," 28.

183. Paul, *Principles of the History of Language,* 2.

184. Paul, *Principles of the History of Language,* xlviii.

185. Paul, *Principles of the History of Language,* 2–3.

186. Paul, *Principles of the History of Language,* 9.
187. Koerner, "Hermann Paul and Synchronic Linguistics," 36.
188. Paul, *Principles of the History of Language,* xliii.
189. Koerner, *Ferdinand de Saussure,* 112.
190. Paul, *Principles of the History of Language,* xliv.
191. Paul, *Principles of the History of Language,* 3.
192. Hans Aarsleff, "Bréal vs. Schleicher," in *From Locke to Saussure,* 393.
193. Koerner, "French Influences on Saussure," in *Saussurian Studies,* 83.
194. Amserdamska, *Schools of Thought,* 236, 247.
195. Nerlich, *Change in Language,* 6.
196. Michel Bréal, "On the Form and Function of Words" (1866), in Michel Bréal, *Michel Bréal: The Beginnings of Semantics: Essays, Lectures and Reviews* (London: Duckworth, 1991), 50.
197. Bréal, "On the Form and Function of Words," 52.
198. Bréal, "Language and Nationality," in Bréal, *Michel Bréal,* 201.
199. Bréal, "Language and Nationality," 206.
200. Fredric Jameson, *The Prison-House of Language: A Critical Account of Structuralism and Russian Formalism* (Princeton: Princeton University Press, 1972), 139.
201. Ferdinand de Saussure, *Course in General Linguistics,* ed. Charles Bally and Albert Sechehaye, trans. Wade Baskin (New York: McGraw-Hill, 1959), 4.
202. Saussure, *Course,* 5.
203. Saussure, *Course,* 6.
204. Saussure, *Course,* 13.
205. Saussure, *Course,* 14.
206. Saussure, *Course,* 9, 10.
207. Saussure, *Course,* 19.
208. Saussure, *Course,* 14.
209. Saussure, *Course,* 10.
210. Culler, *Saussure,* 35.
211. Saussure, *Course,* 75.
212. Saussure, *Course,* 80.
213. Saussure, *Course,* 81.
214. Saussure, *Course,* 71.
215. Saussure, *Course,* 71.
216. Saussure, *Course,* 72.
217. Saussure, *Course,* 73.
218. Saussure, *Course,* 111.
219. Saussure, *Course,* 117.
220. Saussure, *Course,* 122.
221. Saussure, *Course,* 112.

222. Saussure, *Course,* 112–13.
223. Rosalind Coward and John Ellis, *Language and Materialism: Developments in Semiology and the Theory of the Subject* (Boston: Routledge & Kegan Paul, 1977), 20.
224. Jonathan Culler, *Structuralist Poetics: Structuralism, Linguistics and the Study of Literature* (Ithaca: Cornell University Press, 1975), 27–31.
225. Saussure, *Course,* 232.
226. Saussure, *Course,* 222.
227. Saussure, *Course,* 223.
228. Saussure, *Course,* 16.
229. Saussure, *Course,* 68.
230. Nietzsche, *Friedrich Nietzsche on Rhetoric and Language,* xii.
231. See Jameson, *Prison-House of Language.*

Conclusion

1. Antoine Meillet, “Ce que la linguistique doit aux savants allemands” (1923), in *Linguistique Historique et Lintuistique Générale* (Paris: C. Klincksieck, 1951), 1:159, 157.
2. Meillet, “Ce que la linguistique doit,” 158–59.
3. Christopher M. Hutton, *Linguistics and the Third Reich: Mother-tongue Fascism, Race and the Science of Language* (New York: Routledge, 1999), 15.
4. Hutton, *Linguistics and the Third Reich,* 18; and Utz Maas, “Die Entwicklung der deutschsprachigen Sprachwissenschaft von 1900 bis 1950: Zwischen Professionalisierung und Politisierung,” *Zeitschrift für Germanistische Linguistik* 16 (1988): 263. See also Ulrich Ch. M. Thilo, *Rezeption und Wirkung des Cours de linguistique générale: Überlegungen zu Geschichte und Historiographie der Sprachwissenschaft* (Tübingen: Gunter Narr, 1989).
5. Clemens Knobloch, *Volkhafte Sprachforschung: Studien zum Umbau der Sprachwissenschaft in Deutschland zwischen 1918 und 1945* (Tübingen: Max Nieymeyer, 2005), 49.
6. Maas, “Die Entwicklung der deutschsprachigen Sprachwissenschaft,” 263.
7. Hutton, *Linguistics and the Third Reich,* 17–19.
8. Steven E. Aschheim, *The Nietzsche Legacy in Germany, 1890–1990* (Berkeley: University of California Press, 1992), 52.
9. Aschheim, *Nietzsche Legacy in Germany,* 120ff.
10. Marchand, *Down from Olympus,* 305ff.
11. Marchand, *Down from Olympus,* 261.
12. The *langue* of a given community could be seen as a guarantor of a com-

mon mentality or identity because it supposedly provided all its of members with a shared stock of linguistically communicable ideas. See Roy Harris, *Saussure and His Interpreters* (Edinburgh: Edinburgh University Press, 2003), 203; and Hutton, *Linguistics and the Third Reich,* 18.

13. Hermand, *Geschichte der Germanistik,* 75–76.
14. Cited in Greß, *Germanistik und Politik,* 132, 130.
15. Marchand, *Down from Olympus,* 305.
16. Bernhard Becker, *Herder-Rezeption in Deutschland: Eine ideologiekritische Untersuchung* (Saint Ingbert: Werner J. Röhrig, 1987), 116ff.
17. Marchand, *Down from Olympus,* 310.
18. Sengupta, *From Salon to Discipline,* 117.
19. Knobloch, *Volkhafte Sprachforschung,* 177.
20. Knobloch, *Volkhafte Sprachforschung,* 178.
21. Knobloch, *Volkhafte Sprachforschung,* 179.
22. Hutton, *Linguistics and the Third Reich,* 190.
23. Houston Stuart Chamberlain, *Foundations of the Nineteenth Century,* trans. John Lees (New York: Howard Fertig, 1968), 1:lv.
24. Chamberlain, *Foundations of the Nineteenth Century,* 1:221ff.
25. George Mosse, introduction to Chamberlain, *Foundations of the Nineteenth Century,* 1:xvi.
26. Hutton, *Linguistics and the Third Reich,* 16.
27. Maas, "Die Entwicklung der deutschsprachigen Sprachwissenschaft," 256–57, 260.
28. Maas, "Die Entwicklung der deutschsprachigen Sprachwissenschaft," 262.
29. Knobloch, *Volkhafte Sprachforschung,* 59.
30. Knochloch, *Volkhafte Sprachforschung,* 58–59.
31. Hutton, *Linguistics and the Third Reich,* 236.
32. Knobloch, *Volkhafte Sprachforschung,* 60–64.
33. Hutton, *Linguistics and the Third Reich,* 246.
34. Hutton, *Linguistics and the Third Reich,* 291, 304–5.
35. Hutton, *Linguistics and the Third Reich,* 212–32.
36. Leo Weisgerber, "Sprachwissenschaft als lebendige Kraft unserer Zeit," in *Zur Grundlegung der ganzheitlichen Sprachauffassung Aufsätze 1925–1933,* ed. Helmut Gipper (Düsseldorf: Pädagogischer Verlag Schwann, 1964), 388–91.
37. Alan D. Schrift, *Nietzsche's French Legacy: A Genealogy of Poststructuralism* (New York: Routledge, 1995), 5.
38. François Dosse, *History of Structuralism,* trans. Deborah Glassman (Minneapolis: University of Minnesota Press, 1997), 1:60, 66.
39. Dosse, *History of Structuralism,* 392.
40. Dosse, *History of Structuralism,* 388.

41. Dosse, *History of Structuralism,* xix.
42. Claude Lévi-Strauss, *The Savage Mind* (Chicago: University of Chicago Press, 1962), 246–47.
43. Lévi-Strauss, *Savage Mind,* 252.
44. Dosse, *History of Structuralism,* 333.
45. Michel Foucault, *The Order of Things: An Archaeology of the Human Sciences,* trans. R. D. Lang (New York: Pantheon Books, 1970), 386–87.
46. Foucault, *Order of Things,* 387.
47. In Foucault's words: "a history of the different modes by which, in our culture, human beings are made into subjects." Michel Foucault, "The Subject and Power," afterword to H. L. Dreyfus and Paul Rabinow, eds., *Michel Foucault: Beyond Structuralism and Hermeneutics* (Chicago: University of Chicago Press, 1982), 208.
48. Foucault, *Order of Things,* 305.
49. Foucault, *Order of Things,* 305. See also Schrift, *Nietzsche's French Legacy,* 45.
50. Schrift, *Nietzsche's French Legacy,* 375.
51. Schrift, *Nietzsche's French Legacy,* 4.
52. Schrift, *Nietzsche's French Legacy,* 5.
53. Michel Foucault, "The Order of Discourse," in *Language and Politics,* ed. Michael J. Shapiro (New York: New York University Press, 1984), 124–25.

Bibliography

Primary Literature

Adelung, Johann Christoph. *Aelteste Geschichte der Deutschen, ihrer Sprache und Litteratur, bis zur Völkerwanderung*. Leipzig, 1806.

———. *Mithridates oder allgemeine Sprachkunde mit dem Vater Unser als Sprachprobe in bey nahe fünfhundert Sprachen und Mundarten*. Vol. 1. New York: Georg Olms, 1970.

———. *Über die Geschichte der deutschen Sprache, über Deutsche Mundarten und Deutsche Sprachlehre*. Leipzig: Johann Gottlieb Immanuel Breitkopf, 1781.

Altdeutsche Wälder. Edited by Jacob and Wilhelm Grimm. Frankfurt: Körner. 3 vols. 1813–1816. Reprint edited by Wilhelm Schoof. 2 vols. Darmstadt: Wissenschaftliche Buchgesellschaft, 1966.

Ast, Friedrich. *Grundlinien der Grammatik, Hermeneutik und Kritik*. Landshut: Jos. Thomann, 1808.

———. *Grundriß der Philologie*. Landshut: Philipp Krüll, 1808.

———. "Über den Geist des Altertums und dessen Bedeutung für unser Zeitalter." In *Kleine Pädagogische Texte*. Vol. 17, *Dokumente des Neuhumanismus*. 13–31. Berlin: Julius Beltz, 1931.

Bachmann, Johannes. *Ernst Wilhelm Hengstenberg: Sein Leben und Wirken nach ungedruckten Quellen*. 3 vols. Gütersloh: C. Bertelsmann, 1876–92.

Benfey, Theodor. "Ein abschnitt aus meiner vorlesung über 'vergleichende Grammatik der indo-germanischen sprachen.'" *Zeitschrift für vergleichende Sprachforschung auf dem Gebiete des deutschen, griechischen, und lateinischen* 9 (1860): 81–132.

———. *Kleinere Schriften*. Edited by Adalbert Bezzenberger. 2 vols. Berlin: H. Reuther, 1890.

———. *Pantschatantra: Fünf Bücher indischer Fabeln, Märchen und Erzählungen aus dem Sanskrit übersetzt*. 2 vols. Leipzig: F. A. Brockhaus, 1859.

———. *Die persischen Keilinschriften mit Uebersetzung und Glossar*. Leipzig: Brockhaus & Avenarius, 1847.

———. *Ueber das Verhältniss der ägyptischen Sprache zum semitischen Sprachstamm*. Leipzig: F. A. Brockhaus, 1844.

Benfey, Theodor, and Moriz A. Stern. *Ueber die Monatsnamen einiger alter Völker insbesondere der Perser, Cappodocier, Juden und Syrer*. Berlin: G. Reimer, 1836.

Bernhardi, August F. *Anfangsgründe der Sprachwissenschaft*. 1805.

———. *Sprachlehre*. 2 vols. New York: Georg Olms, 1973.

Böckh, Richard. "Die statistische Bedeutung der Volkssprache als Kennzeichen der Nationalität." *Zeitschrift für Völkerpsychologie* 4 (1866): 259–402.

Boeckh, August. *Encyklopädie und Methodologie der philologischen Wissenschaften*. Edited by Ernst Bratuscheck. Leipzig: B. G. Teubner, 1886.

———. *Gesammelte kleine Schriften*. 7 vols. Leipzig: B. G. Teubner, 1858.

Bohlen, Peter von. *Das alte Indien, mit besonderer Rücksicht auf Aegypten*. 2 vols. Königsberg: Gebrüder Bornträger, 1830.

Bopp, Franz. *Comparative Grammar of the Sanskrit, Zend, Greek, Latin, Lithuanian, Gothic, German, and Slavonic Languages*. Translated by Edward B. Eastwick. 3 vols. London: Williams and Worgate, 1862.

———. *Kleine Schriften zur vergleichenden Sprachwissenschaft: Gesammelte Berliner Akademieabhandlungen 1824–1854*. Leipzig: Zentralantiquariat der DDR, 1972.

———. *Über das Conjugationssystem der Sanskritsprache in Vergleichung mit jenem der griechischen, lateinischen, persischen und germanischen Sprache*. Edited by K. J. Windischmann. Frankfurt: Andreäische Buchhandlung, 1816.

———. *Vergleichende Grammatik des Sanskrit, Zend, Griechischen, Lateinischen, Littauischen, Gothischen und Deutschen*. 2nd ed. Berlin: Ferdinand Dümmler, 1857.

———. *Vergleichende Zergliederung des Sanskrit*. Berlin: Druckerei der Königlichen Akademie der Wissenschaften, 1824.

———. *Vocalismus oder sprachvergleichende Kritiken über Jacob Grimm's deutsche Grammatik und Graff's althochdeutschen Sprachschatz mit Begründung einer neuen Theorie des Ablauts*. Berlin: Nicolaische Buchhandlung, 1836.

Bréal, Michel. *Michel Bréal: The Beginnings of Semantics: Essays, Lectures and Reviews*. London: Duckworth, 1991.

Brugmann, Karl. "Zum Gedächtniss W. D. Whitney's." *Journal of the Ameri-*

can Oriental Society 19 (1898): 74–81.

Bunsen, Christian Charles Josias. *Outlines of the Philosophy of Universal History, Applied to Language and Religion.* 2 vols. London: Longman, Brown, Green, and Longmans, 1854.

Burnouf, Eugène. "De la langue et de la littérature sanscrite." *Revue des deux mondes* 1 (1833): 264–78.

Burnouf, Eugène, and Christian Lassen. *Essai sur le Pali, ou langue sacrée de la presqu'ile au-dela du gange.* Paris: Librairie Oreintale de Sondy-Dupré, 1826.

Chamberlain, Houston Stewart. *Foundations of the Nineteenth Century.* Translated by John Lees. 2 vols. New York: Howard Fertig, 1968.

Condillac, Étienne Bonnot de. *An Essay on the Origin of Human Knowledge, Being a Supplement to Mr. Locke's Essay on the Human Understanding.* Edited by Robert G. Weyant. Gainsville, Fla.: Scholars' Facsimiles & Reprints, 1971.

———. *Essay on the Origin of Human Knowledge.* Edited by Hans Aarsleff. Cambridge: Cambridge University Press, 2001.

Cremer, Hermann. *Biblisch-theologisches Wörterbuch der neutestamentischen Gräcität.* Gotha: Perthes, 1872.

Cuno, J. C. *Forschungen im Gebiete der Völkerkunde.* Berlin: Gebrüder Bornträger, 1871.

Curtius, Georg. *Kleine Schriften.* Edited by Ernst Windisch. Vol. 1, *Ausgewählte Reden und Vorträge.* Leipzig: S. Hirzel, 1886.

———. *The Results of Comparative Philology in Reference to Classical Scholarship.* Translated by F. H. Trithen. Oxford: Francis Macpherson, 1851.

———. *Zur Kritik der neuesten Sprachforschung.* Leipzig: S. Hirzel, 1885.

Deissmann, Gustav Adolf. *Bible Studies: Contributions Chiefly from Papyri and Inscriptions to the History of the Language, the Literature, and the Religion of Hellenistic Judaism and Primitive Christianity.* Translated by Alexander Grieve. Edinburgh: T&T Clark, 1901.

———. "Hellenistic Greek with Special Consideration of the Greek Bible." In *The Language of the New Testament: Classic Essays,* edited by Stanley Porter, 39–59. Sheffield: JSOT Press, 1991.

Delitzsch, Friedrich. *The Hebrew Language Viewed in light of Assyrian Research.* London: Williams and Norgate, 1883.

———. *Studien über indogermanisch-semitische Wurzelverwandtschaft.* Leipzig: J. C. Hinrichs'sche Buchhandlung, 1873.

Dorn, Bernhard. *Beiträge zur Geschichte der kaukasischen Länder.* Saint Petersburg: Royal Academy of Sciences, 1841–47.

———. *Beiträge zur Kenntnis der iranischen Sprache.* Saint Petersburg: Royal Academy of Sciences, 1860.

———. *Ueber die Verwandtschaft des persischen, germanischen und griechisch-*

lateinischen Sprachstammes. Hamburg: J. A. Meissner, 1827.

Ewald, Georg Heinrich August. "Abhandlung über den Zusammenhang des Nordischen (Türkischen), Mittelländischen, Semitischen und Koptischen Sprachstammes." In *Abhandlungen der königlichen Gesellschaft der Wissenschaften in Göttingen.* 10:3–80. Berlin, 1862.

———. *Abhandlung über die geschichtliche Folge der semitischen Sprachen.* Göttingen: Dieterische Buchhandlung, 1871.

———. *The History of Israel.* Translated by Russell Martineau. 8 vols. London: Longmans, Green, and Co., 1869.

———. "Plan dieser Zeitschrift." *Zeitschrift für die Kunde des Morgenlandes* 1 (1837), 1–13.

Fichte, Johann Gottlieb. *Reden an die deutsche Nation.* Berlin: Realschulbuchhandlung, 1808.

———. "Von der Sprachfähigkeit und dem Ursprunge der Sprache." In *Sämtliche Werke,* edited by I. H. Fichte, 8:83–222. Berlin: Veit, 1846.

Fick, August. *Wörterbuch der indogermanischen Grundsprache in ihrem Bestande von der Völkertrennung: Ein sprachgeschichtlicher Versuch.* Göttingen: Vandenhoeck & Ruprecht, 1868.

Foucault, Michel. "Nietzsche, Genealogy, History." In *The Foucault Reader,* edited by Paul Rabinow, 76–100. New York: Pantheon Books, 1984.

———. "The Order of Discourse." In *Language and Politics,* edited by Michael J. Shapiro, 108–38. New York: New York University Press, 1984.

———. *The Order of Things: An Archaeology of the Human Sciences.* Translated by R. D. Lang. New York: Pantheon Books, 1970.

———. "The Subject and Power." Afterword to *Michel Foucault: Beyond Structuralism and Hermeneutics,* edited by H. L. Dreyfus and Paul Rabinow, 208–28. Chicago: University of Chicago Press, 1982.

Frähn, Christian Martin. *Indications bibliographiques relatives pour la plupart à la littérature historico-géographique des Arabes, des Persans et des Turcs, spécialement destinées à nos employés et voyageurs en Asie.* Saint Petersburg: Académie impériale des sciences, 1845.

Frank, Othmar. *Das Licht vom Orient.* Leipzig: Besson, 1808.

Fürst, Julius. *Lehrgebäude der aramäischen Idiome mit Bezug auf die Indo-Germanischen Sprachen.* Leipzig: Karl Tachnitz, 1835.

Geiger, Lazarus. "Über die Ursitze der Indogermanen." In *Zur Entwicklungsgeschichte der Menschheit,* 113–50. Stuttgart: I. G. Cotta, 1878.

Gerber, Gustav. *Die Sprache als Kunst.* Hildesheim: Gerog Olms, 1961.

Germania: Neues Jahrbuch der Berlinischen Gesellschaft für deutsche Sprache und Altertumskunde. Edited by Friedrich Heinrich von der Hagen. 10 vols. Berlin: Hermann Schultze, 1836–1853. Reprint, Niederwalluf bei Wiesbaden: Dr. Martin Sändig, 1971.

Gesenius, Wilhelm. *Ausführliches grammatisch-kritisches Lehrgebäude der hebräischen Sprache mit Vergleichung der verwandten Dialekte*. Leipzig: Friedrich Christian Wilhelm Vogel, 1817.

———. *Geschichte der hebräischen Sprache und Schrift: Eine philologisch-historische Einleitung in die Sprachlehren und Wörterbücher der hebräischen Sprache*. Leipzig: Friedrich Christian Wilhelm Vogel, 1815.

———. *Hebräische Grammatik*. Edited by E. Kaustzsch. Leipzig: Friedrich Christian Wilhelm Vogel, 1896.

Gobineau, Arthur Comte de. *Essay on the Inequality of the Human Races*. Translated by Adrian Collins. New York: Howard Fertig, 1967.

Grimm, Jacob. *Deutsche Grammatik*. Edited by Wilhelm Scherer. 4 vols. Berlin: Ferdinand Dümmler, 1870.

———. *Deutsche Grammatik*. Vol. 1. 2nd ed. Göttingen: Dieterichsche Buchhandlung, 1822.

———. *Deutsche Mythologie*. 3 vols. Göttingen: Dieterichsche Buchhandlung, 1835. Reprint, Granz: Akademische Druck-und Verlagsanstalt, 1953.

———. *Deutsche Rechtsalterthümer*. 2 vols. Darmstadt: Wissenschaftliche Buchgesellschaft, 1955.

———. *Geschichte der deutschen Sprache*. 2 vols. Leipzig: Weidmannsche Buchhandlung, 1848.

———. *Kleinere Schriften*. 8 vols. Berlin: Ferdinand Dümmler, 1879–90.

———. *On the Origin of Language*. Translated by Raymond A. Wiley. Leiden: Brill, 1984.

Grimm, Jacob, and Wilhelm Grimm. *Deutsches Wörterbuch von Jacob und Wilhelm Grimm*. Munich: Deutscher Taschenbuch Verlag, 1984.

Grimm, Wilhelm. *Kleinere Schriften*. Edited by Gustav Hinrichs. 4 vols. Berlin: Ferdinand Dümmler, 1882–87.

———. *Über deutsche Runen*. Göttingen: Dieterichsche Buchhandlung, 1821.

Hagen, Friedrich Heinrich von der. "Ueber die Grundsätze der neuen Bearbeitung vom Liede der Nibelungen." *Eunomia: Eine Zeitschrift des 19. Jahrhunderts* 1 (1805): 254–65.

Hamann, Johann Georg. *Briefwechsel*. Edited by Walther Ziesemer and Arthur Henkel. Wiesbaden: Insel, 1955.

———. *Johann Georg Hamann's, des Magus in Norden, Leben und Schriften*. Edited by Karl Hermann Gildemeister. 6 vols. Gotha: F. A. Perthes, 1863–75.

———. *Sämtliche Werke*. Edited by Josef Nadler. 6 vols. Wuppertal: R. Brockhaus, 1999.

Hartmann, Eduard von. *Philosophie des Unbewussten*. Berlin: Carl Duncker, 1873.

Hegel, G. W. F. *Reason in History: A General Introduction to the Philosophy of History*. Translated by Robert S. Hartman. Englewood Cliffs, N.J.: Prentice, 1997.

Herder, Johann Gottfried. *Herders Sämtliche Werke*. Edited Bernhard Suphan. 33 vols. Berlin: G. Olms, 1967–68.

———. *On the Origin of Language: Two Essays*. Translated by Alexander Gode. Chicago: University of Chicago Press, 1966.

Hermann, Gottfried. *Acta Societitas Graecae*. Leipzig: C. H. Funkhänel, 1836–40.

———. *Ueber Herrn Professor Böckhs Behandlung der griechischen Inschriften*. Leipzig: Gerhard Fleischer, 1826.

Humboldt, Wilhelm von. *On Language: The Diversity of the Human Language-Structure and Its Influence on the Mental Development of Mankind*. Translated by Peter Heath. New York: Cambridge University Press, 1988.

———. *Über die Verschiedenheit des menschlichen Sprachbaues und ihren Einfluß auf die geistige Entwicklung des Menschlichengeschlechts*. Edited by Donatella Di Cesare. Munich: Ferdinand Schöningh, 1998.

———. *Werke in fünf Bänden*. Edited by Andreas Flitner and Klaus Giel. 5 vols. Berlin: Rütten & Loening, 1961.

———. *Wilhelm von Humboldts Werke*. Edited by Albert Leitzmann et al. 17 vols. Berlin: B. Behr, 1903–36.

Indische Bibliothek. Eine Zeitschrift von A. W. Schlegel. Bonn: Eduard Weber, 1823–24.

Jahn, Otto. *Gottfried Hermann: Eine Gedächtnissrede*. Leipzig: Weidmannsche Buchhandlung, 1849.

Jones, William. "The Third Anniversary Discourse on the Hindus." In *A Reader in Nineteenth-Century Historical Indo-European Linguistics*, edited by Winfred P. Lehmann, 7–20. Bloomington: Indiana University Press, 1967.

Kalthoff, Johann Heinrich. *Handbuch der hebräischen Altertümer*. Münster: Theissingsche Buchhandlung, 1840.

Kanne, Johann Arnold. *Über die Verwandtschaft der griechischen und teutschen Sprache*. Leipzig: Wilhelm Rein, 1804.

Kant, Immanuel. *Critique of Pure Reason*. Translated by Friedrich Max Müller. New York: MacMillan, 1907.

Klaproth, Heinrich Julius. *Abhandlung über die Sprache und Schrift der Uiguren*. Berlin, 1812.

———. *Asia Polyglotta*. Paris: J. M. Eberhart, 1823.

———. *Geographisch-historische Beschreibung des östlichen Kaukasus, zwischen den Flüssen Terek, Aragwi, Kur und dem Kaspischen Meere*. Wiemar: Landes-Industrie-Comptoir, 1814.

———. "Observations sur la critique faite par M. Sam Lee . . . , par M. le baron Silvestre de Sacy." *Nouveau Journal Asiatique* 5 (1830): 81–96,

241–56, 321–35.

———. *Reise in den Kaukasus und nach Georgien unternommen in den Jahren 1807 und 1808, auf Veranstaltung der kaiserlichen Akademie der Wissenschaften zu St. Petersburg.* 2 vols. Berlin, 1812–14. Reprint, Leipzig: Zentralantiquariat der DDR, 1970.

———. *Tableau historique, géographique, ethnographique et politique du Caucase et des provinces limitrophes entre la Russie et la Persie.* Paris: Ponthieu et C., 1827.

———. (Wilhelm Lauterbach). *Dr. William Schott's vergebliche Übersetzung des Confucius aus der Ursprache, eine litterarische Betrügerei.* Leipzig: Ponthieu, Michelson und Comp., 1828.

Kretzschmer, Johann Karl. *Friedrich Wilhelm III: Sein Leben, sein Wirken und seine Zeit: Ein Erinnerungsbuch für das preussische Volk.* Vol. 2. Danzig: Friedrich Samuel Gerhard, 1842.

Krüger, Karl Wilhelm. *Griechische Sprachlehre für Schulen.* Leipzig: R. W. Krüger, 1875.

Kuhn, Adalbert. "Die sprachvergleichung und die urgeschichte der indogermanischen völker." *Zeitschrift für vergleichende Sprachforschung auf dem Gebiete des Deutschen, Griechischen und Lateinischen* 4 (1855): 115–24.

Lassen, Christian. *Indische Altertumskunde.* 4 vols. Bonn: H. B. König, 1847.

———. "Über Herrn Professor Bopps grammatisches System der Sanskrit-Sprache." *Indische Bibliothek* 3 (1830): 1–113.

Lazarus, Moritz. "Einige synthetische Gedanken zur Völkerpsychologie." *Zeitschrift für Völkerpsychologie und Sprachwissenschaft* 3 (1865): 1–94.

———. *Die sittliche Berechtigung Preußens in Deutschland.* Berlin: Carl Schultze, 1850.

———. "Ueber den Begriff und die Möglichkeit einer Völkerpsychologie." In *Deutsches Museum: Zeitschrift für Literatur, Kunst und öffentliches Leben*, edited by Robert Prutz, 112–26. Leipzig: J. C. Hinrichs'sche Buchhandlung, 1851.

———. "Verdichtung des Denkens in der Geschichte: Ein Fragment." *Zeitschrift für Völkerpsychologie und Sprachwissenschaft* 2 (1862): 54–62.

———. *Was heißt national?* Berlin: Ferdinand Dümmler, 1880.

Lazarus, Moritz, and Heymann Steinthal. "Einleitende Gedanken über Völkerpsychologie, als Einladung zu einer Zeitschrift für Völkerpsychologie und Sprachwissenschaft." *Zeitschrift für Völkerpsychologie und Sprachwissenschaft* 1 (1860/61): 1–73.

Leibniz, Gottfried Wilhelm. *New Essays on Human Understanding.* Translated and edited by Peter Remnant and Jonathan Bennett. Cambridge: Cambridge University Press, 1996.

———. "Unvorgreiffliche Gedancken, betreffend die Ausübung und Verbesserung der Teutschen Sprache." In *History of Linguistics: Eigh-*

teenth- and Nineteenth-Century German Linguistics, edited by Christopher M. Hutton, 1:254–81 (London: Routledge, 1995.

Lévi-Strauss, Claude. *The Savage Mind.* Chicago: University of Chicago Press, 1962.

Link, Heinrich Friedrich. *Die Urwelt und das Altertum erläutert durch die Naturkunde.* 2 vols. Berlin: Ferdinand Dümmler, 1821–22.

———. *Die Urwelt und das Altertum erläutert durch die Naturkunde.* 2nd ed. Berlin: Ferdinand Dümmler, 1834.

Locke, John. *An Essay Concerning Human Understanding.* Edited by Peter H. Nidditch. Oxford: Clarendon Press, 1975.

Lohner, Edgar, ed. *Ludwig Tieck und die Brüder Schlegel.* Munich: Winkler, 1972.

Madvig, Johann Nicolai. *Sprachtheoretische Abhandlungen.* Edited by Karsten Friis Johansen. Copenhagen: Munksgaard, 1971.

Max Müller, Friedrich. *Biographies of Words and the Home of the Aryas.* London: Longmans, Green, and Co., 1887.

———. *Chips from a German Workshop.* 4 vols. London: Longmans, Green, and Co., 1867–75.

———. A *History of Ancient Sanskrit Literature.* London: Williams and Norgate, 1859.

———. *Lectures on the Science of Language.* London: Longmans, Green, and Co., 1866.

———. "On the Relation of the Bengali to the Arian and Aboriginal Languages of India." In *Report of the Seventeenth Meeting of the British Association for the Advancement of Science, 1947,* 319–50. London: John Murray, 1848.

———. *The Science of Thought.* London: Longmans, Green, and Co., 1887.

———. *Suggestions for the Assistance of Officers in Learning the Languages of the Seat of War in the East.* London: Longman, Brown, Green, & Longmans, 1854.

Meinecke, Friedrich. *Weltbürgertum und Nationalstaat: Studien zur Genesis des deutschen Nationalstaates.* Munich: Oldenbourg, 1911.

Meinhof, Carl. *Grundriß einer Lautlehre der Bantusprachen.* Berlin: D. Reimer, 1899.

———. *Grundzüge einer vergleichenden Grammatik der Bantusprachen.* Berlin: D. Reimer, 1906.

Michaelis, J. D. *A Dissertation on the Influence of Opinions on Language and of Language on Opinions.* New York: AMS Press, 1973.

Müller, Karl Otfried. *Die Dorier: Geschichte Hellenischer Stämme und Städte.* 2 vols. Graz: Akademische Druck-und Verlagsanstalt, 1969.

———. *Die Etrusker.* Edited by Wilhelm Deecke. 2 vols. Graz: Akademische Druck-und Verlagsanstalt, 1965.

———. *Geschichte der griechischen Literatur bis auf das Zeitalter Alexanders.* Edited by Eduard Müller. 2 vols. Breslau: Josef Max und Komp., 1841.

———. *Handbuch der Archäologie der Kunst.* Breslau: Josef Max und Komp., 1848.

———. *Kleine deutsche Schriften über Religion, Kunst, Sprache und Literatur, Leben und Geschichte des Alterthums.* Edited by Eduard Müller. 2 vols. New York: Georg Olms, 1979.

———. *Orchomenos und die Minyer: Geschichte Hellenischer Stämme und Städte.* Graz: Akademische Druck-und Verlagsanstalt, 1969.

———. *Prolegomena zu einer wissenschaftlichen Mythologie.* Göttingen: Kandenhoeck und Ruprecht, 1825.

Neumann, Carl Friedrich. *Asiatische Studien.* Leipzig: Johann Ambrosius Barth, 1837.

Nietzsche, Friedrich. *Beyond Good and Evil: Prelude to a Philosophy of the Future.* Translated by Judith Norman. Cambridge: Cambridge University Press, 2002.

———. *The Birth of Tragedy from the Spirit of Music.* Translated by Francis Golffing. New York: Anchor Books, 1956.

———. *Friedrich Nietzsche: Nachgelassene Fragmente, 1885–1887.* Vol. 12 of *Friedrich Nietzsche: Sämtliche Werke: Kritische Studienausgabe,* edited by Giorgio Colli and Mazzino Montinari. Munich: Deutscher Taschenbuch Verlag, 1988.

———. *Friedrich Nietzsche on Rhetoric and Language,* edited by Sander Gilman, C. Blair, and D. Parent. New York: Oxford University Press, 1989.

———. *Friedrich Nietzsche's Frühe Schriften.* Edited by Hans Joachim Mette, Karl Schlechta, and Carl Koch. Munich: C. H. Beck, 1994.

———. *The Genealogy of Morals.* Translated by Francis Golffing. New York: Anchor Books, 1956.

———. "On Music and Words" (1871). Translated by Walter Kaufmann. In *Between Romanticism and Modernism: Four Studies in the Music of the Later Nineteenth Century,* edited by Carl Dahlhaus, 106–19. Berkeley: University of California Press, 1980.

———. *Twilight of the Idols.* Translated by Duncan Large. Oxford: Oxford University Press, 1998.

Nouveaux Mémoires de l'Académie Royale des Sciences et Belle-Lettres (1770). Berlin: Chrétien Fréderic Voss, 1772.

Osthoff, Hermann. "Das physiologische und psychologische Moment in der sprachlichen Formenbildung." *Sammlung gemeinverständlicher wissenschaftlicher Vorträge von Virchow und von Holtzendorff* 327 (1879): 3–48.

———. *Das Verbum in der Nominalkomposition im Deutschen, Griechischen,*

Slavishen und Romanischen. Jena: H. Costenoble, 1878.

Osthoff, Hermann, and Karl Brugman. *Morphologische Untersuchungen auf dem Gebiete der indogermanischen Sprachen*. Vol. 1. Leipzig: S. Hirzel, 1878.

Ouvaroff, Sergei. "Projet d'une Académie asiatique." In *Études de philologie et de critique*, 1–48. 2nd ed. Paris: Didot Frères, 1845.

Paul, Hermann. *Principles of the History of Language*. Translated by H. A. Strong. College Park, Md.: McGrath, 1970.

———. *Prinzipien der Sprachgeschichte*. Halle: Max Niemeyer, 1880.

———. *Prinzipien der Sprachgeschichte*. 2nd ed. Halle: Max Niemeyer, 1886.

Passow, Franz. "Die griechische Sprache, nach ihrer Bedeutung in der Bildung deutscher Jugend." In *Archiv deutscher Nationalbildung*, edited by Reinhold Bernhard Jackmann and Franz Passow, 1:99–140. Berlin: Friedrich Maurer, 1812.

———. *Vermischte Schriften*. Edited by W. A. Passow. Leipzig: F. A. Brockhaus, 1843.

Pott, August Friedrich. *Anti-Kaulen oder Mythische Vorstellungen vom Ursprunge der Völker und Sprachen*. Lemgo: Meyer'sche Hofbuchhandlung, 1863.

———. *Einleitung in die allgemeine Sprachwissenschaft: Zur Literatur der Sprachkunde Europas*. Edited by E. F. K. Koerner. Amsterdam: John Benjamins, 1974.

———. *Etymologische Forschungen auf dem Gebiete der Indo-Germanischen Sprachen, mit besonderem Bezug auf die Lautumwandlung im Sanskrit, Griechischen, Lateinischen, Littauischen und Gothischen*. 2 vols. Lemgo: Meyersche Hof-Buchhandlung, 1833.

———. "Indogermanischer Sprachstamm." In *Allgemeine Encyklopädie der Wissenschaften und Künste*, edited by J. S. Ersch and J. G. Gruber, 2nd ser., sect. 18:1–112. Leipzig: J. F. Gleditsch, 1840.

———. "Researches into the Origin and Affinity of the Principal Languages of Asia and Europe. By Lieut. Colon. Vans Kennedy." *Jahrbücher für wissenschaftliche Kritik*, no. 8 (July 1832): 55–71.

———. *Die Ungleichheit menschlicher Rassen hauptsächlich vom sprachwissenschaftlichen Standpunkte, unter besonderer Berücksichtigung von des Grafen von Gobineau gleichnamigem Werke*. Lemgo: Meyer'sche Hofbuchhandlung, 1856.

———. *Wilhelm von Humboldt und die Sprachwissenschaft*. Berlin: S. Calvary, 1876.

———. *Die Zigeuner in Europa und Asien: Ethnographisch-linguistische Untersuchung vornehmlich ihrer Herkunft und Sprache*. 2 vols. Halle: Ed. Heynemann, 1844.

Prichard, James Cowles. "On the various methods of Research which contribute to the Advancement of Ethnology, and of the relations of that Science to other branches of Knowledge." In *Report of the British Association for the Advancement of Science,* 230–53. London: John Murray, 1848.

Quinet, Edgar. *Oeuvres complète de Edgard Quinet.* Vol. 1, *Le Génie des Religions.* Paris: Librairie Germer-Baillière, 1877.

Renan, Ernest. "Nouvelles Considérations sur le caractère general des peoples sémitique, et en particulier sur leur tendance au monotheism." *Journal Asiatique* (1859): 214–82, 417–50.

———. *Oeuvres Complètes de Ernest Renan.* Edited by Henriette Psichari. 7 vols. Paris: Calmann-Lévy, 1947–58.

Rothe, Richard. *Zur Dogmatik.* Gotha: Perthes, 1863.

Rousseau, Jean-Jacques. "Discourse on the Origin of Inequality among Men." In *The Essential Rousseau,* 203–30. Translated by Lowell Bair. New York: New American Library, 1975.

Saussure, Ferdinand de. *Course in General Linguistics.* Edited by Charles Bally and Albert Sechehaye, Translated by Wade Baskin. New York: McGraw-Hill, 1959.

———. "Souvenirs de F. de Saussure concernant sa jeunesse et ses études." *Cahiers Ferdinand de Saussure* 17 (1960): 12–25.

Scherer, Wilhelm. *Geschichte der deutschen Literatur.* Berlin: Thomas Knaur, 1883.

———. *Zur Geschichte der deutschen Sprache.* Edited by Kurt R. Jankowsky. Philadelphia: John Benjamins, 1995.

Schierbrand, Wolf von, ed. *The Kaiser's Speeches Forming a Character Portrait of Emperor Wilhelm II.* New York: Harper & Brothers, 1902.

Schlegel, August Wilhelm. "De l'origine des Hindous." In *Essais littéraires et historiques,* 441–518. Bonn: E. Weber, 1842.

———. "Miscellen." In *Europa: Eine Zeitschrift,* edited by Friedrich Schlegel, 2:193–204. Stuttgart: J. Cotta, 1963.

———. "Ueber den gegenwärtigen Zustand der Indischen Philologie. Geschrieben im Sommer 1819." *Indische Bibliothek* 1 (1820): 1–27.

Schlegel, Friedrich. *Kritische Ausgabe seiner Werke.* Edited by Ernest Behler. 22 vols. Munich: Verlag Ferdinand Schöningh, 1960.

———. "Über den Anfang unserer Geschichte und die letzte Revolution der Erde, als wahrscheinliche Wirkung eines Kometen. Von. J. G. Rhode." *Jahrbücher der Literatur* 8 (1819): 413–68.

———. *Über die Sprache und Weisheit der Indier: Ein Beitrag zur Begründung der Altertumskunde.* Heidelberg: Mohr und Zimmer, 1808. Reprint, Amsterdam: John Benjamins, 1977.

Schleicher, August. *Darwinism Tested by the Science of Language.* Translated by Alex Bikkers. London: J. C. Hotten, 1869.

———. *Die deutsche Sprache.* Wiesbaden: Martin Sändig, 1973.

———. "Die ersten Spaltungen des indogermanischen Urvolkes" *Kieler Allgemeine Monatsschrift für Wissenschaft und Literatur* (1853): 786–87.

———. "Eine Fabel in indogermanischer Ursprache." *Beiträge zur vergleichenden Sprachforschung auf dem Gebiete der arischen, celtischen und slawischen Sprachen* 5 (1868): 206–8.

———. "On the Significance of Language for the Natural History of Man." Translated by J. Peter Maher. In *Linguistics and Evolutionary Theory: Three Essays by August Schleicher, Ernst Haeckel, and Wilhelm Bleek,* edited by Konrad Koerner, 73–82. Philadelphia: John Benjamins, 1983.

———. *Sprachvergleichende Untersuchungen.* Frankfurt: Minerva, 1983.

Schlözer, August Ludwig. *Allgemeine nordische Geschichte.* Halle: Johann Justinus Gebauer, 1771.

———. *Vorstellung seiner Universal-Historie.* Gotha: Johann Christian Dieterich, 1772.

Schmeller, Johann Andreas. *Bayerisches Wörterbuch: Sammlung von Wörtern und Ausdrücken . . . mit urkundlichen Belegen.* 7 vols. Stutgart: J. G. Cotta, 1827–37.

———. *"Lauter gemähte Wiesen für die Reaktion": Die erste Hälfte des 19. Jahrhunderts in den Tagebüchern Johann Andreas Schmellers.* Edited by Reinhard Bauer and Ursula Münchhoff. Munich: Serie Piper, 1990.

———. *Die Mundarten Bayerns grammatisch dargestellt von J. A. Schmeller.* Munich: Karl Thienemann, 1821.

———. *Sogenanntes Cimbrisches Wörterbuch, das ist Deutsches Idiotikon der VII und VIII Communi in den Venetianischen Alpen,* edited by Joseph Bergmann. Vienna: Kaiserl.-Königl. Hof-und Staatsdruckerei, 1855.

———. "Über die sogenantnen Cimbern der VII und XIII Communen auf den Venedischen Alpen und ihre Sprache." *Abhandlungen der philosophische-philologischen Classe der königlichen bayerischen Akademie der Wissenschaften,* 2, no. 3 (1838): 557–708.

———. *Über Schrift und Schriftunterricht: Ein ABC-Büchlein in die Hände Lehrenden.* Edited by Hermann Barkey. Munich: Bayerische Akademie der Wissenschaften, 1965.

Schmidt, Isaac Jacob. *Forschungen im Gebiete der älteren religiösen, politischen und literärischen Bildungsgeschichte der Völker Mittel-Asiens, vorzüglich der Mongolen und Tibeter.* Leipzig: Zentralantiquariat der DDR, 1972.

———. *Grammatik der mongolischen Sprache.* Saint Petersburg: Kaiserliche Akademie der Wissenschaften, 1831.

———. *Grammatik der tibetischen Sprache.* Leipzig: Leopold Voss, 1839.

Schott, Wilhelm. *Chinesische Sprachlehre: Zum Gebrauche bei Vorlesungen und zur Selbstunterweisung.* Berlin: Ferdinand Dümmler, 1857.

———. *Über die sogenannten Indo-Chinesischen Sprachen insonderheit das*

Siamische. Berlin: Druckerei der königliche Akademie der Wissenschaften, 1856.

———, ed. *Werke des tschinesischen Weisen Kung-fu-dsu und seiner Schüler: Zum erstenmal aus der Ursprache ins Deutsche übersetzt und mit Anmerkungen begleitet.* 2 vols. Halle: Rengersche Verlagsbuchhandlung, 1826–32.

Stalder, Franz Josef. *Probe eines schweizerischen Idiotikons; hie und da mit etymologischen Bemerkungen untermischt.* 1805.

Steinthal, Heymann. *Abriss der Sprachwissenschaft.* Vol. 1 of *Einleitung in die Psychologie und Sprachwissenschaft.* Berlin: Ferdinand Dümmler, 1871.

———. *Die Classification der Sprachen, dargestellt als die Entwickelung der Sprachidee.* Berlin: Ferdinand Dümmler, 1850.

———. *Grammatik, Logik, und Psychologie: Ihre Principien und ihr Verhältniss zu Einander.* Berlin: Ferdinand Dümmler, 1855.

———. *Kleine Sprachtheoretische Schriften.* Edited by Waltraud Bumann. New York: Georg Olms, 1970.

———. *Die Mande-Neger-Sprachen: Psychologisch und Phonetisch Betrachtet.* Berlin: Ferdinand Dümmler, 1867.

———. *Der Ursprung der Sprache im Zusammenhange mit den letzten Fragen alles Wissens, Eine Darstellung, Kritik und Fortentwickelung der vorzüglichsten Ansichten.* Berlin: Ferdinand Dümmler, 1888.

———. "Zur Charakteristik der semitischen Völker." *Zeitschrift für Völkerpsychologie und Sprachwissenschaft* 1 (1860): 328–45.

Thiersch, Friedrich. *L'État actuel de la Grèce et des moyens d'arriver à sa restauration.* 2 vols. Leipzig: F. A. Brockhaus, 1833.

———. "Über die Sprache der Zakonen." In *Abhandlungen der Akademie der Wissenschaften.* Munich, 1835.

———. *Ueber die Epochen der bildenden Kunst unter den Griechen.* 2nd ed. Munich: Literarisch-artistische Anstalt, 1829.

Verhandlungen der Versammlungen deutscher Philologen und Schulmänner. 7 vols. Leipzig: Teubner, 1838–1844.

Verhandlungen der Versammlungen deutscher Philologen, Schulmänner und Orientalisten. Vols. 8–12. Leipzig: Teubner. 1847–1852.

Welcker, Friedrich Gottlieb. *Griechische Götterlehre.* 3 vols. Göttingen: Verlag der Dieterischen Buchhandlung, 1857–63.

———. *Kleine Schriften zur griechischen Literaturgeschichte.* 5 vols. Osnabrück: Otter Zeller, 1973.

———. *Von ständischer Verfassung und über Deutschlands Zukunft.* Karlsruhe: Christian Theodor Groos, 1831.

Whitney, William Dwight. *The Life and Growth of Language: An Outline of Linguistic Science.* New York: Dover Publications, 1979.

Winer, Georg Benedikt. *A Treatise on the Grammar of New Testament Greek:*

Regarded as a Sure Basis for New Testament Exegesis. Translated by W. F. Moulton. Edinburgh: T&T Clark, 1882.

Wolf, Friedrich August. *Allgemeine Grammatik als Grundlage des Unterrichts in jeder besonderen Sprache.* Görlitz: C. G. Anton, 1810.

———. "Darstellung der Alterthumswissenschaft." In *F. A. Wolf's Vorlesung über die Encyclopädie der Alterthumswissenschaft,* edited by J. D. Gürtler, 47–452. Leipzig: August Lehnhold, 1831.

———. "Einleitung in die Alterthumswissenschaft." In *F. A. Wolf's Vorlesung über die Encyclopädie der Alterthumswissenschaft,* edited by J. D. Gürtler, 1–46. Leipzig: August Lehnhold, 1831.

———. *Kleine Schriften in lateinischer und deutscher Sprache.* Edited by G. Bernhardy. 2 vols. Halle: Verlag der Buchhandlung des Waisenhauses, 1869.

Wüllner, Franz. *Über die Verwandtschaft des Indogermanischen, Semitischen und Tibetanischen.* Münster: Theissing, 1838.

Wundt, Wilhelm Max. *Völkerpsychologie: Eine Untersuchung der Entwicklungsgesetze von Sprache, Mythus und Sitte.* 2 vols. Leipzig: Wilhelm Engelmann, 1900–1909.

Zeitschrift der deutschen morgenländischen Gesellschaft. Leipzig: Brockhaus and Avenarius. 1847–67.

Zeitschrift für Völkerpsychologie und Sprachwissenschaft. Edited by Heymann Steinthal and Moritz Lazarus. 20 vols. 1860–1890.

Secondary Literature

Aarsleff, Hans. "The Berlin Academy under Frederick the Great." *History of the Human Sciences* 2 (1989): 193–207.

———. *From Locke to Saussure: Essays on the Study of Language and Intellectual History.* Minneapolis: University of Minnesota Press, 1982.

———. *The Study of Language in England, 1780–1860.* Princeton: Princeton University Press, 1967.

Abrams, M. H. *Natural Supernaturalism: Tradition and Revolution in Romantic Literature.* New York: W. W. Norton, 1971.

Ahlzweig, Claus. *Muttersprache—Vaterland: Die deutsche Nation und ihre Sprache.* Opladen: Westdeutscher Verlag, 1994.

Alter, Stephen. *Darwinism and the Linguistic Image: Language, Race, and Natural Theology in the Nineteenth Century.* Baltimore: Johns Hopkins University Press, 1999.

———. "William Dwight Whitney and the Science of Language." Ph.D. diss., University of Michigan, 1993.

Amsterdamska, Olga. *Schools of Thought: The Development of Linguistics from Bopp to Saussure.* Boston: D. Reidel, 1987.

Anderson, Benedict. *Imagined Communities: Reflections on the Origin and Spread of Nationalism.* London: Verso, 1983.

Appelgate, Celia. *A Nation of Provincials: The German Idea of Heimat.* Berkeley: University of California Press, 1990.

Arenhövel, Willmuth, and Christa Schreiber. *Berlin und die Antike: Aufsätze.* Berlin: H. Heenemann, 1979.

Arens, Hans. *Sprachwissenschaft: Der Gang ihrer Entwicklung von der Antike bis zur Gegenwart.* Munich: Karl Alber, 1955.

Armstrong, Isobel. *Language as Living Form in Nineteenth-Century Poetry.* Sussex: Harvester, 1982.

Asher, R. E., and J. M. Y. Simpson, eds. *The Encyclopedia of Language and Linguistics.* 10 vols. New York: Pergamon, 1994.

Aschheim, Steven E. *The Nietzsche Legacy in Germany, 1890–1990.* Berkeley: University of California Press, 1992.

Assmann, Aleida. *Arbeit am nationalen Gedächtnis: Eine kurze Geschichte der deutschen Bildungsidee.* Frankfurt: Campus, 1993.

Augstein, Hannah Franziska. "Aspects of Philology and Racial Theory in Nineteenth-Century Celticism—the Case of James Cowles Prichard." *Journal of European Studies* 28, no. 4 (1998): 355–71.

———. "Linguistics and Politics in the Early Nineteenth Century: James Cowles Prichard's Moral Philology." *History of European Ideas* 23, no. 1 (1997): 1–18.

Bahder, Karl von. *Die deutsche Philologie im Grundriß.* Paderborn: F. Schöningh, 1883.

Bahner, Werner, and Werner Neumann, eds. *Sprachwissenschaftliche Germanistik: Ihre Herausbildung und Begründung.* Berlin: Akademie-Verlag, 1985.

Bär, Jochen A. *Sprachreflexion der deutschen Frühromantik: Konzepte zwischen Universalpoesie und grammatischen Kosmopolitismus.* New York: Walter de Gruyter, 1999.

Bartels, Claudia. "Deutschunterricht ohne Deutschlehrer." In *Satzlehre-Denkschulung-Nationalsprache: Deutsche Schulgrammatik zwischen 1800 und 1850,* edited by Hans Dietrich Erlinger and Clemens Knobloch, 21–37. Münster: Nodus Publikationen, 1989.

Barth, Karl. *Protestant Theology in the Nineteenth Century: Its Background and History.* Valley Forge, Pa.: Judson Press, 1973.

Bassin, Mark. *Imperial Visions: Nationalism and Geographical Imagination in the Russian Far East, 1840–1865.* Cambridge University Press, 1999.

Baudler, Georg. *'Im Worte Sehen': Das Sprachdenken Johann Georg Hamanns.* Bonn: H. Bourvier u. Co, 1970.

Bayerische Staatsbibliothek. *Johann Andreas Schmeller, 1785–1852: Gedächtnisausstellung zum 200. Geburtsjahr.* Munich: R. Oldenbourg, 1985.

Becker, Bernhard. *Herder-Rezeption in Deutschland: Eine ideologiekritische Untersuchung*. Saint Ingbert: Werner J. Röhrig, 1987.

Behler, Ernst. "Die Sprachtheorie des frühen Nietzsche." In Borsche, Gerratana, and Venturelli, *"Centauren-Geburten" Wissenschaft, Kunst und Philosophie beim jungen Nietzsche*, 99–111. (New York: Walter de Gruyter, 1994.

Beiser, Frederick. *The Fate of Reason: German Philosophy from Kant to Fichte*. Cambridge, Mass.: Harvard University Press, 1987.

Belke, Ingrid, ed. *Moritz Lazarus und Heymann Steinthal: Die Begründer der Völkerpsychologie in ihren Briefen*. Tübingen: J. C. B. Mohr, 1983.

Belzyt, Leszek. *Sprachliche Minderheiten im preußischen Staat, 1815–1914: Die preußische Sprachenstatistik in Bearbeitung und Kommentar*. Marburg: Verlag Herder-Institut, 1998.

Benes, Brigit. *Wilhelm von Humboldt, Jacob Grimm, August Schleicher: Ein Vergleich ihrer Sprachauffassungen*. Winterthur: P. G. Keller, 1958.

Benfey, Theodor. *Geschichte der Sprachwissenschaft und orientalischen Philologie in Deutschland*. Munich: J. G. Cotta, 1869.

Berlin, Isaiah. *Three Critics of the Enlightenment: Vico, Hamann, Herder*. Edited by Henry Hardy. Princeton: Princeton University Press, 2000.

Berman, Antoine. *The Experience of the Foreign: Culture and Translation in Romantic Germany*. Translated by S. Heyvaert. Albany: State University of New York Press, 1992.

Bernal, Martin. *Black Athena: The Afroasiatic Roots of Classical Civilization*. 2 vols. New Brunswick, N.J.: Rutgers University Press, 1987.

Besch, Werner. "Dialekt, Schreibdialekt, Schriftsprache, Standardsprache: Exemplarische Skizze ihrer historischen Ausprägung im Deutschen." In *Dialektologie: Ein Handbuch zur deutschen und allgemeinen Dialketforschung*, edited by Werner Besch et al., 2:961–90. New York: Walter de Gruyter, 1983.

———. "Die Entstehung und Ausbreitung der neuhochdeutschen Schriftsprache/Standardsprache." In Besch, Reichmann, and Sonderegger, *Sprachgeschichte*, 2:1781–1809.

Besch, Werner, Oskar Reichman, and Stefan Sonderegger, eds. *Sprachgeschichte: Ein Handbuch zur Geschichte der deutschen Sprache und ihrer Erforschung*. 2 vols. Berlin: Walter de Gruyter, 1984–85.

Beyer, Arno. *Deutsche Einflüsse auf die englische Sprachwissenschaft im neunzehnten Jahrhundert*. Göppingen: Kümmerle, 1981.

Blok, Josine H. "Proof and Persuasion in *Black Athena I:* The Case of K. O. Müller." In "Black Athena: Ten Years After," edited by Wim M. J. van Binsbergen. *Talanta: Proceedings of the Dutch Archaeological and Historical Society* 28–29 (1996–97): 173–208.

Bohm, Arnd. "Herder and the Politics of Adamic Language." In *Herder*

Jahrbuch, edited by Karl Menger, Regine Otto, and Wulf Koepke, 21–31. Stuttgart: J. B. Metzler, 2000.

Borsche, Tilman, Federico Gerratana, and Aldo Venturelli, eds. *"Centauren-Geburten" Wissenschaft, Kunst und Philosophie beim jungen Nietzsche.* New York: Walter de Gruyter, 1994.

Borst, Arno. *Der Turmbau von Babel: Geschichte der Meinungen über Ursprung und Vielfalt der Sprachen und Völker.* Stuttgart: Anton Hiersemann, 1958–63.

Bouton, Charles P. *Neurolinguistics: Historical and Theoretical Perspectives.* Translated by Terence MacNamee. New York: Plenum, 1991.

Bright, William, ed. *International Encyclopedia of Linguistics.* 4 vols. New York: Oxford University Press, 1992.

Bromiley, Geoffrey W., ed. *The International Standard Bible Encyclopedia.* 4 vols. Grand Rapids, Mich.: W. B. Eerdmans, 1979–88.

Brown, Roger Langham. *Wilhelm von Humboldt's Conception of Linguistic Relativity.* The Hague: Mouton, 1967.

Brubaker, Rogers. *Citizenship and Nationhood in France and Germany.* Cambridge, Mass.: Harvard University Press, 1992.

Brunner, Richard. *J. A. Schmeller: Sprachwissenschaftler und Philologe.* Innsbruck: Institut für vergleichende Sprachwissenschaft, 1971.

Bumann, Waltraud. *Die Sprachtheorie Heymann Steinthals, dargestellt im Zusammenhang mit seiner Theorie der Geisteswissenschaften.* Meisenheim am Glan: Anton Hain, 1966.

Burrow, J. W. "The Uses of Philology in Victorian England." In *Ideas and Institutions of Victorian Britain,* edited by Robert Robson, 180–204. London: G. Bell & Sons, 1967.

Bursian, Conrad. *Geschichte der classischen Philologie in Deutschland von den Anfängen bis zur Gegenwart.* 2 vols. Leipzig: R. Oldenbourg, 1883.

Butler, E. M. *The Tyranny of Greece over Germany.* New York: Macmillan, 1935.

Calder, William M., ed. *Friedrich Gottlieb Welcker: Werk und Wirkung.* Stuttgart: Steiner-Verlag-Wiesbaden, 1986.

Calder, William M., and Daniel J. Kramer. *An Introductory Bibliography to the History of Classical Scholarship Chiefly in the XIXth and XXth Centuries.* New York: Georg Olms, 1992.

Cassirer, Ernst. *The Philosophy of Symbolic Forms.* Vol. 1, *Language.* New Haven: Yale University Press, 1953.

Chadbourne, Richard M. *Ernest Renan.* New York: Twayne, 1968.

Chaudhuri, Nirad C. *Scholar Extraordinary: The Life of Professor the Rt. Hon. Friedrich Max Müller, P.C.* London: Chatto & Windus, 1974.

Chickering, Roger. "Language and the Social Foundations of Radical Nationalism in the Wilhelmine Era." In *1870/71–1989/90: German Unifica-*

tions and the Change of Literary Discourse, edited by Walter Pape, 61–78. New York: Walter de Gruyter, 1993.

Christ, Karl. "Aspekte der Antike-Rezeption in der deutschen Altertumswissenschaft des 19. Jahrhunderts." In *Die Antike in Italien und Deutschland,* edited by Christ and Momigliano, 21–37.

Christ, Karl, and Arnaldo Momigliano, eds. *Die Antike im 19. Jahrhundert in Italien und Deutschland.* Berlin: Duncker & Humblot, 1988.

Clark, Christopher. "Germany: 1815–1848: Restoration or Pre-March." In *Nineteenth-Century Germany: Politics, Culture and Society 1780–1918,* edited by John Breuilly, 40–65. New York: Oxford University Press, 2000.

Cloeren, Hermann J. *Language and Thought: German Approaches to Analytic Philosophy in the Eighteenth and Nineteenth Centuries.* New York: Walter de Gruyter, 1988.

Coward, Rosalind, and John Ellis, *Language and Materialism: Developments in Semiology and the Theory of the Subject.* Boston: Routledge & Kegan Paul, 1977.

Cram, David, Andrew Linn, and Elke Nowak, eds. *History of Linguistics.* Vol. 2, *From Classical to Contemporary Linguistics.* Philadelphia: John Benjamins, 1999.

Crane, Susan A. *Collecting and the Historical Consciousness in Early Nineteenth-Century Germany.* Ithaca: Cornell University Press, 2000.

Crawford, Claudia. *The Beginnings of Nietzsche's Theory of Language.* New York: Walter de Gruyter, 1988.

Culler, Jonathan. *Saussure.* Hassocks, Sussex: Harvester Press, 1976.

———. *Structuralist Poetics: Structuralism, Linguistics and the Study of Literature.* Ithaca: Cornell University Press, 1975.

Darmesteter, James. *Essais Orientaux.* Paris: Librairie Centrale des Beaux-Arts, 1883.

Dascal, Marcelo, Dietfried Gerhardus, Kuno Lorenz, and Georg Meggle, eds. *Sprachphilosophie—Philosophy of Language—la philosophie du langue. Ein internationales Handbuch—An International Handbook of Contemporary Research—Manuel international des recherches Contemporaines.* 2 vols. Berlin: Walter de Gruyter, 1992.

Davidson, Arnold I. "Structures and Strategies of Discourse: Remarks Towards a History of Foucault's Philosophy of Language." In *Foucault and his Interlocutors,* ed. Arnold I. Davidson, 1–20. Chicago: University of Chicago Press, 1997.

Davies, Anna Morpurgo. "Saussure and Indo-European Linguistics." In *The Cambridge Companion to Saussure,* ed. Carol Sanders, 9–29. Cambridge University Press, 2004.

Davies, T. Witton. *Heinrich Ewald, Orientalist and Theologian 1803–1903: A*

Centenary Appreciation. London: T. Fisher, Unwin, 1903.

Delbrück, Berthold. *Einleitung in das Sprachstudium: Ein Beitrag zur Geschichte und Methodik der vergleichenden Sprachforschung*. Leipzig: Breitkopf und Hartel, 1880.

———. *Introduction to the Study of Language: A Critical Survey for the History and Methods of Comparative Grammar of the Indo-European Languages*. Translated by Eva Channing. London: Trübner, 1882.

Denecke, Ludwig. *Jacob Grimm und sein Bruder Wilhelm*. Suttgart: Metzler, 1971.

Dosse, François. *History of Structuralism*. Translated by Deborah Glassman. 2 vols. Minneapolis: University of Minnesota Press, 1997.

Dowling, Linda. *Language and Decadence in the Victorian Fin-de-Siècle*. Princeton: Princeton University Press, 1986.

Droixhe, Daniel, and Chantal Grell, eds. *La linguistique entre mythe et histoire: Actes de journées d'étude organisée les 4 et 5 juin 1991 à la Sorbonne en l'honneur de Hans Aarsleff*. Münster: Nodus, 1993.

Dünninger, Eberhard. "Heimat und Geschichte bei Johann Andreas Schmeller." In Eichinger and Naumann, *Johann Andreas Schmeller und der Beginn der Germanistik*, 197–208.

Dünninger, Joseph. "Geschichte der deutschen Philologie." In *Deutsche Philologie im Aufriß*, edited by Wolfgang Stammler, 1:301–41. Berlin: Erich Schmidt, 1952.

Eckardt, Georg, ed. *Völkerpsychologie—Versuch einer Neuentdeckung: Texte von Lazarus, Steinthal, und Wundt*. Weinheim: Psychologie Verlags Union, 1997.

Eco, Umberto. *The Search for the Perfect Language*. Translated by James Fentress. Cambridge, Mass.: Blackwell, 1995.

Eichinger, Ludwig M., and Bernd Naumann, eds. *Johann Andreas Schmeller und der Beginn der Germanistik*. Munich: R. Oldenbourg, 1988.

Eideneier, Hans. "Hellenen und Philhellenen." In *Griechen und Deutsche: Bilder vom Anderen. Württemburgisches Landesmuseum Stuttgart and Hessisches Landesmuseum Darmstadt*, edited by Kirsten Fast and Jan Peter Thorbecke, 63–75. Darmstadt: H. Anthes, 1982.

Ellis, John M. *One Fairy Story Too Many: The Brothers Grimm and Their Tales*. Chicago: University of Chicago Press, 1983.

Embleton, Sheila, John E. Josepf, and Hans-Josef Niederehe, eds. *The Emergence of the Modern Language Sciences: Studies on the Transition from Historical-Comparative to Structural Linguistics in Honour of E. F. K. Koerner*. Vol. 1, *Historiographical Perspectives*. Philadelphia: John Benjamins, 1999.

Erlinger, Hans Dietrich, and Clemens Knobloch, eds. *Muttersprachlicher Unterricht im neunzehnten Jahrhundert: Untersuchungen zu seiner*

Genese und Institutionalisierung. Tübingen: Max Niemeyer, 1991.

Eschbach, Achim, and Jürgen Trabant, eds. *History of Semiotics*. Amsterdam: John Benjamins, 1983.

Feldmann, Ronald. *Jacob Grimm und die Politik*. Kassel: Bärenreiter, 1971.

Flashar, Helmut. "Die methodisch-hermeneutischen Ansätze von Friedrich August Wolf und Friedrich Ast." In *Philologie und Hermeneutik im neunzehnten Jahrhundert,* edited by Flashar, Gründer, and Horstmann, 1:21–31.

Flashar, Helmut, Karfried Gründer, and Axel Horstmann, eds. *Philologie und Hermeneutik im neunzehnten Jahrhundert: Zur Geschichte und Methodologie der Geisteswissenschaften*. 2 vols. Göttingen: Vandenhoeck & Ruprecht, 1979.

Flemming, K. E. "*Orientalism,* the Balkans, and Balkan Historiography." *American Historical Review* 105, no. 4 (2000): 1218–33.

Formigari, Lia. "Idealism and Idealistic Trends in Linguistics and in the Philosophy of Language." In *Sprachtheorien der Neuzeit I: Der epistemologische Kontext neuzeitlicher Sprach-und Grammatiktheorien,* edited by Peter Schmitter, 230–53. Tübingen: Gunter Narr, 1999.

———. *Signs, Science and Politics: Philosophies of Language in Europe, 1700–1830*. Translated by William Dodd. Philadelphia: John Benjamins, 1993.

Freimark, Peter. "Language Behavior and Assimilation: The Situation of the Jews in Northern Germany in the First Half of the Nineteenth Century." *Yearbook of the Leo Baeck Institute* 24 (1979): 157–77.

Fuchs-Sumiyoshi, Andrea. *Orientalismus in der deutschen Literatur*. New York: Georg Olms, 1984.

Fuhrmann, Manfred. *Brechungen: Wirkungsgeschichtliche Studien zur antik-europäischen Bildungstradition*. Stuttgart: Klett-Cota, 1982.

Gajek, Bernhard. *Sprache beim jungen Hamann*. Bern: Herbert Lang, 1967.

Gambarara, Daniele, Stefano Gensini, and Antonio Pennisi, eds. *Language Philosophies and the Language Sciences: A Historical Perspective in Honor of Lia Formigari*. Münster: Nodus, 1996.

Gans, Rüdiger. "Erfahrungen mit dem Deutschunterricht: Eine Analyse autobiographischer Zeugnisse im Zusammenhang mit der Geschichte des Bildungsbürgertums im 19. Jahrhundert." In *Muttersprachlicher Unterricht im neunzehnten Jahrhundert: Untersuchungen zu seiner Genese und Institutionalisierung,* edited by Hans-Dieter Erlinger and Clemens Knoblauch, 9–60. Tübingen: Niemeyer, 1991.

Gardt, Andreas. *Geschichte der Sprachwissenschaft in Deutschland*. New York: Walter de Gruyter, 1999.

———, ed. *Nation und Sprache: Die Diskussion ihres Verhältnisses in Geschichte und Gegenwart*. New York: Walter de Gruyter, 2000.

Gawthrop, Richard L. *Pietism and the Making of Eighteenth-Century Prussia.* Cambridge University Press, 1993.

Geckler, Horst, Brigitte Schlieben-Lange, Jürgen Trabant, and Harald Weydt, eds. *Logos Semantikos: Studia Linguistica in Honorem Eugenio Coseriu, 1921–1981.* New York: Walter de Bruyter, 1981.

Gérard, René. *L'Orient et la pensée romantique allemande.* Paris: M. Didier, 1963.

Gerratana, Federico. "'Jetzt zieht mich das Allgemein-Menschliche an': Ein Streifzug durch Nietzsches Aufzeichnungen zu einer 'Geschichte der litterarischen Studien.'" In Borsche, Gerratana, and Venturelli, *"Centauren-Geburten" Wissenschaft, Kunst und Philosophie beim jungen Nietzsche,* 326–50. New York: Walter de Gruyter, 1994.

Giesen, Bernhard. *Intellectuals and the Nation: Collective Identity in a German Axial Age.* Translated by Nicholas Levis and Amos Weisz. Cambridge: Cambridge University Press, 1993.

Ginschel, Gunhild. *Der junge Jacob Grimm, 1805–1819.* Berlin: Akademie-Verlag, 1967.

Gipper, Helmut. "Sprachphilosophie in der Romantik." In Dascal et al., *Sprachphilosophie,* 1:197–233.

Gipper, Helmut, and Peter Schmitter. *Sprachwissenschaft und Sprachphilosophie im Zeitalter der Romantik.* Tübingen: Günther Narr, 1979.

Gollwitzer, Heinz. "Zum politischen Germanismus des neunzehnten Jahrhunderts." In *Festschrift für Hermann Heimpel zum 70. Geburtstag,* edited by Hermann Heimpel and Theodor Schieder, 1:282–356. Göttingen: Vandenhoeck & Ruprecht, 1971.

Gossman, Lionel. "History as Decipherment: Romantic Historiography and the Discovery of the Other." *New Literary History* 18 (1986): 23–57.

———. *Medievalism and the Ideologies of the Enlightenment: The World and Work of La Curne de Sainte-Palaye.* Baltimore: Johns Hopkins, 1968.

Gottzmann, Carola L. "Die altnordischen Studien und Publikationen von Wilhelm und Jacob Grimm zur Literatur, Sprache, Ur-und Frühgeschichte, Rechtsgeschichte, Geschichte und Runologie." *Brüder Grimm Gedenken* 7 (1987): 63–88.

Grafton, Anthony. *Defenders of the Text: The Traditions of Scholarship in an Age of Science, 1450–1800.* Cambridge, Mass.: Harvard University Press, 1991.

———. "Invention of Traditions and Traditions of Invention in Renaissance Europe: The Strange Case of Annius of Viterbo." In *The Transmission of Culture in Early Modern Europe,* edited by Anthony Grafton and Ann Blair, 8–38. Philadelphia: University of Pennsylvania Press, 1990.

———. "Polyhistor into Philolog: Notes on the Transformation of German Classical Scholarship, 1780–1850." *History of Universities* 3 (1983):

159–92.

Grafton, Anthony, and Lisa Jardine. *From Humanism to the Humanities: Education and the Liberal Arts in Fifteenth- and Sixteenth-Century Europe.* London: Duckworth, 1986.

Green, Abigail. *Fatherlands: State-Building and Nationhood in Nineteenth-Century Germany.* Cambridge: Cambridge University Press, 2001.

Greß, Franz. *Germanistik und Politik: Beiträge zu einer nationalen Wissenschaft.* Stuttgart: Frommann-Hozboog, 1971.

Gritsch, Eric W. "Luther and the State: Post-Reformation Ramifications." In *Luther and the Modern State in Germany: Sixteenth-Century Essays and Studies,* edited by James D. Tracy, 45–60. Kirksville, Mo.: Sixteenth Century Journal Publishers, 1986.

Grossman, Jeffrey. *The Discourse on Yiddish in Germany from the Enlightenment to the Second Empire.* Rochester, N.Y.: Camden House, 2000.

———. "Wilhelm von Humboldt's Linguistic Ideology: The Problem of Pluralism and the Absolute Difference of National Character—Or, Where Do the Jews Fit In?" *German Studies Review* 20, no. 1 (1997): 12.

Grunewald, Eckhard. *Friedrich Heinrich von der Hagen: Ein Beitrag zur Frühgeschichte der Germanistik.* Berlin: de Gruyter, 1988.

Haar, Michel. "Nietzsche und die Sprache." In *"Jedes Wort ist ein Vorteuil": Philologie und Philosophie in Nietzsches Denken,* edited by Manfred Riedel, 63–75. Cologne: Böhlau Verlag, 1999.

Haas, Walter. *Jacob Grimm und die deutschen Mundarten.* Stuttgart: Steiner, 1990.

Hagemann, Karen. "Of 'Manly Valor' and 'German Honor': Nation, War, and Masculinity in the Age of the Prussian Uprising against Napoleon." *Central European History* 30, no. 2 (1997): 187–220.

Halbfass, William. *India and Europe: An Essay in Philosophical Understanding.* Delhi: Motilal Banarsidass, 1988.

Harpham, Geoffrey Galt. *Language Alone: The Critical Fetish of Modernity.* New York: Routledge, 2002.

Harris, Roy. *Saussure and His Interpreters.* Edinburgh: Edinburgh University Press, 2003.

Harris, Roy, and Talbot J. Taylor. *Landmarks in Linguistic Thought: The Western Tradition from Socrates to Saussure.* New York: Routledge, 1989.

Hauger, Brigitte. *Johan Nicolai Madvig: The Language Theory of a Classical Philologist.* Münster: Nodus, 1994.

Hauser, Christoph. *Anfänge bürgerlicher Organisation: Philhellenismus und Frühliberalismus in Südwestdeutschland.* Göttingen: Vandenhoeck & Ruprecht, 1990.

Heath, Michael. Introduction to Wilhelm von Humboldt, *On Language: The Diversity of the Human Language-Structure and its Influence on the Men-*

tal Development of Mankind, vii–xxxiv. Translated by Peter Heath. New York: Cambridge University Press, 1988.

Heimpel, Hermann and Theodor Schieder, eds. *Festschrift für Hermann Heimpel zum 70. Geburtstag.* 2 vols. Göttingen: Vandenhoeck & Ruprecht, 1971.

Heinrich Hoffmann von Fallersleben: Wollen, Wirken, Werke. Wolfburg-Fallersleben: Hoffman von Fallersleben Gesellschaft, 1974.

Heinrich-Jost, Ingrid. *Anton Heinrich Hoffmann von Fallersleben.* Berlin: Stapp, 1982.

Helbig, Gerhard. *Geschichte der neueren Sprachwissenschaft: Unter dem besonderen Aspekt der Grammatik-Theorie.* Leipzig: VEB Bibliographisches Institut, 1973.

Hellerich, Siegmar. *Religionizing, Romanizing Romantics: The Catholico-Christian Camouflage of the Early German Romantics: Wackenroder, Tieck, Novalis, Friedrich and August Wilhelm Schlegel.* New York: Peter Lang, 1995.

Hentschke, Ada, and Ulrich Muhlack, *Einführung in die Geschichte der klassischen Philologie.* Darmstadt: Wissenschaftliche Buchgesellschaft, 1972.

Hermand, Jost. *Geschichte der Germanistik.* Reinbeck bei Hamburg: Rowohlt Taschenbuchverlag, 1994.

Hess, Jonathan. "Johann David Michaelis and the Colonial Imaginary: Orientalism and the Emergence of Radical Antisemitism in Eighteenth-Century Germany." *Jewish Social Studies* 6, no. 2 (2000):56–101.

Hewes, Gordon. "Disputes on the Origin of Language." In Dascal et al., *Sprachphilosophie,* 2:929–42.

Heyne, Arthur. *Orientalisches Datenbuch: Eine Sammlung von Geburts-und Todesdaten von Orientalisten seit den Anfangen der orientalistischen Sprachwissenschaft bis auf die Gegenwart.* Leipzig: O. Harrassowitz, 1912.

Hobsbawm, Eric J. *Nations and Nationalism since 1780: Programme, Myth, Reality.* Cambridge: Cambridge University Press, 1990.

Hödl, Hans Gerald. *Nietzsche's frühe Sprachkritik: Lektüren zu "Ueber Wahrheit und Lüge im aussermoralischen Sinne."* Vienna: WUV-Universitätsverlag, 1997.

Hoenigswald, Henry M., ed. *The European Background of American Linguistics.* Dordrecht, Holland: Foris, 1979.

———. "Historiography as Source: The Afterlife of Theodor Benfey." In *Lingua et traditio: Geschichte der Sprachwissenschaft und der neueren Philologien,* edited by Hans Helmut Christmann and Richard Baum, 423–28. Tübingen: Gunter Narr Verlag, 1994.

Hoenigswald, Henry M., and Linda F. Wiener. *Biological Metaphor and Cladistic Classification: An Interdisciplinary Perspective.* Philadelphia:

University of Pennsylvania Press, 1987.

Höppner, Wolfgang. *Das "Ererbte, Erlebte und Erlernte" im Werk Wilhelm Scherers: Ein Beitrag zur Geschichte der Germanistik.* Cologne: Böhlau, 1993.

Holub, Robert. *Heinrich Heine's Reception of German Grecophilia: The Function and Application of the Hellenic Tradition in the First Half of the Nineteenth Century.* Heidelberg: C. Winter, 1981.

Horstmann, Axel. "August Boeckh und die Antike-Rezeption im 19. Jahrhundert." In *Die Antike in Italien und Deutschland,* edited by Christ and Momigliano, 39–76.

Hoyt, David, and Karen Oslund, eds. *Language Study and the Politics of Community in Global Context.* New York: Rowland & Littlefield, 2006.

Huber, Wolfgang. *Kulturpatriotismus und Sprachbewußtsein: Studien zur deutschen Philologie des 17. Jahrhunderts.* New York: Peter Lang, 1984.

Hull, Isabel. *Sexuality, State, and Civil Society in Germany, 1700–1815.* Ithaca: Cornell University Press, 1996.

Hundt, Markus. *"Spracharbeit" im 17. Jahrhundert: Studien zu Georg Philipp Harsdörffer, Justus Georg Schottelius und Christian Gueintz.* New York: Walter de Gruyter, 2000.

Hutton, Christopher M., ed. *History of Linguistics: Eighteenth-and Nineteenth-Century German Linguistics.* 8 vols. London: Routledge, 1995.

———. *Linguistics and the Third Reich: Mother-Tongue Fascism, Race and the Science of Language.* New York: Routledge, 1999.

International Encyclopedia of Linguistics. Edited by William Bright. Vol. 2. New York: Oxford University Press, 1992.

Irmscher, Johannes. *Der Philhellenismus in Preußen als Forschungsanliegen.* Berlin: Akademie-Verlag, 1966.

Jäger, Georg. *Zur Geschichte des Deutschunterrichts an höheren Schulen von der Spätaufklärung bis zum Vormärz.* Stuttgart: Metzler, 1981.

Jameson, Frederic. *The Prison-House of Language: A Critical Account of Structuralism and Russian Formalism.* Princeton: Princeton University Press, 1972.

Jankowsky, Kurt R. Introduction to *Zur Geschichte der deutschen Sprache,* by Wilhelm Scherer, ix–xxiv. Philadelphia: John Benjamins, 1995.

———. "Development of Historical Linguistics from Rask and Grimm to the Neogrammarians." In *Sprachtheorien der Neuzeit II: Von der Grammaire de Port-Royal (1660) zur Konstitution moderner linguistischer Disziplinen,* edited by Peter Schmitter, 193–215. Tübingen: Gunter Narr, 1996.

Janota, Johannes, ed. *Eine Wissenschaft etabliert sich, 1810–1870: Texte zur Wissenschaftsgeschichte der Germanistik III.* Tübingen: Max Niemeyer, 1980.

Jay, Martin. "Should Intellectual History Take a Linguistic Turn? Reflections on the Habermas-Gademer Debate." In *Modern European Intellectual History: Reappraisals and New Perspectives,* edited by Dominick LaCapra and Steven L. Kaplan, 86–110. Ithaca: Cornell University Press, 1982.

Jeismann, Karl-Ernst. *Das preußische Gymnasium in Staat und Gesellschaft.* Vol. 2, *Höhere Bildung zwischen Reform und Reaktion, 1817–1859.* Stuttgart: Klett-Cotta, 1996.

Joseph, John E. "Language, Body, Race: From Aristotle and Epicurus to Descartes and Locke." Paper prepared for the Young Scholars' Summer Institute on the Concept of Language, Research Triangle Park, N.C., August 2003.

———. "Saussure's Meeting with Whitney, Berlin 1879." *Cahiers Ferdinand de Saussure* 42 (1988): 205–14.

Kabbani, Rana. *Europe's Myths of the Orient.* Bloomington: Indiana University Press, 1986.

Kalmar, Ivan. "The *Völkerpsychologie* of Lazarus and Steinthal and the Modern Concept of Culture." *Journal of History of Ideas* 48, no. 4 (1987): 671–90.

Kaschuba, Wolfgang. "Deutsche Bürgerlichkeit nach 1800. Kultur als symbolische Praxis." In *Bürgertum im 19. Jahrhundert,* edited by Jürgen Kocka, 2:92–127. Göttingen: Vandenhoeck & Ruprecht, 1995.

Katz, Jacob. *From Prejudice to Destruction: Anti-Semitism, 1700–1933.* Cambridge, Mass.: Harvard University Press, 1980.

Kekulé, Reinhard. *Das Leben Friedrich Gottlieb Welckers nach seinem eigenen Aufzeichnungen und Briefen.* Leipzig: Teubner, 1880.

Kibbee, Douglas. "The 'People' and Their Language in 19th-century French Linguistic Thought." In *The Emergence of the Modern Language Sciences: Studies on the Transition from Historical-Comparative to Structural Linguistics in Honour of E. F. K. Koerner,* edited by Sheila Embleton, Hans-Josef Niederehe, and John E. Joseph, 111–28. Philadelphia: John Benjamins, 1999.

———. "Théorie linguistique et droits humains linguistiques: perspectives tirées de l'histoire des communautés linguistiques en France." In *Divers-Cité,* electronic journal of the Université du Québec à Montréal (1998).

Kieffer, Bruce. *The Storm and Stress of Language: Linguistic Catastrophe in the Early Works of Goethe, Lenz, Klinger, and Schiller.* University Park: Pennsylvania State University Press, 1986.

Kilcher, Andreas. *Die Sprachtheorie des Kabbala als ästhetisches Paradigma: Die Konstruktion einer ästhetischen Kabbala seit der Frühen Neuzeit.* Stuttgart: Metzler, 1998.

Kim, Dae Kweon. *Sprachtheorie im 18. Jahrhundert.* Saint Ingbert: Röhrig, 2002.

Kipper, Rainer. *Der Germanenmythos im Deutschen Kaiserreich.* Göttingen: Vandenhoeck & Ruprecht, 2002.

Kirchner, Hans Martin. *Friedrich Thiersch: Ein liberaler Kulturpolitiker und Philhellene in Bayern.* Munich: Hieronymus, 1996.

Kitagawa, Joseph M., and John S. Strong. "Friedrich Max Müller." In *Nineteenth-Century Religious Thought in the West,* edited by Ninian Smart. 3:179–213. New York: Cambridge University Press, 1985.

"Klaproth." In *Encyclopaedia Britannica,* 8:104–6. 8th ed. 1857.

Klein, Wolf Peter. "Christliche Kabbala und Linguistik orientalischer Sprachen im 16. Jahrhundert: Das Beispiel von Guillaume Postel (1510–1581)." *Beiträge zur Geschichte der Sprachwissenschaft* 11 (2001): 1–26.

Knobloch, Clemens. *Geschichte der psychologischen Sprachauffassung in Deutschland von 1850 bis 1920.* Tübingen: Max Niemeyer, 1988.

———. *Volkhafte Sprachforschung: Studien zum Umbau der Sprachwissenschaft in Deutschland zwischen 1918 und 1945.* Tübingen: Max Nieymeyer, 2005.

Knoll, Elizabeth. "The Science of Language and the Evolution of Mind: Max Müller's Quarrel with Darwinism." *Journal of the History of the Behavioral Sciences* 22, no. 1 (1986): 3–22.

Kocka, Jürgen, ed. *Bürgertum im 19. Jahrhundert.* 3 vols. Göttingen: Vandenhoeck & Ruprecht, 1995.

———. "Das europäische Muster und der deutsche Fall." In Kocka, ed., *Bürgertum im 19. Jahrhundert,* 1:9–84.

Koechly, Hermann. *Gottfried Hermann zu seinem hundertjährigen Geburtstage.* Heidelberg: Carl Winter, 1874.

Koepke, Wulf, ed. *Johann Gottfried Herder: Innovator through the Ages.* Bonn: Vouvier Verlag Herbert Grundmann, 1982.

———, ed. *Johann Gottfried Herder: Language, History, and the Enlightenment.* Columbia, S.C.: Camden House, 1990.

Koerner, E. F. Konrad. *Ferdinand de Saussure: Origin and Development of His Linguistic Thought in Western Studies of Language.* Braunschweig: Friedrich Vieweg & Sohn, 1973.

———, ed. *Linguistics and Evolutionary Theory: Three Essays by August Schleicher, Ernst Haeckel, and Wilhelm Bleek.* Vol. 6 of *Amsterdam Classics in Linguistics, 1800–1925.* Philadelphia: John Benjamins, 1983.

———. *Practicing Linguistic Historiography.* Amsterdam: John Benjamins, 1989.

———. *Saussurean Studies/Études Saussuriennes.* Geneva: Editions Slatkine, 1988.

Kopperschmidt, Josef and Helmut Schanze, eds. *Nietzsche oder "Die Sprache ist Rhetorik."* Munich: Wilhelm Fink, 1994.

Koselleck, Reinhart. "Einleitung—Zur anthropologischen und semantischen

Strukture der Bildung." In *Bildungsbürgertum im 19. Jahrhundert,* edited by Reinhart Koselleck, 2:11–46. Stuttgart: Klett-Cotta, 1985.

Köstlin, Monika. *Im Frieden der Wissenschaft. Wilhelm Grimm als Philologe.* Stuttgart: M & P Verlag für Wissenschaft und Forschung, 1993.

Kroll, Wilhelm. *Geschichte der klassischen Philologie.* Berlin: Walter de Gruyter, 1919.

Kurzweil, Edith. *The Age of Structuralism: Lévi-Strauss to Foucault.* New York: Columbia University Press, 1980.

Landfester, Manfred. *Humanismus und Gesellschaft im 19. Jahrhundert. Untersuchungen zur politischen und gesellschaftlichen Bedeutung der humanistischen Bildung in Deutschland.* Darmstadt: Wissenschaftliche Buchgesellschaft, 1988.

Langewiesche, Dieter. *Nation, Nationalismus, Nationalstaat in Deutschland und Europa.* Munich: C. H. Beck, 2000.

Lauer, Bernhard. *Von Hessen nach Deutschland: Wissenschaft und Politik im Leben und Werk der Brüder Grimm.* Kassel: Weve & Weidemeyer, 1989.

La Vopa, Anthony. *Fichte: The Self and the Calling of Philosophy, 1762–1799.* Cambridge: Cambridge University Press, 2001.

———. "Specialists against Specialization: Hellenism as Professional Ideology in German Classical Studies." In *German Professions, 1800–1950,* edited by Geoffrey Cocks and Konrad Jarausch, 27–45. New York: Oxford University Press, 1990.

Law, Vivien. "Processes of Assimilation: European Grammars of Sanskrit in the Early Decades of the Nineteenth Century." In *La linguistique entre mythe et histoire,* edited by Daniel Droixhe, 250–61. Münster: Nodus-Publikation, 1993.

Layton, Susan. *Russian Literature and Empire: Conquest of the Caucasus from Pushkin to Tolstoy.* Cambridge: Cambridge University Press, 1994.

Lefmann, Salomon. *August Schleicher: Skizze.* Leipzig: B. G. Teubner, 1870.

———. *Franz Bopp: Sein Leben und seine Wissenschaft.* Vol. 1. Berlin: G. Reimer, 1891.

Lehmann, Kornelia. *Die Auseinandersetzung zwischen Wort-und Sachphilologie in der deutschen klassischen Altertumswissenschaft des neunzehnten Jahrhunderts.* Berlin: Humboldt Universität, 1964.

Lehmann, Reinhard G. *Friedrich Delitzsche und der Babel-Bibel-Streit.* Göttingen: Vandenhoeck & Ruprecht, 1994.

Leopold, Joan. *The Letter Liveth: The Life, Work, and Library of August Friedrich Pott (1802–1887).* Amsterdam: John Benjamins, 1983.

Levenson, Jon D. *The Hebrew Bible, the Old Testament, and Historical Criticism.* Louisville, Ky.: Westminster/John Knox Press, 1993.

Leventhal, Robert S. "The Emergence of Philological Discourse in the German States, 1770–1810." *Isis* 77 (1986): 243–60.

———. "Language Theory, the Institution of Philology, and the State: The Emergence of Philological Discourse, 1770–1810." In *Papers in the History of Linguistics: Studies in the History of the Language Sciences,* edited by Hans Aarsleff, Louis G. Kelly, and Hans-Josef Miedereke, 38:349–64. Amsterdam: John Benjamins, 1987.

Lincoln, Bruce. *Theorizing Myth: Narrative, Ideology, and Scholarship.* Chicago: University of Chicago Press, 1999.

Loewe, Hans. *Friedrich Thiersch, Ein Humanisten Leben.* Munich: Oldenbourg, 1913.

———. *Friedrich Thiersch und die griechische Frage.* Munich: Oldenbourg, 1913.

Lütt, Jürgen. "Einleitung." In "Utopie-Projektion-Gegenbild: Indien in Deutschland." Special issue, *Zeitschrift für Kulturaustasuch* 37, no. 3 (1987): 391–93.

Maas, Utz. "Die Entwicklung der deutschsprachigen Sprachwissenschaft von 1900 bis 1950: Zwischen Professionalisierung und Politisierung." *Zeitschrift für Germanistische Linguistik* 16 (1988): 253–90.

Malinovich, Nadia. "Orientalism and the Construction of Jewish Identity in France, 1900–1932." *Jewish Culture and History* 2, no. 1 (1999): 1–25.

Manchester, Martin L. *The Philosophical Foundations of Humboldt's Linguistic Doctrines.* Philadelphia: John Benjamins, 1985.

Mangold, Sabine. *Eine "weltbürgerliche Wissenschaft"—Die deutsche Orientalistik im 19. Jahrhundert.* Stuttgart: Franz Steiner, 2004.

Marchand, Suzanne L. *Down from Olympus: Archaeology and Philhellenism in Germany, 1750–1970.* Princeton: Princeton University Press, 1996.

———. "German Orientalism and the Decline of the West." *Proceedings of the American Philosophical Society* 145, no. 4 (2001): 465–73.

Markley, Robert. *Fallen Languages: Crises of Representation in Newtonian England, 1660–1740.* Ithaca: Cornell University Press, 1993.

Mauro, Tullio de and Lia Formigari, eds. *Leibniz, Humboldt, and the Origins of Comparativism.* Amsterdam: John Benjamins, 1990.

McGetchin, Douglas T., Peter K. J. Park, and Damodar SarDesai, eds. *Sanskrit and 'Orientalism': Indology and Comparative Linguistics in Germany, 1750–1958.* New Delhi: Manohar, 2004.

McNeely, Ian. *The Emancipation of Writing: German Civil Society in the Making, 1790s–1820s.* Berkeley: University of California Press, 2003.

Meillet, Antoine. "Ce que la linguistique doit aux savants allemands." In *Linguistique Historique et Lintuistique Générale,* 1:152–59. Paris: C. Klincksieck, 1951.

Mellor, Chauncy Jeffries. *Scholarly Purpose and National Purpose in Jacob Grimm's Work on the "Deutsches Wörterbuch."* Chicago: University of Chicago Press, 1972.

Menze, Clemens. *Wilhelm von Humboldt und Christian Gottlob Heyne*. Ratingen bei Düsseldorf: A. Henn, 1966.

Mertens, Volker, ed. *Grimms, die Germanistik, und die Gegenwart*. Vienna: Fassbaender, 1988.

Meves, Uwe. "Zum Institutionalisierungsprozeß der deutschen Philologie: Die Periode der Lehrstuhlerrichtung." In *Wissenschaftsgeschichte der Germanistik im 19. Jahrhundert*, edited by Jürgen Fohrmann and Wilhelm Voßkamp, 115–203. Stuttgart: J. B. Metzler, 1994.

———. "Zur Namesgebung 'Germanist.'" In *Wissenschaftsgeschichte der Germanistik im 19. Jahrhundert*, edited by Jürgen Fohrmann and Wilhelm Voßkamp, 25–47. Stuttgart: J. B. Metzler, 1994.

Miller, Robert L. *The Linguistic Relativity Principle and Humboldtian Ethnolinguistics*. The Hague: Mouton, 1968.

Mommsen, Wolfgang. *Bürgerliche Kultur und politische Ordnung: Künstler, Schriftsteller und Intellektuelle in der deutschen Geschichte, 1831–1933*. Frankfurt: Fischer Taschenbuch Verlag, 2000.

Mosse, George. *The Crisis of German Ideology: Intellectual Origins of the Third Reich*. New York: Grosset & Dunlap, 1964.

———. "Jewish Emancipation: Between *Bildung* and Respectability." In *The Jewish Response to German Culture: From the Enlightenment to the Second World War*, edited by Juduha Reinharz, 1–16. Hanover: University Press of New England, 1985.

———. *Toward the Final Solution: A History of European Racism*. New York: Howard Fertig, 1978.

Muhlack, Ulrich. "Zum Verhältnis von Klassischer Philologie und Geschichtswissenschaft im 19. Jahrhundert." In Flashar, Gründer, and Horstmann, *Philologie und Hermeneutik im neunzehnten Jahrhundert*, 1:225–39.

Müller, Daniel. *Wider die "Vernuft in der Sprache": Zum Verhältnis von Sprachkritik und Sprachpraxis im Schreiben Nietzsches*. Tübingen: Gunter Narr, 1995.

Müller, Jorg Jochen, ed. *Germanistik und deutsche Nation 1806–48: Zur Konstitution bürgerlichen Bewußtseins*. Stuttgart: J. B. Metzler, 1974.

Müller-Vollmer, Kurt. "Von der Poetik zur Linguistik—Wilhelm von Humboldt und der romantische Sprachbegriff." In *Universalismus und Wissenschaft im Werk und Wirken der Brüder Humboldt*, edited by Klaus Hammacher and John Pickering, 224–40. Frankfurt: Vittorio Klostermann, 1976.

Naumann, Bernd. "Heymann Steinthals Position in der Geschichte der Sprachwissenschaft." In *Germanistik und Deutschunterricht im Zeitalter der Technologie*, edited by N. Oellers, 1:58–65. Tübingen: Niemeyer, 1988.

Nerlich, Brigitte. *Change in Language: Whitney, Bréal, and Wegener.* New York: Routledge, 1990.

Neufeldt, Ronald W. *F. Max Müller and the Rg-Veda: A Study of Its Role in His Work and Thought.* Calcutta: Minerva Associates, 1980.

Neumann, Friedrich. *Studien zur Geschichte der deutschen Philologie.* Berlin: Erich Schmidt, 1971.

Neumann, Günter. *Indogermanische Sprachwissenschaft 1816 und 1966.* Innsbruck: Sprachwissenschaftliches Institut der Leopold-Franzens-Universität, 1967.

Niedereke, Josef, and Konrad Koerner, eds. *History and Historiography of Linguistics: Papers from the Fourth International Conference of the Language Sciences.* 2 Vols. Amsterdam: John Benjamins, 1990.

Nielsen, Hans Frede. "Jacob Grimm and the 'German' Dialects." In *The Grimm Brothers and the Germanic Past,* edited by Elmer H. Antonsen, 25–32. Philadelphia: John Benjamins, 1990.

Noble, Richard. *Language, Subjectivity, and Freedom in Rousseau's Moral Philosophy.* New York: Garland, 1991.

Norton, Robert E. *Herder's Aesthetics and the European Enlightenment.* Ithaca: Cornell University Press, 1991.

O'Boyle, Lenore. "Klassische Bildung und soziale Struktur in Deutschland zwischen 1800 und 1848." *Historische Zeitschrift* 207 (1968): 584–608.

O'Flaherty, James. *Johann Georg Hamann.* Boston: Twayne, 1979.

———. *The Quarrel of Reason with Itself: Essays on Hamann, Michaelis, Lessing, Nietzsche.* Columbia, S.C.: Camden House, 1988.

———. *Unity and Language: A Study in the Philosophy of Johann Georg Hamann.* Chapel Hill: University of North Carolina Press, 1952.

Olender, Maurice. *The Languages of Paradise: Race, Religion, and Philology in the Nineteenth Century.* Translated by Arthur Goldhammer. Cambridge, Mass.: Harvard University Press, 1992.

Osterhammel, Jürgen. *Die Entzauberung Asiens: Europa und die asiatischen Reiche im 18. Jahrhundert.* Munich: C. H. Beck, 1998.

Otis, Laura. *Organic Memory: History and the Body in the Late Nineteenth and Early Twentieth Centuries.* Lincoln: University of Nebraska Press, 1994.

Park, Peter K. J. "A Catholic Apologist in a Pantheistic World: New Approaches to Friedrich Schlegel." In McGetchin, Park, and SarDesai, *Sanskrit and "Orientalism,"* 83–106.

———. "Return to Enlightenment: Franz Bopp's Reformation of Comparative Grammar." In *Language Study and the Politics of Community in Global Context,* edited by David Hoyt and Karen Oslund, 61–84. New York: Rowland & Littlefield, 2006.

Paul, Hermann, ed. *Grundriß der Germanischen Philologie.* Vol. 1. Strassburg: Karl J. Trübner, 1901.

Pedersen, Holger. *Linguistic Science in the Nineteenth Century: Methods and Results.* Translated by John Webster Spargo. Cambridge, Mass.: Harvard University Press, 1931.

Peppard, Murray B. *Paths through the Forest: A Biography of the Brothers Grimm.* New York: Holt, Rinehart and Winston, 1971.

Perconti, Pietro. *Kantian Linguistics: Theories of Mental Representation and the Linguistic Transformation of Kantism.* Münster: Nodus, 1999.

Petri, Manfred. *Die Urvolkhypothese: Ein Beitrag zum Geschichtsdenken der Spätaufklärung und des deutschen Idealismus.* Berlin: Duncker & Humblot, 1990.

Poliakov, Léon. *The Aryan Myth: A History of Racist and Nationalist Ideas in Europe.* Translated by E. Howard. London: Chatto & Heinemann for Sussex University Press, 1974.

Pollack, Sheldon. "Deep Orientalism? Notes on Sanskrit and Power beyond the Raj." In *Orientalism and the Postcolonial Predicament,* edited by Carol A. Breckenridge and Peter van der Veer, 76–133. Philadelphia: University of Pennsylvania Press, 1993.

Pommier, Jean. *La Jeunesse cléricale d'Ernest Renan.* Paris: Les Belles Lettres, 1933.

Porter, James I. *Nietzsche and the Philology of the Future.* Stanford: Stanford University Press, 2000.

Porter, Stanley E. *The Language of the New Testament: Classic Essays.* Sheffield: Sheffield Academic Press, 1991.

Pozorny, Reinhold. *Hoffmann von Fallersleben: Ein Lebens-und Zeitbild.* Berg: Türmer, 1982.

Pugach, Sara. "Afrikanistik and Colonial Knowledge: Carl Meinhof, the Missionary Impulse, and African Language and Culture Studies in Germany, 1887–1919." Ph.D. Diss., University of Chicago, 2001.

———. "Carl Meinhof and the German Influence on Nicholas van Warmelo's Ethnographic and Linguistic Writing, 1927–35." *Journal of Southern African Studies* 30, no. 4 (2004): 825–45.

Puschner, Uwe. *Die völkische Bewegung im wilhelminischen Kaiserreich: Sprache, Rasse, Religion.* Darmstadt: Wissenschaftliche Buchgesellschaft, 2001.

Raumer, Rudolf von. *Geschichte der germanischen Philologie vorzugsweise in Deutschland.* Munich: R. Oldenbourg, 1870.

Reill, Peter Hans. *The German Enlightenment and the Rise of Historicism.* Berkeley: University of California Press, 1975.

Richter, Joachim. B. *Hans Ferdinand Maßmann: Altdeutscher Patriotismus im neunzehnten Jahrhundert.* Berlin: Walter de Gruyter, 1992.

Ricken, Ulrich. *Linguistics, Anthropology, and Philosophy in the French Enlightenment.* Translated by Robert E. Norton. New York: Routledge, 1994.

———. "Sprachtheoretische und weltanschauliche Rezeption der Aufklärung bei August Friedrich Pott (1802–1887) *History and Historiography of Linguistics,* edited by Hans-Josef Niederehe and Konrad Koerner. 2:619–32. Philadelphia: John Benjamins, 1990.

Riedel, Manfred, ed. *"Jedes Wort ist ein Vorurteil": Philologie und Philosophie in Nietzsches Denken.* Cologne: Böhlau, 1999.

Rimmele, Eva. *Sprachenpolitik im Deutschen Kaiserreich vor 1914: Regierungspolitik und veröffentlichte Meinung in Elsaß-Lothringen und den östlichen Provinzen Preußens.* Frankfurt: Peter Lang, 1996.

Robertson, Ritchie. "*'Urheimat Asien'*: The Re-Orientation of German and Austrian Jews, 1900–1925." *German Life and Letters* 49, no. 2 (1996): 182–92.

Robins, R. H. *A Short History of Linguistics.* New York: Longman, 1990.

Rockinger, Ludwig. *An der Wiege der bayerischen Mundart-Grammatik und des bayerischen Wörterbuches.* Aalen: Scientia, 1985.

Rogerson, John William. *Old Testament Criticism in the Nineteenth Century.* London: Society for Promoting Christian Knowledge, 1985.

Römer, Ruth. *Sprachwissenschaft und Rassenideologie in Deutschland.* Munich: Wilhelm Fink, 1985.

Rosenfeld, Sophia. *A Revolution in Language: The Problem of Signs in Late Eighteenth-Century France.* Stanford: Stanford University Press, 2001.

Rüegg, Walter. "Die Antike als Begründung des deutschen Nationalbewußtseins." In *Antike in der Moderne,* edited by Wolfgang Schuller, 261–87. Constance: Universitätsverlag Konstanz, 1985.

Said, Edward. *Orientalism.* New York: Vintage Books, 1978.

St. Clair, William. *That Greece Might Still Be Free: The Philhellenes in the War of Independence.* New York: Oxford Unviersity Press, 1972.

Sandys, John Edwin. *A History of Classical Scholarship.* Vol. 3. New York: Hafner, 1958.

Scharf, Hans-Werner. *Wilhelm von Humboldts Sprachdenken.* Essen: Reimar Hobbing, 1989.

Schemann, Ludwig. *Gobineaus Rassenwerk: Aktenstücke und Betrachtungen zur Geschichte und Kritik des Essai sur l'enégalité des races humaines.* Stuttgart: Fr. Fromann, 1910.

Scheuerer, Franz Xaver. *Zum philologischen Werk Johann Andreas Schmellers und seiner wissenschaftlichen Rezeption: Eine Studie zur Wissenschaftsgeschichte der Germanistik.* New York: Walter de Gruyter, 1995.

Schlieben-Lange, Brigitte. *Idéologie: Zur Rolle der Kategorisierungen im Wissenschaftsprozess.* Heidelberg: C. Winter, 2000.

———. "Überlegungen zur Sprachwissenschaftsgeschichtsschreibung." In *Europäische Sprachwissenschaft um 1800: Methodologische und historiographische Beiträge zum Umkreis der "idéologie,"* edited by Brigitte

Schlieben-Lange, Hans-Dieter Dräxler, Franz-Josef Knapstein, Elisabeth Bolck-Duffy, and Isabel Zollna, 11–24. Münster: Nodus, 1989.

Schmidt, Siegfried J. *Sprache und Denken als sprachphilosophischs Problem von Locke bis Wittgenstein*. The Hague: Martinus Nijhoff, 1968.

Schneider, Rolf. *Der Einfluß von Justus Georg Schottelius auf die deutschsprachige Lexikographie des 17./18. Jahrhunderts*. New York: Peter Lang, 1995.

Schorsch, Ismar. *From Text to Context: The Turn to History in Modern Judaism*. Hanover: University Press of New England, 1994.

Schrader, Otto. *Sprachvergleichung und Urgeschichte: Linguistisch-historische Beiträge zu Erforschung des indogermanischen Altertums*. Jena: Hermann Costenoble, 1906.

Schrift, Alan D. *Nietzsche's French Legacy: A Genealogy of Poststructuralism*. New York: Routledge, 1995.

Schütte, Hans-Wilhelm. *Die Asienwissenschaften in Deutschland: Geschichte, Stand und Perspektiven*. Hamburg: IFA, 2004.

Schwab, Raymond. *The Oriental Renaissance: Europe's Rediscovery of India and the East 1680–1880*. Translated by Gene Patterson-Black and Victor Reinking. New York: Columbia University Press, 1984.

See, Klaus von. *Barbar, Germane, Arier: Die Suche nach der Identität der Deutschen*. Heidelberg: Carl Winter, 1994.

———. *Deutsche Germanen-Ideologie vom Humanismus bis zur Gegenwart*. Frankfurt: Athenäum, 1970.

Seidl, Wolf. *Bayern in Griechenland: Die Geburt des griechischen Nationalstaats und die Regierung König Ottos*. Munich: Prestel, 1981.

Sengupta, Indra. *From Salon to Discipline: State, University and Indology in Germany, 1821–1914*. Heidelberg: Ergon, 2005.

Sheehan, James J. "What Is German History? Reflections on the Role of the Nation." *Journal of Modern History* 53 (1981): 1–23.

Sheehan, Jonathan. *The Enlightenment Bible: Translation, Scholarship, Culture*. Princeton: Princeton University Press, 2005.

Shuger, Debora Kuller. *The Renaissance Bible: Scholarship, Sacrifice, and Subjectivity*. Berkeley: University of California Press, 1994.

Sieferle, Rolf Peter. "Indien und die Arier in der Rassentheorie." *Zeitschrift für Kulturaustausch* 37 (1987): 444–67.

Siegert, Hans. "Zur Geschichte der Begriffe 'Arier' and 'arisch.'" *Wörter und Sachen: Zeitschrift für indogermanische Sprachverwandtschaft, Volksforschung und Kulturgeschichte* n.s. 4 (1941–42): 73–99.

Skinner, Quentin. "Moral Ambiguity and the Art of Persuasion in the Renaissance." In *Proof and Persuasion: Essays on Authority, Objectivity, and Evidence*, edited by Suzanne Marchand and Elizabeth Lunbeck, 25–41. Turnout: Brepols, 1996.

Smith, Olivia. *The Politics of Language, 1791–1819.* New York: Oxford University Press, 1984.

Smart, Sara. "Justus Georg Schottelius and the Patriotic Movement." *Modern Language Review* 84 (1989): 83–98.

Sonderegger, Stefan. "Zu Grimmelshausens Bedeutung für die deutsche Sprachgeschichte." In *Wahrheit und Wort: Festschrift für Rolf Tarot zum 65. Geburtstag,* edited by Gabriela Scherer and Beatrice Wehrli, 427–35. Berlin: Peter Lang, 1996.

Sorkin, David. *The Transformation of German Jewry, 1780–1840.* New York: Oxford University Press, 1987.

Stache-Rosen, Valentina. *German Indologists: Biographies of Scholars in Indian Studies writing in German.* New Delhi: Max Müller Bhavar, 1990.

Stagl, Justin. "August Ludwig Schlözers Entwurf einer 'Völkerkunde' oder 'Ethnographie seit 1772.'" *Ethnologische Zeitschrift Zurich* 2 (1974): 73–91.

Stam, James. *On the Origin of Language: The Fate of a Question.* New York: Harper & Row, 1976.

Steiner, George. *After Babel: Aspects of Language and Translation.* New York: Oxford University Press, 1975.

Sternsdorff, Jürgen. *Wissenschaftskonstitution und Reichsgründung: Die Entwicklung der Germanistik bei Wilhelm Scherer: Eine Biographie nach unveröffentlichen Quellen.* Frankfurt: Peter Lang, 1979.

Stetter, Christian. "'Über Denken und Sprechen': Wilhelm von Humboldt zwischen Fichte und Herder." In *Wilhelm von Humboldts Sprachdenken: Symposium zum 150. Todestag,* edited by Hans-Werner Scharf, 25–46. Essen: Reimar Hobbig, 1989.

Stocking, George. *Victorian Anthropology.* New York: Free Press, 1987.

Stoeffler, F. Ernest. *German Pietism during the Eighteenth Century.* Leiden: Brill, 1973.

Stoianovich, Traian. *Balkan Worlds: The First and Last Europe.* Armonk, N.Y.: M. E. Sharpe, 1994.

Stubbs, Elsina. *Wilhelm von Humboldt's Philosophy of Language: Its Sources and Influence.* Lewiston: Edwin Mellen, 2002.

Surber, Jere Paul. *Language and German Idealism: Fichte's Linguistic Philosophy.* Amherst, NY: Humanity Books, 1996.

———, ed. *Metacritique: The Linguistic Assault on German Idealism.* Amherst, N.Y.: Humanity Books, 2001.

Sutcliffe, Patricia Casey. "Friedrich Max Müller and Dwight Whitney as Exporters of Nineteenth-Century German Philology: A Sociological Analysis of the Development of Linguistic Theory." PhD diss. University of Texas, Austin, 2000.

Sweet, Paul R. *Wilhelm von Humboldt: A Biography.* Vol. 1, 1767–1808.

Columbus: Ohio State University Press, 1978.

———. "Wilhelm von Humboldt, Fichte, and the Idéologues (1794–1805): A Re-Examination." *Historiographia Linguistica* 15, no. 3 (1988): 349–75.

Taylor, Charles. *Hegel.* London: Cambridge University Press, 1978.

———. *Human Agency and Language.* London: Cambridge University Press, 1985.

Taylor, Talbot J. *Mutual Misunderstanding: Skepticism and the Theorizing of Language and Interpretation.* Durham: Duke University Press, 1992.

Terrall, Mary. *The Man Who Flattened the Earth: Maupertuis and the Sciences in the Enlightenment.* Chicago: University of Chicago Press, 2002.

Thiersch, Heinrich. *Friedrich Thiersch's Leben.* 2 vols. Leipzig: Winter, 1866.

Thomas, R. Hinton. *Liberalism, Nationalism, and the German Intellectuals (1822–1847): An Analysis of the Academic and Scientific Conferences of the Period.* Cambridge: W. Heffer, 1951.

Thomsen, Vilhelm. *Geschichte der Sprachwissenschaft bis zum Ausgang des 19. Jahrhunderts: Kurzgefasste Darstellung der Hauptpunkte.* Translated by Hans Pollack. Halle: M. Niemeyer, 1927.

Timpanaro, Sebastiano. *The Genesis of Lachmann's Method.* Edited and translated by Glenn W. Most. Chicago: University of Chicago Press, 2005.

Toews, John Edward. *Becoming Historical: Cultural Reformation and Public Memory in Early Nineteenth-Century Berlin.* Cambridge: Cambridge University Press, 2004.

Toury, Jacob. "Die Sprache als Problem der jüdischen Einordnung in den deutschen Kulturraum." In *Gegenseitige Einflüsse deutscher und jüdischer Kultur von der Epoche der Aufklärung bis zur Weimarer Republik,* edited by Walter Grab, 75–96. Tel Aviv: Nateev-Printing and Publishing, 1982.

Townson, Michael. *Mother-Tongue and Fatherland: Language and Politics in Germany.* New York: Manchester University Press, 1992.

Trabant, Jürgen. "How Relativistic are Humboldt's 'Weltansichten?'" In *Explorations in Linguistic Relativity,* edited by Marin Pütz and Marjolijn Verspoor, 25–44. Philadelphia: John Benjamins, 2000.

———. "Inner Bleating. Cognition and Communication in the Language of Origin Discussion." In *Herder Jahrbuch,* edited by Karl Menges, Regine Otto, and Wulf Koepke, 1–19. Stuttgart: J. B. Metzler, 2000.

Trask, R. L. *Historical Linguistics.* New York: St. Martin's Press, 1996.

Trautmann, Thomas. *Aryans and British India.* Berkeley: University of California Press, 1997.

Turner, R. Steven. "The Growth of Professional Research in Prussia, 1818 to 1848: Causes and Context." *Historical Studies in the Physical Sciences* 3 (1971): 137–82.

———. "Historicism, *Kritik,* and the Prussian Professoriate, 1790–1840." In

Philologie und Hermeneutik im neunzehnten Jahrhundert, edited by Flashar, Gründer, and Horstmann, 2:450–89.

Tzoref-Ashkenazi, Chen. "The Nationalist Aspect of Friedrich Schlegel's On the Language and Wisdom of the Indians." In McGetchin, Park, and SarDesai, *Sanskrit and "Orientalism,"* 107–30. New Delhi: Manohar, 2004.

Vermeulen, Han F. "Frühe Geschichte der Völkerkunde oder Ethnographie in Deutschland, 1771–1791." In *Völkerkunde Tagung 1991,* edited by Mattias S. Laubscher and Bertram Turner, 1:327–44. Munich: Akademischer Verlag München, 1994.

Vick, Brian. *Defining Germany: The 1848 Frankfurt Parliamentarians and National Identity.* Cambridge, Mass.: Harvard University Press, 2002.

Villers, Jürgen. *Kant und das Problem der Sprache: Die historischen und systematischen Gründe für die Sprachlosigkeit der Transzendentalphilosophie.* Constance: Verlag am Hockgraben, 1997.

Vogt, Ernest. "Der Methodenstreit zwischen Hermann und Böckh." In *Philologie und Hermeneutik im neunzehnten Jahrhundert: Zur Geschichte und Methodologie der Geisteswissenschaften II,* edited by Mayotte Bollack and Heinz Wismann, 103–21. Göttingen: Vandenhoeck and Ruprecht, 1983.

Walravens, Hartmut. *Julius Klaproth (1783–1835): Briefe und Dokumente.* Wiesbaden: Harrossowitz, 1999.

———. *Julius Klaproth: Leben und Werk.* Wiesbaden: Harrossowitz, 1999.

———. *Wilhelm Schott (1802–1889): Leben und Wirken des Orientalisten.* Wiesbaden: Harrassowitz, 2001.

Wardman, H. W. *Ernest Renan: A Critical Biography.* London: Athlone Press, 1964.

Weisgerber, Leo. "Sprachwissenschaft als lebendige Kraft unserer Zeit." In *Zur Grundlegung der ganzheitlichen Sprachauffassung Aufsätze 1925–1933,* edited by Helmut Gipper, 386–93. Düsseldorf: Pädagogischer Verlag Schwann, 1964.

West, David. *An Introduction to Continental Philosophy.* Cambridge: Polity Press, 1996.

Wiedebach, Hardwig, and Annette Winkelmann, eds. *Chajim H. Steinthal: Sprachwissenschaftler und Philosoph im 19. Jahrhundert.* Boston: Brill, 2002.

Wiesinger, Peter. "Johann Andreas Schmeller als Sprachsoziologe." In *Linguistic Method: Essays in Honor of Herbert Penzl,* edited by Irmengard Rauch and Gerald F. Carr, 585–99. New York: Mouron Publishers, 1979.

Wilken, Friedrich. *Geschichte der königlichen Bibliothek zu Berlin.* Berlin: Duncker und Humblot, 1828.

Williamson, George S. *The Longing for Myth in Germany: Religion and Aes-*

thetic Culture from Romanticism to Nietzsche. Chicago: University of Chicago Press, 2004.

Willson, Amos Leslie. *A Mythical Image: The Ideal of India in German Romanticism.* Durham: Duke University Press, 1964.

Windisch, Ernst. *Georg Curtius: Eine Charakteristik.* Berlin: Calvary & Co., 1887.

———. *Geschichte der Sanskrit Philologie und indischen Altertumskunde.* Strassburg: K. J. Trübner, 1917.

Wolf, George, ed. *Michel Bréal: The Beginnings of Semantics: Essays, Lectures and Reviews.* London: Duckworth, 1991.

Wollock, Jeffrey. *The Noblest Animate Motion: Speech, Physiology and Medicine in Pre-Cartesian Linguistic Thought.* Philadelphia: John Benjamins, 1997.

Wyss, Ulrich. *Die wilde Philologie: Jacob Grimm und der Historismus.* Munich: C. H. Beck, 1979.

Zahn, Manfred. "Fichtes Sprachproblem und die Darstellung des Wissenschaftslehre." In *Der transzendentale Gedanke: Die gegenwärtige Darstellung der Philosophie Fichtes,* edited by Klaus Hammacher, 155–67. Hamburg: Meiner, 1981.

Zantop, Susanne. *Colonial Fantasies: Conquest, Family, and Nation in Precolonial Germany, 1770–1870.* Durham: Duke University Press, 1997.

Ziegler, Klaus. "Jacob Grimm und die Entwicklung des modernen deutschen Nationalbewußtseins." *Zeitschrift des Vereins für hessische Geschichte und Landeskunde* 74 (1963): 153–81.

Zimmerman, Andrew. *Anthropology and Antihumanism in Imperial Germany.* Chicago: University of Chicago Press, 2001.

Index

CPSIA information can be obtained
at www.ICGtesting.com
Printed in the USA
LVHW081113160323
741651LV00008B/76

9 780814 333044